ELEMENTS
OF
ECONOMICS
An Introduction to
Microeconomic Theory

C0-AJX-739

John B. Egger
Towson State University

KENDALL/HUNT PUBLISHING COMPANY
2460 Kerper Boulevard P.O. Box 539 Dubuque, Iowa 52004-0539

ELEMENTS OF ECONOMICS

An Introduction to Microeconomic Theory

PREFACE

Readers who understand product differentiation will not consider it necessary for the author of a new textbook in economics to apologize. Still, my own occasional reaction to the simultaneous receipt of a half-dozen sample copies of massive Principles tomes is that just about the last thing the world needs is another Principles book.

This one really is different, though. It had to be. So many accomplished teachers of economics have adopted the same content and style in their books that I am convinced that I could do no better with it than the best of them. What I offer is an approach that is different both pedagogically and theoretically.

Actually, Elements of Economics seeks to maintain the pedagogy of the book from which I taught for many years: Paul Heyne's The Economic Way of Thinking (New York: Macmillan, 1991). Paul's argument that Principles students deserve something other than watered-down graduate micro theory convinced me years ago. My book attempts the difficult task of retaining the nearly-everything that's good about Heyne's text, while emphasizing more strongly a couple of theoretical principles that strike me as essential to a newcomer's appreciation of economics.

Chief among them is subjectivism. Its implications are much more broad and important than our students are normally taught. Everyone (well, almost) teaches that value is subjectively attributed, by individuals, to things. But how about cost? Efficiency? Comparative advantage? If these are value concepts, aren't they, too, subjective? If so, so what?

A direct implication is that knowledge of values is a lot tougher to come by than economists usually convey. It's one thing to pretend that we know everything about individuals' relative preferences so that we can explain the logic of supply and demand. But to confuse this pedagogical assumption-- absolutely necessary at the early stages of analysis--for actual knowledge of the real world is a serious methodological error. To understand what markets do, one must take seriously the nature of the information with which the participating individuals must act. It's far less than we economists routinely assume that we have (though probably far more than we actually do have).

From this it follows that we economists should be far more modest than we often are, about our ability to render judgments about the "success" or "failure" of processes of voluntary exchange. If we truly had some source of knowledge of everyone's values, we could calculate the utility-maximizing pattern of economic activities, and use that as a standard against which to judge as "success" or "failure" the pattern actually produced by individuals' own choices. Although economic theory teaches us a lot about logical interconnections, our only specific knowledge of individuals' values comes from our observation of the objective consequences of their voluntary actions. Where, then, do we get our standard?

The most controversial aspect of this book may be its unabashed advocacy of capitalism. It's pretty tough to thoroughly accept the subjectivist perspective yet advocate an economic system that denies to individuals the greatest freedom to choose and pursue their own values. My thinking about the nature of capitalism has been significantly influenced by the works of Ayn Rand. I identify capitalism as the system of voluntary exchange, and maintain that its philosophy of respect for each and every individual's life accounts both for its efficiency and--more importantly--for its superior morality.

My profound debt, as a teacher, to Paul Heyne has already been acknowledged. This work is an attempt to present in his style the insights of economists identified with the Austrian School. I discovered the works of Ludwig von Mises (whose <u>Human Action</u> (Chicago: Regnery, 1966) is the finest study of economics available) twenty-five years ago, and shortly thereafter those of Friedrich A. Hayek, Murray N. Rothbard, and Israel M. Kirzner. Over the years I have had the privilege of participating in many conferences and seminars focusing on the Austrian approach. I hope that this introductory textbook does justice to it.

John B. Egger
Towson, Maryland

CHAPTER 1

ECONOMICS AND THE PRINCIPLES OF CHOICE

If you want to swim in water that is a little cool for comfort until you get used to it, there are two extreme approaches: dive in, and creep in. Personally, I like to creep for a while, then take the plunge.

Embarking on the study of economics may seem a bit like a swim in that water. You may already find it exciting, and look forward to it. Many students, though, seem to approach it with trepidation. It's something they'd really rather not study at all, but there are business-school and university social-studies requirements, or just three credit-hours that have to be dug up somewhere. People wind up studying economics for all kinds of reasons.

Since economics explains a lot about how a society of individuals functions, it _is_ inherently exciting and important. Its reputation for being tough and boring arises from the way that it is often taught. At the graduate level and beyond, economists use a lot of mathematics and statistics, so some teachers believe that these techniques should dominate a first Principles course. I don't agree. I concentrate on a few fundamental ideas that are key to your understanding of the process of individual choice and the nature of markets. This book expresses and explains these concepts and ideas mostly with plain words, and illustrates them with practical examples. (Caution to extreme mathophobes: Even I use graphs and simple numerical examples when I think they're helpful.)

Everyone quickly forgets most of the specifics that he learns in a course, usually right after the final exam. This course will be no different. My goal is to achieve a simple, perhaps subtle, but permanent change in the way that you think about economic activity. Ten years from now you may not remember a single specific thing from this course...but you may think about people and society a little differently than you otherwise would have.

ECONOMICS, THEORIZING, AND THE <u>POST HOC</u> FALLACY

On the assumption that you share my preference for how to get into the water, let's begin our indirect approach to the study of economics by heading out to a shopping mall.

Enclosed shopping malls, with their hundred or more stores, are--in my humble opinion--one of the great developments of the capitalist system. There's usually one fairly close by. They're cool in hot, humid summers and they're warm in winter. It doesn't rain or snow in there. There are places to sit and drink coffee beside trees and fountains, and lots of interesting shops that encourage you to examine books and clothes and CD players. It's amazing and delightful that one can enjoy all these services without spending a dime. (Except for drinking the coffee...and I guess you could always bring your own.)

Think a little about a parking lot at any particular mall. Every mall that I've ever seen has several entrances. To keep our thinking from getting too complicated, though, let's consider only one of them. This kind of simplifying assumption is common in all intellectual endeavors, economics among them. If it really makes a difference that there are others, we can take them into account later. But first things first: one entrance and its adjacent parking area.

Any particular person driving into the parking lot is free to park wherever he chooses, as long as someone else isn't already parked there. Yet a definite pattern of cars develops. Why?

Of course you're aware that the parked cars tend to be clustered around the entrance door, because people don't like to walk any farther than they have to. If dozens of cars entered the lot, one after the other, and each driver wanted to minimize the distance from his parked car to the mall door, they would produce a semicircular distribution of cars, like this:

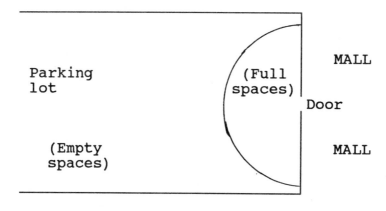

Figure 1.1: Minimizing walking

They would form semicircular rings like the growth rings in a tree, because any driver who deviated from this pattern (parking behind a car that was in a ring only partially completed) would not be minimizing his walking distance.

It's hard to see this pattern from ground level, but it would be apparent from a helicopter or a nearby hill. Besides, the pattern is probably never a perfect semicircle, which makes it even harder to notice.

But you can't argue with the logic: if each shopper wants to minimize his walking distance, his choice of where to park will produce a semicircular arrangement of parked cars, centered on the mall entrance.

Analyzing a mall's parking lot may seem rather strange. For one thing, if you have business in the mall you don't think about--or even care about--this semicircular pattern, and you certainly don't choose your parking spot deliberately to produce it. But, in a way, that makes it even more interesting: it is an <u>unintended consequence</u> of your (and others') goal of minimizing your walking distance. It results from your choice, even though it was not your goal. Such "unintended consequences" are tremendously important in economics: Your decision to buy a new mountain bike instead of new backpacking gear, for example, exerts a thoroughly unintended (and, admittedly, small) effect on the incomes of many individuals who you don't even know.

This mall example may seem strange, too, because it seems pretty trivial. Some things just aren't worth analyzing, as even the brightest and most analytical of people decide, and maybe this is one of them. Of course it's just a way to introduce you to our primary work: the analysis, explanation, and understanding of human behavior. Our examination of mall parking is a step in the process of helping you to understand other things that you <u>do</u> consider important.

If the semicircle seems peculiar because it hardly ever really is a true semicircle, I'm with you there too. When I was an undergraduate studying engineering, we had a joke about a physicist who was paid big consulting money to figure out how much milk a cow could give. His presentation began, "Consider a spherical cow..." I'm not sure what jokes the physics students had about us engineers.

But all that this means is that our first step toward understanding these parking patterns is <u>not enough</u> for a really satisfactory explanation. Our assumption that people just want to minimize their walking distance, oversimplified though it may be, is probably the best way to begin; it provides us with the most understanding per minute spent thinking. Anyone who finds its conclusion inadequate, too unrealistic, is free to make the analysis more complicated (and realistic). But I can't think of any better first step.

What if people partly want to minimize their walking distance, but they also have some preference for parking close to the building rather than farther away from it? They're willing to walk a little farther to get to the door, as long as they can park a bit closer to the building. According to this more complicated behavioral assumption, a person is likely to prefer parking place 100 feet along the side of the building over a spot 75 feet straight out, even though he'll have to walk a little farther to get to the door.

This set of preferences is likely to produce a pattern of parked cars that's a sort of flattened or squashed semicircle. Exactly how flat it is depends on how strong these two preferences are: if people are willing to do a lot more walking to be near to the building, it will be flat and shallow, while only a slight preference would leave it merely a semi-squashed semicircle.

To get the opposite sort of pattern, suppose that people prefer to walk straight to the door, even if it means walking a little farther. This would explain a long, thin pattern of cars sticking out perpendicular to the mall entrance. Here are sketches of these two distributions.

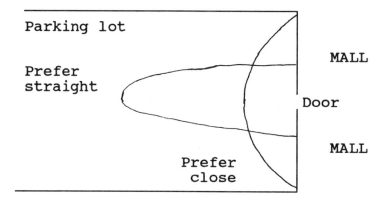

Figure 1.2: Mixed goals in the parking lot

So what's this have to do with economics?

Before anyone gets the idea that economics is the science of shopping-mall parking, let's back away from the specifics of this story for a minute. It's a handy example of the way that economics goes about things, and we'll squeeze more out of it before we're done. But let's think in general terms about what we've done with this mall parking example.

We've made some simple assumptions about other individuals' behavior--their goals, the strengths of different partially conflicting preferences--and combined that knowledge with logic and some understanding of the physical world to explain, understand, and even predict the results (even unintended results) of their behavior. That, in a nutshell, is what we do in economics.

It is actually not easy to define economics in a way that all economists would accept. (Then again, it has been said that if all the world's economists were laid end to end, they still wouldn't reach a conclusion.) There have been whole books written about the changes in the most commonly accepted definition of economics over the years.[1] I don't think this problem of definition is peculiar to economics. Can chemists and physicists specify precisely where the boundary between their subjects lies? Psychologists and philosophers? Sociologists and anthropologists?

The simple definition I prefer is:

Economics is the science of choice.

---

[1] For an especially illuminating study, see Israel M. Kirzner, The Economic Point of View (Princeton: Van Nostrand, 1960).

We have to be careful with this, but it's useful. It correctly implies that there <u>is</u> a certain pattern, a structure, to human action that helps us to explain, understand, and predict it. Human behavior is not simply random, the result of pure chance, with any action just as likely as any other. (In such a situation there would be no pattern whatsoever in the parking lot.) The complex civilization in which we live is clear proof that <u>some</u> kind of guiding principles have directed individuals' choices. You may not entirely understand them yet, but that's one of our goals in this book.

On the other hand, we can't push this science business too far. Choices are made by individual human beings, and no one of us can ever know just what's going on in someone else's mind. It's certainly true that another individual has <u>goals</u>, but when we pretend that we know precisely what they are, we're pretending to have knowledge that we have no way of obtaining. Furthermore, the natural sciences deal with inanimate material. If that's how we tend to think about "science," we should remind ourselves, firmly and often, that the social sciences (like economics) deal with individual human beings who have <u>rights</u> to control over their own lives. The world already has too many scientists who, fascinated with their own brilliance, don't pay much attention to the fundamental philosophical difference between, say, a chunk of granite and a human life.

Back to the parking lot. It's about half full, but there's a vacant parking spot down near the mall entrance, and here comes another car into the lot. Where's he going to park?

The answer is: we don't know.

What we do know is that if he sees the empty spot, and if his only goal is to minimize walking, he'll take it. But there are two very important "if"s there. Perhaps he doesn't know the spot is available. We do, because we're making up this problem, but because he must act on his own (not our) knowledge, we can't very well criticize him if he parks somewhere else.

Then there's the second "if": we have no way of knowing exactly what his goals are. Maybe his car is a freshly restored 1969 Chevy Super Sport 454 with 18 coats of lemon-yellow lacquer. Is he "irrational" to park, at an angle across three spaces, in the farthest corner of the lot, or does someone who makes this judgment not sufficiently understand his goals? Someone whose doctor has told her to get more exercise might well park three-fourths of the way out in a nearly empty parking lot, because to her the walk is desirable.

These two characteristics of human behavior--individuals act on their own knowledge (not yours), and on their own goals and values (not yours)--arise time and time again throughout this book. Although they make the careful economist very modest about his ability to judge or predict individuals' behavior, they are very helpful in his quest for understanding and explanation.

Economics is a science in that it provides us with a set of concepts, a structure, a <u>way of thinking</u> about individuals' behavior and its results. At its core is a set of logically interrelated concepts that has proven to help us understand human behavior. If we insist on getting <u>specific</u>, we have to assume that we know in detail what other individuals' goals and knowledge are (usually on the grounds that they seem reasonable to us). The accuracy of our conclusion then depends on how well we have depicted the thoughts and values of others. This is inherently an "iffy" proposition, and always will be.

What would a world be like in which you could precisely predict the behavior of others, and they could predict yours? It's hard to even think about. I don't think I'd like it.

"Realistic! You gotta be realistic!"

Let's back up to the simplest parking-lot analysis, the one that produces the semicircular pattern of parked cars. As I mentioned, this simplified kind of example makes economics the butt of lots of jokes. (Let me warn you: most jokes <u>about</u> economists aren't very funny, but they tend to be a lot better than jokes told <u>by</u> economists.) Still, it is absolutely essential that our organized thinking about the parking lot begin with such a straightforward and easily understood principle. Sure, it's unrealistic in the sense that it's an incomplete explanation. But don't confuse "incomplete" with false. Whatever its shortcomings, I can't think of any better place to start our analysis.

"Realistic! You gotta be realistic!" I used to hear this a lot from graduate-level business students, especially, older students with jobs who wanted something they could use tomorrow at work. Some of them were quite impatient with general principles, perhaps convinced that such things--if they existed at all--were of no practical use. Every teacher confronts this position, and has to explain (gently) that it is an anti-intellectual attitude that destroys any possibility of rational analysis.

What does it mean, anyway? Are we supposed to think about all of the details of the "real world" at once? After all, if we ignore some trivial little property of something (like the piano-mover failing to notice that the G-sharp above middle C is a little flat), our thought processes aren't accurately capturing "reality."

I'm certainly not smart enough to process every little bit of information in my limited mind simultaneously, and frankly neither you nor anyone else is, either. We all have to pick and choose. We select--on some basis--which attributes are likely to be <u>important</u> to what we're trying to understand, and which probably aren't. The human mind is not capable of thinking about everything at once, so we have to simplify, to dismiss certain characteristics of reality as not significant to our purpose. Only by doing so can we ever hope to understand the <u>important</u> attributes, the characteristics that are mainly responsible for what we're trying to figure out.

This process of selecting important attributes and casting out the "real" but insignificant detail is the process of <u>theorizing</u>. If you're leery of this term, associating it with phrases like "ivory tower" and "isolated from reality," you've probably been exposed either to <u>bad</u> theory or theory that was importantly incomplete. (Our explanation of the parking lot had to <u>start</u> with "minimizing walking distance," but a satisfactory explanation probably wouldn't <u>stop</u> there.)

If you're sure that you just want to march out into the real world and "feel" things, go right ahead. But the very process of <u>thinking</u>, of using your mind to organize and straighten out and identify causes and effects in the world, requires the isolation and analysis of <u>important</u> attributes, the formation of theory.

The very purpose of a college or university, in fact, is to be unrealistic in the sense of providing an environment in which the little details of the real world can be ignored. Enjoy it while you can. You may have trouble ignoring them when you've got a job with lots of responsibilities. Institutions of higher learning are <u>supposed</u> to help you to isolate the principles, the truly important attributes, and to focus solely on them. Our hope, of course, is that this kind of experience will make you better able to cope with the details of the real world, better able to identify what's truly important and better able to think about it.

Our goal: understanding causes and effects

All science is an attempt to identify and understand causality. "If we do this, what are the effects likely to be?" Or "This happened...what caused it?" Often you know what effect you want (higher sales? better grade? healthy and happy children?), and you have to come up with something that's likely to cause it. We searched for cause-and-effect relationships between individuals' preferences and parking-lot patterns, for example.

The process of theorizing about causality requires us to imagine that only one thing changes, and to explore what would be likely to happen if that were the case. We must assume that nothing else changes simultaneously, or we won't know what causes what and will probably find the analysis so complicated that we can't think it through at all. This method of assuming that only one change occurs at a time is called:

<u>ceteris paribus</u> ("other things the same").

It's pronounced SET-er-iss PAIR-eh-buss. You'll see it a lot, because it is absolutely essential to the process of theorizing, of thinking about the world.

If you suspect that more than one thing actually did or might change, you can then do a <u>ceteris paribus</u> analysis on the second factor, and see what its effect alone is likely to be. Then you can combine the two changes' effects--sometimes merely adding them, but sometimes there are more complicated interactions between them that must be considered. The time to get into these complications, though, is obviously after you understand the effect of each change <u>ceteris paribus</u>.

Short cuts? Everybody loves them. When they work, they help us to achieve our goal more economically. But watch out: if you want to understand cause and effect, there is no way around a process of careful, one-thing-at-a-time (<u>ceteris paribus</u>) theorizing. The hopeful but futile search for a short cut around this process leads to the most common mistake in economics.

How to avoid the most common mistake in economics

In my two and a half years as an economist with a Washington, D.C. think-tank, I found this error committed by high-level business executives, accountants and lawyers, and by Congressmen and their staffers. These are highly respected people who work hard, dress well, graduated from good schools, and make important decisions. Except for the government workers, they probably make well over $100,000 a year. But when they talk economics, they often fall into a trap that every student of economics is warned about near the start of his Microeconomic Principles course.

Actually, it's a simple error in reasoning that has nothing to do with economics per se. It's a general logical fallacy known by its Latin name:

`post hoc ergo propter hoc` : "after this, therefore because of this."

Don't forget that this is a FALLACY. It is wrong, a mistake. Most of the things that I highlight in this book are the truth, so if you're memorizing don't forget to tack a little red flag onto this one.

If B follows A, so the fallacy goes, then A caused B.

The problem is that, everywhere except in a carefully designed laboratory experiment, many things change at once. That creates some problems for anyone who is searching for causes and effects.

Suppose, for example, that you have a flat tire and have trouble getting home, but shortly after you get there the mail arrives notifying you of a scholarship for next year. Before you advise other applicants for scholarships to grab icepicks and puncture their own tires, please consider that even though B follows A, B could result from some of the many other changes that were also going on, and be completely independent of A.

Even if A and B are usually found together, though, you can't infer that one causes the other. Each of them may simply have the same cause. When the ice in your iced tea melts on an unexpectedly hot summer day, then a car out on the highway overheats, you wouldn't infer that you could have prevented the driver's breakdown by insulating your glass.

Sometimes it's even the opposite of appearances: A actually makes B less likely to happen, but this effect is swamped by some other changes that, by themselves, make it more likely. Suppose that the owner of the car had just installed the correct amount and type of new coolant (a good thing to do, reducing the chance of overheating) but an unforeseen mechanical failure (water pump, head gasket) occurred too. Identifying the coolant as the cause (because it came earlier) is more nearly the opposite of the truth.

This is where the ceteris paribus method comes in. It helps us to avoid the post hoc fallacy. What if the only change had been that you got a flat (you hadn't submitted those extra letters of recommendation), your ice melted (the way you set your reading glasses on the table focused the sun on your iced tea, even though the air temperature is only 65 degrees), or he changed the coolant (the fan belt hadn't broken)? What, then, would have happened? We are forced to try to find some logical connection, some process rooted in physics or logic or purposive human choice-- something other than the simple fact that one followed the other.

If you think I'm exaggerating, because wealthy, successful attorneys, accountants, and Congressmen wouldn't commit a fallacy described in the first chapter of most Micro Principles textbooks, let's take a look at some examples.

The minimum-wage battle goes on. Economists, almost unanimously, argue that if an inexperienced, unskilled worker can produce only $4 worth of services per hour, an employer who is legally required to pay him at least $4.50 per hour will not hire him. Proponents of a rise in the minimum wage, however, claim to have "solid, factual proof" that it won't cause unemployment: When it has been increased in the past, total employment has actually risen. This argument will be accompanied by stunning graphs and charts, and complicated statistics showing employment data and computing ratios of one kind or another to several decimal points.

Everyone tends to look first at the math and statistics, and it's natural to conclude that if there are no errors there then the conclusion must be right. Statistics are flashy and impressive, and it seems to be widely believed that anyone who can throw them around must be brilliant and "scientific." Often, though, they're camouflage (deliberate or accidental? I've seen both) for the simple error of post hoc. Suppose, for example, that the imposition of the new wage floor coincided with the start of a major economic boom. We then have a situation like the broken fan belt and the new coolant.

One of the battles I fought over and over again, in Washington, dealt with the effectiveness of the investment incentives in the Economic Recovery Tax Act (ERTA) of 1980. Certain critics repeatedly claimed that the accelerated depreciation and investment tax credit in ERTA failed to stimulate investment as the supply-siders claimed they would. Their evidence? In the first couple of years after ERTA was enacted, some measures of investment went down. (Other measures went up, but that's another story.) The critics' reports were peppered with tables of numbers, and fancy computer-generated graphs. They were widely quoted in Congress and in the press as having "solid factual evidence."

Of course it's the post hoc fallacy again. The critics didn't bother to mention that the period covered by their studies coincided not only with ERTA but with our most severe post-World War II recession and with plenty of other changes. Only a ceteris paribus theoretical analysis is capable of isolating the effects on investment of changes in tax law. Naturally, they didn't bother with that, probably suspecting that it would confirm our common sense that reducing the tax on an activity generally tends to encourage it. The think-tank I worked for did such analyses, mostly using theory not much different from what you learn in this and later courses. I'm afraid we had little effect on the press. Despite our best expository writing, our reasoning placed greater demands on the reader than did our critics' simple graphs, and didn't have the pseudo-scientific aura that seems to linger in the air above random piles of statistics.

A final example that I'll cite is from an economist I respect a great deal. It was a brief disagreement in <u>The Wall Street Journal</u> about whether foreign-exchange rates (the price of one country's currency in terms of another's) should be fixed (by the governments) or floating (determined by the market). Disagreeing with Jack Kemp, Milton Friedman ("Letters to the Editor," October 29, 1987) quotes Kemp as saying that it's clear that fixed rates are better. He then cites "the facts," comparing three macroeconomic variables in 1987 with those in 1971 (they're all good, and they're all higher in 1987), concluding with the "score" of Kemp 0, floating rates 3. That's it.

My point is not to try to resolve long-standing debates about whether exchange rates should be fixed or floating, but to examine the case that Friedman presents in his brief letter. He is a brilliant and energetic economist, but in this letter he takes an anti-theoretical, <u>post hoc</u> position. (Theory? Why bother? Here are the facts: after we got floating rates, things improved.) His numbers prove nothing, even to those who like floating rates. (Well, I guess they prove that floating rates and the data he cites are not mutually exclusive. That's not much of a point!)

These three examples are supposed to convince you that the <u>post hoc</u> fallacy is big-league stuff. It is the most common mistake in economics. Congressmen are making law based on this fallacy. Nobel laureates in economics are lured into it when its distortions go their way. It is the most sweeping and common error that you will find in people's efforts to understand economic reality.

So what's the key to avoiding this most seductive of logical errors in economics? Simple to state, tougher to practice: Don't ever let anyone's citing of "facts" and statistics substitute for well-reasoned theoretical argument using <u>ceteris paribus</u>, even when they confirm your position. Remember that the understanding for which economists and all other scientists search is a discovery of <u>causality</u>. Knowing facts is important, of course; they provide the raw material with which we work. (The fan belt broke; the ice melted; the dog barked; etc.) But the whole point of <u>post hoc</u> is that causality can never be determined strictly from facts.

There are no short cuts around the careful process of reasoning using the method of <u>ceteris paribus</u>. Understanding this is a lot of what differentiates a trained, disciplined thinker from someone who's just pretty smart. When you understand, use, and advocate this process of reasoning, you'll have the satisfaction of knowing that you're defending scholarship, intellect, and reason against those who sneer at its impracticality. Besides, you'll be right a lot more often than the "practical" man who thinks he can "let the facts speak for themselves."

SOME PRINCIPLES OF CHOICE

Economics is the science of choice. If we think about the concept of choice, we can draw out a set of principles that will prove to be useful throughout our study. Although these principles are pretty basic, and may seem obvious to you, they provide us with the foundation on which our later work is built.

```
1) Every human action implies a prior choice.
```

It's fairly common to associate "choice" only with consciously thought-out decisions, even those (like where you're going to eat lunch) that aren't very important in the broad stream of civilization. But even relatively trivial action involves at least an implicit choice. You suddenly feel a mild itch on your left forearm. Do you scratch it? Whichever way you go--scratch or not--you have made a choice to pursue one course of action and not another.

"No choice"? We all can think of situations in which we seemed to have "no choice" but to act as we did. Well, whenever there truly is no choice, then there is no scope for, or relevance of, economics. Before we reach that rash judgment (which, after all, could be extended to the ridiculous extreme that there's no use for my teaching services), we should examine carefully the notion of "no choice." Invariably it simply means that it was _easy_ to make the choice, that all imaginable alternatives were so much less attractive that they were easily dismissed. That is _not_ the same as "no choice."

The only things that we cannot truly choose to do are to commit logical contradictions or to violate other natural laws of one type or another. (And even here, you can choose to _try_.) A reflex (your foot moves when the doctor taps your knee with a rubber hammer) is not considered "human action," nor is what happens to you in the second or so after you step vigorously on a banana peel. All of our choices are constrained by natural law which we have "no choice" but to obey.

Fortunately for those of us who work in the field of economics, though, the scope for choice within the limitations of the laws of physics and logic is wide indeed.

```
2) "Choice" implies the existence of
   alternatives.
```

As we've mentioned, if there truly _aren't_ any alternatives, then no choice is involved, and economics has nothing to do with the situation and should gracefully bow out. If there is really only one thing you can do, what's the problem? There's no decision to make, and no thinking could possibly help. You may not like what you have to do, but if it's truly the only option open then whether you like it or not is irrelevant.

Sometimes the genuine alternatives are hidden, one level down from where we're thinking at the moment. Perhaps you know of only one way to make the Dean's List this semester, and that's to get an A in Economics. There's no alternative; given the criteria that identify a student as "Dean's List," the laws of logic require you to have an A. But as much as you desire it, there is no rule of physics or logic that states that it is impossible for you not to make the Dean's List. There _is_ an alternative to "earning an A and making the Dean's List"; it's "earning a B and _not_ making the Dean's List."

When we know of only one means to a particular end, as long as we take that end for granted we have "no choice," no alternative. But there are invariably other goals. Depending on the alternatives open to us, we can choose either other means of achieving the same goal, or different goals. A commuter who has "no alternative" but to risk a speeding ticket and an accident if he's to make the 6:10 commuter train may have the alternative of making the 6:50 instead.

We all think, occasionally, that we have no alternative. We find, though, that as what seemed to be the only possible course of action becomes more and more unattractive, we begin to realize that the end we felt compelled to seek is itself only one among alternatives.

There is a corollary to this second principle:

> 2a) Individuals can choose only from alternatives of which they know.

Again, perhaps this sounds a little silly. How could anyone even consider an alternative that he doesn't know exists? Our shopper has to choose from among the spaces that he knows to be empty, which may or may not cover all of the ones that really are empty.

You're right--this should be obvious and not even necessary to state. But it is not at all uncommon, in either everyday life or in economics, for one person to judge a choice made by another person without considering that the person doing the judging may know more (or less!) about the available alternatives than the person who made the choice.

Have you ever made a choice, based on your knowledge at the time, that you later regretted? Who hasn't? Have you ever seen someone else take an action that you consider unwise, because you're convinced that he would never have made that choice if he knew what you know?

There are a couple of implications of this way of thinking.

First, it suggests that we should be cautious about criticizing another individual's choice. It may simply be that his knowledge of the alternatives available to him differs from ours. Our knowledge of the options open to him can be either greater, less, or simply different from his own knowledge--yet it's his own knowledge on which he has to act. Every individual must act on the basis of his own knowledge of the alternatives. If you want to criticize him for not knowing as much as you do, or to argue that he somehow should have known of other alternatives, feel free. But most of us who long ago learned to accept our own non-omniscience have developed a reluctance to criticize others' lack of some particular bit of knowledge.

Second, if complete knowledge of all alternatives is not automatically provided to everyone with the snap of the fingers, there is some value to economic institutions that help to make information available. Consider advertising--perhaps a large billboard just outside of town. It may not do you any good, because you already know about the fast-food restaurant that it advertises, but it may convey very important information to an out-of-town traveler.

If you often find yourself judging <u>someone else's</u> choice on the basis of <u>your</u> knowledge, please re-examine your attitudes. Sometimes it's reasonable to assert that he should have known what you know; often it isn't. Economists, unfortunately, sometimes don't resist the temptation to commit a particularly extreme form of this error: They judge individuals' behavior and the market outcomes that it produces not by what they (the economists) actually know (which really isn't much more than everyone else knows), but by the standard of perfect, complete knowledge that they are able to <u>assume</u> they have. We'll discuss this frequently throughout the book.

A second corollary to "choice implies the existence of alternatives" is:

> **2b) Individuals can choose only among alternatives that are truly available now.**

Wishing won't make it so. We all can imagine alternatives that are far superior to those actually confronting us at any particular time. We sometimes improperly identify an alternative that's available, thinking that it's something it really isn't.

What happens if you "choose" an alternative that isn't really available? Suppose Frank and Joe each invites you to spend Saturday afternoon with him. You'd prefer Joe rather than Frank, but you'd even more rather spend the day with Mike. You don't want to ask him, and unfortunately, he hasn't asked you and there is no chance that he will. If you turn down both Joe and Frank, in preference for the nonexistent "Mike" alternative, you wind up watching reruns of "Magnum, P.I." on television, alone. You have, by default, wound up with an alternative you consider much less attractive even than spending the day with Frank. That's what happens: when you try to choose an alternative that isn't really there, you wind up--by default--with one of the ones that <u>do</u> exist. It may or may not be the best of the existing alternatives.

We have to be a little careful with this corollary. If you believe there still <u>is</u> a chance that Mike will ask you, there's nothing at all wrong with considering "the chance of spending the afternoon with Mike" to be a real opportunity, and to prefer it to "the certainty of going with Joe." If Mike doesn't ask you, and you wind up electronic images of Thomas Magnum, you may regret not accepting Joe's invitation. But your decision was made on the basis of your best knowledge at the time. You took a chance and it didn't pay off. Who doesn't <u>that</u> happen to, every day? There's nothing wrong with deciding that the alternative that consists of a 20 percent chance of spending the day with Mike and an 80 percent chance of spending it at home alone is preferable to the alternative that consists of a 100 percent chance of an afternoon with Joe.

This corollary is not an insistence that you know the future or be omniscient. It just points out that our current choice is always among currently available alternatives. If we misunderstand what they are, or construct phony ones by pretending that we have options that we don't really have, we often wind up making choices that make us less well off than we could have been.

One of the things that economics can do for you is to help you to identify accurately the alternatives that are really open to you. There are certain mistakes that people commonly make when they try to conceive of the options confronting them, and we'll discuss them in several upcoming chapters.

> 3) Choice requires a process for ranking alternatives. That process is called "valuation."

Suppose that we have developed a list of alternatives open to us at a particular time. (I don't mean to treat this step lightly; often it's not easy to decide exactly what our real options are.) If we're going to decide what to do, we must have some criterion, some basis or rule, for deciding among them. We have to have some way to decide which one to pick, and which--therefore--to reject.

What we do is assign value to each of the opportunities open to us. Here's the process.

From those alternatives currently available to you, imagine taking Action A. (Maybe it's going hiking with Frank, or buying a Toyota Corolla, or scratching your chin.) Think about what your future would be like if you chose that action. What would your life be like? Try to get a firm grip on that feeling, that sense of how well-off you'd be. Economists throughout history have used the word utility to describe that sense of well-offness. Set that feeling aside, temporarily, in a brain file marked "Action A."

Now perform a similar thought experiment with Action B, another currently-available alternative. What would your future be like if you were to choose this action? Most things would undoubtedly be the same as if you'd chosen A, but some things would be different. How well-off would you feel? That's the utility of action B. There's no way you can put a number on it, but try to develop a sense of what your own future would be like if you chose B, and file that sense away under "Action B."

You'll have to do the same with each of the other alternatives open to you. Since the number of alternatives that are actually available is virtually infinite, this may seem like a daunting task. (You could, for example, spend the next hour neither studying economics nor anthropology, but standing on your head out on the sidewalk, or beginning a walk to Afghanistan.) The fact that most of them are so ridiculous that you don't even bother to think of them means that the process of valuation is implicitly involved even in the very conceiving of your available alternatives.

Valuation is the process of assigning value (the same as the economist's word utility) to the alternative actions open to you at a particular time. The value or utility of an action is the sense of how well-off you'll be if you choose that action. Since the alternatives among which we must choose are actions, valuation is always associated with an action, not with a "thing." (Sometimes this distinction seems a little strained, but we attribute value to "buying, owning, and/or using this fishing rod" and not to "this fishing rod.") Value is determined by the act of imagining the future.

Perhaps you enjoy the study of art, and are thinking about becoming a museum curator. But you also love to rip around on off-road vehicles, and are considering a career as a professional driver in Baja-style races. These radically different careers appeal to different aspects of your personality; the reasons that each of them produce value are different. Nonetheless, you must decide which of them is more attractive, which of them offers <u>more</u> value. It's often tough because the specific sources of value are so different. Fortunately, all that's necessary is a sense of "more" and "less." It's neither necessary nor possible to identify cardinal numbers with the alternatives ("curator, 87.5; driver 79.2").

Even though your future may be quite different if you choose A (become a plumber?) rather than B (go to Cornell Med School?), you must be able to compare the senses that you've developed about how well-off you think you'd be under each alternative. That's the whole purpose of the valuation process--to provide you with a way to compare the alternatives and decide which is preferable. You say you can't compare having the extra money (med school) to having the more relaxed lifestyle (plumber)? Sorry, but you have to compare them somehow if you are to make a decision between them.

What you have to do is to rank the alternatives, in order of decreasing value. It is not necessary to assign specific numbers to the "amount" of value that you attribute to each action. (Since it's not possible, it's a good thing that it isn't necessary!) But in your own mind, by imagining what your future would be like (maybe the next ten seconds or the rest of your life, depending on the actions involved) if each action were chosen, you must rank them according to their desirability.

I like to depict the result of your valuation process with little diagrams called "value scales." There will be a different one for each decision you have to make, of course, but here's a general one:

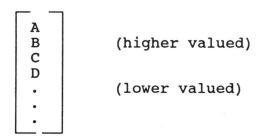

Figure 1.3: A schematic "value scale"

All that this little diagram is intended to show is that, in the current situation, you believe that your future would be better if you were to choose action A than if you were to choose action B. Either of these would produce a better future than choosing C, D, or any of the lower-ranked alternative actions.

> 4) We choose the highest-valued alternative, and forego each of the others.

Choice is the selection of one of the available alternatives, and the foregoing of each of the others. You can't have more than one; your alternatives must be identified as true alternatives. (If it were really possible to have B _and_ C together, for example, then our value scale above is not correctly constructed. We should be comparing A not to B and to C, but to the single alternative "B and C." The alternative actions ranked on a value scale must be _mutually exclusive_: if you pick one, you can't have any of the others.)

It's not surprising that choice involves going for the alternative that, in your own judgment, makes your own future look brighter than do any of the other alternatives. Beware of any inference of narrowly conceived, materialistic selfishness. Depending on your own attitudes, buying that new BMW convertible may rank about fifth and making a big contribution to the local homeless shelter may be the option that makes your own future seem the brightest. However you determine it, you always go for the highest-valued alternative.

Any _other_ choice would require you to sacrifice an alternative that could have made you better off than the one actually selected. If we have properly conceived of what "better off" means to you, such an action doesn't make sense.

This step sounds kind of mechanical, maybe, or automatic. That's because it is. In this logical structure for analyzing individuals' choices, once the alternative actions have been conceived, and values have been attributed to them, the work is over: the decision is automatic, not requiring any further thinking. You go for the highest-ranked action, and that's it.

But haven't you known that all along? The tough part of life is _not_ deciding how to act when we have already conceived of our alternatives and have determined the consequences and value of each. What's difficult is conceiving of our options in the first place, and then imagining and assigning value to their consequences. What do you do if you've always wanted to go to a particular concert, but suddenly a close friend or family member asks you to visit that evening and will be sadly disappointed if you refuse? No economist can help you much with that.

We will be using these "principles of choice" continually in our further study, returning to them and adding new insights (and, perhaps, restrictions or qualifications) as we explore their implications. They don't tell us everything we need to know to understand human behavior, by a long shot, but they provide us with an essential, not-to-be-missed, framework or _way of thinking_ about individuals' choices.

YOU SHOULD REMEMBER...

1. Economics is the science of choice.

2. It provides a set of logically interrelated concepts to help us think about human behavior.

3. Unlike the physical sciences, the objects of our study have their own minds and their own individual rights.

4. Our goal is to trace causes and effects.

5. Ceteris paribus ("other things the same") is our way of insisting, "One thing at a time, please!"

6. Post hoc ergo propter hoc ("after this, therefore because of this") is the most common mistake in economics.

7. People who try to "let the facts speak for themselves" are usually committing the post hoc fallacy.

8. Economists use the ceteris paribus method to protect against the post hoc fallacy.

9. Every human action implies a prior choice.

10. "Choice" implies the existence of alternatives.

11. Individuals can choose only from alternatives of which they know.

12. Individuals can choose only among alternatives that are truly available now.

13. Choice requires a process for ranking alternatives. That process is called "valuation."

14. We choose the highest valued alternative, and forego the others.

PROBLEMS

1)   It's 2 AM and you're driving alone across desolate stretches of west Texas and New Mexico. Your car, the best you could afford, is old and you don't think it's in very good condition. You're really worried that--any minute now--it might start running badly or overheating, stranding you in this awful place. Besides, a good job awaits you, but only if you arrive by 7 AM. You <u>need</u> that job, you <u>need</u> to get there, and your car <u>can't</u> break down, you tell yourself. Please analyze the relevance of these "needs" to whether or not your car breaks down. You can probably make mechanical failure less likely by driving more gently.

2)   Napoleon Hill, decades ago, wrote a book called <u>Think and Grow Rich</u>. His main point was that an almost sure-fire way to get rich is desperately to <u>want</u> to be rich. Adopt getting rich as your "definite chief aim," using various psychological ploys like repeating it aloud ten times every morning ("I will do everything in my power today to become rich" or something like that), pasting it on your bathroom mirror, etc.

   a)   You may not know Hill's work yourself, but do you think it's likely that he believes that you can get rich <u>just by thinking</u>?
   b)   What, if anything, would you suspect is the connection between his kind of "thinking" and "growing rich"?
   c)   Please defend the claim that a lot of people aren't rich simply because they don't <u>want</u> to be rich.
   d)   If you were to ask some guy sprawled in his recliner, drinking a beer and watching "Married...with Children" whether he wants to be rich, he'll probably say "yes." Hill might respond that he doesn't <u>really</u> want to be rich. What do they mean?

3)   A flying rock has just punctured your car's radiator. You just passed the sign that says "Exit 48 Murraysville, 1/2 mile." A new song by Van Halen just came on the radio, and you just spilled a Big Gulp in your lap. A few miles down the road, you notice that your car is overheating.

   a)   Which of the events listed above is the most likely cause of your car's overheating?
   b)   Think about why you answered (a) as you did. What kind of knowledge--incomplete and imperfect though it may be--led you to that answer?
   c)   Give an <u>incorrect</u> answer (that is, attributing the cause to something other than what you identified in (a)) that commits the <u>post hoc</u> fallacy.
   d)   Now: Formulate an answer that identifies the cause as the punctured radiator but which, nonetheless, commits the <u>post hoc</u> fallacy. [Don't

forget the essence of the fallacy! Simply giving me some incorrect reasoning doesn't necessarily commit this particular fallacy.]

    e)   What is the point of this question, anyway?

4)   Two people have asked you for a date for Saturday night, and you told each of them that you'd have an answer later today. What do you think about in trying to make up your mind? By examining the mental processes you go through, see if the concepts of expectations, benefits, and foregone opportunities are involved. How are your past experiences with these two individuals relevant, if at all?

5)   You're trying to find out what causes a particular disease. By thorough examination of many years' statistics, you find that the development of the disease usually followed event A. (It might be drinking a certain kind of water, visiting a particular country, or taking some other kind of action.)

    a)   Does this "prove" that A caused the disease?

    b)   Might this information help you to determine the cause?

    c)   What, in general, is the relationship between "facts" and causality?

    d)   Suppose that you discover that everyone who took action A got the disease, and no victim of the disease did not take action A. Would this be enough to prove that A caused the disease?

    e)   What kind of discovery would be necessary to convince you that you had, indeed, found the cause of the disease?

CHAPTER 2

THE CONCEPT OF DEMAND

WANTS, NEEDS, AND DEMANDS

You've been making choices all of your life, and probably been doing a pretty good job at it. Without thinking much about the process, you have been conceiving of your options, imagining what your future life would be like if you selected each of them, and selecting the current action that you believe will lead to the most appealing of these alternative futures.

Our point in studying this process is not to improve your decision-making. It can help, maybe, but not much. That's why economics is not primarily a business subject. It's a social science, one of the liberal arts. Its goal is to help you to <u>understand</u> the functioning of a society of free individuals. Since the building block of this understanding is the set of principles of choice that each of us applies, they are essential in our quest for an understanding of how a free society functions.

Besides, as obvious as these "principles of choice" may seem, people sometimes act in ways that seem to deny their validity. We've already talked a bit about the problem of the phony alternative, trying to choose an option that isn't really there and therefore, by default, rejecting the best of the truly available opportunities. Another, perhaps more important, is the mistake of denying that there are alternatives at all.

Some of the language that we use every day, unfortunately, suggests ("implies" is too strong a term here) that there <u>are no</u> alternatives. One of the greatest benefits that the study of economics can offer is to make you critical of such language, to watch for subtle, hidden meanings in everyday words and phrases that nudge you down the path to this error.

Tricky terminology: "wants" and "needs"

One of the first concepts, and probably one of the first words, that a baby learns is "want." The concept of want is important; it implies that the individual has used his imagination to determine that he would be better off if he had this gadget than if he didn't. In this sense, "wanting" is the same as attributing value, and we all do that as an essential part of the process of choosing among alternatives. As long as we realize that we must choose among our alternative wants, and if we pick one of them we have to go without the others, then the term is OK. We want A and we want C, but we can't have them both and we want C more, so we choose to go without A.

The problems come from denying the existence or relevance of <u>competing</u> or alternative wants. When the simple fact that you want something is taken as sufficient for determining your action, you're pretending that mutually exclusive alternatives do not exist. You're behaving as if your action did not require you to give up any other alternative action. This is the attitude of the immature child, who either has not yet learned to conceive of the concept of foregone alternatives or trusts that he will be protected by his parents from any adverse consequences.

This denial of the existence of alternatives is childish. I do not mean that as a criticism of children; there are some things that it's not reasonable to expect a child to know or understand. It's perfectly normal for a genuine child to behave "childishly." But the process of maturing is in part a process of accepting that you can't have everything, and that if you have one thing you have to go without something else. This isn't a particularly happy discovery, and people too immature to accept it can be found of all ages. Jerry Rubin's slogan of the hippie days, "If it feels good, do it!," is an example.

"Need" is a term that must be used even more cautiously. Although it has a long history in economics, it is wise to be suspicious of it because it suggests that there is "no alternative," no choice. Since that is almost never the case, the word has the effect of encouraging us not to think about the alternatives that are really there.

Is a need anything more than a strong want? Don't we all say revealing things like, "Well, I need this...but I need that more, and I can't afford both of them"? Interpreted in this way, when we attribute value to alternatives we rank them according to how much we "need" them; we choose the one that we need the most, and deliberately sacrifice the options that we don't need as much.

This view of "need" is far too benign, though. The very concept of need suggests logical necessity, no alternative conceivable. That would make even <u>thinking about</u> alternatives nonsensical. No choice would be possible.

Beware! If there really were no alternative, of course, nobody would have to talk about how much we need this, or we need that. Going without it would be impossible. The reason people talk so much about "needs" is precisely that there <u>are</u> alternatives, but they don't want you to realize that and to think about them. Remember that, the next time you hear a politician identifying his legislation as "meeting a need."

But what about your own needs? You need a notebook for taking notes, you need this course to meet certain requirements, you need your morning coffee. Think back, though, to our discussion of alternatives. Is there truly no other way you could take notes than in a notebook? (When I was a student--to use the term loosely--in high school, I took my entire semester's notes in a sociology course on the flap of the book cover, about six square inches. Based on my own experience, this is not recommended for anyone who wishes to do well.) Scrap computer paper works great.

There's nothing wrong with deciding that using a notebook is the best of your alternatives. Indeed, it's the normal suggested course of action. But you should reach that conclusion after at least a cursory consideration of alternatives, or at least a recognition of their existence.

There's no "need" to obliterate the word "need" from our vocabularies, or to chop it out of our dictionaries. It comes in handy sometimes. But it's usually a good idea to quickly interpret it, in your mind, as a strong want. Even when a particular action is the only way you know to achieve a particular goal (like making the Dean's List), there is nothing logically necessary about the goal itself.

The only genuine "needs," the only situations in which there truly are no alternatives, deal with requirements of the laws of logic or the physical universe. We need to obey the law of gravity and the rules of arithmetic. In these circumstances, human action is not present.

Any language that discourages you from thinking about action as a choice among alternatives simply makes the understanding of human behavior more difficult. Economics is complex enough as it is; why further burden yourself with misleading concepts and terminology?

The economist's concept of demand

The economists' concept of <u>demand</u> has the virtue of emphasizing, rather than hiding, the fact that if we select one alternative we must forego others. Our feelings of wants or needs are built into the concept of demand, but it requires us to realize that it is the relative strengths of different wants or needs that determines how we're really going to act.

The general idea behind the concept of demand is that your willingness to choose action A is affected by the attractiveness of the alternative action, B. If we mentally leave action A alone but imagine something to cause the attractiveness of action B to rise or fall, it's easy to understand that while we'll choose A when B is fairly unattractive, the strength of our preference for A diminishes as we imagine B becoming more attractive, and if B becomes (in our imagination) attractive enough, we may actually prefer it to A.

Let's get specific.

You go over to the bookstore because you want (or "need") a notebook. Unfortunately there are lots of other things you want (or need) too, so there's a trade-off about how you use your money. If you buy the notebook, you'll have to go without some other thing you could have bought with the money that the notebook costs. If you choose this alternative use of your money instead, you'll have to go without the notebook.

Here's the pile of notebooks. The bookstore says that you may take one away if you leave $2.69 with them. You do a quick mental scan over the other things you could buy with this $2.69, decide that having the notebook is more important than the best of these alternatives, and you go ahead with the purchase.

Before we go on, think about how you arrived at your decision. You examined the notebook to learn about its physical properties (how many pages, divisions, quality of paper, spacing between lines, sturdiness). You imagined your future use of it, picturing it full of neat and detailed notes on which you will draw, periodically, for the rest of your life. Finally, you developed some judgment about how "well off" having those notes is likely to make you. You then thought about what else you could do, instead, with the $2.69 that you are being asked to give up: eat lunch, buy a magazine, go to a (cheap) movie, buy a tube of toothpaste. You imagined what your future would be like if you were to pursue each of these alternatives, compared those imaginary futures with the imaginary future of the notebook, and decided that you preferred the latter.

That's enough for your "buy or no buy" decision, and if you've got other things to do with your time and brain (Who doesn't?), you'll stop there. But we economists ask you for a little work: Run through the same analysis if the purchase of the notebook required you to give up $2.70 worth of other things. Not much difference. How about $2.71? $2.80? As the quality of the lunch you are asked to forego becomes greater (you can buy a nicer lunch for $2.80 than for $2.70), or the tube of toothpaste that you would have to sacrifice becomes larger, the relative appeal of the notebook shrinks. As the hypothetical price we're asking you to imagine rises, so does the value of the best of the alternatives that you must sacrifice if you're to buy it. At some point, the value of what you would have to go without becomes greater than the value of the notebook itself. At that price, you say "Woah, hold it, too much, keep it," and go spend your money on whatever it is that ranks above the notebook on your own value scale.

Suppose, in fact, that you would have been willing to pay up to $2.83 for the notebook, but that the best alternative use of $2.84 looks more attractive than the notebook itself. Apparently a little piece of your value scale looks like this:

```
┌                             ┐
│ Best other use of $2.84     │
│           Notebook          │
│ Best other use of $2.83     │
│ Best other use of $2.82     │
│              .              │
│ Best other use of $2.69     │
│              .              │
│              .              │
└                             ┘
```

Figure 2.1: The notebook on your value scale

This is just a little diagram of the information that we've stated above about your relative valuation of the notebook and the alternatives of which you are aware. You'd buy it (but just barely) if it were $2.83, you wouldn't (but just barely) if it were $2.84, and you are fairly pleased to be able to get it for only $2.69.

The figure $2.83 is sometimes called your "demand price."

> An individual's DEMAND PRICE for a
> unit of a good is the maximum price
> he would be willing to pay for it and
> still choose to buy it.

It is the maximum price that you would be willing to pay, the highest price at which "buying the good" is still preferable to "not buying the good."

We can draw a little diagram of your values regarding this notebook and its alternatives. Let's assume that you have no interest whatsoever in a <u>second</u> notebook. You can imagine no use for a second one, and wouldn't take it even if it were free. Then if we plot the "number of notebooks you'll choose to buy" on the horizontal axis, and identify each and every conceivable "money price per notebook" (from zero on up, in one-cent increments) on the vertical axis, we get a little diagram like Figure 2.2:

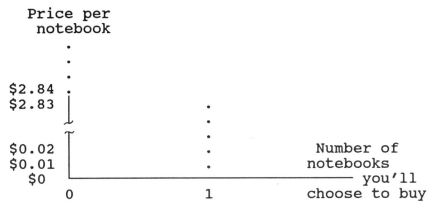

Figure 2.2: A discrete demand "curve"

All that this accomplishes is to provide us with a little picture, a visual sense, of what we've already said about your judgments of value. It does not add any new information. It's simply a different way of expressing what we've already discussed, first in words and then in our little value scale.

Most economists prefer to make this graph a little neater and cleaner, though less realistic, by connecting all of the dots with straight lines. Figure 2.3 shows the result.

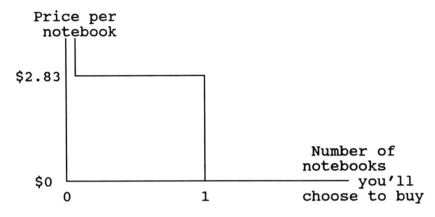

Figure 2.3: A simplified demand for a notebook

There are actually a few problems with taking this graphical step, though. It suggests that both the price and quantity are infinitely divisible, and they really aren't. We can't have prices like "two dollars and 59.83576 cents." And we have only two options: buy none, or buy one. Yet that horizontal segment across the top of the rectangle suggests that we could buy half a notebook, 27 percent of one, or 0.49218 notebooks. Furthermore, what does this thing tell us that we'll do if the price is exactly $2.83? Every quantity between (and including) zero and one lies on that horizontal line segment.

Despite its problems, we'll be OK if we understand that since the horizontal line shows our demand price, we actually are willing to buy one at that price (and, of course, at any lower price) but not at any price that is even slightly higher.

The diagrams that we've just drawn are <u>demand curves</u>. They're the first of many that you will see in this course, so try to become comfortable with them. Your "demand for notebooks" is the relationship between any imaginable money price per notebook and the number of notebooks that you will choose to buy at that price.

An individual's QUANTITY DEMANDED, at a particular price per unit, is the number of units that he will choose to buy.

The phrase "quantity demanded" always refers to a specific number of units of a good (one notebook, five shirts, whatever) and to one specific price ($2.69 each, $13.99 each, etc.).

If we imagine changing the notebook's price, <u>ceteris paribus</u> so that the <u>only</u> change is this hypothetical change in its price, we can determine your "quantity demanded" at each and every conceivable price per notebook.

> An individual's DEMAND for a good is
> the set of his "quantities demanded"
> at each conceivable price, with all
> other things assumed to be unchanged.

Demand is the relationship between all imaginable prices and the quantity demanded at each of them. At a price of $2.17, for example, our "quantity demanded" was "one." At a price of $3.32 our "quantity demanded" was "zero." There is no number that measures "demand," because the word denotes a whole lot of pairs of numbers. Each pair consists of a hypothetical price and its associated "quantity demanded."

In our little example, we simplified the problem by making your "quantity demanded" only zero or one. More generally, we construct "demand" by imagining the money price of the good to take on all kinds of different values ($0.23, $18, $2.75, whatever) and, by taking a peek at your value scale, determine how many units of the good you would choose to buy at that hypothetical price. That's another way of asking how many units of the good you value more than you value the best alternative that you would have to forego. (If Sears informs you that you must give up $1.75 for each pair of athletic socks that you buy, how many pair meet the test of being worth more to you than the best alternative use of $1.75?)

Economists like the concept of demand because, unlike "want" or "need," it brings the necessity of choice among alternatives right to the foreground. We put the good you're considering buying on one axis, and some measure of the things you'll have to sacrifice on the other axis. There's no way to gloss over the fact that if you want one, you have to give up the other. It may be very interesting that you "want" a notebook, but your action depends on whether you want it more than you want the most attractive of the other stuff you'll have to sacrifice.

DEMAND, QUANTITY DEMANDED,
AND THE LAW OF DEMAND

If you want to determine your demand for a notebook, you have to imagine all feasible prices that you might be charged for one. At each of these imaginary prices ($0.50? $10?), you evaluate the alternatives that you would have to forego if you actually paid that price, consider the value of the notebook itself, and decide which is greater: the value of the notebook, or the value of the best of the alternatives that you could pursue if you did not buy the notebook. At the particular price you're imagining, this process determines your quantity demanded. In our simplified example, it's either zero or one. Now imagine that the price (but only the price) is different, and find its "quantity demanded." The whole collection of hypothetical prices and the "quantity demanded" associated with each of them, with everything else that could conceivably affect your attitude toward notebooks assumed to be unchanged, is referred to as your demand for notebooks.

Words, words, words. Aren't we just nitpicking over words here? What difference does it make if we refer to "one" as your "quantity demanded at a price of $2.69" or simply as your "demand"? Don't businessmen and ordinary people, whose minds haven't been warped and confused by a course in economics, just refer to the number of things that people buy at a particular price as "demand"?

They sure do. And we economists have some obligation to defend our use of this awkward phrase "quantity demanded" instead of the much more common and easy-to-say "demand."

I don't want to seem too snobbish about this. The ordinary language that people use evolves, it changes over time and develops in ways that generally prove useful. In a lot of circumstances, referring to something as "demand" when precise language would call it "quantity demanded" does no harm whatsoever.

But remember what we're trying to do. We're developing an approach, a way of thinking about individuals' choices, that will help us to understand the functioning of a society. Sometimes we need language that's more precise than is used--perfectly adequately--by people who aren't seeking this goal of understanding. When you're out socializing with friends, you can sling the term "demand" around however you wish. But if you want to communicate something significant about people's choices and their effects, you have to be a lot more careful with your terminology.

Figure 2.4 might help to drive the point home.

Price	Quantity Demanded
.	0
.	0
$100	0
.	0
.	0
$3	0
.	0
.	0
$2.84	0
$2.83	1
.	1
.	1
$2.69	1
.	1
.	1
$1	1
.	1
.	1
$0	1

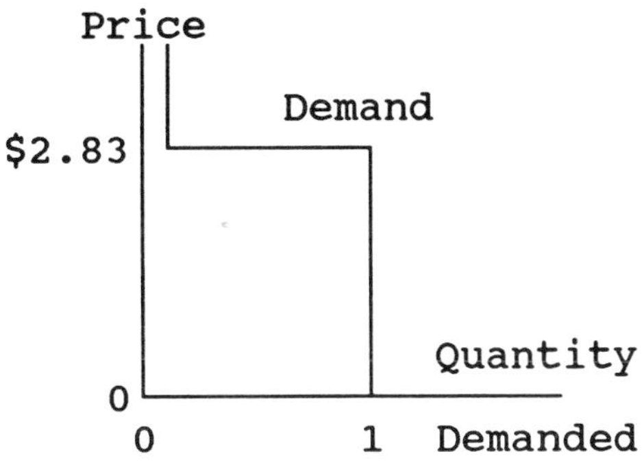

Figure 2.4: Demand as a schedule and as a curve

If the price of the notebook were raised from $2.69 to $2.75, your demand for notebooks wouldn't change. But if the price were raised from $2.69 to $2.99, your demand for notebooks wouldn't change either. Something would change. You still would have bought one at $2.75 but you won't at $2.99. Something dropped from "one" to "zero" when we imagined a price of $2.99 rather than one of $2.75. That "something" was not "demand," however: it was "quantity demanded."

Try to think of the word demand as identifying this whole schedule or table of related numbers, or the entire curve in the graphical diagram. (Mathematicians can think of demand as a set of ordered pairs, with each consisting of a price and its associated "quantity demanded.") Then you're more likely to understand that we can jump around, sliding up or down the schedule or the curve, without doing anything whatsoever to the schedule or curve itself.

As we jump, slide, or climb around, we change (or imagine to be changing) the notebook's price and the quantity of notebooks that we demand. But demand is the mountain that we're climbing up and running down, and none of our cavorting changes it in the slightest.

*So "demand" implies that people
care only about money? Wrong!*

The concept of demand is sometimes accused of implying that the only thing that you think about, when deciding whether or not to buy a notebook, is its price. Look at the graph or the schedule. There's nothing there but the price of the notebook and the related "quantity demanded." Or is there? Looks can be deceiving.

Where did those numbers, or that curve, come from, in the first place? How did "demand" get to be what it is? We went through a long and arduous discussion about imagining the future, valuing alternatives, and so forth before we were able to obtain these "demand" numbers. The numbers that we obtained (such as the "demand price" of $2.83) depended importantly on all of the considerations involved in that decision process, and there are many things that might have changed our choices.

Is there a new magazine that the bookstore didn't previously carry? That may change the value of the best alternative that you must forego to purchase the notebook, and might reduce the maximum you'd pay for a notebook to, say, $2.35. Did you break a shoelace just as you walked into the bookstore, or see a newspaper headline that students who take organized notes get better grades and therefore better jobs and therefore make a lot more money? The broken shoelace may make you less eager to buy a notebook, since that would require you to go around with a flopping shoe, but the promise of wealth and riches probably makes you more eager.

No economist would ever deny that your choice is importantly affected by considerations like these. Some of them involve the alternatives, the other opportunities, that you evaluate; there may be more or fewer of them, or something may have happened to cause a change in your estimate of their value. Perhaps something has happened that leads you to revise your judgment of the value that you attribute to the notebook itself.

As you might imagine, there is hardly anything under the sun that could not, conceivably, change an individual's attitude toward a particular product. It starts to rain in northwest China, a guy in Missouri hears about it on the news, develops a fear of flooding in his own neighborhood (no, not from that particular rain but from a possible future one in his area), and decides to spend his money on sandbags rather than notebooks. You can make up your own semi-fanciful stories that, in principle, relate almost anything to almost anything else.

Be careful not to let this lead you into an "anything goes" attitude. It's true that these decisions all depend on people's ideas and personal judgments, and just about anything <u>could</u> make them change their minds. But we couldn't say, for sure, where any one person was going to choose to park, either. The social sciences deal with human beings who have the ability to change their minds, and no other individual will ever be able to specify precisely how, why, and when. If we're going to try to predict how people are really going to act, to some extent we have to be content with <u>probabilities</u>. (It isn't very likely that this Missouri flood-fearer is representative of other people, for example.) But we do need a logical structure, a set of concepts, that is broad enough to permit us to think about even remote possibilities.

All of the other considerations--rain in China, broken shoelaces, good jobs--affect an individual's willingness to purchase the notebook even if its price were unchanged. When one or more of these changes occurs, the individual has to re-evaluate his alternatives. He'll probably come up with a whole new schedule or curve relating the notebook's price to the quantity he is willing to buy. When something happens that causes him to change the values that he assigns to either the notebook or to its alternatives, we must construct an entire new set of relationships between hypothetical prices and quantities demanded. We must construct a new <u>demand</u>.

> ```
> The PURPOSE of the concept of DEMAND
> is to isolate the effect, on the
> quantity that one is willing to buy,
> of changes in the good's own price.
> ```

To build a demand curve or schedule, we have to assume that there is only one thing changing: the good's own price. If we say, "Let's suppose the price drops to $2.53, but he breaks his shoelace and it starts to rain in China and an attractive young woman says 'Hi' to him and...," then who knows what he's going to do? We can't think of all of these things at once. Nobody's smart enough to do that.

But maybe we can pick these effects apart, and analyze them one at a time. That's what our <u>ceteris paribus</u> method advised, a bit earlier.

Imagine that the <u>only</u> change is this hypothetical change in the good's own price. Everything else remains the same: your income, the weather in China, the state of your shoelaces and of the magazines that you have to walk past, your knowledge and judgment about all of these things. Then we can isolate the effect, on your notebook-purchase decision, of changes in the notebook price alone. What we get is your demand for notebooks.

In the real world, of course, at least some of these other things really are changing, so we'd better be able to take account of that somehow. Because these changes--even just one of them--may make us either more or less willing to buy a notebook, at any particular price, than we were before, we identify the result as a <u>change in demand</u>.

> ```
> A CHANGE IN DEMAND may result from
> a change in anything except a change
> in the good's own price.
> ```

Figure 2.5 shows a change in <u>demand</u>.

<u>Price</u>	Old Quantity Demanded	New Quantity Demanded
$100	0	0
.	0	0
$3	0	0
.	0	0
.	0	0
$2.84	0	0
$2.83	1	0
.	1	0
.	1	0
$2.69	1	0
.	1	0
$2.53	1	0
$2.52	1	1
.		1
$1	1	1
.	1	1
.	1	1
$0	1	1

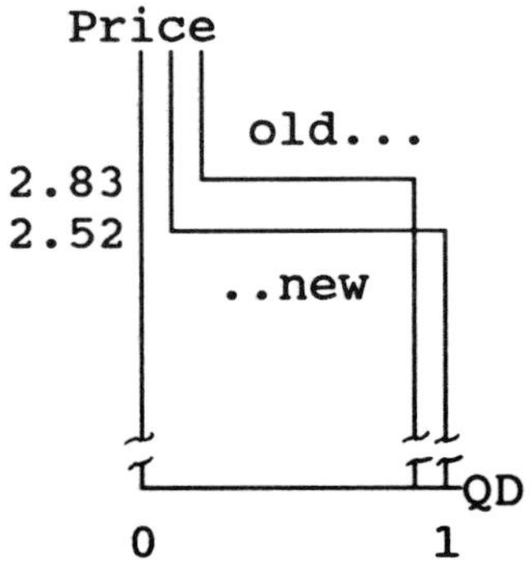

Price

old...

2.83
2.52

..new

0   1   QD

Figure 2.5: A change in demand (schedule and curve)

The "Price" column and the "Old Quantity Demanded" column make up the old "demand," while the "Price" column and the "New Quantity Demanded" column make up the new "demand." For many of the prices, the quantity demanded under the new circumstances is the same as that which was demanded before the shoelace broke, the woman was friendly, or whatever. But as long as even one of them is different (say, the quantity demanded at $2.75), we must recognize that <u>demand</u> has changed.

The purpose of the concept of demand is to isolate the effect, on the amount someone will choose to purchase, of changes in that good's own price. Isolating that effect requires us to assume that it's the only change. Any particular demand curve or schedule is constructed on the basis of a particular set of knowledge of alternatives and individual attitudes about them. If we wish to examine the effect of changes in any of these things (including the prices of other goods, our income or wealth, our knowledge of the good or its alternatives, for example), then we do so by constructing a whole new demand.

When it's only a change in the good's own price that affects our choice, we refer to that as a change in <u>quantity demanded</u>. (It isn't a change in demand, because we've just moved from one point to another on the demand schedule or curve.)

> A change in the good's own price
> may cause a CHANGE IN QUANTITY
> DEMANDED. It <u>cannot</u> cause a change
> in "demand."

But if there is a change in one of the underlying conditions that we had assumed to be constant when we constructed our demand curve or schedule, then that curve or schedule doesn't work any more. It can't be trusted to tell the truth. We have to construct a new one, and we call that a change in <u>demand</u>.

Remember that the word "demand" refers to the entire schedule or curve relating a good's own price to the quantity demanded of it. Just moving around on it can't change demand. But if we must construct a whole new schedule or curve, that is indeed a "change in demand."

So economists do not deny that lots of things matter besides a good's own price. It is precisely those "lots of things" that make <u>demand</u> what it is, and a change in any of them can and probably will change demand. But a good's own price is clearly a pretty important determinant of how people act regarding that good, so it's helpful to have a concept that highlights, emphasizes, isolates all by itself, the effect of changes in a good's own price (and <u>only</u> those changes) on the "buy or no-buy" decision. That's what "demand" does for us.

The market demand

The demand curve that we've been working with is important and interesting. It's the foundation of all other kinds of demand curves. But it isn't the sort that we're going to be working mostly with in this course.

I hate to break this to you, but the bookstore is not particularly concerned with your demand, personally. As a business matter, the managers are concerned about the demand for their notebooks by all students, and not specifically about your demand.

To make the transition from your demand to the "market demand," consider Sam. He (or she) runs through a thought process much like your own, although his specific alternatives and the values he places on them are different. He concludes, let us say, that his own demand price is $2.63 (and, like you, he can imagine no use for a second notebook). We can then imagine a range of different prices, just as before, and find the "quantity demanded" at each of these prices by "you and Sam." It's just a matter of adding together the "quantity demanded" of each of you. At prices above $2.83, neither of you demands a notebook so the "quantity demanded" by the two of you is zero. At prices between $2.64 and $2.83, you'll demand one but he won't, so the "quantity demanded" by the pair of you is "one." At prices at or below $2.63, each of you demands one so the total "quantity demanded" is "two."

Notice the change in the shape of the demand curve. The extra step results from the combination of the two demanders who have different demand prices. (If Sam had also had a demand price of $2.83, our combined demand curve would have looked just like yours alone, but with a bigger step.)

Price	You	Sam	Both	
$100	0	0	0	
.	0	0	0	
$3	0	0	0	
.	0	0	0	
$2.84	0	0	0	
$2.83	1	0	1	$2.83
.	1	0	1	$2.63
.	1	0	1	
$2.69	1	0	1	
.	1	0	1	
$2.64	1	0	1	
$2.63	1	1	2	
.	1	1	2	
$1	1	1	2	
.	1	1	2	
.	1	1	2	
$0	1	1	2	

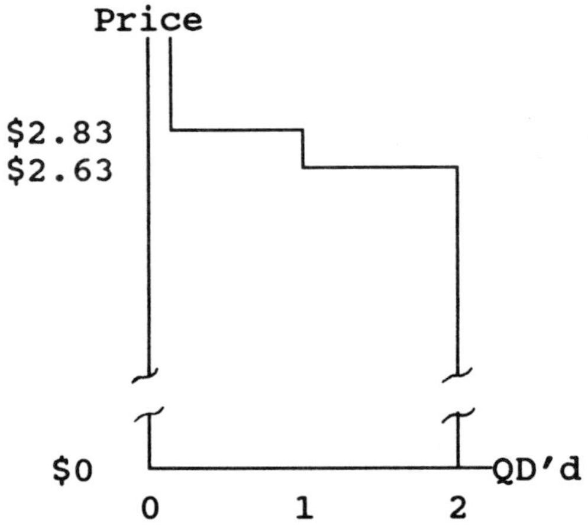

Figure 2.6: Demand by two individuals

Now imagine adding in Sally, whose demand price is $2.13, Jenny (demand price $2.93), Frank (demand price $2.43), and Joe ($3.13). The demand curve that graphically depicts these six students' demand for notebooks has six steps (because each of their demand prices is different).

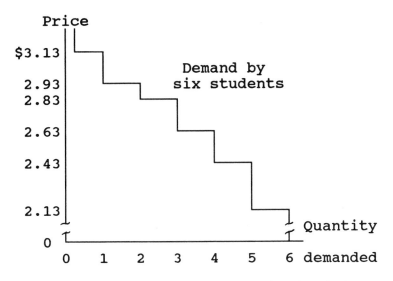

Figure 2.7: Demand by six individuals

There's no difference in principle with increasing the number of students to, say, a few thousand. (Relax--we aren't actually going to consider them one by one.) The number of steps increases, the distance between them decreases, and the demand curve begins to take on a much more smooth kind of shape. We have to shrink the horizontal axis to accommodate the thousands of students in the same space we used to devote to you alone, but that's no particular problem.

What we wind up with is a demand curve by "the market," or a "market demand curve," depicting the demand by all of the people in whom the bookstore is interested, that looks something like this:

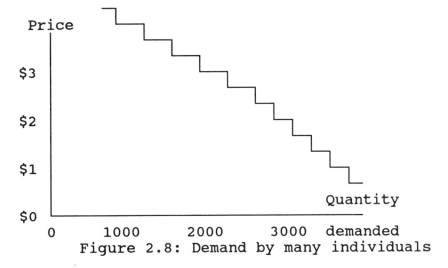

Figure 2.8: Demand by many individuals

36

This is a fairly realistic market demand curve, but we could make it even more so by eliminating both the little horizontal and vertical line segments, leaving simply a pattern of dots like Figure 2.2. Each would show us exactly how many notebooks our school's students would purchase at the particular price we've hypothesized.

The primary characteristic of this demand curve in which we're interested, though, is the simple fact that it has a downward slope. The quantity demanded is smaller at high prices than it is at lower prices. If we're willing to accept some further degree of unrealism for the sake of simplicity, we can approximate this many-stepped demand curve by a downward-sloping smooth line. That's what nearly all economists do, and this is what it looks like:

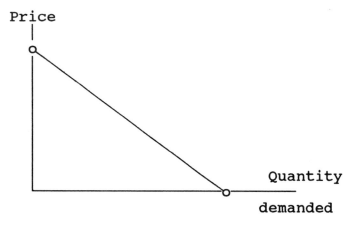

Figure 2.9: A simple linear demand curve

This line can be steep or relatively flat, and it can be straight or curved. Since the straight line is easiest to draw, and it captures the main point about demand--that a good's own price and the quantity of it that is demanded are inversely related to each other--we might as well draw the demand curve as a straight line. You'll run into situations, later in your study of economics, in which a straight line is clearly not right. When you do, you can make it as fancy as you wish.

The law of demand

This essential property of demand is, indeed, called "the law of demand":

> The LAW OF DEMAND: the "quantity
> demanded" of a good is <u>inversely</u>
> related to its own price.

Specifically, when the price of a good goes up, the quantity demanded of it falls, and when its price falls the quantity demanded rises. In yet other words: demand curves slope downward.

This "law of demand," simple as it is, is one of the most important lessons of economics. The money price of any good tells something about the alternatives that anyone buying the good will have to forego. The higher the good's money price, the greater the value of the alternatives that a purchaser will have to sacrifice. I hope it makes sense, therefore, that higher prices make it less and less likely that any particular individual will value the good more than he values that ever-increasing set of alternatives.[1]

A FEW MORE LESSONS ON DEMAND

The Law of Demand is so important that we ought to become more familiar with it, and some of its implications, before we move on.

A good's own price, and the "quantity demanded" of it, are inversely related. Demand curves, in other words, slope downward.

Let's see how that applies to some of the cases we've already considered...and to some new ones. I've tried to present a number of questions that thoughtful students often raise, and then advance a sensible answer to each.

1)   About one person's demand for a notebook: For many price changes, the "quantity demanded" doesn't change. How can you say they're "inversely related"?

According to your own estimates of the value of one notebook and the value of the alternatives to it of which you are aware, you'd be willing to pay $2.83 but not $2.84. The actual price, in our example above, was $2.69 so, of course, you'd buy one. But what if that price were to rise to, say, $2.75? You'd still buy one. There has been no reduction in your "quantity demanded" even though the price is higher. Doesn't that contradict the law of demand?

Well, I hope not, because your behavior is perfectly sensible. What's happening here is that the price increase does make the notebook less attractive, relative to your known alternatives, than it was before. But while the "value of the alternatives" is gaining on the "value of the notebook," the notebook is still ahead. The price increase wasn't enough to actually flip your decision from "buy" to "no buy."

Nothing in the law of demand is intended to deny that demand curves may have vertical sections, price ranges over which the quantity demanded doesn't change.

---

[1] Some of you will learn, later, about a strange exception called the Giffen good (after the British economist Robert Giffen (1837-1910)). I'm mentioning it so that you (any my colleagues) don't think that I don't know about it. If I were to explain it, you'd get an exaggerated sense of its importance. It isn't anything that Principles students should be concerned about.

The law <u>does</u> imply that, even for a single individual like you, a there is some rise in price (it may be large or it may be small) that leads you to switch your choice.

Certainly as we consider a <u>market</u> demand, the demand for the bookstore's notebooks by "six students" or "five thousand students," the likelihood of a significant vertical segment--a large range of prices over which the quantity demanded by the market does not change--becomes much more remote. You don't change your action when the price rises from $2.69 to $2.75...but someone else does.

2)   What if something else, besides just the good's own price, changes? Is the law of demand still valid?

Some economists invoke the <u>ceteris paribus</u> (other things remaining the same) condition when they express the law of demand: a good's own price and its "quantity demanded" vary inversely, assuming that <u>only</u> the good's own price changes.

That's OK, but it seems a little redundant. The <u>ceteris paribus</u> condition is implicit in the very concept of demand. If some other change coincides with the change in the good's own price, like sudden widespread fears of a depression, then we have a confusing mixture of "change in demand" and "change in quantity demanded." Who knows what might happen? There's certainly no "law" to describe it.

The law of demand refers to an important property of each and every demand curve. Pick a demand curve, any demand curve. But you have to stick with it. The law of demand tells us <u>nothing</u> about the relationship between the quantity demanded at $2.69 on one demand curve, and the quantity demanded at $2.75 on some other demand curve.

So yes, certainly it's still valid. Quantity demanded and price are inversely related along the new demand curve, just as they were along the old. The law is simply not applicable to changes in <u>demand</u>.

You must not say, or even think, that changes in demand "violate" the law of demand. Would you say that the principle that a victim of overheating should be immersed in a tub of cool water is rendered invalid, "violated," or "falsified" by the fact that this is the exact opposite of what should be done for a victim of hypothermia (excessively low body temperature)? I hope not.

3)   "The price went up, and people bought more. Surely <u>that</u> violates the law of demand."

Well, how much confidence do you <u>have</u> in that law, anyway? If you've followed the above discussion through a consideration of the value attributed to the alternatives that must be foregone, and agree that (unless something else changes) a higher price calls for the sacrifice of greater-valued alternatives, then the law of demand should seem pretty solid. People buying more when the price rises implies that, even though the value attributed to the good itself doesn't change, an <u>increase</u> in the value of the alternatives that must be foregone leads more people to decide that these alternatives are <u>less</u> valuable than the good itself. That, I submit, doesn't make much sense.

Yet sometimes we do, indeed, observe the behavior that we're being asked about. What's the solution?

Look back at our comments on Question #2. It is perfectly possible for a higher price to correspond to a higher "quantity demanded" if some other change has resulted in an increase in <u>demand</u>. Figure 2.10 gives you some pictures.

Apparently something has caused people to re-evaluate this good and/or its alternatives, and--at any particular price--to attribute more value to it than they used to. They're more willing to sacrifice alternatives than they used to be. At any particular price, the market's "quantity demanded" is larger than before.

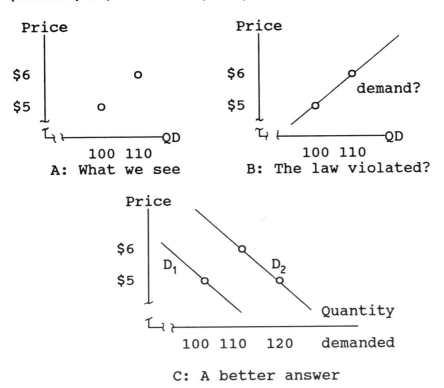

Figure 2.10: So you think you saw an upsloping demand?

Take a look at C, our "better answer." Suppose that the price had remained at $5, despite the increase in demand. The quantity demanded would have increased from 100 to 120. But the rise in price cut that 120 back down to 110--reducing the "quantity demanded" just as the law of demand says it does.

The difficulty here is that the final result is a combination of two causes: the increase in demand (which specifies that, at some or many prices the quantity demanded increases, and at no price does it decrease), and the rise in price (which, according to the law of demand, reduces the quantity demanded). The increase in demand moves us over to the new demand curve, and the law of demand--combined with the price increase--moves us back up this new curve. We don't move all the way back to our original quantity (100), though, so the net result is a higher price ($6) and a higher quantity demanded (110).

Notice how limited our powers of direct observation are. We can see only that 100 units per week were sold when the price was $5 each, while 110 units per week were sold when the price was $6 each. The rest of our story came from our theorizing, our understanding of action as choice among alternatives. The law of demand, which says that demand curves slope downward, tells us that these two observed combinations of price and quantity cannot lie on the same demand curve. (It would slope upward.) Therefore, something must have happened, although we may have no idea exactly what, to cause people to value this good more intensely, relative to its alternatives, than they used to. That is the only explanation for our observed data that is consistent with the law of demand.

4)   What are some of the things that are likely to change demand?

Actually, there's only one thing that can't: a change in the good's own price. That's because of the way that demand is defined, and the purpose of the concept of demand in economic thinking. The purpose of the concept of demand is to isolate the effect, on the amount that someone will choose to buy, of a change in the good's own price. If demand itself could be affected by a change in the good's own price, the concept wouldn't be doing its job. It would be like a rubber ruler, whose "inch" markers got closer together or farther apart, depending on whether the thing you're trying to measure is small or large.

It may sound pretty strange that the demand for a good cannot be affected by a change in its own price.[2] If it does sound wierd, you're still using ordinary everyday language (failing to distinguish between demand and "quantity demanded") that simply isn't accurate enough for economic understanding. Try to get comfortable with this statement:

---

[2] If a surprising and significant change in a good's price provokes you to learn more about alternatives, your demand may be affected. It's best to identify the cause of the change in demand as your new knowledge.

> There is only one thing that, by
> definition, cannot change the demand
> for a good. That's a change in the
> good's own price.

That said, everything else is fair game. We talked about the rain in China. (How about the rain in Spain, that falls mainly on the plain? Or is that "plane"?) I asked you to think about some strange possibilities for causal relationships. Can a mongoose sneezing in Pakistan affect the demand for snowblowers in Bangor, Maine? I'm sure it _could_, but I'll let you make up a story about how, if you wish.

There are, however, certain types of changes that are more likely than others to affect demand in predictable ways.

Complements and substitutes

Imagine a change in a price of some good that is normally used with the good we're considering. Goods that are normally used together are called _complements_. Coffee and sugar may be examples, or automobiles and gasoline, or dress shirts and neckties. An increase in the price of sugar makes "sugared coffee" more expensive, and leads people to buy less of it--less sugar (a reduction in its "quantity demanded") _and_ less coffee. Buying less coffee, even though the price of _coffee_ hasn't changed, means that our _demand_ for coffee has fallen.

> A change in the price of a COMPLEMENT
> to a good is likely to change the
> demand for that good in the opposite
> direction.

Goods that can typically be used in place of each other are called _substitutes_, like--to some extent--tea and coffee, cotton and wool, or automobiles and bicycles. A rise in the price of a substitute reduces the attractiveness of the alternatives to the good that we're considering, making it appear _relatively_ more valuable. A rise in the price of coffee does not affect the demand for _coffee_ (What--about coffee--does it affect?), but it is likely to bump some borderline coffee-drinkers over into tea instead, thereby increasing the demand for tea. A significant rise in the price of gasoline may increase the demand for bicycles.

> A change in the price of a SUBSTITUTE
> for a good is likely to change the
> demand for that good in the same
> direction.

Normal and inferior goods

Suppose you suddenly become richer than you used to be. You get a raise, or you win a lottery. Goods of all types are more accessible than they used to be. For many of them, you may be inclined to buy more (or be willing to pay more, if you had to) than before. Economists refer to such goods as "normal goods," reflecting the belief that this is typical behavior. If a good is "normal," a change in one's income produces a same-direction change in his demand for that good. Here's an example.

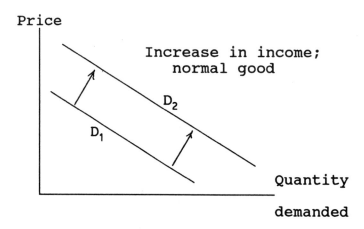

Figure 2.11: A normal good and a change in demand

There are other goods, however, that you buy basically because they're cheap and you're poor, and you wouldn't go near them if you could afford anything better. (Consider your apartment. Your car. Ah, the list goes on and on!) When an increase in your income expands the range of alternatives open to you, and you re-evaluate your actions in the context of this expanded set of opportunities, there will be some goods that just don't make it any more. In the old days when most people felt obliged to eat red meat once a day, economists used hamburger as an example. Presumably when you become more wealthy, you graduate to genuine un-ground beef. Your demand for hamburger actually falls when your income rises. Goods like this, for which your demand moves oppositely to changes in your income, are called "inferior" goods. Here's a picture of an "inferior" good.

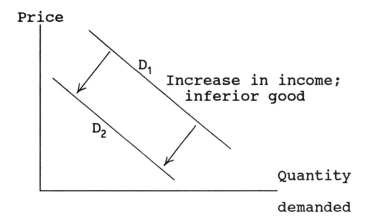

Figure 2.12: An inferior good and a change in demand

Whether a particular good (say, turnips) is normal or inferior depends entirely on the attitudes, the values, of the individual who's making the determination. What is inferior to you may be normal to me, and vice versa. When we try to select examples like the one above, or to make general statements about how "people in general" respond, we're thinking about our own reaction and those of the people that we know, and suggesting that maybe these are representative of "people in general." Well, maybe...and maybe not. Whether or not the generalization is valid, we have to remember that no such generalization applies to each and every individual, and it is the right of each individual to decide how he's going to act.

> The demand for a NORMAL good varies directly with income. The demand for an INFERIOR good varies inversely with income.

Expectations of price changes

We've already warned you that the <u>one</u> thing that, by definition, <u>cannot</u> cause a change in the demand for a particular good is a change in the price of that good itself. But suppose that someone gets the idea that the <u>future</u> price of the good is going to be different from what he'd been imagining. Fred makes some money waxing cars, and uses 5 sponges each week. They cost him $2.49 each. If Fred reads some news story about a sponge-divers' strike or a political coup in the region that produces them, he may develop the fear that the price of each sponge will rise sharply soon. Since they're easily stored (don't try this with ripe bananas), he may stock up on them now, preferring to spend, say, an extra $49.80 (four weeks' worth) now rather than much more later.

Because the change in Fred's action has not been caused by a change in the current price of a sponge, but rather by a change in one of the conditions that we assumed to be held constant when we constructed his demand, we must identify this as an increase in demand. Its cause was a change in Fred's belief about the future. Even if the current price were to remain unchanged at $2.49, Fred would demand a larger quantity than before.

How would Fred's current behavior be likely to change if he began to expect that this good was likely to become much less expensive soon?

> The expectation of a future change in
> the price of a good is likely to cause
> the current demand for the good to
> change in the same direction.

5)   "You draw all these curves as if they just shifted in, or out, parallel to the original one. Can't they become steeper or flatter? And what if the new curve crosses over the old one?"

Technically, a "change in demand" can be considered, unambiguously, an "increase in demand" if (and only if) there is no price at which the quantity demanded is smaller than it used to be. If the quantity demanded at each and every imaginable price is larger than before, I presume nobody would have any problem identifying that as an "increase in demand." I think we should be a little more liberal in our terminology here, and accept cases in which, at some or perhaps even most prices, the quantity demanded remains the same. If your demand price for the notebook rises from $2.83 to $2.95, we should be able to call that an "increase in demand" even though you used to demand zero at ten bucks each, and you still do.

Similarly, a "decrease in demand" refers to a situation in which there is no imaginable price at which quantity demanded has increased but at least one price-- and probably many--at which quantity demanded has decreased.

Certainly the new demand curve can be shaped differently, and it very likely will be. Our practice of always drawing them as parallel shifts conveys, to some extent, a misleading impression. But it's a bit like our drawing of smooth-line demand curves in the first place: just as the simplified but unrealistic smooth curve captures the essence of the law of demand, the main ideas that we want to get across with the concepts of increases or decreases in demand come through just fine with parallel-shifted curves. Some less-significant characteristics of changes in demand may not fare so well, but we can take them into account whenever it seems advisable, and for most purposes the simplification seems worth its cost.

But...if the new straight-line demand curve is steeper or flatter than the old one, they're going to cross each other somewhere. That means that at <u>some</u> prices "quantity demanded" has fallen while at others it has risen, and at one price it hasn't changed. Now has demand increased, decreased, or remained constant?

I do not know how economists have dealt with this question. I "handle" it by just saying that demand is <u>different</u>, and that the terms "increase" or "decrease" can't be applied unambiguously. Perhaps one can say that demand has increased in some price ranges, and decreased in others. I don't like that, because the term demand relates quantity demanded to all imaginable prices. So...demand is just "different," as far as I'm concerned.

Here are a few drawings of some changes in demand that don't conform to the usual parallel-shift practice.

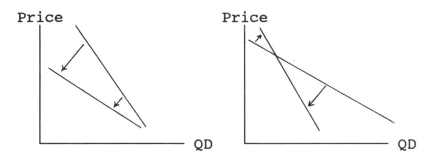

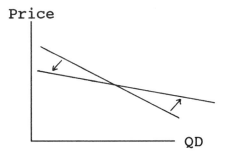

Figure 2.13: Some non-parallel changes in demand

6)   "Aren't there some cases where quantity demanded changes a lot when the price is changed, and others where it only changes a little, or maybe even not at all?"

You bet. Economists use the concept of the <u>elasticity of demand</u> to describe how sensitively "quantity demanded" responds to a change in price.

Suppose you sell widgets for a living, and at your normal price of $20 each the quantity demanded per week is 150. But perhaps many people's demand prices are clustered around your current selling price. There are another 30 potential customers whose demand prices lie between $19 and $20, and the demand prices of 30 of your current customers lie between $20 and $21.

In this case, a $1 price cut would raise the quantity demanded (and the quantity that you sell) by 30 units per week, while a $1 price increase would reduce it by the same number. Expressing these changes in percentage terms removes the arbitrariness that's involved in other forms of measurement (30 tons of wheat? or 3 trillion grains of wheat?), so let's do that: The $1 price changes are 5% of $20, and the 30-unit changes are 20% of 150, so we find that whether we raise or lower our price by 5%, "quantity demanded" changes by 20% (in the opposite direction, of course).

Let's take an opposite sort of case. Perhaps the demand prices of only 3 of our current non-customers lie between $19 and $20 (so the quantity demanded would rise by only 2% if we cut our price by 5%), and only 3 of our 150 current customers have demand prices between $20 and $21 (so the quantity demanded would fall by only 2% if we raised our price by 5%). In this case, people's demand prices are <u>not</u> clustered near our current selling price, so a change in that price would affect the purchase decision of only a few of them.

As you can imagine, it's pretty important to any particular seller which of these stories is closer to the truth. Would the seller benefit by a price increase? We'll investigate the details along about Chapter 6, but the answer is likely to be "no" in the first case and "yes" in the second. How about a price cut? Reverse the probable recommendations.

The official definition is:

> The ELASTICITY OF DEMAND is the
> percent change in quantity demanded
> divided by the percent change in
> price, times (-1).

(Price and quantity demanded always change in opposite directions, so we use that "minus 1" to make our elasticity a more comfortable positive number.)

In our examples above, elasticity was 4 (that's 20/5) in the first case and only 0.4 (that's 2/5) in the second.[3]   When this number is <u>greater</u> than one, we call demand "elastic." When it's <u>less</u> than one, demand is "inelastic." It all depends on whether a lot of people's demand prices are clustered around the price at which we're evaluating the elasticity.

Whether or not they're clustered like this isn't just a matter of chance, as a final example will illustrate.

```
Elasticity of demand is determined
primarily by the ATTRACTIVENESS of
the AVAILABLE ALTERNATIVES.
```

Consider an intersection between two busy streets, with a gas station on each corner. These four gas stations are literally right across the street from each other, and they each have large signs advertising their prices. Any particular customer may have a strong, long-standing, belief that Mobil is far superior to Shell, but many drivers don't much care and are likely to be quite sensitive to price differences that are easily perceived with a turn of the head. When each station charges $1.25 per gallon, customers may be about evenly distributed among them. But because many customers find the available alternatives to be nearly as attractive as their current gas, most people's demand prices for their current station's gas are likely to be clustered around $1.25. If any one station (and only one! <u>ceteris paribus</u>! no price wars permitted) were to lower its price by a nickel a gallon, its sales would probably skyrocket, and if it (alone) were to raise its price, its sales would drop dramatically. Competition makes the demand for any seller's product very elastic.

Here's another gas station. It's on the west Texas highway described in a problem in Chapter 1, the only gas station for a hundred miles either way. Your gauge has been pinned on "E" for thirty miles. As you roll in, with your fingers crossed, you find the price is $1.35, a dime a gallon more than you'd been paying (and perhaps nine cents more than your demand price) at the Exxon on the busy intersection back home.

A price like that would have caused you to go across the street immediately. But what's across the street here? Sagebrush and gopher holes. Your demand price for the Exxon gas back home ($1.26) was strongly affected by your knowledge that you could get Shell, across the street, for $1.25. Out here in the desert, your demand price is determined by how much you would pay to avoid the only alternative you can think of: "abandon the car and hitchhike." Most people find that far less appealing than

---

[3] When economists measure the elasticity between two points on a demand curve (like ($19,180) and ($20,150)), they prefer to express the changes ($1, 30 units) as a percentage of the <u>average</u> of the new and old amounts. (It's a 5.128% price change ($1/$19.50) and a 18.18% change in quantity demanded (30/165), for an elasticity of 3.545.) This keeps the percentage changes (and therefore the elasticity) from being different if we move from $19 to $20 than if we move from $20 to $19. This procedure also makes the elasticity between $20 and $21 greater (it would be 4.555--work it out!) than that between $19 and $20.

crossing the street and switching brands, so their demand prices will be far above $1.25 or even $1.35 per gallon. The demand for this gas, at these prices, will be very inelastic.

If Mr. "Last Chance Gas" decides to make use of his location to raise his price, he will eventually begin to encounter your and his other customers' demand prices. Suppose they're mostly clustered around, say, $7 per gallon. Although his demand was extremely inelastic (perhaps nearly zero) at $1.35, he will find that it's <u>elastic</u> up around $7. This illustrates the important point that:

> Elasticity VARIES along a demand curve. It is low (and demand is INELASTIC) at low prices, and it increases as price rises (with demand becoming ELASTIC at high prices).

Exactly what "low" and "high" mean depend on the circumstances; $1.35 was "high" to the competition-encircled Exxon station and "low" to "Last Chance Gas."

We won't be using the concept of elasticity much in the next few chapters, but it will be important to us in Chapters 6 and 7, especially. We'll have more to say about it then.

YOU SHOULD REMEMBER...

1. Be careful with terminology (like "need") that discourages you from thinking of action as choice among alternatives.

2. An individual's DEMAND PRICE for a unit of a good is the maximum price he would be willing to pay for it and still choose to buy it.

3. An individual's QUANTITY DEMANDED, at a particular price per unit, is the number of units that he will choose to buy.

4. An individual's DEMAND for a good is the set of his "quantities demanded" at each conceivable price, with all other things assumed to be unchanged.

5. Language that is just fine for casual conversation is often not sufficiently precise for careful reasoning.

6. The PURPOSE of the concept of DEMAND is to isolate the effect, on the quantity that one is willing to buy, of changes in the good's own price.

7. A change in the good's own price may cause a CHANGE IN QUANTITY DEMANDED. It cannot cause a change in the demand for the good.

8. The LAW OF DEMAND is that the "quantity demanded" of a good is inversely related to its own price.

9. The law of demand applies to any one demand curve, but it does not apply to comparisons between two different demands.

10. A change in the price of a good's SUBSTITUTE is likely to cause the demand for the good to change in the same direction.

11. A change in the price of a good's COMPLEMENT is likely to cause the demand for the good to change in the opposite direction.

12. When income changes, the demand for a NORMAL good changes in the same direction, and the demand for an INFERIOR good changes in the opposite direction.

13. The expectation that a good's own price is going to change in the future is likely to affect its demand in the same direction.

14. The ELASTICITY OF DEMAND is the percentage change in quantity demanded, divided by the percentage change in price, times minus one.

15. If elasticity is GREATER than ONE, demand is "elastic." If it's less than one, demand is "inelastic."

16. Demand will be elastic at a particular price if many people's demand prices are CLUSTERED around that price.

17. Elasticity of demand is determined primarily by the ATTRACTIVENESS of the AVAILABLE ALTERNATIVES.

Problems

1. Here is a list of a few persons' demand prices for widgets. Each person is interested in purchasing only one.

Frank:	$ 1.00
Lauren:	$ 4.50
Alicia:	$ 0.75
Bud:	$ 2.00
Wilma:	$ 3.25

a) Construct a step-type demand curve for widgets, with "price per widget" on the vertical and "quantity demanded" on the horizontal axes. Your graph doesn't have to be of draftsman quality, but try to follow the usual rules: equal distances on the graph always correspond to equal amounts (e.g., 1 inch = $1), price and quantity demanded are both 0 at the origin, etc.

b) If the price charged for each widget is $1.50, how many widgets will be bought and BY WHOM?

c) If the price remains at $1.50 each, how much more would Wilma have been willing to pay, than the amount that she actually pays, to obtain a widget?

d) Someone convinces Frank that widgets are good for him, and he changes his demand price to $1.75. What will this do to the demand curve that you drew, and how many widgets will now be sold at the $1.50 price?

e) Return Frank to his original valuation (forget (d)). Now suppose that the widget owner has only three widgets, and he decides to sell them according to this scheme: He announces that he will start at a price of zero, and raise it a penny at a time until he finally reaches a price at which only three bidders are left. Each of those three will then each get a widget at that price. What is that price, and how much money will he get from the sale of the three?

f) Suppose, instead, that the owner of the widgets announces that he'll start with a price of $100 each, and move it down (a penny at a time) until he reaches a price at which exactly three bidders express a willingness to purchase. He will then sell each of them a widget, at that price. What will that price be, and how much money will he get?

g) Compare your answers to (e) and (f). Explain why you found them to be different (if you did) or the same (if you did).

2. Draw a simple downward-sloping straight-line market demand curve for apples. Now, suppose that the price of oranges rises sharply. Show what is likely to happen to the market demand curve that you drew for apples if...

a) apples and oranges are substitutes.

b) apples and oranges are complements.

c) apples and oranges are completely unrelated.

d) Which of these three alternative possibilities do you think describes most people's attitudes about apples and oranges?

3. In its quest for tax receipts, your state slaps a heavy new tax on gasoline. This is likely to raise the price of gasoline (though not necessarily!). Consider the effect of a sharp increase in the price of gasoline on the demand for bicycles.

a) Would your demand for bicycles be affected by a 30 percent rise in the price of gasoline?

b) Let's assume that you answered "no" to (a). Does it follow that the market demand for bicycles is likely to be unaffected?

c) Explain why the market demand might rise even if your demand does not. [Hint: what's the difference between "you" and "the market"?]

4. You go to the grocery store, planning to buy one jar of instant coffee, and discover that the price has been reduced by fifty cents. You buy two jars. Did the lower price cause you to double your demand? Explain.

5. Henry was about to buy a computer, when he suddenly discovered that their prices have been declining for many years. He decided to wait until they got even cheaper. Explain what happened to his current demand for computers, and why.

6. President Bush announced, with some humor, that he does not like broccoli. Could his revelation of his personal preference cause the demand for broccoli to rise, or perhaps to fall? Can you imagine a causal connection?

7. Is your demand for the services of a furnace repair man likely to be more elastic in the summer or in the winter? Explain, using the concept of the value of the best alternative.

8. Advertising that is seen by people who already use the advertised good isn't necessarily wasted. Suppose you already drink a certain brand of cola, but its

appealing advertising convinces you that it is even more superior to its competition than you had thought. This advertising doesn't lead you to drink more of "your" cola, but it may affect the elasticity of your demand for it. How, and why?

9. You normally drink Coke but are convinced, by excellent advertising for Pepsi, that Coke is nowhere near as superior to Pepsi as you had believed. At current prices you'll continue to drink Coke, but what is this advertising likely to do to the elasticity of your demand for it? Why? Is this problem (and answer) consistent with that of number 8?

10. Here are two conceivable situations:

i) You normally buy Morton's Salt, but you discover that its price has gone up by 30%. You are shopping in your usual food store, and there are 8 competing brands of salt nearby on the shelf.

ii) You normally buy Morton's Salt, but you discover that its price is 30% higher than you've been used to paying. You are on a camping trip, shopping in a small country store, where Morton's is the only salt to be found.

a) Is your response to these discoveries about price likely to differ in these two cases? Why or why not?

b) What (if anything) does this imply about the elasticities of the market demand for Morton's Salt (in the price range involved here), in these two cases? After all, it's "Morton's Salt" in each situation.

CHAPTER 3

THE CONCEPT OF SUPPLY

AN INTRODUCTION TO SUPPLY
AND "RESERVE DEMAND"

How do you train a parrot to be an economist? You teach him to say, "Supply and demand, supply and demand."

The British economist Philip H. Wicksteed (1844-1927) might have disagreed with this old joke. In a speech delivered in 1913, he stated:

> But what about the "supply curve" that usually figures as a determinant of price, co-ordinate with the demand curve? I say it boldly and baldly: There is no such thing.[1]

The concept that economists call supply, he believed, is simply another way of looking at what we have already analyzed as demand, so there is little value to introducing the new idea.

Although it's clear (even from our parrot) that the economics profession has not followed Wicksteed's implicit advice about terminology, his point is interesting and important. Our introduction to supply builds on it.

There may appear to be a fairly sharp difference. Based on our own experience, it may seem as if demand, like that for notebooks, is determined by individuals who attribute value to actually using the demanded good. But most of the goods that we buy are supplied by large retail stores, at prices determined by "business" things like costs and profit in which the value that the store clerk (or store manager) attributes to actually using the good plays no noticeable role at all.

Good point. By the end of this chapter, though, you'll see that this difference is more apparent than real. In fact, business costs and prices and profits (things that we normally associate with "supply") are also determined by the individual valuations of people like you.

---

[1] Philip H. Wicksteed, "The Scope and Method of Political Economy in the Light of the 'Marginal' Theory of Value and Distribution," Economic Journal XXIV, 93 (1914), reprinted in Wicksteed, The Common Sense of Political Economy (Clifton NJ: Kelley, 1933), p. 785.

To highlight the essential similarity between demand and supply, let's start with a simple yard-sale kind of story in which the seller <u>does</u> have some personal use for the good.

The Veggie Whacker at the yard sale

Your neighborhood holds a community yard sale every year, and it's coming up. Suddenly you notice, in a corner of the kitchen, that old Veggie Whacker that you bought from a TV ad a few years ago. On impulse, you set it out with some other things, and someone (Peter) offers $5 for it. Do you accept his offer? More interestingly, how do you decide whether to accept it or not?

We've actually been through this already. You have two mutually exclusive alternatives: the extra $5, or continued ownership of the Veggie Whacker. You'd been putting off this valuation process, but now you can't avoid it. You scan over, in your imagination, how important the continued ownership of this kitchen appliance might be to your future; you try to think about what you could do with the $5 if you had it; and you compare how "well off" you believe you would be in these two alternative future situations. Depending on your anticipation about the future, you accept or reject Peter's offer.

Although there is nothing here that we have not already analyzed, you have just made a decision about "supply." You have decided either to supply Peter with this wonderful Whacker at a price of $5, or not to. Perhaps your judgments about the future led you to conclude that you must receive at least $7 for the appliance, if "sacrificing it and obtaining money" were to be preferable to "keeping it." You would <u>not</u> supply the Whacker if the price offered were below $7, but you would supply it if the price were $7 or above. You prefer the Whacker to the best alternative that you could obtain with $6.99, but with $7 you could acquire an alternative good that is preferable to it.

In Figure 3.1 we have a graph that depicts your preferences in the situation we've been describing.

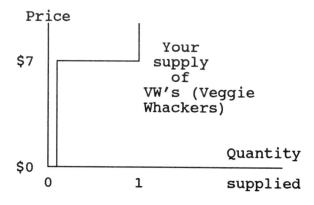

Figure 3.1: Your supply of Veggie Whackers

Notice that the general shape of this graph--a couple of vertical lines connected by a short horizontal line segment--is similar to that of the demand curve we've discussed before. That's no coincidence, because the reasoning process we went through to describe your decision whether or not to "supply" the Whacker to Peter was exactly like your decision whether or not to demand a notebook.

The only thing that's really different is that before, when we were talking about demand, you owned the good depicted on the vertical axis (money) and were evaluating the action of giving it up in return for the good on the horizontal axis (notebooks). Now, when we're discussing supply, you already own the good that's on the horizontal axis (the VW) and are evaluating the action of giving it up in return for the good on the vertical axis (money).

That's why demand and supply are so similar in principle: they involve the very same action, considered from the viewpoints of the two individuals who are involved. Our choice of which axis we use to identify which good you already have, with the other axis depicting the good you're thinking of acquiring, makes a difference in the appearance of the curve, but it can hardly be very significant to the ideas.

You express your demand for a particular good (perhaps a notebook but let's identify it in general terms as "A") by your willingness to sacrifice some other good (perhaps money, but to keep the discussion general let's call it "B") in return for it. The very act of <u>demanding</u> one good consists of the <u>supplying</u> of the other. Your action in this exchange consists of demanding A by supplying B, while Joe demands B by supplying A.

Think back, for a moment, about buying that notebook at the bookstore. In our new way of thinking about the trade, you demanded the notebook by supplying money, while the bookstore demanded money by supplying the notebook.

The money price of the good still indicates something about the alternative to the good. If you're <u>demanding</u> the good by supplying money, you want to minimize the alternatives that you must sacrifice: you like to find a low price. If you're <u>supplying</u> the good by demanding money, you prefer to obtain as attractive a range of alternatives, in return for the good, as you possibly can: you prefer a high price. In either case, the money price is an index of the alternatives to the good. But the good's demander has to give them up, while the good's supplier receives them.

Wicksteed explained that you can actually be said to exercise a demand for your own Veggie Whacker if the price is below $7.00. This minimum-acceptable price is often called a <u>reserve price</u> (they're fairly common at auctions--see the little excerpt, below, from a report on an antique-car auction), and at prices below it the owner is said to be exercising <u>reserve demand</u> for his own good.

A RESERVE PRICE is the lowest price at which the owner of a good will prefer to sell, rather than keep ("reserve"), the good.

Your "quantity reserve-demanded" is "one" at prices below $7.00, and "zero" at prices of $7.00 and above. Because your "supply" of Whackers is just another way of expressing your own "reserve demand" for it (the quantity that you supply, at any particular price, is the difference between the number that you actually have and the quantity that you "reserve demand"), Wicksteed saw the concept of supply as superfluous.

"At a Puyallup auction held in July, Silver offered an immaculate 1957 Chevrolet 3124 Cameo pickup, equipped with a 283 cid V-8 and an automatic transmission, that had been garaged for 30 years. It was bid to $9,000 but didn't sell because the seller insisted on $13,000." (Old Cars Weekly, January 10, 1991, p. 20)

--A reserved Cameo--

Demand and supply, "stock," and "reserve demand"

Some time ago, we discussed a set of related concepts: demand price, quantity demanded, and demand. There is a similar collection of concepts associated with the supply decision.

An individual's supply price of a unit of a good is the minimum price at which he will prefer to sell the unit rather than not to sell it. (Reserve price is a special case: it is the individual's supply price if he already owns the good. Nobody can "reserve" a thing, like the '57 Chevy pickup, unless he already owns it.)

To determine an individual's quantity supplied, we run through the same kind of mental experiment that allowed us to find his "quantity demanded." We select a particular price per unit ($7.98, say). We then ask him to assume that he can sell as many units as he wishes at that price, and to decide how many units he would choose to sell under those conditions. That's his "quantity supplied." It's always a particular number of units (such as 147 blodgets per week), and it is associated with one particular price per unit (such as $7.98 per blodget).

The individual's supply of the good is the set of relationships between each conceivable price per unit, and the "quantity supplied" at each of those prices.

Look back at your supply of Veggie Whackers. Since you only have one, and you have no plans or ideas to obtain others, you can supply only either zero or one of them. Suppose a voice comes out of the air, stating that the price is $5.25. We find that price on the price (vertical) axis, consult the supply curve at that price, and find a quantity supplied of zero at $5.25. If the voice now says, "Price is now $6.38," our quantity supplied is still zero. But if it says "Price is now $8," our quantity supplied jumps to "one."

Our <u>supply</u> of VWs has not changed. We have not had to draw a new supply curve, or to construct a whole new set of relationships between "price" and "quantity supplied." We simply moved from one point on the supply curve, to another point--on the same supply curve.

There is only one change that, by its very nature, cannot change the SUPPLY of a good. That is a change in the GOOD'S OWN PRICE.

The number of units of the good that you already own (here, one Whacker) is called your "stock." Since your reserve demand is the number that you prefer to own at each conceivable price, we can draw the curves of Figure 3.2 that illustrate the relationship among stock, reserve demand, and market supply.

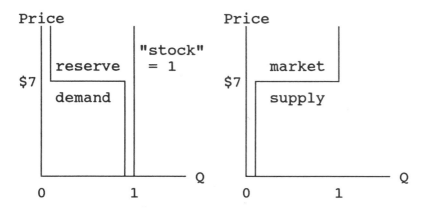

Figure 3.2: Supply, stock, and reserve demand

Your "supply price" is $7. You already own the good, in this example, so $7 is also your "reserve price." Since it's pretty tough to sell something you don't already own (and it's probably against the law), you might wonder how there can be "supply prices" that <u>aren't</u> "reserve prices." They are the minimum prices at which you would be willing to sell the good if you first have to acquire (perhaps by producing) it. Once you <u>have</u> acquired or produced it, your supply price does, indeed, become your reserve price. We'll get into this soon, mostly in Chapter 5. For now, back to the matter of the vegetable chopper that you already own.

With a fixed "stock" (one Whacker), anything that changes your "reserve demand" makes your "supply" change in the opposite direction. That's just an economist's way of saying that if you decide that you value your own good more, you become more reluctant to sell it.

Since your "reserve demand" is determined by exactly the same kinds of things that determine others' "market demand" for your chopper (namely, the value of its ability to chop things), any changes that affect others' market demand are likely to affect your reserve demand in the same way. A doubling in the price of all vegetables (complementary goods to the VW) makes using the device more costly and therefore less attractive to potential customers (reducing the market demand), but also to you (reducing your reserve demand). A recession may increase both market and reserve demand, since a manual VW is probably an "inferior good," especially compared to imported electric food-processors.

Our interesting conclusion is that whatever makes the device more attractive to others (increasing their demand for it) also makes it more attractive to you (reducing your supply of it). When the supplier and the demander both value the good for the same reasons (specifically, personal use), then anything that changes the market demand for the good also changes the market supply, in the opposite direction.

Sellers with no personal use for the good

What if you truly place no value whatsoever on the possibility of using the Veggie Whacker yourself in the future? On your value scale, it lies right down there on the bottom, a little below "the best alternative use of one cent." Your "reserve demand" is a vertical line at zero (it lies right on top of the vertical (price) axis) and your supply is identical to your stock: a vertical line at a quantity of "one." This is the case of a "no reserve" auction; the good goes to the highest bidder, even if it's for a nickel. Any of the changes that may affect market demand by making the good more or less attractive to use will have no effect on you, since you have no intention of using it anyway.

This example is raised because, in a modern mass-production economy like our own, many goods are supplied by individuals who have no personal use for them. How many Chryslers can Lee Iaccocca drive (or be chauffeured around in)? A building-supply wholesaler views the 2,457th fifty-pound sack of concrete mix, back in the warehouse, about the same way that you look at your old Veggie Whacker: you want to get as much as you can for it, but it would only take a penny to bid it away from the best use to which you could personally put it.

When those who produce, own, and sell a good have little or no personal use for it, considerations that affect the market demand for it have little or no effect on its reserve demand--and, hence, on its market supply. In this case, the factors that affect the demand for a particular good have little or nothing in common with the factors that affect the supply of that good.

It's our ability to treat the market demand and market supply of a particular good as approximately independent that makes the distinction between "demand" and "supply" useful. Why only "approximately"? There are always some pesky roundabout effects, sometimes weak and sometimes strong, that operate through the markets for other goods and make the independence only partial. To the extent that it's proper to assume that changes in demand for a particular good do not require us to draw a new supply curve for that good too, that independence arises from the fact that in a modern economy characterized by specialization and division of labor, people produce goods far in excess of their own ability to use those goods. Some of the important factors that change the market demand for a good may have only a trivial effect on the willingness of its current owner(s) to supply it on the marketplace.

COST AND SUPPLY

One of the reasons that I like to start my discussion of supply with a small-scale everyday example like the notebook or the Veggie Whacker is to nudge you away from thinking that ordinary people (like us) demand, while big businesses supply. Any trade involves two goods and two people; each of you evaluates what you're considering giving up and what you're considering obtaining, and acts according to this judgment of value.

If we focus our attention on one of the goods (A), then one person (Joe) demands it and the other (Sally) supplies it. If we decide, instead, to look at the other good (B), then we find Sally the demander and Joe the supplier. How can our decision about which good to concentrate on, as we read in the library or sprawled in an old armchair somewhere, have <u>any</u> significance to the basic nature of what's going on? It can't, and it doesn't.

Besides, if you didn't "supply" that big retailer with something (like, money?), it wouldn't be too eager to supply you with socks and light bulbs. Furthermore, where does it get the services of its sales clerks and stockboys? Of course it demands these labor services (by supplying occasional paychecks).

> In every exchange, each party demands
> one good and supplies another.

So we all--from the least wealthy individual to the largest corporation--demand and we all supply. Demanding and supplying are just looking at the same activity (exchange) from two different directions. In every exchange, one party demands one good and supplies another, while the second party demands the good that the first party supplies and supplies the good that the first party demands.

Supplying a good that you don't own yet

What if you don't already <u>have</u> a Veggie Whacker, but you know that Peter wants one? What would it take to make it worth your while to <u>obtain</u> one yourself, and then sell it to him? Our little story above is fine if you already have it, but the real world is one of continual production, not just yard-sale exchanges of things that already exist.

Assuming that you aren't interested in simply doing Peter a favor, this little exchange will be beneficial to you only if you are able to obtain the VW yourself for less than Peter is willing to pay you for it. If you know where to get it for $4.99, and he's willing to offer you $6, then it's worth your while to buy it and resell it to him.[2] This exchange makes you better off (you can enjoy $1.01 worth of other goods, unavailable before) but it also makes him better off (he valued the Veggie Whacker more than he valued his best alternative use of $6). He would, surely, have been even <u>more</u> "better off" if he could have obtained the appliance, as you did, for $4.99, but apparently you knew something that he didn't. We can choose only among alternatives of which we have knowledge.

The $4.99 is your monetary cost of providing Peter with the Veggie Whacker. (Our example is simpler, and the point comes across more clearly, if we assume that you incurred no taxi fares or advertising expenses or any other monetary outlays not already included in the $4.99.) We'll be going into the concept of "cost" at considerable depth in Chapter 5, but for now let's try to get along with a sort of minimalist notion of it.

```
The COST of an action is the value
of the best (highest-valued)
alternative action that the actor
must forego.
```

The phrase "monetary cost" refers to the amount of money that one must sacrifice-- either give up, or not receive--to take a particular action. (Of course it derives its significance from the alternative ways of using it that must be sacrificed.) Here, apparently, if you are to sell Peter the kitchen device that he wants, first you have to buy it yourself, and that'll require you to hand over $4.99.

Reselling this Whacker would actually make you better off if you could get any price of $5 or more for it. (Remember that we assumed absolutely zero hassles or

---

[2] The fact that <u>your</u> demand for the Whacker is derived from <u>his</u> demand for it illustrates "the principle of derived demand" that will be discussed in Chapter 9.

costs of any other kind. We're trying to keep the example as simple as possible.) Figure 3.3 shows a graph of your market supply of this particular Veggie Whacker.

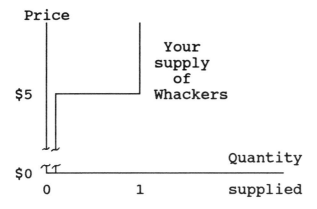

Figure 3.3: Supplying a good you do not yet own

You only know where you can get one, and you have no personal use for it yourself. This is strictly a business proposition, designed to make money. If you can get enough (price) to more than cover your cost ($4.99), "supplying one" makes you better off and you'll do it. If you believe that you won't be able to sell the device for more than your $4.99 cost, then you won't get into this little endeavor at all: you'll supply "zero." In this example, $5 is your supply price of this Veggie Whacker.

This example illustrates the general proposition that:

> An individual's SUPPLY of a good is determined by his COST of supplying it.

In our example, with no taxi fares or labor on your part, that's just your cost of buying it yourself.

Exploring the principle...

We can go a long way toward a general understanding of supply just by applying this reasoning, also, to your supplier.

If you're going to be able to buy the appliance yourself for $4.99, someone else is apparently willing to supply it to you for $4.99. That means that it must have cost that supplier less than $4.99, or the exchange wouldn't benefit him. We could follow this example through various levels of retailers, wholesalers, distributors, and so forth, but it's easiest simply to suppose that you buy it directly from the manufacturer.

The manufacturer's willingness to supply you with a VW is determined in exactly the same way as was your willingness to supply Peter with one: the manufacturer must anticipate receiving a price that is greater than his own cost of producing it. Only then will the act of "producing and selling the VW" be preferable to simply holding onto the money that the production would have cost, and using it for the next-best investment.

So if the manufacturer can produce the Veggie Whacker for a sum as high as $4.98, he benefits (though not much) when you purchase it for $4.99, and you benefit (though not much) if you supply it to Peter for $5.00. Naturally you would prefer that Peter pay much more, and the factory prefers that you pay much more, but the figures clustered around $5 are the minimum prices at which production and exchange are beneficial to all of the parties involved.

About the only problem left is to explain what determines the $4.98 that may constitute the manufacturer's cost. To answer that, we have to think about the manufacturing process.

The producer of the Veggie Whacker has to purchase (<u>demand</u>) many kinds of inputs: plastic parts, labor for assembly, rubber wheels, advertising services, electricity, warehouse space, transportation. Each of these inputs, however, has other uses, and other people (or businesses) demand them for their own purposes. If our producer--the Vegco Company--is going to be able to obtain the resources that it needs to build our machine, it has to <u>outbid</u> the other offers for these resources. It has to offer enough for these resources that the resource owners find the sale to Vegco to be <u>their</u> best alternative.

This could seemingly go on forever, but we don't need to carry it much farther. If our producer knew he could get $4.99 for a machine, he would be willing--if necessary--to offer as much as $4.98 for the resources needed to produce it. But the producers of other goods--knife sharpeners, roller skates, can openers, you name it--feel exactly the same way. If the resources needed to produce the Veggie Whacker could be used to produce some other good that consumers are willing to pay $4.50 for, then other producers will be willing to offer $4.49 for the inputs. That means that Vegco will have to offer at least a little more than that.

The cost of producing any good (Veggie Whackers included) is determined by the value that consumers attribute to the most-valuable of the other goods that could have been produced with the same resources. The reason our company must pay at least $4.50 is that some other producer is willing to pay $4.49, and the reason he's willing to do that, is that he knows he can sell the good that he produces with these resources for $4.50.

This is one of the most important things you can learn about cost:

> The cost of producing any good is
> determined by the value that
> consumers attribute to the most-
> valued of the other goods that could
> have been produced with the same
> resources.

After all, if our VW is going to be produced, somebody somewhere is going to have to go without some other good. Only if we're willing to pay more for the Whacker than that other person was willing to pay for the other good, will our manufacturer be able to bid the necessary resources away from his manufacturer.

This is a very powerful principle that explains a great deal about how a capitalist (free) economic system functions, how actions are interconnected. Let's consider another simple example.

The Adirondack chairs and the mini-deck

Here's a pile of redwood lumber, a bunch of zinc-coated (non-rusting) bolts, and a skilled carpenter. With this very same pile of resources, the very same skills, and the very same amount of time, this carpenter could build either a small (OK, very small) deck or four Adirondack lawn chairs. We'd like him to build the chairs, and we're willing (though he doesn't know this) to pay up to $100 each for them. The question is: what determines the minimum that we will have to pay, to get him to build the chairs for us?

Well, what's his best alternative? That's what we have to outbid. Suppose he can imagine no other earthly use for any of these materials, but he likes watching soap operas so much that it would take $50 to get him to sacrifice them long enough to build the chairs. Since his monetary estimate of his cost of building the chairs is apparently $49.99 or so, we must offer him a little more than that if he's going to prefer "building the chairs" to "watching TV." Our minimum cost is determined by his cost. What we actually pay will be somewhere between $50 and $400, determined by our bargaining abilities.

Another neighbor suddenly sees the redwood and the loafing carpenter, and decides that he ardently wants a tiny redwood deck. He considers his income, wealth, and alternative uses for his money, and decides that he would be willing--if necessary--to pay as much as $324.99. Suppose he's not a very good bargainer, or believes it's immoral, and simply offers $324.99 for a deck.

The carpenter's best alternative is suddenly no longer $49.99 worth of "The Edge of Night" and "The Bold and the Beautiful": it's $324.99 for building a deck. If we want him to choose, instead, the action "building the chairs," the alternative action that we must now outbid is "building the deck," and that's going to take at least $325. The cost <u>to us</u> of the chairs has suddenly risen from $50 to $325, because that's what has happened to the cost <u>to the carpenter</u> of producing them, the monetary value of the most-valuable alternative to the chairs.

Consider the carpenter's supply of Adirondack chairs. In this example, the quantity supplied is either zero or four. If we're willing to pay $325 or more, there are four chairs supplied. At a price (of the four chairs all together) of $324.99 or less, zero chairs (but one deck) are supplied. Before the neighbor butted in, the quantity of chairs supplied jumped from zero to four when the price (for four) reached $50. His entry into the market increased the cost to the carpenter of producing chairs, and therefore our cost of buying them. It reduced the supply of chairs.

Here's the principle again. Apply it to the deck and the chairs. The cost of producing any good is determined by the value that consumers attribute to the most-valuable alternative goods that could have been produced with the same resources.

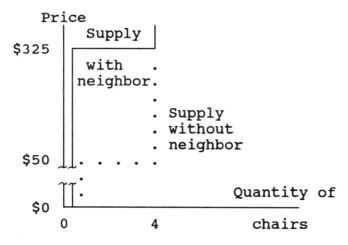

Figure 3.4: The supply of Adirondack chairs

A LITTLE MORE ON SUPPLY

There's another way of expressing that principle about the cost of producing one good being determined by people's valuations of other goods. It may help you to understand cost and supply.

> If you want someone else to take a particular action, you have to make sure that he perceives it as the best of his current alternatives.

You have to make it worth his while. Whatever his next-best alternative is, you must outbid it.

You want the carpenter to build the chairs for you. If <u>he</u> doesn't view "building the chairs for you" as <u>his</u> best available action, he won't do it. Sometimes all you have to do is ask, but in this case there are alternatives that you have to outbid. First there were the TV shows, which took at least $50 to outbid. (The carpenter considered "seeing the shows and having the same amount of money" preferable to "missing the shows but having $49.99 more," but not preferable to "missing the shows but having $50 more.")

Then there was the nosy neighbor--some nerve he's got, making the carpenter a great offer and therefore making it necessary for you to increase your own offer. The carpenter's best alternative is now "miss the shows, build the deck, and have $324.99 more," and <u>that's</u> what you have to outbid if you want the chairs. Since we've assumed that he's indifferent between building a deck and building four chairs, the only difference is money. To make "building the chairs" the best of his available opportunities, all you have to do is offer at least $325.

You must outbid the best alternative use...

This principle can be applied all throughout the economic system, as our example about the Veggie Whacker implied. If the carpenter does not already have the lumber and hardware, he would have to obtain it. That means he'll have to make sure that "selling to him" is the best of the resource owners' available alternatives: he must outbid the offers of others who also want the lumber and hardware. He will be willing to increase his offer (though reluctantly) as necessary, as long as it's still less than we're willing to pay for the chairs.

We can imagine our carpenter at the lumber company, with us on the telephone for authorization: "I gotta have $50 for my time, and they want $337 for the other stuff. Will you pay $387 for the chairs?" "Great...oops, somebody else just offered the lumber company $340 for the materials. Will you pay $390 for the chairs?" If it looks as if the resources (including the carpenter's time) will cost more than $400, we are no longer able to outbid the next best use of the resources. The chairs just aren't worth as much money to us as some other good, producible with those resources, is worth to somebody else.

If we're to get the chairs, the carpenter must make sure that the owners of the lumber and hardware perceive "selling the resources to him" as the best among their alternatives. But that requires <u>us</u> to make "buying the resources," at a price sufficient to make <u>selling</u> them the best option open to the lumber company, the best alternative available to the carpenter. Ultimately, what we must outbid is the best alternative offer for the resources, and that's going to be coming from someone who wants to use them in some other way. That next-best offer, the one that we have to outbid, is determined by the amount that some other consumer is willing to offer for some other good that can be produced with these resources.

Maybe there's one pile of lumber and hardware at the local lumber company, and they're willing to sell it to the highest bidder. Your friend the carpenter is bidding to build you some chairs, while the guy who wants the deck has found another carpenter (who also evaluates his own time at $50) who is bidding too. Your carpenter will be able to make "selling to him" the preferable of the lumber company's options, outbidding your neighbor's carpenter, as long as you are willing to offer your carpenter more for the chairs than your neighbor is willing to pay his carpenter for the deck.

This principle is a little tougher to follow when one considers some really complex goods that are produced in today's economy. What does it cost General Motors to produce a Buick Roadmaster? I don't have any idea, but the inputs required include computer chips, glass, rubber, plastic, steel, aluminum, electricity, labor, transportation, the services of a huge variety of complex machines, and all kinds of other things. There is probably no other single good that uses exactly this same combination of inputs. (That was a simplifying assumption in our "deck vs. chairs" example.) If GM is going to buy these inputs, the company must offer at least enough to outbid other demanders of the plastic, of the rubber, of the computer chips, etc. No one buyer is bidding for all of these, but someone is bidding for each of them, and those are the people that GM must outbid. Their offers determine GM's cost of producing the Roadmaster. And those offers are, in turn, determined by the judgments that the managers of other businesses make of the value that their customers attribute to the use of the input.

"If we used this plastic, our can openers would be more attractive. How much more would our customers pay for them?," wonders the owner of a can-opener factory. His answer sets an upper limit on how much he can offer for the plastic. If GM doesn't think that amount of that kind of plastic is likely to contribute at least that much value to Roadmasters, the plastic is going into the can openers.

The issues involved here can get very complex. (How would you try to determine the contribution of this particular plastic to the sales revenue GM is likely to receive from sales of Roadmasters?) It's a part of economics known as "marginal productivity theory," which we'll discuss in Chapter 9. For now, it's enough for you to see that some judgment on these issues is necessary. If Buick didn't think the plastic added some appeal, why would it be willing to incur any expense whatsoever for it? But surely Buick wouldn't spend $5,000 per car for it. Where's the line? Somehow it has to depend on what benefit Buick expects from the use of the plastic.

We don't have to go into all of the details now. (Good thing!) But it is important that you appreciate that the conclusions of our little examples about Adirondack chairs and tape recorders apply to far more complex and realistic processes of production in the real-world economy. Whether we're talking about the carpenter and the deck, or GM and the Buick Roadmaster, the cost of producing a particular good is determined by the value that consumers attribute to the other goods that could have been produced with the same resources.

Supply of one, and demands for others

The relationships between cost and supply, and between "value" and demand, suggest another way of expressing this conclusion.

> The SUPPLY of a particular good varies INVERSELY with individuals' demands for OTHER goods that could have been produced with the same inputs.

Think about the effect on the carpenter's supply of chairs, of an increase in your neighbor's demand for a deck. When his demand increases (he's willing to pay a higher price), your supply decreases (for some prices at which the carpenter was willing to supply you with the chairs, he no longer is willing).

If there's an increase in the demand for plastic-handled can openers, there will be a reduction (probably pretty tiny) in the supply of Roadmasters that use this kind of plastic. That's another way of saying that because Buick's cost has risen slightly, individuals who want to buy a Buick will have to pay a slightly higher price than before.

Note that it's individuals' demands for <u>other</u> goods that affect supply. The supply of any one good is still largely independent of the demand <u>for it</u>. When there's a change in the demand for a good, the "quantity supplied" of that good probably changes--we move up or down along the supply curve--but the "supply" itself doesn't.

We'll return to some of the implications of this proposition shortly. You might think about what it implies about what happens to the supply curve of "locally raised range-fed beef" when the adjacent city experiences a business boom and rapid population growth that brings a big increase in the demand for new single-family houses in the suburbs.

Supply curves slope upward

Another important characteristic of supply is the upward slope of the curve that depicts it graphically. We've already discussed that, at the level of the individual who already owns the good and has some reserve demand for it. To the potential seller, "price" indicates the range of alternatives that is available, and "more is better." If the good itself is of <u>some</u> use, it takes some minimum price (reserve price) to make the seller judge that the best alternative use of the money is now superior to retaining the good itself. Because "reserve demand" slopes downward just like "market demand," market supply slopes upward.

When the individual doesn't own the good yet, his supply decision hinges on the cost of producing the goods. A buyer must offer enough to cover the seller's cost, or the seller won't find the production and sale to be desirable.

Remember how a supply curve is constructed. We imagine an increase in the price that the seller receives for each unit of the good that he offers, and ask how the quantity that he finds it desirable to sell is affected by this hypothetical increase in the price received for each of them. Suppose that a seller has been selling 93 widgets per week when the price was $15. We ask him to tell us how many he'd be willing to sell each week if he could get $16 each, how that new "quantity supplied" would differ (if at all) from 93.

We can't give a precise number without knowing a great deal more about the facts, but there is something we can say.

At the previous price of $15, we were offering the producer enough to make it "worth his while" to produce every widget that cost him less than $15. We were providing him with the incentive, and the money, to bid resources away from other uses that other individuals--somewhere in the economy--valued less than $15.

Now, at the $16 price, units that would have cost the manufacturer more than $15 but less than $16 are profitable for him. It benefits him to produce and sell any unit that he can produce for less than $16. That includes all of the units that cost him less than $15, plus any that cost between $15 and $16. He now has both the incentive and the money to bid additional resources away from their other uses--those resources that could be used to produce other goods that other people valued more than $15 but less than $16.

When the price of each widget was $15, those additional resources were used-- and, economists generally would agree, were best used--to produce those alternative goods. We simply didn't value widgets enough to be willing to outbid the other consumers who demanded the other goods producible with the resources that our extra widgets would have required. They were willing to outbid us, and they did so.

That's the simplest explanation of why supply curves slope upward. A higher price for a particular good (widgets) provides both the incentive and the money for a supplier to bid resources away from alternative uses that were previously valued higher than the additional widgets. If we imagine offering a supplier a higher price per unit, he is both willing and able to bid more of the resources needed for production away from their alternative uses. The quantity that he is willing to supply increases. Figure 3.5 offers a graphical representation of what's going on.

Underlying this analysis are two basic ideas. First, the bland term "resources" hides a lot of differences. No one acre of land is exactly like any other, and no two individual workers are the same. (One person may prefer a certain mix of physical and mental responsibilities, or working with people vs. "things," while another is most comfortable with a slightly different mix.) Some iron ore contains small amounts of other trace minerals, other ore doesn't. These differences make particular resources especially well suited to the production of particular products.

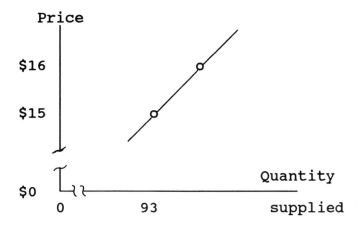

Figure 3.5: A simple upward-sloping supply curve

If you want to produce widgets, you naturally seek out those resources especially well suited to widget production. It will be easy for you to bid them away from alternative uses (where their special properties mean little or nothing), and very attractive for you to do so. If you wish to expand production, however, you must resort to resources that are progressively less well suited to the production of widgets, and more well suited to other things. That generally means that you're going to have to bid more for them; your costs rise. A higher price per unit will be necessary if it is to be worth your while to bid such resources away from their increasingly valuable alternative uses.

A related consideration arises from other individuals' valuations of the other goods they will have to go without. If you are to expand the production of widgets, they will have to sacrifice an increasing number of units of other goods. Think back to our discussion of demand. If an individual is asked to give up only one unit of a good, he'll sacrifice the least-important use that he is currently satisfying with a unit of that good. If he's asked to give up two units, he'll sacrifice the least- and the next-to-least important uses, and the latter is necessarily more important than the former. As the widget producer attempts to bid resources away from an increasing number of alternative uses, the value--to other individuals--of those alternative uses increases. They become more reluctant to make the sacrifices, so the widget producer--if he's going to outbid their demands for resources--is going to have to pay more.

Exactly how a particular producer in a particular situation responds to a higher, or a lower, price depends on a lot of things. Is it easy (low-cost) for him to outbid alternative uses for the resources he needs? If so, a slightly higher price may result in a large increase in "quantity supplied" and the supply curve will be pretty flat. If we apply our elasticity concept to supply, such a supply curve is called elastic: the quantity supplied responds dramatically to a change in price. (In a manner parallel to our discussion of the elasticity of demand, if the percentage change in "quantity supplied" is greater than the percentage change in "price" that caused it, supply is called elastic.)

For some goods it's very difficult (read "costly") to expand production, so the inducement of a higher price causes a relatively small increase in quantity supplied and the supply curve is steep. When the percentage change in "quantity supplied" is less than the percentage change in price that caused it, supply is called inelastic. "Quantity supplied" just isn't very responsive to price. In the extreme, perhaps it's absolutely impossible to produce any additional units of the good ("genuine Mona Lisas" is a traditional example), so the quantity supplied can never exceed the stock already on hand. But don't forget that its owner can exercise "reserve demand." The "quantity supplied" to the market is likely to be different at a price of $10 (undoubtedly zero) and at $200 million (probably one). If the owner truly has a "quantity reserve-demanded" of zero at all prices (like a "no reserve" auction), then the market "quantity supplied" is equal to the stock regardless of price. When a change in price produces no change whatsoever in quantity supplied, as it would in this "no reserve" situation, supply has zero elasticity.

Between these extremes of easy to expand (very high elasticity) and impossible to expand (zero elasticity) are all ranges of difficulty. Real-world supply curves are generally neither horizontal--very easy to draw resources from alternative employments--nor vertical--impossible to attract the necessary resources at any price. We'll usually draw supply

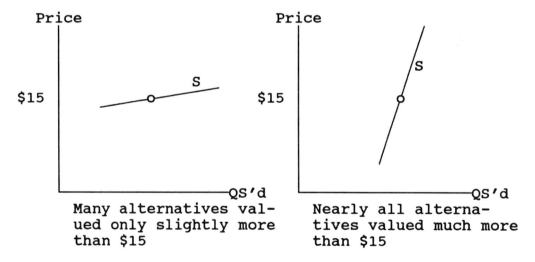

Figure 3.6: The elasticity of the supply curve

curves with about a 45-degree upward slope, but don't let that mislead you. Sometimes it's important whether their upward slope is steep or slight. But the <u>most</u> important thing is simply that they slope upward.[3]

---

[3] A <u>lower</u> price and a <u>larger</u> quantity supplied (and demanded and sold) are often found together. Personal computers offer a dramatic modern example, as did automobiles about 75 years ago. But think back to our Chapter 2 question about the demand curve that apparently sloped upward: that example provides the key here. Our upward-sloping supply curve is a <u>ceteris paribus</u> construction with production technique and technological knowledge assumed constant. If demand (and therefore price) are higher than expected, or technology advances, producers' actions may make our <u>ceteris paribus</u> analysis importantly incomplete, by adopting new production techniques. That means that our whole supply curve shifts to the right. It is perfectly possible to have upward-sloping supply curves, a lower price, and a larger quantity supplied--but only if there was also an <u>increase in supply</u>.

YOU SHOULD REMEMBER...

1. In every exchange, each party demands one good and supplies another.

2. "Supply" and "demand" are both determined by individuals' valuations of alternatives.

3. Reserve demand is an owner's demand to retain his own good.

4. An individual's "supply price" of a unit of a good is the lowest price at which he will be willing to sell it.

5. An individual's "reserve price" is his supply price of a good that he already owns.

6. An individual's "quantity supplied" at a particular price per unit is the number of units that he would choose to sell, if he knew that he could sell as many as he wished at that price.

7. An individual's supply of a good is the set of his "quantities supplied" at all conceivable prices, ceteris paribus (only the good's own price permitted to change).

8. The cost of any action is the value of the highest-valued alternative action that must be foregone.

9. If you want someone to take a particular action, you must make sure that he perceives it as the best of his own alternatives.

10. To get someone to supply you with a good, you must outbid others who value different uses of the resources.

11. The supply of any good is determined by the value that individuals place on other goods that could have been produced instead.

12. The SUPPLY of a particular good varies INVERSELY with individuals' demands for OTHER goods that could have been produced with the same inputs.

13. Supply curves slope upward: as we imagine the price increasing (ceteris paribus), the quantity supplied increases.

Problems

1.   Mother and Father have been on a cruise and have left you in charge of the estate. They're getting home tomorrow. You have let the place get rather messy, but there's nothing that some energetic teenagers' labor couldn't clean up. You happen to know of five kids who could handle the various cleanup duties (equally well) today, but of course they all have other opportunities. The monetary value they place on the best of the other uses of their time today is as follows:

Joe: $74.99 (lounging around the country club pool)
Wendy: $24.99 (flipping hamburgers at a fast-food joint)
Barbara: $36.99 (studying for a summer-school course)
Sam: $14.99 (watching reruns of Knight Rider)
Alice: $94.99 (sorting out a local company's computer problems)

a)   Use these data to construct a supply schedule of "persons' worth of estate-cleaning labor services today." Plot the data with "number of persons working for me today" on the horizontal axis (this is our "quantity") and "daily wage per person for today's labor" on the vertical axis (this is our "price"). Assume that you pay the same wage to each person that you hire. Use axes like those below, and construct and label your scales properly. Hint: imagine offering a very low wage (say $1 per day), gradually increasing it, and tracing out the number of people willing to work for you. (The $20 marks do not mean that your offered wage can change only by $20 increments.)

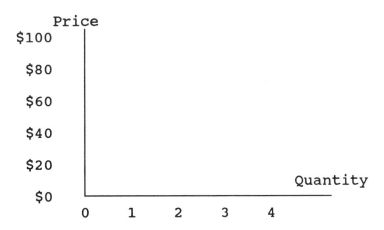

b) Suppose you are a bit short on cash and decide the place can be put into tolerable shape with only one worker's labor. Will you hire Barbara to do it? Why or why not?

c) Would it be reasonable to say that your answer to (b) explains why this supply curve slopes upward? Discuss.

d) If you must pay each worker that you hire the same wage (perhaps out of some sense of fairness), and decide that the estate can be made respectable with 3 teenagers' labor today, who will you hire? What is the minimum that you can pay each of them? (Remember: each worker is paid the same amount.)

e) The monetary value of <u>which individual's</u> best alternative determines how much you will have to pay <u>each</u> of the three workers?

f) Joe and Barbara are equally skilled at helping to clean the estate. Why, then, does he require $38 more for his services than she requires for her (identical) services?

g) Suppose you decide that you can afford to spend as much as $80 to make the place look as good as possible. Who will you hire, and how much will you have to spend? (Each person that you hire receives the same wage, and no partial days--only full days--are allowed.)

h) If you offer a daily wage just barely high enough to induce 3 of these teenagers to come to work for you, how much <u>more</u> do you pay Sam than was necessary to drag him away from Knight Rider?

i) If you pay the same wage to each worker that you hire, how much would you have to spend if you wanted to hire three workers? Four workers? Why such a dramatic difference? (We'll see this situation again, in Chapter 9.)

j) If these young folks' abilities at cleaning up the estate are really identical, as we've been assuming, why are the minimum amounts they're willing to accept for these identical cleaning services so different? Is that right or fair, since the cleaning services are identical? (Although it may not seem like it, this is one of the most important questions that I ask you to consider in this course.) Discuss.

2. Suppose that it takes the same kind of fairly special land and climate to grow either pomegranates or oranges. If you grow one kind of fruit, you can't grow the other.

a) What (if anything) will an increase in the demand for oranges do to the supply of pomegranates?

b) What will a rise in the price of oranges do to the supply of oranges?

c) If pomegranates and starfruit are generally considered to be substitutes, what will happen to the demand for starfruit, and why?

3. For years, you've been saving up to buy a nice few acres in the Green Mountains of Vermont. You've almost got enough saved when about a million rich lawyers and doctors decide they want to own rural Vermont property too. What does that do to your cost of obtaining some Vermont real estate for yourself, and why? Is it fair?

4. Suppose that you suddenly decide to increase your demand for blodgets. How might your action reduce the supply of some other good that you don't even know about? What effect is this likely to have on the people (you have no idea who they are) who have been buying this other good?

5. What typically happens to the supply of Saturday-night babysitting services, as most of the young people in a neighborhood begin to reach their teenage years? Explain, by considering the need to outbid best alternatives.

6. Business and industry are getting more "technical" by the year, offering more--and more lucrative--employment opportunities for individuals with skills in math, science, and engineering.

a) What effect does this tend to have on the supply of people with these skills to the teaching profession?

b) If no adjustment is made in the wage offered to teachers with these skills, what is likely to happen to the number of math and science teachers?

c) Would it be fair to pay different wages to teachers of math and of history, if they work equally hard?

7. A radical group of environmentalists succeeds in passing legislation that requires companies to apply for permission before they can cut each and every individual tree, and to justify the action. What would this do to the supply of paper? Draw some curves.

8. What happens to the supply of land to be used for drive-in movie theaters, as the suburban population expands and the demand for land for other uses

increases? [Hint: Think about the landowners' best alternatives. What is happening to the minimum that a prospective drive-in operator will have to bid? What does this imply about the supply curve of land to him?]

9. Your neighbor, an elderly man, has a 1957 Chevrolet that he no longer drives. He was about to give it to you, when Tim offered him $5,000 for it. When you approach him about the car, he says, "Golly, I'm sorry, but you'll have to pay more than $5,000 if you want it." What has Tim's offer done to your neighbor's supply of '57 Chevys to you? Is it fair, when the car's owner has zero use for it himself?

10. Suppose that computer programmers can develop software for either operating system A, or operating system B. A major computer company adopts operating system A for its popular computers, sharply increasing the demand for programs written for that system. What will this do to the supply of programs written for system B? Explain, drawing curves and discussing the concept of the value of the best alternative.

CHAPTER 4

USING "SUPPLY AND DEMAND TO ANALYZE MARKETS

"SUPPLY AND DEMAND, SUPPLY AND DEMAND"

There's that parrot again. Great humor never dies, at least not in this book. Now that we understand a little about the general nature of demand, and about the general nature of supply, we can put our insights together to form some understanding of what markets actually accomplish. It's a fascinating exercise.

The minimalist market: one demander, one supplier

This simplest market has two people (one to buy and one to sell), and two goods. Let's make one of them money, because so many of our daily exchanges involve it.

I like to start with these simplest-conceivable examples, because they highlight the _essence_ of the idea. If you get a firm grip on the essential nature of an economic concept, you have a foundation that you can count on when you decide--as you surely will--to make the analysis more "realistic" (and complicated and interesting) by gradually dropping some of the simplifying assumptions (like "only walking distance matters" or "the bookstore will not bargain"). Make your analysis as realistic and complex as you wish, but first get the basics right.

Felix has some money. He has scanned over the various alternative ways that he could use it, carefully considered what he could do if he had a wodget, and has determined that his demand price for a wodget is $13. He values one wodget more than the best alternative use of $13, but not as much as the best alternative use of $13.01.

Oscar has a wodget. He has scanned over the various things that he could do with different amounts of money, carefully considered what he could do if he kept his wodget, and has determined that his supply (actually reserve, since he already owns the good) price is $10. He values his one wodget more than the best use to which he could put $9.99, but not as much as the best use of $10.

If they get together and communicate (always necessary if a market is to exist), they are likely to discover that there is a range of prices at which each of them (that is, both of them) benefits. Let's draw a picture (Figure 4.1) of their supply and demand curves.

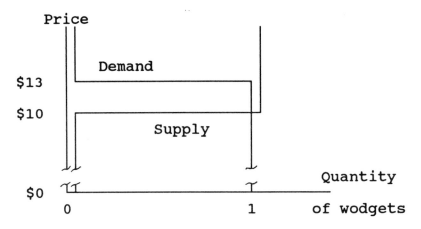

Figure 4.1: The minimalist market

Consider a price of $7. Felix (the potential buyer) would be delighted to get the wodget for that low a price, so the "quantity demanded" in our little market is "one" (that's him). But that price is so low that Oscar won't sell, preferring to keep and use the wodget himself: the "quantity supplied" is "zero."

How about a hypothetical price of $16? Oscar (the potential seller) would be thrilled (quantity supplied is "one") but Felix wouldn't go for it (quantity demanded is "zero").

There is a range of prices, however, at which exchange would benefit each party. These are the prices that are $10 or above, but $13 or below. Let's pick one of them, say $12, for illustration.

A price like $12 meets the following essential criterion: Oscar values $12 more than he (Oscar) values the wodget, while Felix values $12 less than he (Felix) values the wodget. An exchange of "one wodget for $12" therefore makes each individual better off. Each receives something in the exchange (Felix the wodget, Oscar the $12) that he himself values more than he himself values what he gives up (Felix the $12, Oscar the wodget).

What would have happened if Felix's demand price had been $10 and Oscar's supply price had been $13? I'm going to let you think that one through, but here's the punch line: There is no sum of money that Oscar values more than the wodget but that Felix values less than the wodget. No exchange can take place. [This sub-example is now over. Please switch back to Oscar at $10 and Felix at $13.]

Graphically, the interesting property of prices in this $10-to-$13 range is that "quantity demanded" is equal to "quantity supplied." Each is "one." That, of course, means that Felix is willing to <u>buy</u> one at any price in this range (or lower), while Oscar is willing to <u>sell</u> one at any price in this range (or higher). Since an exchange requires a willing buyer <u>and</u> a willing seller, trade can occur only between $10 and $13.

We can't say exactly what price emerges from Felix and Oscar's discussion. That depends on their bargaining abilities. Obviously Oscar is going to try to get a high price, but it can't go over $13 or Felix won't buy. Felix wants a low price, but it can't go below $10. Who outfoxes whom, here? You know some of the ploys: "There's another guy coming back in 15 minutes with $12.75 cash...," or "I already have one of these, but I might go as high as $10.50 for a spare..." Such strategies are risky and not always advisable, but the point for us is that it's pretty tough to say exactly where the price will wind up. What we <u>can</u> say, however, is that it will be between $10 and $13.

One seller, multiple potential buyers

The next step in our process of understanding markets is to see what happens when a second potential buyer is introduced. It's easy, then, to imagine a third or forty-seventh of them.

Our seller is still Oscar, with his $10 supply price. Felix still has his demand price of $13. But suppose now that Marilyn has come along, and her examination of her own value scale has produced a demand price of $12.

Oscar would be willing to sell to either of them: prices above $10 but below $12 would benefit all three of these people. But there's only one wodget, and if Oscar wants to get the highest price that he can for it, he won't sell it to either Marilyn or Felix at a price below $12. He will let Felix and Marilyn bid against each other for it, and they will drive the price up until Marilyn is no longer willing to buy. The price must be above $12 (to outbid Marilyn's highest offer) but below $13 (so that Felix benefits). Figure 4.2 illustrates the market with supply and demand curves:

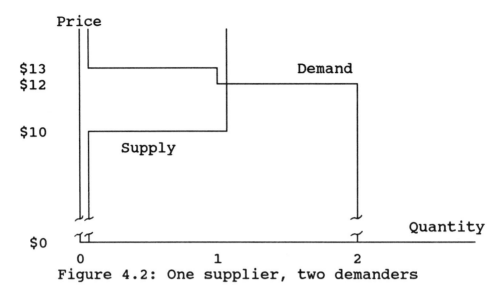

Figure 4.2: One supplier, two demanders

If there's going to be a sale, the price must be above the seller's supply price of $10, so that the quantity supplied is "one." But it must also be high enough that there's only one demanded. At a price of, say, $12.25, Felix still values the wodget more than he values the money, but neither Marilyn nor Oscar does. Competition between Felix and Marilyn has driven the price up until the person with the lower demand price (Marilyn's $12) has dropped out. Now both the quantity supplied and the quantity demanded are equal to "one." The successful buyer (Felix) is the one with the highest demand price, and the price that he has to pay is <u>now</u> in the range of $12 to $13.

If there were, say, 38 other bidders, or 953, but each of them happened to have a demand price below $13, the principle would remain the same. Felix would still have to outbid the second-highest offer for Oscar's wodget. With that many other bidders (remember our restriction of "below $13"), it's not going to be Marilyn's $12, but probably someone else's $12.99. The more bidders, the narrower the range of prices at which "quantity demanded" equals "quantity supplied" (each simply "one" here), and the closer the price gets to the <u>highest</u> demand price among the folks who want to buy. Felix gets the wodget (at a price of, say, $13) only because he's the individual who, among all of these people, is willing to give up the most money for it.

One buyer, many would-be sellers

Let's put Felix in a somewhat more enviable position. Instead of having to out-compete hordes of other buyers (who drive up the price that he has to pay), we'll consider him the beneficiary of competition among a number of potential sellers...not just Oscar.

Felix wants one wodget and is willing to pay up to $13 for it. Now suppose that Blanche has a wodget and, having considered and evaluated all of her alternatives, has selected a supply price of $9.

At a price like $11, Felix is willing to buy, but both Oscar and Blanche are willing to sell. Blanche is especially eager; that price is well above her supply price. Trying to make sure that he is the successful seller, Oscar chops the price a little (to $10.75), hoping to drive Blanche out of the market. But the strategy backfires, because when she adopts it their competition for Felix's money drives the price down below $10. (Felix is grinning with delight, naturally.) Finally, a price is located (perhaps $9.80) at which Felix and Oscar each value a wodget more than the money, but Blanche doesn't. Since Oscar already has a wodget, the trade is between Felix and Blanche.

Figure 4.3 shows the supply and demand curves that depict this situation. Once again, notice that they overlap (quantity demanded equals quantity supplied) only in this particular price range: $9 to $10. Both supply prices (Oscar's $10 and Blanche's $9) meet the criterion of being acceptable to Felix (below his $13 demand price). But competition between the sellers will drive the price down until it is still <u>above</u> the lowest supply price, but is <u>below</u> the second-lowest supply price.

This story is the mirror-image of the multiple-demanders story that we investigated above. Suppose there are 274 other individuals each with a wodget to sell, and each of their supply prices just happens to be <u>above</u> $9. Competition among them will narrow the range of prices at which quantity supplied equals quantity demanded (both equal to "one" here), and the price will fall toward the <u>lowest</u> supply price among those who wish to sell. The way this example is constructed, that's Blanche. She sells the wodget, at a price of probably $9, because of all of these people, she's willing to accept less than is any of the others.

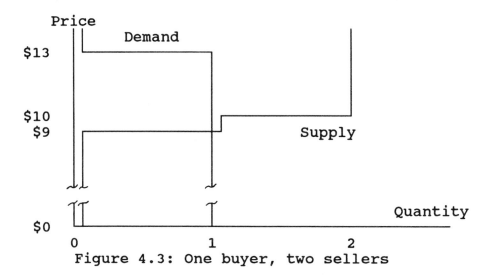

Figure 4.3: One buyer, two sellers

Two-sided competition: many buyers and sellers

We've now had a chance to think a bit about a market with one seller but competing buyers, and about a market with one buyer and competing sellers. It's time to combine these perspectives into a market with many buyers and sellers.

Actually, there's not much to it. Back in Chapter 2, when we expanded our demand curve from one or two or six students to "many," all that we did was to draw a smooth downward-sloping demand curve in place of the ones with steps. We imagined that each conceivable price ($3.41? $0.92?) was some individual's demand price, and brushed aside the remaining little steps that arise from the fact that prices have to change by at least one cent, and quantities by at least one unit.

To pull a similar maneuver with supply, we assume that each and every price is the "supply price" of some particular unit. That gives us a smooth, upward-sloping supply curve like those of Chapter 3.

Figure 4.4 provides an illustration of our smoothed-out, many-buyer and many-seller supply and demand curves.

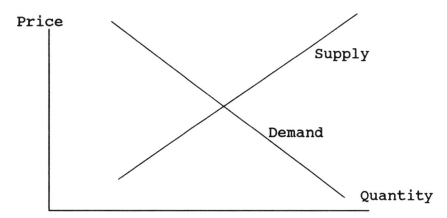

<u>**Figure 4.4: Many buyers and many sellers**</u>

Economists very much prefer this kind of supply-and-demand example over that involving few traders, because there is no longer any doubt about the exact price. As our examples showed, an expansion of either the number of buyers, or of the number of sellers, is likely to shrink the range of prices at which the demand and supply curves overlap, the set of prices at which "quantity supplied" equals "quantity demanded." If we imagine a sufficiently large increase in the number of traders, the curves become smooth and they only overlap at one point. There is then <u>only one price</u> at which "quantity supplied" equals "quantity demanded," so we no longer have to explain, apologetically, "Well, it's between $10 and $13 but we don't know where, because that depends on bargaining."

Markets that are appropriately described with smooth curves like these, intersecting at only one point, are sometimes called "perfect" markets. I don't much like that term, because it improperly suggests that there's something <u>wrong</u> with a market that consists of only a few buyers and sellers. As we'll see in our Chapter 7 discussion of "monopoly," whether the number of traders in a market is "good" or "bad" depends entirely on the nature of the <u>process</u> by which that number of traders was determined.

EQUILIBRIUM AND ITS SIGNIFICANCE

There's obviously something special about the point (or range) at which the demand and supply curves cross. At that price (or range of prices), the number of units that some people want to <u>buy</u> is precisely equal to the number that certain other people want to <u>sell</u>. Every individual who actually wants to buy (at that price) therefore can (there's a seller for him); every individual who actually wants to sell (at that price) therefore can (there's a buyer for him).

This particular price <u>coordinates</u> the plans of the buyers and the sellers. It is the only price at which the plans of the demanders and the suppliers are mutually compatible. Remember that if you're actually going to be able to buy, someone else has to be willing to sell... and <u>vice versa</u>. At any higher price, suppliers won't be able to sell as many units as they want to sell, because demanders won't buy that many; at any lower price, demanders won't be able to buy as many units as they want to buy, because suppliers won't sell that many. Only at the price at which the curves cross, at which quantity supplied equals quantity demanded, are the plans of the suppliers and of the demanders consistent.

> A good's EQUILIBRIUM PRICE is that price at which its quantity demanded and quantity supplied are equal.

Figure 4.5 shows a few supply-and-demand graphs with prices depicted that are above, below, and at equilibrium.

At the above-equilibrium price, shown in Figure 4.5A, the quantity supplied is greater than the quantity demanded. Because the price is "too high," sellers are enthusiastic but buyers are reluctant. Since nobody can sell unless someone else buys, the quantity that will actually be bought and sold is limited to the smaller quantity: the quantity demanded.

At the below-equilibrium price, shown in Figure 4.5B, the price is "too low" so the buyers are eager but the sellers reluctant. The quantity actually exchanged will be limited to the quantity supplied.

> The number of units of a good that are actually bought and sold is the SMALLER of the "quantity supplied" or "quantity demanded."

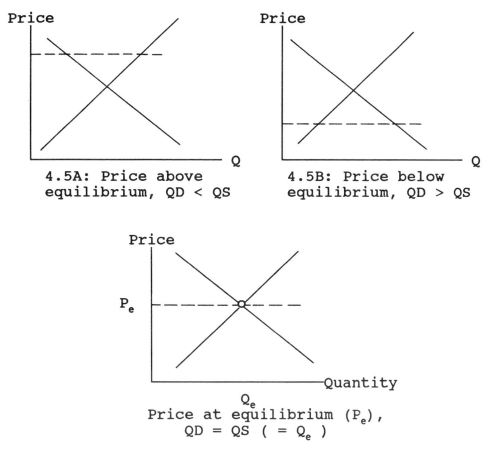

Figure 4.5: Above, below, and at equilibrium

It's natural, of course, to think of equilibrium simply as "where the curves cross." I have my own little "Egger's Law of Economic Graphs." It states that whatever the graphs that you see on the board in an economics course, there is almost always some reason why whatever it is that's being described should be at the point where the curves cross. Feel free to use this "law" in the future. It's good for brownie points, allowing you to answer professors' questions in this and upper-level economics courses when you really have no idea what's going on. I take no responsibility, of course, if he asks you to explain why one should be at the crossing point!

Individuals bring a market to equilibrium

How does a market get to its equilibrium? As you might infer from our stories of Felix and Blanche, the process is simply the self-interested entrepreneurial actions of the individuals involved.

Suppose that the market price ($16) is above equilibrium ($12), so that the weekly quantity supplied is 175 units while the quantity demanded is only 85 units. Since the suppliers know that only 85 units could actually be sold at that price, their desire to sell 90 of them will be disappointed (that's 175-85): they want to sell that many more at $16 than they are able to. (see Figure 4.7 on page 91.)

Some clever, entrepreneurial, seller is bound to get the idea that his success as a seller will be assured if he makes his good more attractive than his competitors' by shading the price a little--say, to $15.90. Some buyer, too, may infer that he can offer less than $16 and still get the good. Of course their actions attract imitators and self-defenders. As the price falls, sellers find that it no longer covers the cost of selling some of the units; that's why the quantity supplied falls. Meanwhile, the lower price attracts new buyers: the quantity demanded increases. These pressures continue until the market reaches equilibrium, at $12 and 125 units.

If the market price ($10) is below equilibrium, so that the quantity supplied is 100 and the quantity demanded 145, frustrated buyers try to assure their success by bidding the price up and clever sellers perceive that they can sell even at higher prices. As these individuals bid the price up, it crosses over some individuals' demand prices, so the quantity demanded falls; meanwhile, the higher price exceeds the cost of selling a larger number of units than did the old lower price (quantity supplied increases). These upward pressures on price continue until equilibrium is reached.

Equilibrium exerts a great fascination for economists, and properly so. But we must never forget that markets are not "automatically" in equilibrium. They don't fly there instantly, in the split-second after a shift in demand or supply. A market in disequilibrium is brought toward equilibrium by the clever insights of particular individuals, who perceive that a lower (or higher) price might make them better off.

Equilibrium in a broader perspective

To get a broader understanding of the meaning of equilibrium, let's step back a little and re-examine some of the properties of demand and supply.

Figure 4.6 shows a demand curve, with some made-up numbers to help to clarify the point.

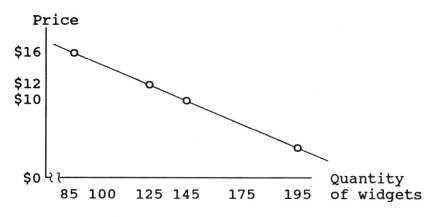

Figure 4.6: A demand curve

The height of this demand curve, corresponding to any particular widget, is the <u>demand price</u> for that widget. (We investigated demand prices in Chapter 2.) The reason that the demand price for the 145th widget is $10, is that the person with the 145th-highest demand price values a widget just slightly more than his best alternative use of $10. There are 144 people with higher demand prices, of course, and they form the portion of the demand curve that's above $10.

Joe's demand price for a widget is the price of the highest-priced alternative that Joe barely considers giving up for a widget. He makes that determination by comparing the <u>values</u> of the widget and the alternatives that are available for different sums of money. It is reasonable, then, to interpret Joe's demand price as an indicator of the value of the alternative that he is just willing to sacrifice.

> The height of the DEMAND curve, corresponding
> to a particular unit, is a measure of the
> highest-valued alternative that individuals
> <u>would be willing</u> to sacrifice for that unit.

If we think, now, about the supply curve, we can develop a similar interpretation. The supply price of any particular unit--the minimum price at which it will be offered for sale--is determined by its monetary cost. That, in turn, is determined by the amount of money that people are willing to spend for the most valuable alternative good, something that they will have to go without if our unit is produced and sold. (See Chapter 3 on this.) If the supply price of unit number 438, for example, is $6.72, that indicates that the largest sum that anyone is willing to offer for some good that would have to go unproduced if number 438 is to be produced, is about $6.72. (OK, maybe a hair less.)

This association between a unit's "supply price" and the value of the best alternative that people would have to give up if that unit were to be produced, gives us the "supply" part of our picture:

> The height of the SUPPLY curve, corresponding to a particular unit, is a measure of the highest-valued alternative that individuals <u>would have to</u> sacrifice for that unit.

Figure 4.7 adds these interpretations of supply and demand to Figure 4.6. Since the value that an individual attributes to a particular widget determines that value that he would be willing to sacrifice to obtain it, we can interpret the height of the demand curve as an indicator of the value of the unit of the good itself, and the height of the supply curve as the value of the best alternative that would have to be given up if that unit is to be produced.

Pick a unit like the 100th widget. Its supply price is $10, and its demand price is $14.25. Someone values that widget just a little more than he values $14.25 worth of alternatives. But the suppliers can make it available at a cost of only $10, and that tells us that if it is produced other individuals must go without alternatives that they value at only $10.

A simple way to express this point is that each widget (like the 100th) for which the demand curve lies above the supply curve is valued <u>more</u> than alternatives, while each widget whose demand price is less than its supply price is valued <u>less</u> than alternatives. This terminology is a little sloppy, in part because the numbers on the demand and supply curves are amounts of money and not "values," which can't be quantified like this. But I think the main point of the story is right, and maybe the simplification is worth its cost in rigor.

This interpretation explains the comments at the bottom of the graph in Figure 4.7.

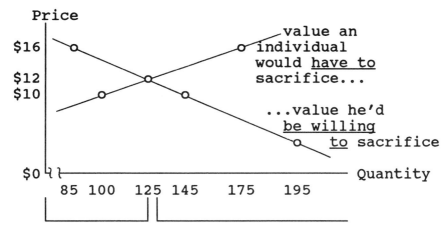

Figure 4.7: Equilibrium and values

Notice that for each unit to the left of the equilibrium quantity, the demand curve lies above the supply curve: these units' demand prices exceed their supply prices. For each unit to the right of the equilibrium quantity, the supply curve is higher: these units' supply prices exceed their demand prices.

If you could play the role of benevolent dictator, choosing how many widgets your economy should produce to make your subjects as well-off as possible, how many would you order to be produced? You wouldn't want 175 or 195 or any other quantity above 125, because then some widgets would be produced that are not as valuable as the other goods that other people would have to go without. You wouldn't want only 85 or 100 or any other quantity less than 125, because then some other goods would be produced that people value less than they value the 40 or 25 additional widgets. You would want to produce precisely 125, the equilibrium quantity, because then every widget that is valued more than alternatives is being produced, and no widget is produced that is valued less than alternatives.

If you're tempted to think that people actually want and value widgets numbered 126 and above, well, you're right--in a way. And if we could just snap our fingers and create them out of thin air, that's what we ought to do--and a social system that prevented us from doing it would be undesirable and harmful.

But that's not an accurate depiction of the alternatives available to us. We cannot just create number 126 out of thin air. To obtain it, Frank is willing to sacrifice perhaps $11.90 worth of other things that he could have done with his money. It sure would be nice if he could have this widget, and it seems too bad that somehow he is denied it.

Think again, though. Its production would require the using up of resources that could have produced a <u>wodget</u> that Chet values at $12.08. Frank values the widget, but not enough to be able to make it worthwhile for the widget producer to bid the resources away from the wodget producer.

We can't say that Chet values the wodget more than Frank values the widget, because values cannot be compared between individuals. But it is likely that the resource owner values $12.08 more than he values $11.90, so Chet is going to be able--indirectly--to bid the widget away from Frank. Frank is willing to give up only $11.90 worth of <u>his</u> alternatives, while Chet is willing to give up $12.08 of <u>his</u>. Those of us who thought it would be nice if Frank could have the widget (that he values at $11.90) may view things a little differently once we recognize that Chet would have to go without the wodget (that he values at $12.08).

Whether or not you consider market activity in general to be "fair," I hope you agree that there's something appealing or desirable about a system that tends to produce every unit of every good that some individual values at more than its cost, and no unit of any good that is worth less than it costs.

But that is precisely what a market in equilibrium does. To emphasize this delightful property of markets, I've reproduced Figure 4.7 with some additional commentary: it's Figure 4.8.

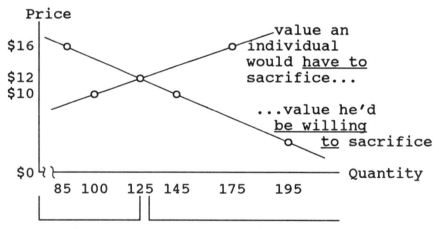

These units are valued more than alternatives, and they <u>are</u> produced.

These units are valued less than alternatives, and they <u>are not</u> produced.

Figure 4.8: Equilibrium, values, and production

When this market has adjusted to its equilibrium, we find that every widget for which someone is willing to pay more than its cost is likely to be produced, and no widget for which no individual is willing to pay more than its cost is produced. Since the cost of producing a widget is the value that individuals attribute to the best alternative that could have been produced with the resources required to produce that widget, we reach the conclusion illustrated by the few additional notes added at the bottom of Figure 4.8.

This is a fascinating property of markets. If any one person had <u>designed</u> or <u>invented</u> a system of cooperation among individuals which, even though leaving each person completely free to make his own choices according to his own values, still manages to produce this outcome, he would no doubt be recognized as one of history's greatest contributors to civilization.[1]

In fact, of course, no one person created the system of interrelated markets that we know as capitalism. Markets emerge naturally, from the choices and actions of individuals who have freedom of control over their own property.

Think back over the process by which the demand and supply curves that we've become familiar with are constructed. They're all rooted in the individual's decision that using his own resources in one way would make him better off than using them in another way. You buy the notebook or use your money for an afternoon movie, and similar decisions by millions of other people determine how many movies and notebooks are produced, their prices, the prices of the resources used to produce them, and millions of other quantities, prices, and costs in our complex market society.

The three functions of price

The money price of the good is a key element in the whole process, as a brief scan over our discussion above shows. Price is sometimes said to have three functions: information, incentive, and rationing.

A money price conveys information about a good's relative scarcity; how much people value it relative to other goods, how much of it they value more than they value the other goods they would have to sacrifice. We cannot <u>see</u> people's values directly, but we can see how much money they offer or ask. A rising or falling money price is a sign that the good has become relatively more or less scarce than it used to be. (If <u>all</u> money prices are rising, that's inflation. All goods are becoming more scarce relative to money, because the government is pumping out new money. Then we have

---

[1] Friedrich A. Hayek, discussing the market mechanism, put it this way: "I am convinced that if it were the result of deliberate human design, and if the people guided by the price changes understood that their decisions have significance far beyond their immediate aim, this mechanism would have been acclaimed as one of the greatest triumphs of the human mind." Hayek, "The Use of Knowledge in Society" <u>American Economic Review</u> XXXV,4 (1945); reprinted in Hayek, <u>Individualism and Economic Order</u> (Chicago: University of Chicago Press, 1948), p. 87.

the problem of determining which goods' prices are rising faster than others'. They're the goods that are becoming relatively more scarce.) As we will see, a society that believes that it must place restrictions on prices, or even make the pricing and market exchange of important classes of goods illegal, suffers from distorted information about people's relative values.

The information that a good is becoming increasingly scarce may be quite interesting, but so what? Who cares? Why should anybody take any particular action based on that information? This is the incentive function of price. You pay prices every day. Nobody has to tell you that "price" is not just an index or abstract number on somebody's computer somewhere. It is actually an amount of money that someone must hand over and that another receives. A rising price, therefore, does more than simply inform us of an increasing scarcity.

If the increasing scarcity resulted from a natural catastrophe like a severe freeze that destroyed most of a crop (a reduction in supply), its rising price provides incentive for those who use the good to use it more sparingly, to find substitutes, to economize on it. If the good is more scarce because of a surge in the demand for it, the rising price provides incentive for those who produce the good to pursue new ways of producing it, not profitable before, calling into its production resources that had previously been used in ways that are now less important and valuable.[2]

As far as you're concerned, it doesn't make any difference whether a higher price is the result of a sharp reduction in supply or a surge in other individuals' demands. The higher price itself provides incentive for you to economize. Nobody has to explain it to you, or convince you of its social desirability.

Finally, the pricing process provides a means of determining who gets what, and how much. When a good is scarce, so that not everyone can have as much as he would like to have, there has to be some way of allocating these scarce goods among all of the individuals who would like to have them. The process of voluntary exchange, which we have been describing with supply and demand curves, jointly and simultaneously determines prices, quantities exchanged, and the demanders and suppliers who are successful.

Those who are successful demanders (buyers) are those who are willing to offer the highest prices. They're the demanders on the upper end of the demand curve. The successful suppliers (sellers) are those who are willing to ask the lowest prices. They're the suppliers on the low end of the supply curve.

---

[2] The classic discussion of this mechanism is Hayek's example of tin. See "The Use of Knowledge in Society" (cited in footnote 1), pp. 85-6.

SCARCITY, RATIONING, AND COMPETITION

Take another look at our supply and demand curves for widgets.

After whatever market adjustments may be called for have taken place, our widget market reaches its equilibrium of 125 per week produced and sold, each at a price of $12.

Now, who gets these 125 widgets, and who goes without them? If their price is $12 each, and that's an equilibrium price, every individual who is willing to sacrifice his own best alternative use of $12 obtains a widget. Those individuals' values are shown on the <u>upper</u> end of the demand curve--the portion of the demand curve that starts at $12 and points upward and to the left.

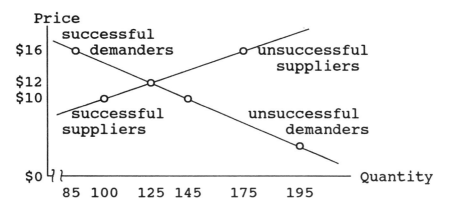

Figure 4.9: Successful and unsuccessful

The individuals who place <u>some</u> (but evidently not enough) value on widgets are out on the lower tail of the demand curve--from $12 on down toward the right. There's Sam out there; she's willing to pay $7.85 for a widget, but that's not enough, and at $12 she has better uses for her money.

I have labelled these portions of the demand curve, to help to drive the point home. Those demanders who "get the good" are the successful demanders, those who actually wind up buying a widget, and they're the 125 who place the highest value on a widget, relative to the value that they themselves place on their own best alternative use of the money. The demanders who "don't get the good" are unsuccessful demanders, who do not buy a widget because "it's too expensive" or they "can't afford it." These phrases simply mean that these individuals had better things to do with their money or time. They didn't value widgets highly enough, relative to the alternatives that they themselves perceived.

As we explained about Frank and Chet, it's too bad that some of the people who "want" a widget, perhaps even some who say they "need" a widget, aren't going to get one. But widgets must be produced, and the resources required for their production--labor, electricity, magnesium, whatever goes into these imaginary goods--could be used for other things. If a particular widget gets produced, something else can't. Sympathize, if you wish, with the unsuccessful widget demander, but if he were accommodated you might need even more sympathy for the other people who would have to go without other goods. Our "widget" graph hides these other goods and people from view, so it's easy and tempting to forget them. If you do, though, you'll make a serious mistake in judging and understanding what markets accomplish.

> A thing is SCARCE if you would be
> better off with more of it.

Imagine simply being handed a wristwatch, free of charge or obligation of any kind. Would you consider yourself "better off" than before the magical gift? If so, wristwatches are scarce for you.

As long as wristwatches are scarce, you would be willing to sacrifice something else (maybe not much) of value to obtain another. The reason that you don't is that the opportunity isn't there: the price is so high that the value of what you would have to give up exceeds that of the second watch. If you didn't consider wristwatches to be scarce, you wouldn't even bother picking one up if they were free.

In a world of trade and markets, the scarcity judgments of one individual are linked with those of others. Perhaps you can imagine no use for a second wristwatch, but if you know that I (or someone else) can, the fact that we consider it to be scarce opens up a trading opportunity for you. Because the watch is scarce to us, if you perceive the trading opportunity it will be scarce to you. If you don't think anyone else will consider wristwatches scarce, or if you simply have no idea how to find out who does, you will attribute no value to the watch: it won't be scarce for you.

It's easy to identify scarcity with quantity, but be careful. Scarcity is a judgment of value. If the individuals who live on an island with few bananas and lots of pineapples hate bananas and love pineapples, they could well find pineapples scarce and bananas a worthless nuisance. This was often the fate of crude oil in the mid-1800s, when it was considered a largely useless byproduct accompanying the discovery of natural gas.

Something for which nobody conceives any value is not scarce, no matter how few of them there are. There are probably more good than rotten eggs, but the former are scarce and the latter aren't. Sellers are always trying to convince us how scarce (and therefore valuable) their product is, because there are so few of them. "There are only three of these 1917 Weirdo automobiles in existence," we can imagine reading in an ad in an antique-car magazine. Great. But maybe only two people in the world would even be willing to accept a 1917 Weirdo as a gift.

You might try to consider a world without scarcity. (Occasionally there's a spate of pop economists writing paperbacks that warn us to beware of the imminent "post-scarcity" age. If these guys are trying to cash in on the popularity of "doomsday" books, they need to be straightened out a little on the basics.) Everyone could just snap his fingers and have anything he wants. Actually, since finger-snapping requires some exertion and trouble, even that would not be necessary.

I'll let you work out the details. What if two individuals have logically contradictory desires--Sierra Zeke wants a thousand square miles of desolate wilderness and Yuppie Biff wants a well-stocked condo every hundred yards along the trail? Would a universe in which each individual could have whatever he wished for, just by imagining it, be desirable? Is it even conceivable? Maybe I'd better let the philosophers and science-fiction writers deal with this one. But one thing's for sure: there would be no choice, no human action as we know it, because there would be no need to sacrifice any alternative. That's because there would be no "alternatives": you can have them all!

Whatever kind of world this would be, it surely isn't the one that we live in.

> RATIONING is the process that deter-
> mines how scarce goods are allocated
> among individuals and uses.

Scarcity implies rationing. If something is scarce, not everyone can have as much of it as he would like, and there must be some way of determining whose desires for it get satisfied, and whose don't. There has to be some kind of rationing criterion, some principle or rule, so that individuals who meet the rule or satisfy the criterion get the good, and those individuals who don't, don't.

Kristin has a problem. She's a friendly, pleasant woman who has been asked for a date this Saturday night by two different men. Television sitcoms in which the lead character dates two or three different people in the same evening spring to mind (Mike Seaver of "Growing Pains" or Sam Malone of "Cheers," perhaps), but either the logistics are too complicated or she's just too nice to want to try that. So here's a scarce good--a date this Saturday with Kristin--that must be allocated somehow. She'll use some kind of rationing criterion, involving her own expectations about what an evening with each of these two men would be like, then select one and reject the other. One of them will be a successful demander, the other--who did not meet the rationing criterion--an unsuccessful demander.

How does a coach allocate scarce positions on a varsity sports team? Twenty-five positions and three hundred hopeful student-athletes; what rationing criterion does he use? How about the admissions officers of a prestigious private liberal-arts college, with ten thousand applicants for fifteen hundred freshman openings? Various rationing criteria probably include high-school grades, SAT scores, willingness to pay lots of money, and range of extracurricular activities. (Many of these work by affecting the college's expectations of the prospective student's future effect on the reputation of the college.) Who gets a parking space in the nearby lot or garage--what is the process by which these scarce goods are rationed?

```
COMPETITION is the act of attempting
to meet a rationing criterion.
```

Wherever there's a scarce good, people are willing to sacrifice alternatives for it. The nature of the alternatives that they must sacrifice is determined by the rationing criterion that the owner of the scarce good uses to determine what gets done with it. As soon as the rationing criterion becomes known, individuals who value the good will attempt to meet the criterion by outbidding others who have the same goal. This process of trying to outbid, out-do, others who are also attempting to meet the rationing criterion, is competition.

If our two men really want to go out with Kristin, they are likely to make some sensible guess about her rationing criterion and try to determine what she likes and to be extra pleasant to her for some period before asking her out. They may not know each other, or know that both asked for a date, but they may consider it likely that they're only one of several possible companions and that she's likely to pick the one who she thinks is the nicest. They may or may not identify their actions as competition, oriented toward a particular rationing criterion for a particular scarce good, but that's what it is.

The would-be varsity athletes, of course, work hard in the tryouts; the would-be college students try to achieve good grades in high school; those who seek parking spots schedule 8-o'clock classes and arrive at seven, or try to outguess other waiting and idling drivers as to which row contains someone who's about to leave. The shopkeeper knows that consumers allocate their money according to the best value that they perceive, and tries to offer them something more attractive than other retailers are offering. In a mile run in which the "scarce good" is one winner's trophy, the rationing criterion is "getting to the finish line first" and the competition--well, that's obvious.

We have presented a sequence of linked definitions of concepts that are vital to economics.

```
The very existence of human action
implies scarcity. Scarcity implies
rationing, and rationing implies
competition.
```

If you think that modern society is "too competitive," I agree--in a sense. What I mean is that, according to my values, a lot of people seem to undervalue certain things that don't require much competition with other people, like time spent with their families, and time spent reading important books, listening to good music, and thinking about issues that have been important to man for centuries. Inexpensive radios and paperback editions of great books make rich culture available to anyone who wants it. If one isn't picky about leather bindings and so forth, the words of Shakespeare are available so cheaply that they're hardly scarce any more.

Competition among individuals arises, of course, when many of us want goods whose supply is much less elastic--like nice houses in attractive areas, safe and comfortable and reliable cars, high-quality medical care... even widgets. Some of the reasons that people want these things seem a little silly to me--like prestige, trying to show off how rich and important they are. Others don't seem so silly: wanting a safe neighborhood for one's children, or minimal danger while travelling.

In any case, our disagreement is really with these individuals' values. We can attempt to convince others that our values are better than theirs, that they should back off and smell the roses (a scarce good?), and we might be able to achieve a society with less competition among individuals. (Don't forget, though, that time is scarce: your own gardening "competes" with your reading of Plato.) But a world without scarcity is inconceivable, and as long as there's scarcity, there's going to be some form, and some degree, of competition.

SHORTAGES AND SURPLUSES; NON-PRICE RATIONING

When you go to the bookstore for that notebook, you're going to find that it's a scarce good that is rationed by price. A good that is sold to anyone who is willing to pay the seller's price is said to be rationed by price.

You may hear the term "rationing" used more narrowly, to apply only to situations in which governments attempt to overrule price rationing and allocate scarce goods by coupons or some other scheme. In World War II, people were given gas rationing stickers to put in their car windshields, entitling them to purchase a certain number of gallons each week (at a fixed, government-set, price). This is, indeed, one form of rationing, but the concept of rationing is much broader and includes the method that many buyers and sellers prefer when they are free to choose what to do with their own goods: they are exchanged at a market-clearing price. Those willing to pay it get the goods, and those who aren't don't.

As we have seen, this system has some interesting properties. Every unit of the good that some individual values more than he values the best alternative that he would have to forego to have it produced, does in fact get produced. If some other individual values the good, but not as much as he values the other things that he would have to give up to make its production worthwhile, that individual prefers the alternative and his unit of this good is not produced. The pricing process not only determines which individuals obtain units of this good; it also determines how many-- and what kind of--resources are used in this way, rather than in the production of other goods. This is the rationing function of price.

An increase in demand, resulting from individuals' judgments that this good is more valuable (relative to alternatives) than before, raises its price--a change that simultaneously demonstrates the good's greater relative scarcity (that's the information function of price) and makes it worthwhile for producers to increase the "quantity supplied" (that's the incentive function of price).

Legislative interference with pricing

For one reason or another, though, sometimes governments do not permit price rationing to do the whole job. When there are restrictions placed on the range that a particular good's price can take on, the price of a good is no longer capable of carrying out its three functions (information, incentive, and rationing). What happens in these cases is quite interesting.

First of all, please note:

> A restriction on the price that he can charge is a violation of the property rights of the owner of the good.

If I "own" a coffee mug, it surely is an implication of my ownership that I get to decide how much money it would take to get me to part with it. I have a cute one that was given to me by colleagues at a place where I used to work. (It says, "This mug contains the terrible coffee they make at my office.") It has some sentimental value to me, and I wouldn't part with it for less than $15. If someone comes up, declares that a similar one can be bought new for $5 and therefore that $3 is a "fair" price (mine is used), tosses me $3 and takes my cup, he has stolen from me just as surely as if he had simply taken the thing. We'll return to this point later, but for now you should note that the best reason not to restrict price rationing is that the restrictions violate the property rights of the individuals who own or seek to buy the scarce good.

Figure 4.10 presents a diagram of a legal price floor, set at $11, a little above the equilibrium price of $10. A "floor" is something that is below the permitted range of prices.

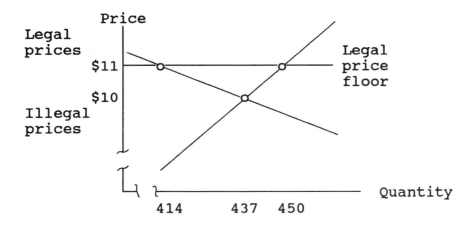

Figure 4.10: A legal price floor

> A legal price FLOOR sets a minimum
> level below which a good's price
> cannot legally go.

Here, the "legal prices" are identified as those of $11 or more; any price below $11 is illegal. An example is a minimum-wage law: a covered employer cannot legally pay less than $4.25 for each hour of labor service. Another is our country's system by which the government supports the prices of agricultural crops.

It is perfectly possible for the legal price floor to be set <u>below</u> equilibrium. There are people who are convinced that if the minimum wage were suddenly changed to 3 cents per hour, nearly every inexperienced and/or unskilled worker in the country would have his wage reduced instantly to 3 cents per hour. (If this were true, why do fast-food outlets often plead for help at wage rates that are well above the legal minimum?) A legal minimum price that's below equilibrium affects people's behavior only to the extent that they expect that, in the future, a drop in the equilibrium price might put it below the legal minimum. In other words, they're afraid that a situation like the one shown in our graph might develop.

The market-clearing price of the good in this graph is $10, with the quantity supplied (and demanded! That's what makes it an equilibrium.) 437 units per week. But if the price at which the good may be sold is not permitted to fall below $11, producers would like to sell 450 per week (their "quantity supplied") while buyers are willing to purchase only 414 per week.

We've talked about what happens in an unhampered market when a price of $11 pops up although the equilibrium is $10; the actions of the individual suppliers and the individual demanders both tend to move that price downward toward equilibrium. But here, that's not legally permitted. The sellers are not allowed to bid against each other for buyers (by reducing their asking prices), and the buyers may not be allowed to try to buy at less than $11.

The result of this legal floor, above equilibrium, is a permanent gap between "quantity demanded" and "quantity supplied." Economists often refer to this gap as an "excess supply," but a more common term for it is <u>surplus</u>.

A SURPLUS is the amount by which
quantity supplied exceeds quantity
demanded.

Take a look at any normal supply-and-demand diagram. Over what range of prices does the quantity supplied exceed the quantity demanded? Only those prices that are above equilibrium.

Neither buyers nor sellers know everything, and it may take a while for sellers to discover that the price they're charging is "too high," above equilibrium. In a free market, both the buyers and the sellers have incentive to <u>discover</u> that it's above equilibrium, and to begin chopping away at it. These things don't happen instantaneously, so we frequently find temporary--usually small--surpluses of particular goods. For various reasons sellers are usually reluctant to cut their asking prices (believe it or not, they're also usually reluctant to raise them), until it becomes obvious that demand has really fallen. Remember: you and I have these nice curves, we can see exactly what's going on, but a retailer only sees trickles or waves of customers--one or two at a time--and has to <u>infer</u> what's going on with demand. We shouldn't criticize him for not knowing what we, the omniscient designers of this example, know (or pretend to know).

Persistent surpluses are ALWAYS
caused by legal restrictions that
hold a good's price above its
equilibrium level.

Why not just identify a "surplus" as "too much" of something? I'll buy that, as long as we understand that how much of something we want depends on its price. In a free market, as the price comes down people begin to "want" (that is, demand) more of it, and others become less willing to provide it (the quantity supplied falls). An important aspect of your education in economics is to understand that whether people perceive that there's "too much" or "too little" of something depends importantly on its price.

You have to be careful with terminology like that ("too much"), though. It's widely used in casual, imprecise ways that have little or nothing to do with "quantity supplied exceeds quantity demanded because price is above equilibrium." As I've mentioned several times, a lot of language that works just fine in our normal everyday lives is just not precise enough to permit us to think carefully about the economic organization of a society.

We run into a similar problem with shortage.

A SHORTAGE is the amount by which quantity demanded exceeds quantity supplied.

Figure 4.11 gives us a diagram of a shortage, caused by a legal price ceiling that holds the price below equilibrium.

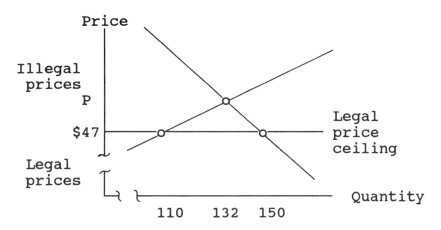

Figure 4.11: A legal price ceiling

The quantity demanded (150) exceeds the quantity supplied (110) at the legal price ceiling, which is set below the good's equilibrium price. (A ceiling sets an upper limit, it's at the top of the legally permitted range of prices.) An example is the recent imposition of price controls on gasoline, resulting in the long lines of cars waiting at gas stations, during the late 1970s. Rent controls offer another example.

There are 150 units of the good demanded at the ceiling price of $47, indicating that individuals value 150 units more than they value the best alternative use that they can conceive for their $47. But there are producers of other goods bidding for the necessary resources, and this price of $47 makes it advantageous to the suppliers to outbid only enough of these other demands for resources to produce 110 units.

So there's "not enough" of the good, or "too little" of it, right? Well, again, right--in a carefully defined sense. "Not enough" has no <u>absolute</u> meaning; it has to refer to a relationship between how much people have and how much they want. But both of these quantities depend on the good's <u>price</u>, and there's "not enough" when the price is below its equilibrium (market-clearing) level.

> ```
> Persistent shortages are ALWAYS
> caused by legal restrictions that
> hold a good's price below its
> equilibrium level.
> ```

Whenever you hear the claim that there's a "shortage" of something, look closely at its market. Is there some kind of legal restriction that prevents the kind of rise in price that's needed to reduce the quantity demanded, and increase the quantity supplied, until everyone who's willing to pay the price is able to obtain a unit of the good?

If you find no evidence of such a restriction, then it's likely that someone is using the charge of "shortage" as a self-serving argument for some kind of government action. Usually, to put it bluntly, it means "I can't get the good at a price that I am willing or able to pay." This person occupies part of the lower tail of the demand curve. If he can persuade a few influential politicians that this constitutes proof that "the market isn't working," we can expect legislation that takes resources away from the individuals who have earned and own them, and devotes those resources instead to an increase in the supply of this "shortage" good.

Restricted prices can't do their jobs...

Legal restrictions on market prices prevent them from serving their three functions.

First, the <u>information</u> conveyed by restricted price is inaccurate. A good's price is no longer a reliable indicator of its relative scarcity, of people's valuation of the good relative to their valuations of other goods. A price held above equilibrium conveys the information that the good is more scarce than it really is; a price below equilibrium indicates that it's less scarce than it really is.

Neither suppliers nor demanders are stupid. Suppliers know that if a legal floor holds price above equilibrium, they may not be able to sell all of the units that they can produce at a cost that's below this floor price. (These are all of the units that lie below the floor price, along the supply curve.) Whether they try to increase their good's appeal to consumers or just take a chance that they'll be successful sellers, the posted legal price is no longer a trustworthy guide: lots of other things have to be considered.

Similarly, if you know that gasoline is legally restricted to prices below $1.50 per gallon even though the market-clearing price is well above that, simply having $15 is no guarantee that you're going to be able to fill your 10-gallon tank. And imagine the accountants trying to compute a business's costs. "We'll need 1,450 of these things and they're $7 each, but who knows what we'll have to do to actually get them..." What does he write down as their cost, and what does that do to the trustworthiness, the certainty, and the predictability of the business plan?

Second, the incentive is altered by these restrictions. A below-equilibrium price ceiling ($47, here) provides incentive only for the production of the 110 units that cost less than $47. If you look at the range of quantities for which the demand curve lies above the supply curve, however, you'll note that there are another 22 units that individuals value more than the cost of their production. These willing customers are legally prohibited from offering a price that exceeds those units' cost.

An above-equilibrium price floor provides incentive (if the producers anticipate successful sales) to produce "too much" of the good: units for which the cost of production (the height of the supply curve) exceed what people are willing to pay for them (the height of the demand curve) are produced anyway. Again, the reason is that the legally restricted price presents false information about relative values.

This limitation of the incentive function of price carries with it a disturbing implication. Price ceilings below equilibrium are typically imposed on goods that are considered to be especially important; "we have to make sure everyone can afford these vital necessities." But look back at our "shortage" graph to see what such a ceiling does to the quantity that is actually exchanged. Remember: it's the smaller of "quantity demanded" or "quantity supplied." At a market-clearing price, more people would have obtained the good than suppliers are willing to offer at the enforced below-equilibrium price. The quantity of this "vital necessity" that is produced and sold actually falls. More people can afford the money price, but a legally restricted price is no longer an accurate measure of the good's scarcity and availability.

Third, the rationing function of price is hobbled. Who gets the good, or who successfully sells it? The answer is no longer "anybody who wants to, at the market price," because a market price doesn't exist any more. At a legal price ceiling of $47, there are 150 people who are willing to purchase and only 110 units offered for sale. Clearly only 110 of those 150 willing demanders are actually going to obtain the good. What process determines which 110 out of the 150 succeed? This is rationing again, but it can't be accomplished by price. Some other rationing criterion has to emerge.

Price rationing isn't completely inoperative here. Look at the people down on the tail of the demand curve, out beyond 150 and below $47. They aren't even willing to pay the legal ceiling price, so they're "rationed out" by even that "low" price. A free market would slide the price on up until everyone southeast of the equilibrium point was "rationed out" by price, but that isn't permitted here. What kind of process might ration the 110 units that producers are willing to supply at $47, among the 150 people who are eager to obtain them at that price?

Well, you name it. It could be almost anything. First-come, first-served? Then the rationing criterion is "willingness to pay $47 and wait in line," and among those willing to pay the money competition emerges to meet the other part of the criterion. People set their alarms for 5 AM to get to the gas station just after the tanker truck has delivered the station's quota. Music or sports fans camp out for three nights on the sidewalk in front of the ticket office.

How about "pay $47 and be here when I feel like opening"? If a retailer can sell all of the units that he can obtain under the price restriction during any particular two-hour period during the day, why not open just when there's nothing on TV that he wants to see? In a free market, shopkeepers of course have other things they'd like to do with their time, but the prices that we offer bid them away from those alternatives. If we're not allowed to offer those prices, can we blame the retailer for pursuing his own best alternative?

Lots of other criteria are possible, and some of them aren't especially praiseworthy. In a market free of legally restricted prices, a seller who voluntarily restricts his customers to those of a particular race, sex, religion, or range of ages is likely to lose money because of his prejudices; the demand by those who meet his criteria is almost certain to be smaller than the total market demand. If he is not permitted to charge a market-clearing price, though, there may be more than enough demand by those individuals who fit his particular prejudices to purchase all that he is able to supply at the ceiling price.

Does price rationing seem harsh and cruel to you? Unfortunately there are plenty of individuals and families who are so poor that price "rations them out" of many of the things the rest of us take for granted. Please consider this: if price rationing precludes the poor from obtaining some of these goods, the problem isn't necessarily with price rationing. Perhaps the real problem is that some people are simply too poor. (To figure out exactly what that means, and what it implies about action, we have to do a lot of thinking that would take us a bit off the track at this point. We'll return to it, a little, in Chapter 9.)

Those who criticize rationing by price have to realize this:

```
If a scarce good isn't rationed by
PRICE, it will be rationed in some
other way.
```

You can't criticize the price system for preventing everyone from having everything; it's <u>scarcity</u> that prevents that. Scarcity requires rationing, and if it isn't going to be price rationing, it's going to be some form of non-price rationing.

Critics of the price system who compare it with a never-never-land in which scarcity does not exist simply don't deserve to be taken seriously. It's up to those critics to explain the superiority of their own alternative rationing criteria.

That's quite a trick. Can you come up with another rationing criterion that (simultaneously) also performs the functions of conveying accurate information about people's values and providing incentives for production and consumption to adapt to those values? Nothing except a market price, determined by suppliers and demanders free from legal price restrictions, even comes close.

Benjamin M. Anderson, an economist best known for his financial history of the early 20th century America, <u>Economics and the Public Welfare</u> (Princeton: D. Van Nostrand, 1949; p. 550), offered a comment that it would be wise for all of us to think about: "Prices have work to do... Prices must be free to tell the truth."

THE FAIRNESS OF MARKETS

By now, you have a pretty good idea of what markets do and how they do it. Every individual bids against every other individual for the use of scarce resources. If you are willing to sacrifice $10 worth of other things for a wodget, and nobody else is willing to sacrifice more than $10 for the other things that could have been produced with the resources needed to make the wodget, you get it. (That's because its cost of production will be less than $10, and some producer is likely to notice that he can sell for $10 something that costs him less than that to produce.) When you realize that this works for everybody, and for every good (including things like your labor services), you can begin to appreciate the three functions of price: rationing, information, and incentive.

But is it fair?

That's a nagging question that has been raised time and time again, and it's a good thing that it has. People should be concerned about fairness. Treating other individuals fairly is good, both on a broad scale (it's important to the future of civilization) and at the personal level (it makes us feel better about ourselves).

There are observers of contemporary America who perceive a decline of concern about being "fair" to others. I think there's something to that. If indeed there is such a trend, we should all buck it by placing the fair treatment of others high on our personal value scales.

The great problem, though, is in knowing what constitutes "fair treatment of others." I neither want to, nor can, address that issue thoroughly here, but I do have to comment on some of the "fairness" questions related to markets and exchange.

A "process" versus an "end-state" view

One of your neighbors has a new car, and you don't. Is that fair?

The simple fact that he possesses the car and you don't is referred to as an "end state." It is a small portion of the state of the universe at a particular moment of time, and it's at the end of some kind of causal sequence or process that produced it. If you wanted to capture an end-state on film, you would need only a standard camera. A still photograph would do just fine.

I hope that most of you would agree that determining the fairness of this state is a lot more complicated than simply observing that he has it and you don't. What we have to examine is how he got it, and how you happened not to have one.

> The fairness of an END-STATE is
> determined by the fairness of the
> PROCESS that produced it.

Did your neighbor work overtime every Saturday, while you watched football games on TV? Did he go into massive debt, committing himself to hundreds of dollars a month of payments, while you have the comfort of no such obligation? Perhaps he's going without the modernized kitchen, on which you just spent about the same amount of money.

On the other hand, maybe he stole the car. Maybe he bought it with his secret income as a drug dealer. Perhaps he saw an elderly couple driving it, lied to them that it was so dangerous that their lives were in imminent peril if they kept driving it, and kindly took it off their hands for two hundred bucks.

The point of this example is that we cannot determine whether an end-state is fair simply by examining it, no matter how deeply we probe into its details. We have to evaluate it according to the process of which it is the end.

Applying this principle to situations that are more important than who owns a new car will try your convictions sometimes. What if he has a bigger house than you? Let's get extreme: What if he has a multimillion-dollar Beverly Hills mansion while you're homeless?

It's fine to be a little disturbed by such an end-state, and to wonder if there isn't something wrong with the process that produced it. We all see situations that we just can't imagine resulting from a legitimate and fair process.

The proper response is to investigate the process that produced the end-state that strikes us as prima facie unfair. What was the sequence, the pattern, of actions that produced it? Were the actions that make up that process fair or unfair? That's what a proper judgment has to rest on.

Voluntary exchange is the essence
of market action

There's more to life than the exchange of goods and services in the marketplace. There's also more to fairness than observing the minimum essential rules of market exchange.

But if we are to judge "the fairness of markets," or to evaluate the arguments of others who do, we have to consider exactly what is the essence of market activity.

Any discussion of supplies and demands involves judgments about ownership and property rights. Remember your jaunt to the bookstore? The store owned the notebook. One attribute of its ownership was its right to determine its reserve price, the minimum amount of money it would accept in return for the notebook. The store's manager determined that receiving this sum or anything greater (and giving up the notebook) would make him better off, while if he were offered less then keeping the notebook would be the preferable alternative.

By the same token, it's your money. The bookstore cannot force you to give it up. It can specify the terms of any exchange that will make it better off, but unless those terms also make you better off you'll simply walk out with your money intact.

This is the principle of voluntary exchange. Each of us has certain assets of which we are the rightful owner. If another individual wants one of our assets, he must make it worth our while (the best of our available alternatives) to transfer its ownership to him. He must offer us something in return, something that we value more than we value the asset that he's asking for. We saw this, earlier, in the principle that "if you want someone to take a particular action, you must make sure that he considers it to be the best of his alternatives."

It is this principle on which capitalism is based. The "voluntary exchange" principle is a natural consequence of the fact that individuals have rights of ownership. If you want someone else's lawn mower, it's his right to establish a rationing criterion and it's your obligation to meet it. If you don't think his asking price is fair, don't pay it; he evidently values the mower more (relative to his alternatives) than you do (relative to yours).

What would his "ownership" mean if you could take his mower, against his will, simply by offering him something that you think is fair? ($5?) What would your "ownership" of your money mean, if--despite your maximum offer of $40--he could load the mower into your car and then throw you to the ground and take $60 because that's what he considers "fair"?

The concept of voluntary exchange, according to which each party must himself perceive the trade as beneficial, is inseparable from the concept of individual rights.

Capitalism

The term "capitalism" has been subjected to such a smear campaign, since its origin with Karl Marx over a century ago, that some economists who appreciate the properties of free markets and voluntary exchange have suggested that it be avoided.

Since I guess that I don't agree with them, let's try to get a grip on its basic nature.

> "Capitalism is a social system based on the recognition of individual rights, including property rights, in which all property is privately owned."[3]
>
> -- Ayn Rand

Contrary to what is often taught, capitalism is <u>not</u> a system in which "big business" can do anything it wants; a big company would not be permitted--any more than any of us individuals would--to take anyone's property by force or fraud. It is not a system in which anyone could pollute anyone else's property; it requires the enforcement of the pollutee's (and everyone else's) property rights. Capitalism is not a system that promotes war; rights-respecting voluntary exchange is inherently a peaceful activity. (Don't confuse the "defense industry" with the process of voluntary exchange on which private business operates.) It is not prone to severe depression and mass unemployment; the sensitive adjustments that we've been studying sharply limit the severity and duration of these problems unless the government interferes--which it did, in spades, in our Great Depression of the 1930s. Capitalism does not permit "the rich" to "oppress" the poor, since the rights of the poor are precisely as inviolate as those of the rich.

Some of the popular confusion about capitalism arises, no doubt, from the identification of the United States as "capitalist." Basically, it is. But before you saddle the concept of capitalism with the various social problems that you see all around you, think a bit about the implications of that word "basically." It suggests--and properly so--that while the United States was founded on the principle of "unalienable individual rights" (this phrase is from the Declaration of Independence) and individuals' rights are better protected here than anyplace else in the world, our government deviates from the principle of inviolate individual rights in substantial and important ways.

We've seen some of them already: price controls, laws that prevent an owner of a good from exchanging it at prices that are legally declared to be too high (in some cases) or too low (in others). Minimum-wage laws are an example, as are agricultural crop price supports. Government control of the money supply (responsible for depressions and wide-scale unemployment) and of the educational system (responsible for all kinds of problems, perhaps including high-school graduates who can't read this) constitute other deviations from a purely capitalistic society. Rent controls and other restrictions on landlords and developers contribute significantly to homelessness,

---

[3] The quote is from Ayn Rand, "What is Capitalism?," in her <u>Capitalism: The Unknown Ideal</u> (New York: New American Library, 1966), p. 11. All italicized in the original.

and while under capitalism neither landlords nor developers could do "anything they want" they would be substantially more free to respond to demands for different types (qualities and costs) of housing.

Keep in mind the principle underlying capitalism: Individual human beings have rights; each of them has the same rights; the single most important of those rights is ownership; from the individual's right of ownership (often called "private property rights") follows the principle of voluntary exchange.

The <u>real</u> problem with legislative interference with the price mechanism is not that it "distorts information" or provides "perverse incentives" or "inefficient rationing." The real problem is that it violates individuals' rights. Price restrictions essentially take away individuals' freedom to act in certain ways that are fully their <u>right</u>. Restrictions on some individuals' freedom invariably work to the benefit of others. These restrictions constitute government-condoned and government-enforced <u>theft</u> from those individuals whose property rights are violated, with the booty doled out to other individuals.

Only voluntary exchange can be fair

Is any voluntary exchange between consenting adults necessarily fair?

Perhaps, but I don't think that I want to make this claim. There is probably more to "fairness" than this. It is a complex issue, one that I hope you will investigate by studying philosophy during your college career.

While the voluntary nature of an exchange may not be <u>sufficient</u> to make it fair, this "voluntary" property is a <u>necessary</u> condition. Since no individual has the right to violate (that is, to take without consent) the life or property of another individual, no action that fails this test can be fair, though perhaps not all actions that do pass it are. (To illustrate "necessary" vs. "sufficient": four tires are necessary if you're going to be able to drive a car, but they sure aren't sufficient.)

Since voluntary exchanges are those in which no individuals' property rights are violated, we can restate this condition:

```
A necessary condition for an action
to be FAIR is the it violate no
individuals' rights.
```

Again, this may not be a <u>sufficient</u> condition. (Actually, I suspect that it is, but I don't want to come out that strongly until I've worked on it a bit more.) But we should never consider an action to be fair if it violates the rights to life and property of some other individual.

The process of voluntary exchange that constitutes <u>capitalism</u> passes this test.

The rationing of scarce resources that results from the functioning of the market is the consequence of the voluntary choices of individuals whose actions involve only the exercise of their legitimate individual property rights. You really can't very well criticize the results of a process that involves nothing but the free exercise of rights that you accept as legitimate.

Here's an example. You consider Joe Blow to be a thoroughly detestable individual and you have as little to do with him as possible. He's obnoxious, uncultured, crude, gross, inconsiderate, foul-mouthed, dirty--you name it. Unfortunately (in your opinion), he happened upon an idea for a product that millions of people wanted to buy at prices far above his costs, and he became fabulously rich. Meanwhile, you're a thoroughly admirable person with all of the virtues that Joe lacks, but as you drive your old rusty car past his mansion every day you succumb to a little envy, muttering how "unfair" life is.

There's no way that we can simply look at Joe's situation and determine whether or not it is "fair." (He could have murdered the owner of the mansion and simply moved in, or bought the place with millions of dollars that he embezzled from some financial institution somewhere.) We have to examine the process that produced his wealth.

Now suppose that Joe began life with no advantages that can properly be considered unfair. His family's wealth, whatever it was, had been earned through productive exchange in the marketplace.[4] Suppose further that he really thought up this idea himself (he didn't steal it from some starving inventor), that he borrowed the money without misrepresentation from investors who perceived it as a good deal, that he paid prices for resources that the owners of those resources voluntarily accepted, and that his millions of customers each truly perceived his product as more than worth the price he asked.

What's the problem? Joe has benefitted everyone with whom he has come in contact here. If the starting point of this process was fair, and the process itself consisted of nothing but a sequence of strictly voluntary, mutually-beneficial exchanges, the outcome of this process meets at least the necessary condition for being fair.

The reason that many of us have trouble accepting this proposition is that we may not like the result of these millions of individuals' choices. You think Joe is a jerk and you're sorry that he's rich. But he became rich because of the way in which he and other individuals chose to exercise their legitimate property rights, and to find something wrong with Joe's wealth you have to find something wrong with these actions. Was it "unfair" of someone who valued the gizmo at $12 to willingly purchase at Joe's price of $9? Was it "unfair" for Joe to pay resource owners only $7 when he knew he could sell the product for $9 (even though many of them would have been willing to sell their resources to him for $6)?

---

[4] Inheritance is a voluntary transfer, a legitimate exercise of the right of the donor. Perhaps you don't think Joe deserves his father's money any more than you do, but his father deserves to choose who gets it.

If you don't like Joe and don't think he <u>should</u> become rich, feel free to try to convince his potential customers, who believe their lives would be significantly easier if they had his product, that they shouldn't buy it, because that would make him rich and <u>they</u> shouldn't want that to happen. But you're obligated to observe their (and Joe's) individual rights. As much as you may--personally--be offended by his wealth, legislation that <u>interferes</u> with the voluntary process that produced it would violate the necessary condition for fairness. There's no fairness in a law that prevents another person from trading with Joe (at a mutually agreeable price) simply because <u>you</u> don't like the consequences of that trade.

Voluntary exchange is the only kind of action among individuals that can be <u>fair</u>. It involves nothing but the legitimate exercise of individuals' rights to life and property. We don't always have to like what it produces--after all, don't we all sometimes feel that others are foolish for holding the values that they do?--but fortunately others don't have to ask our permission for their every act. (Of course that implies that we don't have to ask theirs, either. That's what freedom means.)

One must have something to offer

It is unfortunate that some individuals have little or nothing of value to offer in exchange. These individuals are poor, and the fact that they have little of value to offer is more a definition of poverty than an explanation or cause of it. If we are sympathetic (and we should be), we might contribute--voluntarily--to charity. Perhaps our view is that fairness requires something more than the minimum condition of "not violating another's rights."

But can we blame someone for not paying $35 for a good that's worth only $23 to him? Would <u>you</u> hire someone who--as far as you knew--has absolutely no mechanical experience or skills, to do a major overhaul on your car's engine simply because he was poor and needed a job? Plenty of people who would answer "Of course not!" will then criticize "the capitalist system" for not presenting this guy with work as an auto mechanic.

The distribution of wealth, in capitalism, results from choices made by millions of individuals just like you and me. Few of them either know or care about their decisions' effects on the incomes of unknown people perhaps thousands of miles away. Each of them simply perceives benefit in a particular exchange. Income earned in the market is not a reward for moral virtue and should never be interpreted as such. The inherent <u>fairness of markets</u> arises simply from the unfairness of interfering with markets, the unfairness of forcefully preventing individuals from exercising certain of their legitimate property rights.

An individual leaves the ranks of the poor when he obtains a skill (often it's just the habit of showing up for work at a regular time each day) that someone else values and is willing to pay for. Those who are concerned about the number of poor should find out why they lack marketable skills. Sometimes the answers lie in restrictions on markets themselves, like minimum-wage or union-shop laws or mandated-benefit legislation that require anyone who actually hires somebody to provide him with a whole range of costly benefits. Sometimes the markets are OK, but there aren't any skills. The answer then is education--usable, practical training.

The individual who criticizes the fairness of markets usually simply doesn't like the way that other individuals choose to act. They don't value the same things that he does, they spend their money on things he considers frivolous junk and worthless entertainment, and they make rich the people who provide it. This sort of elitist attitude ("I know better than you how you should live your life") is characteristic of a lack of respect for other human beings. Respecting the lives and property of other individuals is the first step toward understanding the inherent fairness of a system that is governed, at every step, by "unalienable individual rights" and their corollary, voluntary exchange.

YOU SHOULD REMEMBER...

1)   The height of a particular good's DEMAND curve indicates the value of the marginal unit of that good.

2)   The height of a particular good's SUPPLY curve indicates the value of the best <u>alternative</u> to the marginal unit of the good.

3)   A good's EQUILIBRIUM PRICE is that price at which quantity demanded and quantity supplied are equal.

4)   At equilibrium, each unit of the good that is valued MORE than alternatives is produced, and no unit is produced that is valued LESS than alternatives.

5)   The actions of individual buyers and sellers tend to bring markets to equilibrium.

6)   The three functions of price are: information, incentive, and rationing.

7)   A thing is <u>scarce</u> if you would be better off with more of it.

8)   <u>Rationing</u> is the process that determines how scarce goods are allocated among individuals and uses.

9)   <u>Competition</u> is the act of attempting to meet a rationing criterion.

10)   A restriction on the price that he can charge is a violation of the property rights of the owner of the good.

11)   A SURPLUS is the amount by which quantity supplied exceeds quantity demanded.

12)   A SHORTAGE is the amount by which quantity demanded exceeds quantity supplied.

13)   Persistent shortages or surpluses are ALWAYS caused by legal restrictions that hold the market price below or above equilibrium.

14)   If a scarce good isn't rationed by PRICE, it will be rationed in some other way.

15)   "Prices have work to do. Prices must be free to tell the truth." (B. M. Anderson)

16) The fairness of an END-STATE is determined by the fairness of the PROCESS that produced it.

17) Capitalism is the socioeconomic system that emerges when individuals' natural rights to life and property are recognized and enforced.

18) The United States deviates from capitalism in many ways.

19) A <u>necessary</u> condition for an action to be FAIR is the it violate no individuals' rights.

20) Only the process of voluntary exchange that defines capitalism meets this necessary condition of FAIRNESS.

Problems

(1-6) Figure 4.12 presents some supply and demand curves, old and new. Please identify the graph (A, B, C, or D) that best depicts the primary effect of the changes listed below. Assume that the supply or demand curve (whichever is not shown in the particular problem) has the usual upward or downward slope, and determine what is likely to happen to the equilibrium <u>price</u> and <u>quantity</u> in each case.

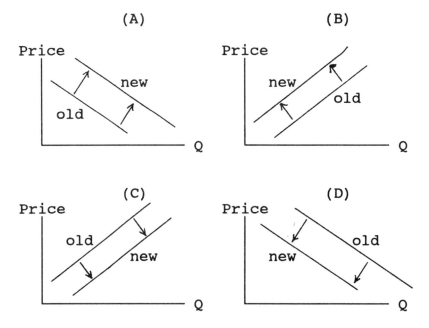

Figure 4.12: Problems of shifts in supply and demand

1)   Oranges, when much of the apple crop (a substitute for oranges) has been unexpectedly destroyed:

2)   Oranges, when frost unexpectedly hits southern Florida (where oranges are grown):

3)   Corn syrup sweetener (it is made from corn, not from sugar), following the imposition of price supports that suddenly double the domestic price of sugar:

4)   Corn syrup sweetener, if the domestic price of sugar were allowed to fall back to the level of world sugar prices:

5)   Logs from National Forests, after the U. S. Forest Service agrees to bear 90
        percent of the costs of the logging:

6)   Electricity, after acid-rain legislation requires generating plants to install
        expensive scrubbers on their smokestacks:

(7-12) Figure 4.13 is a diagram of a market that may be (depending on the problem)
subjected to some legal restriction. Please identify the <u>point</u> (a, b, c, d, e, f, g, or h)
on the graph that answers the relevant question. (Each of your answers should be
simply one of these letters.) Nothing is labelled in Figure 4.13. This is generally not
good practice, but here it's part of the problem.

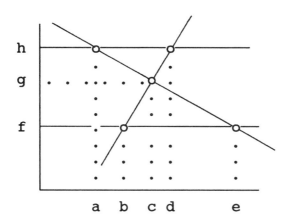

Figure 4.13: The problem of the unidentified points

7)   The number of widgets that individuals value more than they value the other
        things that could have been produced with the resources needed to produce
        <u>that number</u> of widgets:

8)   The number of pounds of cheese that will actually be purchased by individual
        consumers each week, when the price of cheese is held by law above
        equilibrium:

9)   The number of rent-controlled apartments that people want to rent, at the
        below-equilibrium legal rent ceiling:

10)   The number of rent-controlled apartments that landlords will make available,
        at the below-equilibrium legal rent ceiling:

11) The number of apartments that landlords would make available in the absence of the rent control:

12) The price (rent) at which they would make this number available (in #11):

CHAPTER 5

PROBING DEEPER INTO
THE CONCEPT OF COST

COST AND ACTION: PAST, PRESENT AND FUTURE

Now that we have a handle on the general way that a market system functions, it's time to get more specific about the nature of cost--and especially its relationship to business decision-making. Although it is true that economics is not <u>primarily</u> a business subject, its application to business is important and interesting.

Back up to some of the things we've already said about choice and cost.

The cost of an action is the value that the actor attributes to the best of the alternative actions that he must forego. (The value he attributes to the action itself is often called its "benefit.") The actor determines these values--benefit and cost--by imagining what his future would be like if he were to choose each of them. Benefit is the value of one action (the one he's considering), cost the value of another action (the best of the ones he's not considering).

As our early discussion of the "principles of choice" emphasized, good decisions depend on the accurate identification of the alternatives. That's what this chapter is about. As an illustration, here's one kind of problem that you may have encountered yourself. It's certainly familiar to me.

Good hammers are useful. They last forever and the heads don't fly off. You decide to buy one, and stride into a hardware store with $15. But the store also has a nice hand saw priced at $15, a boxed set of pliers for $15, a collection of screwdrivers for $15, and a pair of adjustable wrenches for $15. You value each of these tools more than the best non-tool alternative use of your $15, but you value the hammer more than any of the others.

Nonetheless, many of us (well, at least one of us), as we approach the cashier with our hammer and money, have had a moment of "buyer's regret." We think of <u>all</u> the other things we're giving up to buy that hammer. A veritable toolbox full of alternative tools! The pliers, the saw, the wrenches... If we view the cost of buying the hammer as the satisfaction we were likely to obtain from this whole collection of tools, no wonder the thought strikes us that buying the hammer was a mistake.

This is a simple--but not uncommon--example of misidentified alternatives. We don't forego <u>all</u> of those other tools; we only forego each of them. Our alternatives are not "the hammer" or "the saw <u>and</u> the pliers <u>and</u> the screwdrivers <u>and</u> the wrenches." Our options are "the hammer" <u>or</u> "the saw" <u>or</u> "the pliers" <u>or</u>... If we <u>could</u> obtain the entire non-hammer collection for $15, no doubt it would be the preferred alternative. But as long as the hammer is more valuable to us than any one of the other tools, we have no cause for regret.

The importance of carefully identifying the alternatives that are truly open to us may suggest that we must be thorough in specifying each of them. Although the intentions are good, there's a problem, as we can see from this little example.

Silly example #1: the brown eyes

You're trying to decide where to eat lunch today, and the alternatives you consider feasible are the Student Union or the Snack Bar. To help make the choice, you write them out on a piece of paper:

A: Eat at Student Union

B: Eat at Snack Bar

But you want to be conscientious about this--after all, you're studying economics--so you decide you'd better specify all of the properties of these two alternatives. For some reason the first thought that strikes you is that you happen to have brown eyes:

A: Eat at Union, have brown eyes

B: Eat at Snack Bar, have brown eyes

Something seems a little strange about this procedure, so you decide to think a bit before you go farther. After all, why stop with brown eyes? Why not include the fact that Annapolis is the capital of Maryland and that the square of the hypotenuse of a right triangle equals the sum of the squares of its two sides? Each of these remains true if you eat at the Union, or if you eat at the Snack Bar. You could wind up with an entire listing of the total of human knowledge. There's obviously something wrong with this.

The reason that it's a silly exercise is that you continue to have brown eyes (and Annapolis remains the capital and the Pythagorean Theorem remains true) regardless of which alternative you choose. You do not have to sacrifice "having brown eyes" if you eat at one place or the other. And because you do not have to sacrifice the brown eyes if you eat at the Snack Bar, whatever satisfaction arises from having them is not a relevant part of the cost of eating at the Snack Bar.

Characteristics that are common to each alternative cannot affect their relative desirability.[1]

---

[1] This can get a little tricky sometimes. Perhaps the Union is holding a "free bag of chips to anyone with brown eyes" day, or you're meeting a friend there who really likes your brown eyes. These circumstances create differences between the alternatives that are relevant only because you have brown eyes.

> Only characteristics that DIFFER
> between two alternatives can affect
> their relative desirability.

We don't have to illustrate this with something as ridiculous as "brown eyes." If the quality and price of the sandwiches are the same at either place, then your decision has to hinge on other considerations. What's different? Only those characteristics can affect the relative attractiveness, the relevant cost and benefit, of eating at the two locations. One's closer than the other. Service is faster at one. There's more room at the other. I don't know exactly how you're going to weigh these things, but only the differences between the two are relevant to your choice.

Silly example #2: the high school

"Having brown eyes" is clearly a proxy, in Silly Example #1, for all of the attributes that are the same whichever choice you make. There's a related set of characteristics which--as ridiculous as it seems at first--gets us a bit closer to some real economic problems of cost.

Some time ago you went to Lincoln High School in Buffalo (I have no idea if there really is such a school), and decide to identify your alternatives like this:

A: Eat at Union, have gone to Lincoln High School

B: Eat at Snack Bar, have gone to Lincoln High School

This is almost as silly as the brown eyes. Since LHS is a characteristic of either option, it cannot affect their relative desirability. Your experiences there may have important effects on your choice, but you do not--and can not--accept or reject those experiences by choosing one alternative or the other. Just as the question of whether $(X + A)$ is greater than $(Y + A)$ is determined solely by whether X is greater than Y, we can and should "cancel out" the Lincoln High School.

You did a lot of other things in your past, too: falling off your bike when you were eight, moving to Dubuque at the age of three, getting bawled out for breaking your brother's wagon when you were six, and so forth. "Have gone to Lincoln High School" is representative of all of the particular things that you did in the past. These characteristics are present whichever place you choose to eat lunch today. If you're trying to figure out the cost of "eating at the Snack Bar," there are certain things you'll have to sacrifice, but "having moved to Dubuque at the age of three" is not one of them. Indeed, you couldn't sacrifice it even if you wanted to.

Action can affect only the future. That's why our concepts of value (cost and benefit) are "future-oriented," based on how appealing the actor believes his life will be if he chooses one or the other. (That's <u>will be</u>, future tense.) Your current action cannot probe back into the past, undoing choices you now believe to have been mistakes. Here's a little diagram that depicts this point:

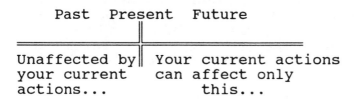

Figure 5.1: Action can affect only the future

I hope this doesn't sound too fatalistic or depressing. We've all done things we regret, and we cannot change the fact that we did them, because that's in the past. But most actions--whenever they were taken--have effects that stretch out into the future. It may be possible, with appropriate action now, to alter (perhaps offsetting and preventing) the effects of past action that still lie in the future. You can't change the fact that you've lived in Dubuque for the past seventeen years, but you don't have to <u>keep</u> living there. It's never too late to apologize for mistreating another person; although it can't erase past years of ill will, it may improve the future.

To a large extent, the kind of individual you are--the kind of values and tastes you hold, the degree to which you respect yourself and others and are considerate of them, even whether you like the seashore or the mountains--is a complex product of your past, especially the choices that you yourself made.[2] Nothing you do today can affect any of that. But the kind of person you are <u>tomorrow</u> depends in part on the actions you take today, and because you haven't taken them yet, those actions are still under your control.

Regret that you are not the person you wish you were is self-defeating; the key to becoming a better person (by your own standard) is to accept the past but to choose current actions of which you're proud. The detrimental effects on one's self-esteem of having for many years worked far below one's potential can't be reversed

---

[2] Ben Ames Williams, in his 1920 short story "Another Man's Poison," made this point: "The moment marked, in a fashion, a milestone in Andy's life. He was confronted by alternatives. He might follow the wagon, retrieve it, save what remained of the victuals that had been in his charge. Or he might follow the men, with some risk to himself, with some faint chance of recovering their stolen goods. When a man faces a choice, and chooses, he shapes himself by the choice for good or ill. Character is the product of such choosings, whether for better or worse." The story is reprinted in his <u>Fraternity Village</u> (Boston: Houghton Mifflin Company, 1949), p. 16.

instantly. But if spending an hour between classes playing pool in the Union usually makes you feel a little guilty, while an hour studying in the library gives you a small sense of pride, the way to begin is clear.

The drawing identified here as Figure 5.2 depicts the general idea. The blob-shaped figure identified as "YOU" is the collection of your past experiences, and the "A" and "B" are two current candidates for incorporation into the blob: two current opportunities for choice.

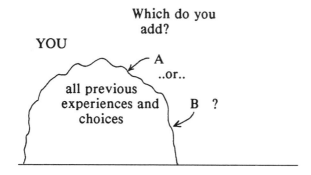

Figure 5.2: You, your past and present

Whichever you pick then becomes a characteristic of tomorrow's blob, when you will be faced with different alternatives. Lincoln High School lies somewhere deep within the current set of experiences, and your brother's broken wagon lies even deeper. Your current choice can determine only what is added at the edge.

Characteristics of your currently available alternatives that consist of your past (Lincoln High) are already part of your collection of experiences. Characteristics that are the same for either alternative (the quality and price of the sandwich, for example) are _effectively_ already part of your life, since you know you're going to pick either A or B and you obtain these characteristics whichever of them you select. All that you haven't decided on, yet, are the differences between A and B.

Economists use the term _margin_ to indicate this edge. (I always remember English teachers who refused to accept laboriously typed papers unless the blank spaces on the edges were the proper width.)

Let's get marginal

The economist's term "marginal" is used to denote the characteristics that are "on the edge" or _different_ between alternatives. Only such differences can affect the _relative_ values of alternatives, and therefore your choice.

If your alternatives are A and B, your _cost_ of choosing A is the value you believe you would have obtained from B, the sense of how "well off" you would have been if you were to choose B instead. Your <u>marginal cost</u> of choosing action A rather than action B is determined only by what's different between B and A. It's the value that you attribute to the <u>differences</u> between A and B.

> Your MARGINAL COST of choosing action A rather than action B is the value that you attribute to characteristics that B possesses but A does not.

Want to see how that differs from the simple "cost" of taking action A? Drop off the last four words. The concept of cost does not "net out" the things that are the same between alternatives, while the concept of marginal cost does.

Your "cost" of eating at the Snack Bar would include everything, including having brown eyes, that you would have experienced by eating at the Union. Your "marginal cost" of eating at the Snack Bar would include only the value that you attribute to the things that make the Union different from the Snack Bar.

> Only MARGINAL costs and marginal benefits are relevant to decision-making.

Economists have identified a number of <u>types</u> of cost, identified by some adjective. Besides our just-plain, no-adjective cost, we've already seen marginal cost. There are also total, fixed, variable, sunk, average, average variable, short-run-total, and others. Most of them, we'll have no use for and won't bother with. That's because whenever it seems as if one of these other kinds of cost is important to action, it either isn't, or in the context it is fundamentally marginal.

Let's consider some examples.

You bought a used motorcycle a few months ago for $1,500. Since then you've learned a thing or two about motorcycling and decided that you don't like it as much as you had hoped. In fact, keeping it is now only as desirable to you as the best alternative that you could obtain with $800. You greatly regret the purchase, of course, but what's done is done.

But someone suddenly comes up and offers you $1,000 for the bike. What are the monetary benefit and cost of selling to him? (To make the problem simpler, assume that you expect no other offers.) The alternatives can be depicted like this:

A: Sell for $1,000; have paid $1,500

B: Keep (worth $800); have paid $1,500

Note that whatever you do now, you have paid $1,500 for the bike. Just like Lincoln High School, the history of how you acquired legal ownership (including how much you paid) is in the past and no current action can change it. This sum is therefore <u>irrelevant</u> to your current choice; the problem would be no different if the amount had been $3 or $47,000. The monetary cost of selling is $800 and the monetary benefit is $1,000, so you should do it.

The best way to look at this transaction is as a $200 net benefit. If you insist on calling it a $500 loss, you should be aware that if you <u>hadn't</u> accepted the offer you would have incurred a $700 loss. Relative to what you <u>would have</u> lost, it's a $200 gain. Realizing that the entire episode has left you $500 poorer has some learning value--as parents are fond of saying, "Let that be a lesson to you..."--so we don't want to dismiss this interpretation completely.

If you interpret this "loss" notion incorrectly, though, you're likely to make a basic error: pretending you have alternatives that don't really exist. To turn the offer down because you "can't afford to take a loss" implies that you have the alternative of getting your $1,500 back. If you <u>could</u> exchange the bike for $1,500, selling it for $1,000 would indeed involve a loss and you wouldn't and shouldn't do it. But if you pretend that the offer of $1,500 exists when it doesn't, and turn down the $1,000, you are left <u>by default</u> with a motorcycle that is worth only $800 to you. Selecting a non-existent alternative and rejecting the best of the existing ones has left you, by your own error, with an option that is less attractive (by $200) than the best that was available.

"Sunk costs" are not costs at all

Economists use the term "sunk costs" to refer to sacrifices made in the past. The $1,500 is a "sunk cost" in this example. Because a past sacrifice is not a currently available opportunity for choice, it is not a cost at all. There's a quick little phrase that can be helpful if it's interpreted properly:

> ## Sunk costs are irrelevant.

Of course the problem is identifying what they're irrelevant to. They certainly help us to understand the history of how you came to be a motorcycle owner, for example; they aren't irrelevant to that. But they are irrelevant to the relative attractiveness of currently available opportunities, and therefore to the process of choice.[3]

Another example involves a simplified notion of apartment rental. Suppose it's the 10th of the month. You pay your rent on the first and that entitles you to the

---

[3] How about regret? Rejecting the offer helps us to preserve the facade that we didn't make a mistake. There's no doubt that we all do that sometimes. Is it a good way to act?

apartment for one month. You have no lease or deposit to think about, but you cannot get any of your current month's rent back if you should leave and are not permitted to sublease the apartment to anyone else. (I know real apartment contracts aren't this simple, but we can put complications in later if we wish. The purpose here is to illustrate a point about cost.)

The rent is $750 per month, which averages out to $25 per day. (All economists' months have 30 days; they're easier to do arithmetic with.) What is your monetary cost of remaining in your apartment for the remaining 20 days of this month?

The natural impulse seems to be to take that $25 per day average, multiply it by 20 days, and get $500. It may seem natural, but it's wrong. We obtained the $25 by dividing our monthly rent of $750 by the number of days in the month (30). But on the 10th, today, that $750 is long since sunk. We paid it on the first, and cannot get it back. It's no longer relevant to anything, and dividing it by 30 gives us another number that isn't relevant to anything.

Check the math if you wish; that seems to be natural, too. But don't forget the computer folks' saying: Garbage In, Garbage Out. If the cost concept on which you base your calculation (the sunk $750) is invalid, then even the most precise mathematical manipulation won't create a nonexistent validity. All you get is another "cost" number that isn't a valid cost at all because it does not represent the value of a currently available opportunity.

A good common-sense way to look at this is to imagine that you want to stay the next 20 days, and ask how much cash you have to hand over to the landlord so that he'll allow you to do that. $500? $25 each day? Of course not. That's what the $750 was--your payment for the right to remain (if you wish) in the apartment until the end of the month. Furthermore, if you decide to leave now, you can't get $500 back from the landlord or from a friend who wants to sublease. (If you could, then remaining would indeed cost you $500.) So the $500 is nothing you have to pay if you stay, and nothing you can get back if you leave. It's just irrelevant. It's not a cost at all.

Cost is future-oriented

Perhaps you look ahead, though, to next month. Suppose it is now the evening of the 30th and you have to decide whether to pay and stay, or move.

With respect to this decision, the $750 is indeed a cost. This $750 still lies in the future, and can be avoided by choosing differently. It is "on the edge," a marginal cost with respect to the action you are evaluating. You must sacrifice the best alternative use of $750 if you rent the apartment for the coming month, and can avoid that sacrifice by not renting it.

If we divide this genuine $750 cost by the number of days in the upcoming month (30, of course), we again obtain the figure $25 per day. Although I find this number a little misleading because it suggests that we can rent on a day-by-day basis when we really can't, it doesn't suffer from the problem of invalidity that plagued our

$25 a couple of paragraphs above. Since the $750 on which it is based is now a genuine (marginal) cost, there's nothing wrong with expressing this cost on a per-day average basis. You have to remind yourself that you can get this daily average only by purchasing 30 of these days at once, nonrefundable and in advance, but as long as you keep that in mind this "average cost" is simply another way of expressing the "marginal cost" of renting the apartment.

"Average cost" is a term that economists often associate with the action of producing a number of units of something, like days in an apartment or widgets turned out by the assembly line. It is determined by dividing the action's "total cost" by the number of units produced. (Here, $750/30 days = $25 per day.) The validity of the "average cost" concept is determined by the validity of the "total cost" from which it is derived. If that "total cost" is entirely a genuine cost, still completely in the future (like our next month's $750) and none of it yet sunk, then both "total" and "average" are legitimate concepts of cost.

Watch out, though, for "average costs" that are obtained from some notion of "total cost" that is partly true future-oriented cost and partly sunk. Suppose you have to pay the landlord $450 on the first, plus $10 each day. That still adds up to $750 each month, but if we're talking about this month then $15 of our $25 daily average is sunk and only the other $10 is a true cost.

COST AND PRODUCTION

We've discussed a bewildering collection of "cost" concepts already: sunk, marginal, average, total, and "true" cost (the actual, real, genuine article--whatever word you want to use to denote it; I prefer no adjective at all). A bit later we'll summarize all of these things in a concise form that will help you to remember the important lessons about them.

You can never go wrong thinking of the cost of an action as the value of the highest-valued alternative action that you would have to forego. In many cases, though, it's important to know something about sums of money that might be obtained or that must be sacrificed. It is never all that matters. In a modern, developed economy like the capitalism (impure though it is) of the United States, businesspeople typically scan the moral and legal implications of general categories of action. (Is it ethically OK for me to aid in the production of can openers? Sausage? Pesticides? To work for Gordon Gekko, the corporate raider played by Michael Douglas in the movie "Wall Street"?)

Often there are complex matters of personal taste involved, as in an owner's steadfast insistence on locating a new factory near the slums where he grew up, or his absolute refusal to build it in a certain state no matter what the financial incentives it offers. When the moral and legal status of many alternatives seem about equal, so that matters of law and ethics have no effect on the relative attractiveness of the alternatives, and matters of taste have been taken into account, judgments of cost and benefit generally depend on sums of money.

Even when questions of personal taste arise, such as the preferential hiring of employees of particular races or sex, it is useful for the decision-maker to know how much money it's costing him to satisfy that preference. (I will not deny that there are trade-offs between morality and money. It's easier to be steadfastly moral when it apparently isn't costing you anything than when it is.)

In any case, monetary measures of costs and benefits are important, so we should carry forward the investigation of them that we began with the motorcycle and the apartment rental. Our further examples will get only a little more complicated.

> Cost is always associated with an
> action, and never with a thing.

When we speak of "the cost of 1,000 widgets," we usually mean "the cost of producing 1,000 widgets." That's OK, but the monetary alternative that has to be sacrificed depends on the circumstances, and we've got to be pretty careful to specify them correctly. Consider the following example.

For $25, you could buy a license that permits you to produce up to 100 widgets. Once you have the legal authority, all of the other materials, electricity, and labor (in short, everything else you need) can be obtained for $3 for each and every widget that you produce. If, for some reason known only to you, you just want to have the license but don't want to produce anything, it'll cost you $25. If you want to legally produce one widget, be prepared to spend $28; two, $31; etc. Your total monetary outlay will be

$$\text{Total monetary outlay} = \$25 + (\$3 \times Q),$$

where Q is the number of widgets you want to produce (up to 100, which is the maximum you're licensed for).

Compared to what?

Two old friends are talking on the sidewalk. When one of the middle-aged men casually asks the other "So, how's your wife?," he barks back "Compared to what?"[4]

I've been fond of this relic of a joke for many years, and before we can answer a question like "What's the monetary cost of producing 40 widgets?," we ought to think about the joke a bit. Compared to what? In other words, what are the

---

[4] I have recently seen this famous old vaudeville joke attributed to Henny Youngman. It is used, just as I use it, by another witty economist: Todd G. Buchholz, New Ideas From Dead Economists (New York: Penguin Books, 1989), p. 141.

alternatives that are available? If "producing 40 widgets" is where we want to go, the sacrifice that lies ahead of us depends a lot on where we are already.

Perhaps we aren't even in the business yet. To produce 40, we'll have to buy the license ($25) and spend $120 (40 x $3) on materials, labor, and other inputs. That's $145, the cost of producing 40 widgets compared to not even having the license.

But maybe we do have the license; we just haven't begun production yet. Then the $25 license fee is sunk, not a cost at all, and only $120 represents the true cost of producing 40 widgets (compared to "being in the business but producing none").

Perhaps we not only have the license, but are already planning to produce 39 widgets. Our alternatives, as far as we're concerned, are "produce 40" or "produce 39," and we're not even considering other possibilities. In this case, clearly the $25 license fee is sunk, but the $117 (that is, 39 x $3) is _also_ sunk, in a sense. Here's a way to look at our alternatives:

A: Produce 39, spend $142

B: Produce 40, spend $145

Pursuing action B (producing 40) only requires us to spend $3 more than action A requires. There's a more dramatic way to look at these alternatives (even if, at first, it looks a little silly).

A: Produce 39, spend $117, also spend $25

B: Produce 40, spend $3, also spend $117,
also spend $25

Whether you produce 39 or 40, you have to buy the license and you also have to buy materials (etc.) sufficient for producing 39. Those are the $25's and the $117's, and the reason I rewrote the alternatives this way is to show you that they're just like your "brown eyes" or "Lincoln High School." Since they are common to each of the alternatives you're considering, they can be cancelled out or erased because they can have no effect on the relative desirability of the two options. If you are taking for granted the production of 39 and trying to evaluate the cost of producing 40 instead, the answer is simply $3.

"Gimme a simple answer, not a lot of economists' gobbledegook!" Economists hear this all the time, from people who don't recognize the complexity of the problem. Well, give it a try. What's the monetary cost of producing 40 widgets? Is it $145, or $120, or $3?

The answer is: "Yes. It depends." (This is a good answer for students of economics to remember. It almost always works, and even when it doesn't it buys you a little thinking time.) That's not what he wanted to hear, but the fact is that his question is simply not sufficiently precise to make a one-number answer possible. Things could be even worse: The cost of producing 40 rather than 38 is $6, rather than 17 is $69, etc.

Economists would identify the $145 as the "total cost" of producing 40 widgets.

> The TOTAL COST of an action is defined
> as the cost of taking that action
> rather than some specific zero-base
> alternative.

In our monetary context, the "total cost" of producing Q units is the monetary sacrifice required to produce them rather than not being in the business or having any of the necessary resources at all. This is our "ground zero," our baseline, and "total cost" is the corresponding "from scratch" measure.

If we aren't really starting from scratch, so that some this "total cost" has already been incurred, it will not be relevant to current production decisions and is not an accurate measure of cost. Economists are well aware of this, and it prevents us from being able to identifying "total cost" as the same thing as "cost."

The term "fixed cost" identifies sacrifices that are required simply to enter the business and set up for production.

> A FIXED COST is a sacrifice that does
> not vary with the quantity produced.

Our $25 is a "fixed cost." It's rather curious in that it can be avoided by the decision not to enter the business (so it isn't "fixed" in the broadest sense), and to those who have already incurred it, it's sunk and therefore no longer a cost. We'll be OK if we identify it simply as a cost of entering the business and remember that it is independent of the actual quantity that we produce.

> A VARIABLE COST is a sacrifice that
> does vary with the quantity produced.

The cost of producing Q units rather than being in the business but producing none, is the "variable cost" of producing Q. (By "being in the business" we mean having all necessary licenses, machines, factory buildings, professional contacts. It's what we get for our "fixed costs.") We can avoid variable costs completely by simply not producing anything, and they increase with each unit that we produce. In this example, they increase by $3 for each additional unit that we add to our production. (The real world, and many economists' examples, are not this conveniently simple.) The "variable cost" of producing 40 is $120, the cost of "producing 40 rather than being in the business but producing zero."

> TOTAL cost is the sum of FIXED cost and VARIABLE cost.

After all, the former is the cost of getting into the business in the first place, and the latter is the cost of producing once you're in. The sum of the two is the cost of producing a specific quantity starting from scratch, from the position of not even being in the business at all. (That's the usual baseline or "zero base" when we're talking about businesses' total costs.) For example, the "variable cost" of producing 23 widgets is $69 (that's 23 x $3), the "fixed cost" of producing them is $25 (of course this is also the "fixed cost" of producing zero or 100 or anything in between), and the "total cost of producing 23 widgets" is $94.

What about the $3, the cost of producing 40 rather than 39? Well, this is what economists usually mean by <u>marginal cost</u>.

> In production, the MARGINAL COST of a particular unit is the cost of adding that unit to our level of production.

When we're discussing marginal costs in the context of production, our assumed alternatives are "produce one more" or "stay where we are." The marginal cost of a particular unit of output is our cost of adding it (and only it) to our (assumed) existing level of output.

The "marginal cost of producing widget number 40" is the cost of producing 40 widgets rather than 39. It's determined solely by what's different between producing 40 and producing 39, and can be obtained--as we did above--by eliminating the sacrifices that are common to these two quantities (the $25 and the $117, leaving the $3). If you know, or are told, what the "total costs" of producing various quantities are (for example, $142 for 39 and $145 for 40), what's different is literally the difference: subtract the total cost of 39 ($142) from the total cost of 40 ($145), and you find the difference that widget number 40 makes. It's $3, the marginal cost of number 40.

Please be cautious about this "production" terminology. It's more restrictive than the way I like to use the term "marginal." I insisted earlier that the term refers to any "edge," so that <u>all</u> costs that are relevant to action are "marginal." They are determined only by differences between the considered alternatives; they are sacrifices that must be incurred if (<u>and only if</u>) the action is taken; the "and only if" means they are completely avoided if it is not. I'll have more to say about this later.

For now, it's enough to note that most economists restrict the term "marginal cost" to the action "producing one more unit."

A numerical example

If we take the problem of widget production just described and construct a little table of some of the numbers involved, we can pull a few interesting points from it. To remind you how "average costs" are determined, the process is explicitly illustrated for a couple of them.

Quantity Produced	Fixed Cost	Variable Cost	Total Cost	Marginal Cost	Average Cost	
	$	$	$	$	$/unit	
0*	0	0	0	---	----	*not in business
0**	25	0	25	---	----	**in the business
1	25	3	28	3	28	
2	25	6	31	3	15.50	
3	25	9	34	3	11.33	(= $34/3)
4	25	12	37	3	9.25	
5	25	15	40	3	8.00	
6	25	18	43	3	7.17	
7	25	21	46	3	6.57	(= $46/7)
8	25	24	49	3	6.13	
9	25	27	52	3	5.78	
10	25	30	55	3	5.50	

We could, of course, continue this table on out to a quantity of 40 or 100 or even beyond (which would be kind of interesting, since we'd have to buy a second license), but I think this will be enough to make the point.

Look first at the "average cost" if we produce 5 widgets. It's $8 per widget. Please recall my warnings about this number, though. All it really means is that, starting from scratch, our cost of producing 5 widgets is $40. If we read anything more into it, we're almost certain to run into problems.

If we're producing 5, could we save $8 by cutting back to 4? No, we'd save only $3. If we're producing 4, would we have to spend another $8 to expand to producing 5? No, only another $3. As long as we're already in the business, that $8 has nothing to do with currently available alternatives because the $40 "total cost" that we used when we derived it (dividing it by 5) is nearly all sunk. In fact, $5 of that $8 is sunk.

Here's a simple example of the kind of mistake we can make by treating this "average cost" as a genuine alternative. Suppose we've already decided to produce 4 (why, how, or whether this is the best quantity isn't relevant at the moment) and have promised them to specific customers when someone rushes up and says, "I desperately need a widget. I'll give you $7 if you'll produce that extra one for me." Your alternatives are to produce 4 and tell him "no," or produce 5 and tell him "yes."

You know the "benefit" of producing and selling number 5. It's just $7. The question is, what's the cost of this action? Maybe you figure that if you were to produce 5 widgets, each of them--on average--would cost $8, so this $7 "isn't covering your cost" and the fellow should be told "no." On the other hand, maybe you figure that the cost of producing and selling number 5, given that you're already producing and selling the first four, is only $3; his $7 offer is well above cost, so you tell him "yes" and go ahead. Which is right? Is the proper measure of cost $8, or $3? The answer obviously determines what you'll choose to do, and if you pick the wrong concept of cost you'll make the wrong decision.

Go with the $3. If you reason as if the $8 "average cost per unit" represents a sum that truly must be sacrificed to produce number 5 and can be avoided by not producing it, you're making a mistake that I cautioned you about very early in this book. You're misidentifying the available alternatives, labelling this guy's offer as less attractive than it really is by falsely believing that producing his widget will cost you $8. In choosing the best of the alternatives that you mistakenly believe are available (sticking with 4), you wind up rejecting the best that truly is available (producing 5), selecting an alternative less attractive (by $4) than an available one that you rejected.

Whether it's a good idea to be in this business at all is something I haven't given you enough numbers to figure out. But if producing and selling 4 is a good idea, then producing (for $3) and selling (for $7) a fifth to this new customer is an even better idea (better by $4).

Covering your costs

An individual takes an action when its benefit exceeds its cost. (These terms refer, of course, to future states that the individual anticipates if he selects the action or its best alternative.) The benefit from business activity like producing widgets is normally considered the money it brings in from customers, and the cost... well, that depends on what your alternatives are.

Swing back to our 40-widget discussion. Suppose you have invested the necessary $25 in the license and can't get it back. You've tentatively decided not to bother producing any widgets at all, though. Suddenly Joe comes up and offers you $132 for 40 widgets. Not one for making rash judgments, you think a bit and come up with a batch of numbers.

The "total cost" of producing 40 widgets is $145, while Joe is offering only $132. The "average cost" of producing 40 is $3.63 each (that's $145/40, rounded off), while Joe is offering only an average of $3.30 each (that's $132/40). That's a 33-cent loss on each widget, or a $13 loss on the bunch. You've got yourself pretty well convinced that it's a bad deal.

Think again. Garbage In, Garbage Out. What is the proper cost of producing 40 widgets, rather than none, if you're already in the business? Not $145, because the $25 "fixed cost" is sunk. What lies in the future is only your "variable cost," the $120 of that $145 that you can avoid by choosing not to produce. The true cost of the action you're evaluating, then, is only $120, while its benefit is $132. (If you insist on averages, you're getting $3.30 each and your cost is only $3 each.) In fact, the benefit (to you) of the action "produce 40 rather than being in the business but producing zero" is greater than its cost if Joe offers you as little as, say, $120.01.

Now let's suppose that you are not in the business yet. Your "fixed costs" are now true costs, because they are sacrifices that must yet be made. They lie in the future and can be avoided by choosing differently. To make "producing 40 widgets" worthwhile, Joe must--as before--"cover your costs." But now your true cost of producing 40 widgets is the full $145 "total cost," and if he doesn't offer you at least that, your best alternative is to decline his offer.

Here's the opposite extreme. Suppose you entered the business and produced 40 widgets "on spec," speculating that buyers would eventually show up. You were wrong, and have become convinced that nobody will ever buy them. You have no personal use for the things. Suddenly Joe comes in and offers you $5 for the entire lot. As long as you truly expect no better offers, your cost of producing and selling the widgets to Joe is zero. The entire $145 "total cost" is sunk, irrelevant to your current choice, and the only alternative of which you're aware is continuing to store them yourself (which we assume, for simplicity, has neither costs nor benefits to you). You should jump up and click your heels that he offered five bucks, because even a penny would have been enough to make the sale desirable to you.

Despite all of the terminology, the principal lessons are those we learned earlier. If someone wants you to take a specific action (like produce 40 widgets and sell them to him), he must make that action the best of your currently available alternatives. That means he must offer more than your cost of taking the action. The minimum that he must offer is a lot different if you are not even in the business yet, if you are but perceive your best alternative as producing zero, or if you've already produced the things and perceive only a valueless alternative for them.

FURTHER APPLICATIONS OF THE CONCEPT OF COST

We've covered the basics of cost, but these basics have a number of interesting implications. We're going to look into some of them now.

A sacrifice made in the past is no longer a cost. It was once, before it was made. And if it's part of a recurring pattern, maybe you'll face the decision again and then it'll be a cost. If it's March 10, your March rent is not a cost; it was, though, on

February 30 (remember economists' months!); and your <u>April</u> rent will become a cost when you face the decision at the end of March.

A precisely identical problem faces any business with "fixed costs." Suppose you have just leased a building and equipment for one month, at a price of $10,000. You have been planning to produce 4,000 wodgets per month, each of which will require you to spend $8 on materials, labor, and electricity. No other sacrifices are required. (How you decided on 4,000, instead of perhaps 2,853, is a matter we'll investigate in the next chapter.) Now: how much money must you expect to receive from your wodget customers, to make "producing and selling 4,000 wodgets" preferable to "not producing at all"?

Well, your benefit must exceed your cost. The "benefit" is the money you expect to receive, and your cost...?

If we're talking about <u>this</u> month, the $10,000 is sunk. (We assume that you can't get a refund or sublease the industrial space if you decide not to use it yourself.) Your alternatives are not "go into the wodget business and produce 4,000" or "don't go into the wodget business," because you're already in it. Your options are "use these resources to produce 4,000" or "just let the resources sit here." Whichever you do, you have already paid the $10,000. You now have a pile of resources sitting in front of you; your question is not "How did these things get here?," but rather "What is the best thing to do with them?" Let them sit until you have to give them back at the end of the month, or spend yet more money to actually use them?

The answer is that you must expect the revenue from your customers to exceed the cost of using the resources that you already have. That cost is $32,000, the expenditure that still lies ahead and that you can avoid by not producing at all. Since you've already incurred the fixed cost, the <u>cost</u> of producing 4,000 wodgets is simply their variable cost.

Perhaps you expect to be able to sell these planned 4,000 wodgets for a total of $36,000. (That's an average of $9 each.) Since the cost of producing the wodgets-- given that you already have the building and equipment--is only $32,000 (an average of $8 each), you should go ahead. The fact that you aren't covering your "total cost" of $42,000 is irrelevant to your current choice: $10,000 of that $42,000 is not a legitimate cost at all, because it's sunk.

Along about now some of the more thoughtful students sometimes ask: "Hold it a minute. Maybe in <u>economics</u> you're gaining $4,000, but in <u>reality</u> aren't you losing $6,000?" Every economist has faced such a charge that "economics is one thing, but reality is another," especially from business students. The answer to it lies in keeping clear exactly what action we're talking about, what action we're evaluating the costs and benefits of. Comparing the benefit of one action with the cost of a different action is--as you might imagine--an almost sure-fire route to error...and maybe bankruptcy.

Knowing the past helps us in the future

First of all, doing this month after month is <u>not</u> a sure key to getting rich. That's the old joke about taking a loss on each unit but getting rich by "making it up on volume." But let's take a look at <u>next</u> month. (Only the planners for businesses that are in the most desperate straits don't look at least that far into the future, especially if it's the 10th already.)

Unless you have reason to believe that demand will rise substantially, it's natural to use this month's results as a predictor of next month's and to infer that you won't be able to get more than $36,000 then either. Since your cost of producing 4,000 wodgets <u>next month</u> is $42,000, a decision to go ahead would indeed produce a $6,000 loss. You'd be that much poorer at the end of next month than you were at its beginning. The cost of "producing 4,000 wodgets next month" exceeds the action's benefit, so you won't and shouldn't do it. Investigate the widget business instead.

If we take a retrospective look at the current month, using what we now know about the state of the wodget market, it is clear that we never should have taken out that $10,000 lease in the first place. (We can't make <u>that</u> decision again since it's in the past and already done, but if we ever have a chance to make a <u>similar</u> decision, which we will at the start of <u>next</u> month, we won't do it.) The best that we can do this month is to lose $6,000. But what's the alternative? If we produce nothing, we lose $10,000. "Producing" makes us better off than "not producing" by $4,000 this month.

It is important that our monthly operation be identified as resulting in a $6,000 loss, because that conveys information that may be useful in the future. It's the old "Let that be a lesson to you" again. (Why would we ever care about the past, unless we believed that it might help us to deal with the future?) But one-third of the way through the month, the actions of the first 10 days have already been taken, and the managers' problem is how best to use the next 20. Producing is better than not producing by $4,000, and whether the month's overall loss is $6,000 or $187,473 doesn't change that. If you want to interpret producing, under these circumstances, as "loss minimization," that's fine. Just make sure you approve of the action.

Benefit (that is, expected revenue) must exceed cost. Producing any particular quantity Q is a bit like taking a journey. Before you've begun, the relevant cost of getting to your destination includes everything ("total cost"), and you will begin only if you expect the result to be worth at least this much. If you've already travelled part of the way (perhaps only metaphorically, by doing all of the planning and getting the car packed), then going on to your destination requires that it seem more appealing only than the sacrifices that still lie ahead of you.

A business must "cover its costs," as any action must. But the relevant costs are what we normally call "total costs" only if none of them has yet been incurred. That portion of "total costs" that has been incurred is now <u>sunk</u>, not a cost at all, and a business that acts as if even "sunk costs" have to be covered is bound to make errors-- perhaps fatal ones (in the business sense).

Selling "below cost"

Recently, an imported car dealership just up the road from my University was offering "brand new" Italian sports convertibles for under $8,000. These cars, although they had never been sold, were four years old. The brand had developed a reputation for shoddy quality, so the cars had remained unsold for four or five years.

I have no idea what the dealership originally paid for each of the cars, but let's say it was $11,000. (After all, I have a point to make here about economics and costs; this course isn't about the auto business.) Would the dealer be justified in advertising that he's "selling these cars way below dealer cost"?

Remember that cost is always associated with an <u>action</u>, not with a <u>thing</u>. Furthermore, the cost of any action (X) is the value that the decision-maker attributes to the highest-valued action (say, Y) that he will have to forego if he chooses the considered action (X). Cost refers to currently available opportunities for action, and is determined by anticipating what the future would be like if the best alternative were selected instead.

So what is the action whose cost we are evaluating? It's the dealer's action. Is it "selling the car" rather than "not selling the car"? Well, what alternative use for the car is open to the dealer, other than selling it? If he could get a refund of, say, $3,500 from the importer or manufacturer for each car returned (which I doubt), his cost of selling would be $3,500. If the best alternative currently available is $75 from an auto salvage yard (which I suspect is more likely), then the dealer's cost of selling the car-- that is, the best alternative that he sacrifices by selling the car to a new-car customer--is only $75. In either case, of course, the $8000 is way <u>above</u> his true cost of selling the car. The $11,000, as you've realized by now, is long since sunk and not a cost of his current action at all. His best current course of action would be no different if he had paid either $1,800 or $27,000 for the vehicle.

> No individual EVER takes an action
> whose cost exceeds its benefit.

These costs and benefits are determined by the individual at the time of his choice, and if the benefits are "below cost" the action is simply not taken. The dealer is offering to sell <u>now</u> below what his cost of selling once was, sure enough, but that's not what his cost of selling is now.

If the action we're evaluating is, however, "selling to Harry," the dealer may believe that his best alternative is "selling to Pam." If he believes that there might be more than one bidder for the car, then his cost of selling to Harry is determined by his guess at the best alternative offer. If he thinks Pam would be willing to pay $8,300, then he would have to sacrifice this opportunity if he were to sell to Harry. A sale to Harry for $8,000 would indeed be "below cost" and the dealer wouldn't do it. If he thinks Pam would offer $7,800 tops, then the relevant cost of selling to Harry is the $7,800 that he will have to forego from Pam. This is the sum that Harry must outbid; if he offers $8,000 he's offering more than the dealer's cost ($200 more).

Suppose you buy a pickup truck load of good-looking bananas for 25 cents a pound. But you misprice them, asking too much, and they don't sell. They're now kind of yellow and brown--more brown than yellow--and you now believe you can sell them only at 10 cents a pound. That's below what the cost of selling them was once upon a time, before you purchased the truckload. (To sell them, when you didn't even own them yet, required that you first buy them yourself--an action that cost you 25 cents per pound.) But whether it's below your cost of selling them _now_ is determined by currently available alternative uses. For over-ripe bananas, there probably aren't many. In fact, if your best alternative is to pay a garbage collector $5 to haul them away, your cost of selling them could even be negative. If you find a customer who will take them all if you pay him $3, you're "selling" them for $2 more than your "cost of 'selling' them"!

Exactly how good are you at mind-reading?

This whole matter of "selling below cost" is full of confusion and misinterpretation. Nobody ever "sells" when the "benefit of selling" is below the "cost of selling." Plenty of people take an action when the benefit of taking that action is less than the cost of taking some _other_ action. But so what? Remember what the benefits and costs of any action are. They're subjective anticipations about the future that are formulated by the decision-maker at the moment that he makes his choice.

> To determine someone else's benefit
> and cost, you would have to be able
> to READ HIS MIND.

I don't know for sure about you, but mind-reading is something that I haven't figured out how to do (yet).

Often when we judge another's behavior we impose on the actor our own beliefs about costs and benefits. If he had shared _our_ judgment of cost and benefit, he never would have taken the action. Therefore, we too often conclude, the action was a mistake, it was shortsighted and stupid, and he never should have taken it. Because our benefits of this action would have been smaller than our costs, we mistakenly judge that his benefits must be smaller than his costs too.

But we can't read others' minds, and we know that their knowledge of alternatives and their values differ from ours. It should hardly surprise us that others interpret costs and benefits differently than we do, and often choose actions that we never would. Indeed, the only direct evidence that one individual can have of another's values (costs and benefits) is to observe his voluntary action.

> All that we can really know about
> another individual's cost and benefit
> is that if he took the action
> voluntarily, he judged the benefit
> to exceed the cost.

"Voluntary," of course, means without force or fraud that violates his individual rights.

The case of the "loss leader"

"Your first visit free!," blares the TV ad for some lawyer or psychiatrist. Hmmm. Is that "selling below cost"? Surely there are costs involved in providing you with that consultation for which you are not charged. Suppose it's $50. In the time that the lawyer spends with you, she could have earned $50 from someone else.

If it seems to you as if this is a clear case of "benefit less than cost," apparently a lot of sellers interpret things a little differently than you do, because this is a common practice. A convenience store sells milk at a price below the price it had to pay to its own wholesaler. And how about "second pair of shoes free!"? (I'm sure these retailers have faced wiseguys who say, "I'd just like one of those second pairs, please.")

If you want to interpret the "benefit" of selling the item strictly as the money received from it (the first office visit, the gallon of milk, or the second pair of shoes), and the "cost" as the money you will have to sacrifice to provide the item, please feel free to. You will, of course, conclude that the cost of these activities exceeds their benefits and will choose not to engage in this kind of business behavior. But the simple fact that others do, is itself evidence that they see things a little differently.

Clearly nobody would take these actions if they viewed costs and benefits as you do. The reason that some sellers offer these "loss leaders" (I've also heard them called "merchandising items")[5] is that their interpretation of benefits is much broader than yours. The lawyer anticipates establishing a long relationship with a client who she might never have seen without the "first visit free" offer. The convenience store

---

[5] The simplest definition of a "loss leader" or "merchandising item" is a good that is offered for sale at a price that is below its explicit monetary cost (such as the price that the retailer paid to the wholesaler).

may hold a similar expectation, or simply hope that the guy who drops in for cheap milk will buy ten bucks worth of snack food too. The shoe retailer apparently hopes to sell far more "first pairs" than he would have without the "second pair free" offer.

Are these wise business strategies? In retrospect, did the sellers' benefits really outweigh their costs? Well, I certainly don't know. When the future--and other people's decisions--are involved, there's always uncertainty and we often find actual results that don't meet our expectations. Then there's the ceteris paribus problem that the retailer can't really hold "other things the same," so he can't be sure what caused a sales increase. But at the moment of the choice, the actor anticipated benefits exceeding costs. Maybe nobody else did, but he's the one who matters because it's his action.

Sometimes rival sellers accuse a competitor of "selling below cost" to drive them out of business, a strategy known as "predatory pricing." Like a wolf ripping apart a sick moose, the "predator" is alleged to be viciously destroying his competitors by selling at prices that are not only below their prices, and not only below their costs, but even below his own costs.

Even if we accept this strategy at face value, the firm offering the low prices does so in anticipation of benefits in the future: no longer having any competitors, and being able to charge much higher prices then. Since his own perceived benefit from selling at these low prices has to include the belief that the action will produce higher prices later, that benefit exceeds his own perceived cost of selling cheap now.

In fact, though, what's usually happening is that the low-pricing seller's costs really are lower than those of his competitors. That means he's able to sell at a price that's below their costs, but that covers his own current costs of production. The other sellers don't like it, or can't understand how his costs could be lower than theirs, so they attempt to marshall public disapproval of his action. Perhaps they can convince the government to take antitrust action against him. All that's really happening is that he's out-competing them and they don't like it.

As we'll see later, this is what was going on in the most renowned tale of "predatory pricing" in our nation's history: John D. Rockefeller's Standard Oil in the late 1800s. The folklore is that Rockefeller viciously destroyed his competitors by selling below his own cost of production. But that tale mostly originated from unsuccessful competitors. The truth is that his own cost of production, because he was such an innovative and courageous businessman, was much lower than theirs.

Can others bear the cost of your action?

We know that a person will take an action only when he perceives its benefit to exceed its cost. The relevant benefit and cost are those anticipated by the actor. But what if someone else bears some of the costs? Is that even possible, if we are careful about how we use our words?

Gwen is a college student who has been so busy with her work that her parents have decided to encourage her to attend football games. A season ticket is $100, and they've volunteered to pay $60 if she will pay the other $40.

Her parents' offer will change her choice only if her demand price for the season ticket had been between $40 and $100. (If it had been higher, she would have gone anyway; if lower, she won't go even with the offer.) Even though the ticket's price is $100, Gwen is likely to act as if the cost of the ticket is only her best alternative use of $40.

Now... did buying the ticket "really" cost $100, but Gwen only had to bear 40% of it because her parents bore the other 60%? Did her decision to buy the ticket "impose a cost" on her parents? Or should we truly insist that the cost of her choice was only the $40 that she, herself, had to sacrifice? If so, what about the other $60?

The best way to think about this matter is to remind ourselves that cost is always associated with an action, and it is determined by the actor as part of the process of choice. From this perspective, Gwen's parents obtained a benefit and bore a cost when they chose to make the offer. (Whether the money involved is $60 or zero depends on Gwen, but they're prepared for either outcome.) The cost of Gwen's purchase is, truly, only $40.

The issues seem to be more complex when parties are involved who apparently made no choices. What if I choose to wear a necktie that is so ugly, in your judgment, that just seeing it upsets your whole day? On a more serious note, what if you paint your house orange with purple polka-dots, George dumps his car's used oil in the creek that runs behind your house, or a local government's incinerator spews foul odors and soot all over your property?

Economists often use the phrase "private cost" to identify the cost borne by the decision maker. Harm that the decision causes for others, who were not involved in the choice, is identified as an "external cost." The sum of these two, which is--in a sense--the overall negative impact or "downside" of your choice, is called your action's "social cost." (Your action may have "external benefits," too--advantages that others enjoy. Planting flowers in your front yard might offer an example. Then your action's "social benefit" exceeds its "private benefit.")[6]

Although such "external" effects certainly exist, my own judgment is that we should keep the concept of cost well away from them.

---

[6] Of course, if others find the flowers to be ugly, they would impose an "external cost." The difficulty of finding some measure of the size of external effects--and sometimes even whether they're positive or negative--is only one of the problems with this attempt to extend the concepts of cost and benefit to "society."

> The only concept of cost that is relevant to an actor's choice is that of the value that he himself must sacrifice.

If an individual is environmentally sensitive, or simply considerate of others' feelings, he will take these things into account: an alternative that harms the environment or treats others unfairly will not be very attractive to him. If I learn (and care--but of course I do!) that you hate that tie, my cost of choosing it rises. If Gwen knows that her parents are poor and she doesn't think they "can afford" the $60, she will consider their sacrifice as part of her cost.

If an action truly violates others' legitimate individual rights, it should be proscribed by law. What's wrong with it is <u>not</u> that it makes others "worse off"; that happens simply when I wear the ugly necktie, or when you cleverly outguess others and snatch the newly vacated parking space. What's wrong with rights violations is simply that they violate rights. They fall outside the category of voluntary action.

If an action simply makes someone else feel less well off than he otherwise would have, without violating any of his rights, then perhaps the term "harm" could appropriately identify the effect. What we should do with such a concept is another matter, as well as how we manage to evaluate it in an manner that respects the subjective nature of value.

In any case, to mix it up with the concept of cost that we've developed (the value that the decision maker attributes to the best of the actions that he must forego) is unwise. Whatever this notion of social effects might be, it clearly is something quite different from cost. According to our subjectivist, action-oriented concept of cost, there is indeed no such thing as a cost that is not borne by the individual who makes the decision.

YOU SHOULD REMEMBER...

1) The COST of an action is the value that the actor attributes to the best of the alternative actions that he must forego.

2) Only characteristics that DIFFER between two alternatives can affect their relative desirability.

3) Because action can affect only the future, our concepts of value, benefit, and cost must be FUTURE-ORIENTED.

4) Your MARGINAL COST of choosing action A rather than action B is the value that you attribute to characteristics that B possesses but A does not.

5) Your MARGINAL BENEFIT of choosing action A rather than action B is the value that you attribute to characteristics that A possesses but B does not.

6) Only MARGINAL COSTS and MARGINAL BENEFITS are relevant to choice.

7) A SUNK COST is a sacrifice made in the past. It is not the value of a currently available alternative, so it is NOT A COST AT ALL and is irrelevant to choice.

8) Cost is always associated with an action, and never with a thing.

9) The TOTAL COST of an action is defined as the cost of taking that action rather than some specific zero-base alternative, such as "not even being in the business."

10) A FIXED COST is a sacrifice that does not vary with the quantity produced. If it has already been paid, it is SUNK and no longer a cost at all.

11) A VARIABLE COST is a sacrifice that does vary with the quantity produced.

12) In business production, MARGINAL COST is the cost of ADDING a particular unit to our level of production.

13) Only sacrifices that have NOT YET BEEN MADE, and can therefore be avoided by choosing differently, can be COSTS.

14) We study the PAST (including our own sunk costs) to help us to make better choices when similar opportunities again become available.

15)   COVERING YOUR COSTS simply means that you perceive the benefit of the action to exceed its cost.

16)   No individual EVER takes an action whose cost exceeds its benefit. Despite the advertising, nobody ever "sells below cost."

17)   Because they are both "values," to determine another individual's cost and benefit you would have to READ HER MIND.

18)   All that one person can know about another person's cost and benefit is that if she took the action VOLUNTARILY, she judged its benefit to exceed its cost.

19)   If COST is to identify a sacrifice evaluated, chosen, and borne by the actor, negative effects imposed on others (without their choice) should be identified as HARMS, not costs.

Problems

We're considering entering (or are already involved in, depending on the problem) the quark business. Consider the following data (I haven't bothered with quantities between 0 and 42). An occasional answer is provided as assurance (or warning).

```
Number of              Total monetary outlay
quarks produced          to produce this number
     0* ------------------- $0        *no assets, not even in business
     0** ----------------- $1000      **ready to produce but none yet
    42 ------------------- $4200
    43 ------------------- $4257
    44 ------------------- $4312
    45 ------------------- $4365
    46 ------------------- $4420
    47 ------------------- $4477
```

1)   Find the monetary cost of producing...

43 rather than 42:

44 rather than 43:

45 rather than 44: [Answer: $53]

46 rather than 45:

47 rather than 46:

(These are the numbers that economists usually refer to as the marginal costs of the particular units (e.g. of quark number 46).)

2)   Find the "average cost" (that is, total monetary outlay divided by the number produced) if the quantity produced is:
        42 _____; 43 _____; 44 _____ ;

        45 _____; 46 _$96.09_; 47 _____

3)   Suppose that a major customer has a long-standing contract to purchase 42 quarks per month for $4,200. (That's $100 each, exactly equal to your average cost of producing them.) Suddenly an individual comes up, pleading for one quark and offering $75 for it. If your major customer has no objections, would you be better off producing and selling number 43 to this individual,

or not? _____ If your accountant says, "But that's less than our cost!," which cost is he referring to? _____

4) Suppose the $1,000 is a lease payment on a machine that you must have if you're to produce at all. If you have already leased the machine (and can't back out or sublease it to someone else), what is the monetary cost of producing 45 quarks rather than none? _____What is the monetary cost of producing 45 rather than none, if you haven't leased the machine yet? _____

5) You have already leased the machine, and there's no way you can get your $1,000 back. How much must you expect to be able to sell 44 quarks for (your total expected sales revenue from all 44 of them), to make "producing and selling 44 quarks" more attractive than "producing and selling none"?

6) Answer (5) again, this time assuming that you have not already incurred the $1,000 lease expense.

7) If you expect to sell each one of these 44 quarks for the same price, what minimum selling price must you expect to receive for each quark to make "producing 44" preferable to not producing at all, in the case of question (5) $75.28 ? In the case of question (6) _____ ?

8) Suppose you have leased the machine, and then become convinced (by thinking about demand) that you will have to charge no more than $80 each if you want to sell 44 quarks. Are you better off producing and selling 44 at $80 each, or not producing at all?

9) Does this $80 price allow you to "cover your costs," given that you've already leased the machine?

10) Would it allow you to cover them if you hadn't already incurred the lease expense?

CHAPTER 6

DETERMINING THE BEST
QUANTITY AND PRICE

PRICE TAKERS AND MARGINAL REVENUE

When we began our study by discussing a shopping mall's parking lot, we made a very simple hypothesis about people's behavior (they just want to minimize walking distance) and found that the cars would be parked in a semicircular pattern centered on the door. It wasn't, by itself, a very good description of reality, but it was the place to start.

One of the purposes of that example was to convince you that it's not only OK but absolutely necessary to follow a procedure of "decreasing abstraction." We make a lot of simplifying assumptions so that we can focus our attention on some basic principle. Once we think we understand that principle, we can drop one of the simplifying assumptions and see what happens. As soon as we figure out this more complex analysis, we can drop another of our assumptions. We continue this process until we judge its benefit (a further increase in the realism of our analysis) to no longer exceed its cost (the increase in the difficulty of understanding what's going on).

Our analysis of cost in the preceding chapter proceeded like that, making use of several examples like this one. Starting from scratch, producing 50 hooeys would require the expenditure of $8,000. But if you've already irretrievably spent $4,500 of that ("fixed costs" like a license and property lease), the relevant cost of producing the 50 hooeys is only the remaining $3,500, and "producing 50" is better than "producing zero" if you expect to get at least $3,500 for them (an average of $7 each). If you haven't spent the $4,500 yet (or have but can get it all back, which is about the same as not having spent it at all yet), it's not yet sunk and is still part of your true cost of production. In this case, "producing 50" rather than "producing zero and staying out of the hooey business" is the superior choice only if you expect to be able to receive at least $8,000 for them (an average of $16 each).

Where did that "50" come from? We may be able to determine the conditions under which 50 is better than zero, but how do we know that 50 is better than 49 or 197 or 13? Well, the "50" came from the same place that provided the problem's other numbers: I made it up. Assuming that your only choice was either fifty or zero was a simplification designed to help you to get a grip on the basic idea. Now it's time to drop that simplification, permit you to select any quantity, and examine the logic of the process by which you make the choice.

Since we've just spent a chapter on the cost side of things, let's keep you in the role of a producer but turn our attention first to the sales side of your decision. That means the demand for your product. Could you sell fifty for $3,500 or more?

Could you get at least $8,000 for them? Maybe 50 isn't even the best quantity to sell at all.

The price taker

Economists have found some advantages to working with a demand curve that isn't much like the ones with which we dealt in Chapters 2 through 4. Those demand curves were sometimes discrete (steps) and sometimes smooth, but they always sloped downward, illustrating the "law of demand" that there's an inverse relationship between the "quantity demanded" and the price of any good. A larger quantity demanded requires a lower price, and a higher price is associated with a smaller quantity demanded.

Suppose, however, that there are such perfect substitutes for your product that none of your customers perceives anything unique about it. It has absolutely no advantages that would lead anyone to prefer it over the products of your competitors.

This assumption is utterly unrealistic, and it's important that you remember that. Neither your specific location (you're near a particular residential area and no other seller is) nor any personal characteristics of you or your staff (you're a trout-fly fisherman, and two of your long-standing customers like that) are permitted to have any relevance to even one of your customers.[1]

Under these conditions, as long as all of the producers of these identical goods offer them at the same price, no buyer has any reason to prefer any seller over any other. If you (or any other particular seller) were to raise your asking price even the tiniest amount, you would lose all of your sales because your (previous) customers perceive nothing about your product that would make it worth paying the higher price for.

If you wished, for some reason, to increase the quantity that you sell, it would take only the tiniest imaginable price cut to achieve that. After all, the customers of your competitors perceive nothing unique about their products either, so they'll drop their sellers like a hot potato when they see your minutely lower price. Just as the tiniest imaginable price increase would cause your sales to fall to zero, the tiniest imaginable price decrease would cause them to increase by any amount you're willing to supply--up to, and perhaps including, the entire market.

If we were to draw a graph of the demand for your product, we'd get a line that's just about horizontal at the current market-clearing price. Economists normally take the final step in the construction of this abstract model and eliminate the "just about," pretending that the demand curve truly is precisely horizontal. (Those of you with some math training can use the concept of the limit as the magnitude of the price change necessary to reduce the quantity demanded to zero, or increase it by any specific large amount, approaches zero.)

---

[1] "Especially remarkable in this connection is the explicit and complete exclusion from the theory... of all personal relationships existing between the parties." Friedrich A. Hayek, "The Meaning of Competition," in his Individualism and Economic Order (Chicago: University of Chicago Press, 1948): pp. 96-7.

As you may recall from Chapter 2, the term <u>elasticity</u> refers to the sensitivity of quantity to a change in price. The elasticity of demand is formally defined as (-1) times [the percentage change in quantity demanded divided by the percentage change in price]. The demand curve that we're discussing here is price-sensitive in the extreme.

The elasticity of a horizontal demand (or supply) curve is INFINITE.

Elasticity is determined by the attractiveness of the available alternatives, and in this case they are precisely as attractive as the good itself. (You might wonder, then, how each seller winds up with a certain number of customers, since none of them cares in the slightest which seller he buys from. I don't know. Pure chance?) Mathematically, the elasticity is infinite because even the tiniest imaginable percentage change in price produces wide swings (between zero and "the whole market") in quantity demanded. (Again, in the limit: what happens to "percentage change in quantity demanded divided by percentage change in price" as "percentage change in price" approaches zero?)

If there is only one other seller, though, or even several, it's probably unrealistic to think that some action of yours will leave "the market" unaffected. If you raise your price by 20%, your competitors are certainly going to notice, and might raise theirs, too. If they simply try to handle a big influx of your (former) customers, their costs will rise.

So, we stick in another condition: each seller has <u>a lot</u> of competitors, producing goods among which customers have absolutely no preference at all. That way, the actions of any one seller (raising or lowering his price) will probably not even be noticed, and--in any case--will have no noticeable effect on the overall market.

In this case, the market-clearing price of your commodity (and "commodity" is a good word, for mostly only agricultural commodities like wheat come even close to this kind of situation) is determined by the demands by all of the buyers and the supplies by all of the sellers (including you). The <u>market</u> demand and supply curves have the normal downward and upward shapes, but you (or any other one seller) are such a small frog in a big pond that any decision that you might make about quantity would have a negligible impact on the overall market-clearing price. Whether you were to decide to go out of business or triple your output, your action has such a small impact on the market-clearing price that it is ignored. That's where we get the horizontal demand curve.

Figure 6.1 illustrates the situation, with some rather extreme numbers that I made up to try to make the reasoning dramatic.

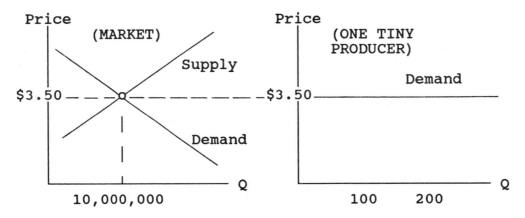

Figure 6.1: The market, and one price-taking producer

The market-clearing (equilibrium) price and quantity were originally $3.50 each and 10,000,000, with you accounting for 100 of them. Suppose that you then arbitrarily decide to double your output to 200. (No, I don't know why either.) The market supply curve will shift to the right by the 100 extra units that you insist on producing, and the equilibrium price will fall. But the increase in quantity supplied at $3.50 is only from 10,000,000 to 10,000,100, and the fall in price needed to equilibrate the market under these new conditions is surely far less even than one whole cent. A microscopic examination of the diagram of the overall market might show a reduction in the equilibrium price of, say, a thousandth of a cent. Since the quantity demanded of your output is 100 at $3.50 each, and 200 at $3.49999 each, it's clear why economists typically just identify the demand for your output as horizontal at $3.50.

Any particular seller in this kind of market is called a "price taker" because he simply "takes" his price from "the market." No action of his, from closing up shop to quadrupling his output, can have any effect on that price.

The "price taker" model has some nice properties that make it attractive to economists, particularly to teachers. There are certain problems that disappear, or become much easier to deal with, when we assume that a demand curve is flat, horizontal, rather than downward-sloping. Learning about this model is an important step in your education in economics.

We must never forget, however, that it is a simplified abstraction, an imaginary construction that we use to make certain problems easy by sweeping aside certain real-world complications. In particular, we cannot base recommendations about real-world economic policy on the "price taker" model. It is wrong to conceive of this model as some kind of ideal, and to argue that real-world markets have somehow "failed" if they don't seem to produce its results. (I raised a related issue back in Chapter 2, in a comment about economists' use of the term "perfect" to describe markets with smooth, non-stepped, demand and supply curves.) This is a very real problem to which we'll return in Chapter 7.

The concept of marginal revenue

One of the main reasons that economists like the price-taker model is that there's no problem deciding what price the seller should ask. If he tries to charge a price that's above the market equilibrium he'll sell nothing, and there's no point to charging anything less because he can sell all that he wants to at the market equilibrium price. He simply "takes" his selling price from the market. (That, of course, is why he's called a "price taker.") If he should decide that he wants to sell one unit more, or to triple his output and sell that, he does not have to concern himself with the matter of what this increased supply might do to the price that he can receive: it won't do anything.

> A seller is a PRICE TAKER if the
> demand for his product is a horizontal
> line (infinitely elastic) at the
> market price of the good.

(A <u>buyer</u> is a price taker if the supply of the good <u>to him</u> is a horizontal line. For all practical purposes, you're in this position when you go to the bookstore to buy notebooks. Again, a small frog in a big pond...)

It's pretty obvious what price such a producer should charge, but he still has to decide on the best quantity to produce. If the market equilibrium price that he "takes" is $3.50 per unit, the monetary <u>benefit</u> of producing 100 units rather than none is simply 100 x $3.50, or $350. (We'll talk about cost later.) The monetary benefit of producing 101 units rather than none is just 101 x $3.50, or $353.50. The monetary benefit of "selling 101 rather than 100" is, therefore, $353.50 minus $350, or $3.50. In fact, the monetary benefit of "producing and selling one more," whatever level he's starting from, is always $3.50, because that's the amount by which his sales revenue increases when he offers one more unit to the market.

> The MARGINAL REVENUE of any particular
> unit is the amount that it adds to the
> seller's sales revenue.

This concept of "marginal revenue" is the monetary benefit of the action "add this unit (and only it) to our previous level of output and sales," and can be determined by finding out how much the additional unit changes the seller's total sales revenue. (Note that the new unit will have costs of production and marketing; we haven't considered those yet here. An action is determined by a comparison of its benefit with its cost, and "marginal revenue" is concerned with the "benefit" part of that comparison.)

Whenever a price taker cares to, he can sell one additional unit (increasing his production level by one) with no effect whatsoever on the market-clearing price. A little algebra can be used to generalize our example of unit number 101:

$$MR_{n+1} = [P \times (n+1)] - [P \times n]$$
$$= P,$$

and this is true for any particular unit (n+1) that the price-taker cares to consider. Unit number 1 increases his sales revenue from zero to $3.50. Unit number 77 raises it from $266 (that's $3.50 x 76) to $269.50 (that's $3.50 x 77), another increase of $3.50. If you're comfortable with the algebra, you don't need these numerical examples because you're already convinced.

The derivation above depends crucially on the price-taker assumption. That's what allows us to assert that the price (P) at which the slightly larger quantity (n+1) could be sold was the same as the price (P) at which the previous quantity (n) had been sold. If our seller had found that the demand for his product was not horizontal but rather downward-sloping, he would have found it necessary to cut his price a little to sell that additional unit. Our derivation would then have had two <u>different</u> prices in it and we couldn't have just subtracted the one "P x n" from the other "P x n", the way we did above.

> For a price taker, marginal revenue and price are identical.

Since the demand curve traces out the relationship between quantity demanded and price, and price is identical to marginal revenue, the same curve also shows the marginal revenue of each individual unit. The demand and marginal revenue curves are identical, indistinguishable horizontal lines lying right on top of each other at the market equilibrium price. Remember: This is for a price taker. Figure 6.2 presents a picture.

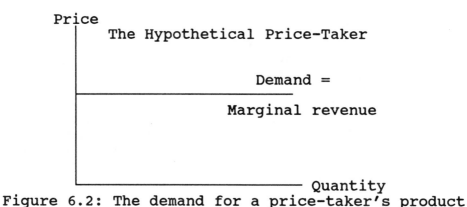

Figure 6.2: The demand for a price-taker's product

The price taker finds his quantity

Suppose you're thinking of going into business as a price-taker, but haven't incurred any of the costs yet. You're planning ahead and trying to figure out the best quantity to plan to produce and sell. (Whether it's sensible to want to go into business in a price-takers' market is another story. We'll have a little to say about it in Chapters 11 and 12.) You want to produce that quantity which maximizes the difference between your total sales revenue and your total costs, a difference that's often called your "profit." (No matter how complicated the concept of profit gets--we'll see a lot more of it in Chapter 11--it never loses its basic nature as "revenue minus cost.")

One way to do it would be simply to list your sales revenue and your total costs at each potential quantity of output, subtract the two to find a relationship between the quantity of output and profit, and pick the quantity at which profit is the biggest. I call that the "brute force" approach, and it always works.

A better technique, however, works even when it's tough to get the data required by the brute-force approach. It relies on marginal revenue (the monetary benefit of expanding production by one unit) and marginal cost (the monetary cost of expanding production by one unit).

Assume that you're already "in the business," having incurred the necessary fixed costs (which are now sunk and therefore not costs at all), but you aren't producing anything yet. Consider the action "expand production and sales by one unit." What are its benefit and cost?

Since you're starting from zero, you have to determine the marginal revenue and the marginal cost of unit number 1. If you find that unit number one brings in more than it costs, then you have to decide whether to stay there or to go on to number two. You'll continue with the process, increasing your planned level of output and sales by one unit, as long as the additional unit's marginal revenue (the benefit of your action) exceeds its marginal cost (the cost of your action). Here's an example.

Quantity	Price	Total Revenue	Marginal Revenue	Total Cost	Marginal Cost	
0*	---	0	---	0	---	*Not in business
0**	---	0	---	$10	---	**In the business
1	$3.50	$3.50	$3.50	10.50	$0.50	
2	3.50	7.00	3.50	11.50	1.00	
3	3.50	10.50	3.50	13.00	1.50	
4	3.50	14.00	3.50	15.00	2.00	
5	3.50	17.50	3.50	17.50	2.50	
6	3.50	21.00	3.50	20.50	3.00	
7	3.50	24.50	3.50	24.00	3.50	
8	3.50	28.00	3.50	28.00	4.00	
9	3.50	31.50	3.50	32.50	4.50	
10	3.50	35.00	3.50	37.50	5.00	

Note that I've made <u>marginal</u> cost increase with each additional unit produced--not just <u>total</u> cost, but the size of the jumps in total cost. This is a realistic assumption, and something like this has to happen for the problem, and the real-world situation it describes, to make any sense. (It doesn't usually increase by the same amount with each unit, like my fifty cents, though.)

The marginal revenue, the amount by which total revenue changes when each additional unit is sold, is always $3.50; that's because of the price-taker assumption. The horizontal demand curve shows up in the fact that any quantity we wish to specify is associated with a price of $3.50. The $10 is some kind of fixed cost, like a license fee.

The brute-force method involves finding profit by subtracting total cost from total revenue, for each quantity. It starts out at a $10 loss (profit is -10) at a quantity of zero, a $7 loss at a quantity of 1, a loss of $4.50 at a quantity of 2, and so forth. The largest profit (a positive $0.50) results when either 6 are produced ($21 - $20.50 = $0.50) or 7 are produced ($24.50 - $24.00 = $0.50). If we think about producing more, we'll find that our profit at 8 has disappeared completely, at nine it's a $1 loss, and if we were to produce and sell 10 we'd do so at a loss of $2.50. Clearly the best quantity to produce and sell is either 6 or 7, and it doesn't matter which.

Let's get marginal...again

If we set aside what seems like the simple, straightforward approach for a minute, we can investigate how economists believe it really ought to be done. We aren't brute-forcers; we're suave, subtle, and sophisticated. (Sure.)

Consider the action "produce and sell one" rather than "be in the business but sell zero." The action you're considering adds $3.50 to your sales revenue (that's its "benefit"), but only fifty cents to your costs (that's its "cost"). You're better off by three bucks if you produce one instead of zero. (You brute-forcers can check: your loss drops from $10 to $7.)

How about "produce two" instead of "produce one"? The benefit of this action is again $3.50 (the marginal revenue of number two), while its cost is only $1.00 (the marginal cost of number two). Looks as if number two makes you $2.50 better off than you would have been if you'd stayed at one. (Sure enough, your loss drops from $7 to $4.50.)

We could keep this example going by examining each individual unit, but this is probably enough to get the point across. You should produce and sell every individual unit whose marginal revenue exceeds its marginal cost. You should produce and sell no units that, individually, cost you more than they bring in: avoid those whose marginal cost exceeds their marginal revenue. (An example: number 8, which reduces your profit by fifty cents, from $0.50 to zero.)

Don't be concerned about the fact that the "marginal profit," or the amount by which marginal revenue exceeds marginal cost, is getting smaller. Each unit for which

MR exceeds MC by even a little adds <u>something</u> positive to your profit. Unit number one added $3.00 while unit number five added only $1.00, but five's contribution was a buck that we wouldn't otherwise have had.

What about number seven? Our brute-force approach concluded that either six or seven was an equally good number to produce; do we reach a similar conclusion using our marginal approach? Well, number six adds 50 cents to our profit (its MR is $3.50 while its MC is only $3.00), so we should definitely expand from producing only five to producing six. Should we go on, to number seven? Its MR is $3.50 but its MC is, too. Although it doesn't <u>help</u> us (that is, it doesn't increase our profit), it doesn't <u>hurt</u> us (reduce our profit) either. Since number seven is a matter of indifference, so is the problem of whether to produce six or to produce seven. Flip a coin. Figure 6.3 illustrates what's going on, and has a simplified general version beside it.

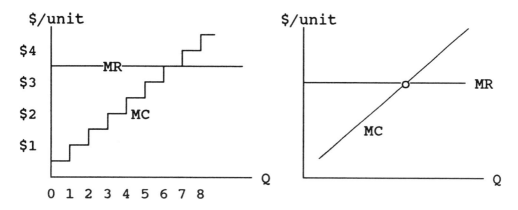

Figure 6.3: The price taker finds his quantity

So here's our rule: Produce and sell each unit for which marginal revenue exceeds marginal cost. Produce no unit for which marginal cost exceeds marginal revenue. If there's a unit for which they're equal, toss a coin--who cares?

There is a simpler version of the rule, though.

> Produce that quantity for which
> marginal revenue equals marginal cost.

If you realize that MC usually starts out below MR and goes up, while MR usually starts out above MC and comes down (though it stays constant for price takers like our example here), or at least take a glance at the "simplified general version" graph above, you can understand why this "MR=MC" rule works. It will automatically direct you to produce every individual unit for which MR exceeds MC (units one through six here), and none of those for which MC exceeds MR. Now it <u>does</u> direct you to produce the one that's right on the border, like number seven, when in fact it's a matter of indifference, but that can't do any harm. And "MR equals MC" is easier to remember than the more extended version.[2] Besides, it confirms--once again!--my "Law of Economic Graphs."

And what about those "fixed costs"?

If you're going to produce anything at all, you should make sure that you produce each unit that adds more to your sales revenue than it adds to your costs. That means you should produce any unit whose MR exceeds its MC, and no unit with an MC greater than its MR. A quick and easy rule for achieving this is to produce that quantity for which MR equals MC.

Very interesting. But this addresses only the problem of selecting the best quantity to produce if your "fixed costs" are not relevant (because you've already incurred them). To show how irrelevant they are, consider what happens in our previous problem if those fixed costs had been not $10, but $15.

Every "total cost" number would be $5 greater, but the "marginal cost" numbers wouldn't change a bit. (Remember why?) Since "marginal revenue" is derived strictly from the demand curve, it doesn't change either. With changes in neither MR nor MC, we should still find that either six or seven should be produced. Our best profit will no longer be a positive $0.50, though, but a negative $4.50.

Our lessons about the true nature of cost should help to clarify this result. Sure, even with the cleverest "MR=MC" reasoning the overall endeavor makes you $4.50 poorer than you were before you went into the business, and in retrospect that was a bad decision. But you have already spent the $15 to go into the business, and if you don't produce at all, you'll be poorer at the end by the whole $15--as a quick thought about your "profit" at a quantity of zero will show. In fact, producing any quantity other than six or seven will result in an overall loss that's greater than $4.50.

Unit number one brings in $3.50 and costs $0.50, so it adds $3.00 to your profit. Unit number two adds $2.50, unit number three adds $2.00, four adds $1.50, five adds $1.00, six adds $0.50, and seven adds zero. If we add up these contributions to profit, we get $10.50. That's the profit contributed by the first seven units. Not coincidentally, the difference between $10.50 and $15 is $4.50. Businesspeople often talk about "covering their overhead" or fixed costs, and in this problem producing six or seven units manages to get $10.50 of it "covered." (In fact, you can think of the amount by which any individual unit's MR exceeds its MC as that unit's contribution

---

[2] In my examples, MC always starts low (below MR). Many realistic situations aren't like that. It often starts out high, falls, and rises again. Suppose the MCs of, say, units 1 through 7 exceed their MRs, while for units 8 through 56 MR exceeds MC. You'd produce only the 8th through 56th if you could, but you can't, so you have to see if the positive contribution of numbers 8 through 56 more than offsets the negative contribution of numbers 1 through 7 (as well as your fixed costs, if any are involved). A comparison of total revenue and total cost, at a quantity of 56, will do this for you.

to fixed costs.) When your fixed costs were only $10, you were able to more than "cover" them and your operation was slightly profitable. With fixed costs of $15, even the best choice of quantity doesn't come close. But any choice other than six or seven would be even worse.

Before you've committed yourself by incurring those fixed costs, they are genuine non-sunk costs and are significant to your decision. Your proper approach is to imagine yourself in the business, use the MR=MC rule to determine the best quantity to produce (if you were in the business), and see if your profit at this quantity (which is the best that it can be) is positive. If it is, then you can more than cover your fixed costs and they're worth incurring. If it isn't, you shouldn't go into this business at all because even the very cleverest operation of it will still be a loser.

Your decision before you've gone into the business is a little more complicated than the one you face if you already have (and can't get out), because there's an extra cost to consider. The cost of "producing seven, having incurred my fixed costs already" rather than "producing zero, having incurred my fixed costs already" properly ignores those fixed costs--just as we ignored the brown eyes or the Lincoln High School. But the cost of "producing seven, and (necessarily) incurring fixed costs" rather than "producing zero, and not incurring fixed costs" clearly has to include them: Here, the fixed costs are genuine costs because you can avoid them by selecting the alternative.

So you (the producer) should determine the quantity at which MR = MC. That's the best quantity to produce if you've already sunk your fixed costs (you've irretrievably incurred them already). If you haven't yet, then you still have the option of hanging onto your money. Check to see if the cleverest selection of a level of output (MR=MC) will produce positive profit, and go ahead only if it does. You still have this choice; the guy who's already sunk his fixed costs doesn't.

GETTING REAL WITH THE PRICE SEARCHER

When a seller realizes that the demand for his product slopes downward, he has something besides quantity to consider. None of the principles that we've discovered in our analysis of cost and the price taker is changed, but the evaluation of marginal revenue is a little more complicated. Because modest changes in price do not cause his sales to fly immediately to zero or infinity, the price that he should charge is not so obvious, and he has to figure it out. He's called a price searcher, searching for the best price to charge (and, simultaneously, quantity to sell).

The price searcher

Let's begin our discussion of the price searcher with an example. Suppose that when you charge $10 per widget you normally sell 100 of them each week. If you wanted to sell 101 instead, you believe you'd have to reduce your asking price to $9.99. (There's one individual lurking about who would be willing to pay $9.99, but isn't willing to pay $10.) Now $9.99 isn't very different from $10, but when you're selling roughly a hundred of the things a one-cent change can make a difference.

You were originally taking in sales revenue of $1,000 (that's $10 x 100), and with the new price and additional unit sold your revenue will be... let's see, what's $9.99 times 101?... that's $1,008.99. The sale of unit number 101 resulted in an increase of $8.99 in your sales revenue. The marginal revenue of unit 101, therefore, is $8.99.

If you decide to do a little detective work and keep an eye on your cashier, you'll find that someone actually pays $9.99 for unit number 101. (There he goes now.) Since you didn't even sell it at all, before, it might seem as if this new unit of sales obviously adds $9.99, its full sales price, to your sales revenue. So how can its marginal revenue be only $8.99? Did we make a $1.00 error somewhere?

You do, indeed, take in $9.99 from the new customer, and if you want to identify this as the additional sales revenue of the new unit "itself," I guess that's OK. But remember that you have 100 other customers. You used to sell widgets to each of them for $10, and now you're selling each of those 100 widgets for only $9.99. That's where the buck comes from: you do indeed take in $9.99 on unit number 101 itself, but to sell it you had to reduce the price by one penny to each of your other 100 customers so your revenue from them falls by $1.00. The result: unit number 101 adds only $8.99, not its price of $9.99, to your sales revenue.

You had no such problem when you were a price taker. (You would also not have this problem if you could reduce the price only to the 101st customer. That's price discrimination, which we'll get to soon. We'd better first learn how to handle the case of a non-discriminating price searcher, who charges the same price to every customer.) When the demand for your product was a horizontal line, you could sell unit 101 for the same $10 price at which you sold the first 100. Unit number 101 brings in $10 itself, but the first 100 continue to bring in the same $10 each, too. There's no reduction in price and therefore no loss of revenue from previous customers.

A little algebra might clarify what's going on. As I mentioned earlier, it's a bit more complicated than the price-taker's algebra (where we found that MR = P), but it's not too bad.

The seller's "old" sales revenue is:

$$\text{Old revenue} = P_o \times Q_o,$$

and his "new" sales revenue, after he lowers his price to P_n, is:

$$\text{New revenue} = P_n \times Q_n,$$

so the change in his sales revenue is:

$$\text{Change in revenue} = (P_n \times Q_n) - (P_o \times Q_o).$$

If we now insist that the quantity sold increases by only one unit (the economist's conventional meaning of "marginal revenue"), then Q_n is just $(Q_o + 1)$, and we can rewrite the change as:

$$\text{MR of unit n} = [P_n \times (Q_o+1)] - [P_o \times Q_o].$$

Grouping together the terms that contain Q_o, we find that:

$$MR_n = P_n + [(P_n - P_o) \times Q_o].$$

If we note that the size of the price cut that we had to make, to sell this extra one unit, is $(P_o - P_n)$ (remember that the new price is lower than the old one), we can change our formula a little so that it shows the price cut:

$$\boxed{MR_n = P_n - [Q_o \times (P_o - P_n)].}$$

There. The marginal revenue of unit number n is the price at which it can be sold, minus the loss of revenue from our Q_o old customers that results from the price cut. (Note that Q_o is the same as n-1.) The price taker could stop with $MR_n = P_n$, because the new and old price were the same. When that's true, the second term in our new, more complicated, formula simply disappears. The size of the required price cut is zero.

We can check this formula by applying it to the problem we've already discussed. We're evaluating the MR of unit number 101. It should equal $9.99 (the price P_n at which it can be sold--the "new price") minus the revenue lost from our old customers because of the price cut. That's 100 customers (Q_o) at one penny ($10-$9.99, which is P_o-P_n) each, or $1.00. By cutting the price by one penny, we take in $9.99 from the one new customer but lose a penny from each of our other 100 customers (who used to buy 100 at $10 each but are now getting 100 for $9.99 each). Net result? Our sales revenue increases, but by only $8.99.

If you aren't wild about the algebra, Figure 6.4 provides a picture of what's going on.

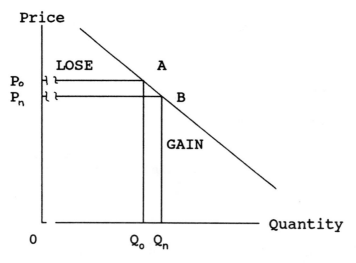

Figure 6.4: The searcher gains some, and loses some

At our original point on the demand curve (A), our total sales revenue was $P_o \times Q_o$, which is the area of the rectangle OP_oAQ_o. When we move to the new point on the demand curve (B), selected so that our quantity increases by exactly one unit, our sales revenue becomes $P_n \times Q_n$, indicated visually by the rectangle OP_nBQ_n.

Consider the differences between these two "total revenue" rectangles. When we move from the old one to the new one, we <u>gain</u> the tall, skinny rectangle on the right and <u>lose</u> the short, flat one on the top. The height of the rectangle that we gain is the new price P_n, the price at which we sell the new unit; the width of this rectangle is--by the way we defined the problem--one unit. Its area, the revenue of the "gain" strip, is therefore just the new price. The height of the short flat rectangle that we lose is the size of the price cut that we had to make (P_o-P_n), and its width is the quantity that we used to sell (Q_o). With its height the price cut offered to each of our old customers, and its width the number of them, its area is the revenue that the price reduction causes us to lose from our previous customers. When we add the area of our tall, skinny "gain" rectangle and subtract the area of our short, flat "lose" rectangle, we get our formula again.

For the price-searching seller, the marginal revenue of a particular unit (other than the first, where they're equal) is always less than the price at which it can be sold. For that lower price must be offered to all customers, not just the new one, so the sales revenue taken in from customers who had been paying the higher price declines. The total effect of the new unit on the seller's revenue must include both of these considerations.

For this seller, the choice is not the price taker's "sell number 101 for $10, and the first 100 at $10 each" or "sell the first 100 at $10 each," where the monetary benefit of selling number 101 is therefore simply $10. For the seller facing a downward-sloping demand curve, the alternatives are either "selling number 101 for $9.99, and the first 100 at $9.99 each" or "selling the first 100 at $10 each." When we compare these two alternatives, the "number 101 at $9.99" is something that's available in one of them that isn't in the other. But we can't simply cancel out the two "selling the first 100"'s, because they're at different prices. We could play around with the way we describe these alternatives, as we did to illustrate sunk costs, and get this problem into the format of our "brown eyes" or "high school" discussion by obtaining common elements that we <u>can</u> cancel out. I guess I'll let you try it if you wish.

As always, it is differences (and only differences) that matter. But the difference between "101 at $9.99" and "100 at $10" is not just the extra one unit at $9.99. It's also the difference between "100 at $9.99" and "100 at $10".

A numerical example

With that basic example as an introduction, we're prepared to handle a somewhat more involved numerical example that illustrates a few things about the price searcher's marginal revenue and how our rule for properly selecting the best quantity (and, now, price) applies to him. I'm going to assume that marginal cost is constant, at $3 per unit, so that we can focus on marginal revenue. (No principle is different with the more-realistic increasing marginal costs, but one thing at a time, please.)

The first two columns identify the demand for our product. We determine marginal revenue by finding the change in total revenue. The move from a quantity of 2 to a quantity of 3, for example, raised total revenue from $16 to $21 so the marginal revenue of the third unit is $5. If we wish to sell nine rather than eight we must cut the price from $2 to $1. That'll cut our sales revenue from $16 to $9, so the marginal revenue of unit number nine is a negative $7.

Price	Quantity	Total Revenue	Marginal Revenue	Total Cost	Marginal Cost
$10	0	0	---	$ 8	---
9	1	9	9	11	$3
8	2	16	7	14	3
7	3	21	5	17	3
6	4	24	3	20	3
5	5	25	1	23	3
4	6	24	-1	26	3
3	7	21	-3	29	3
2	8	16	-5	32	3
1	9	9	-7	35	3
0	10	0	-9	38	3

To determine the best quantity to sell, we can either brute-force it by subtracting total costs from total revenues and finding out where the difference is the largest, or we can use the preferable "marginal" technique.

MR equals MC (both are $3) for unit number 4, so our simple rule tells the price searcher to produce and sell 4. A quick check of the demand curve shows that to sell 4 he should set a price of $6, and his search is over. Price at $6, and sell four.

For those of you who don't fully trust this rule yet, let's first do a brute-force check. Profit at $6 and 4 will be $24-$20 or $4. Profit at 3 ($7 each) is also $4, which we should have expected since unit number 4's MR and its MC are exactly equal (it adds $3 to revenue and $3 to cost, leaving profit unchanged). But profit at a quantity of 5 falls to $2 ($25-$23), as it does at a quantity of 2 ($16-$14). Any other quantity produces an even lower profit.

Now let's examine marginal profits. Unit number one adds $9 to our revenue and $3 to our cost, so it's a winner by $6. Number two contributes another $4 to our profit (that is, its $7 MR minus its $3 MC). We should go on to number 3, because its MR ($5) is still greater (by two bucks) than its MC. Number 4 is a wash, adding $3 to our sales revenue and $3 to our costs, so we can either produce it or not as whim strikes us. As for number five, it adds only $1 to our revenue but $3 to our costs, so it would reduce our profit by $2. Better stay away.

Since our best profit (MR=MC, setting a price of $6 and selling 4) is positive, we should go ahead even if we're not already in the business. Go ahead, sink those fixed costs, spend that eight bucks; you won't regret it. On the other hand, if the fixed costs had been $15 your best profit (still at $6 and 4, because fixed costs affect neither marginal revenue nor marginal cost) is now negative (a negative $3). If you haven't invested yet, you shouldn't. If you have, using the MR=MC rule to produce 4 and sell them for $6 each still makes you $12 better off than you would have been: a $3 loss is $12 better than a $15 loss.

Please note than none of the principles has changed. In the welter of new things to learn about the price searcher's marginal revenue, it's easy to lose sight of that. Same old stuff. Whether a seller is a price searcher or a price taker, he should produce each unit whose MR exceeds its MC, and none of the units for which MC exceeds MR. The easy way to achieve this is simply to produce that quantity for which MR=MC. Once this quantity is determined, the seller consults his demand curve to find out what price to charge. (For the price taker the answer's a little more obvious than it is for the searcher, and determining MR is quite a bit easier, but these are the only real differences.) If the seller's fixed costs are already sunk, that's all there is to it. If they aren't, he'll have to check to see if he can cover them at this "best" quantity and price by determining whether his profit will be positive. If it won't, he'd better sink his money into something else.

A rather peculiar looking graph, Figure 6.5, depicts our problem. Compare it with the data shown in the above table. The demand and marginal revenue curves coincide at $9 and 1 unit, but after that they diverge, with MR falling by $2 for every $1 reduction in price (and 1-unit increase in quantity demanded, on this demand curve). Whenever the graph's marginal revenue curve lies above its marginal cost curve (the horizontal line at $3), that unit should be produced. When MC lies <u>below</u> MR, those units should not be produced. As for the exact crossing point...who cares? Produce it if you like the simplicity of "MR=MC."

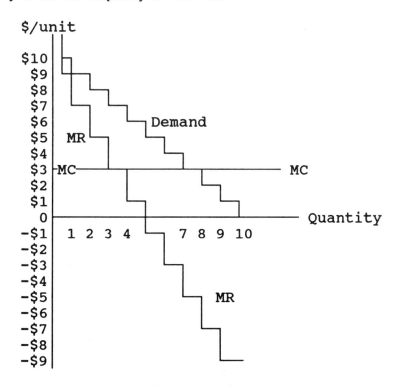

Figure 6.5: Illustrating a price-searcher example

The basic idea, depicted without all of the detail and precision of Figure 6.5, is illustrated in Figure 6.6.

It's no accident that the MR line in Figure 6.6 intersects the Quantity axis exactly half way out, at 1/2 of the quantity at which the demand curve intersects the axis (the numbers 100 and 50 were chosen to dramatize that; 168 and 84 would have worked just as well). They start at the same point on the Price axis, but as we increase the quantity that we sell, the marginal revenue curve falls twice as fast. (In our numerical problem above, the demand curve was constructed so that for each additional unit sold the price fell by $1. Because of that, with each new unit the marginal revenue fell by $2. Look back at those numbers.) That's why it reaches the Quantity axis twice as quickly.

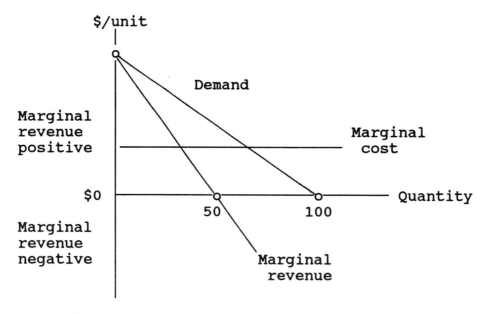

Figure 6.6: The basic price-searcher's problem

This is a mathematical property of the relationship between the demand curve and its associated marginal revenue curve. There's a neat proof, using calculus, that if demand is a straight line with negative slope, so is marginal revenue, with the same vertical-axis intercept but a negative slope that's twice as great. If you take a Calculus course you will almost certainly see it, used there as an example.[3]

---

[3] For calculus students only: Revenue is P x Q. If we write the linear demand curve as $P=a-bQ$, then $R=aQ-bQ^2$. Since $MR = (dR/dQ)$, it is: $MR=a-2bQ$. This curve is linear with the same vertical-axis intercept (a) as the demand curve, but a slope (-2b) that is twice as steep.

We don't have to get into that here, but it's very helpful to remember this method for drawing a marginal revenue curve. It starts from the same point on the Price axis as does the demand curve, but it crosses the Quantity axis at exactly <u>half</u> of the quantity at which the demand curve reaches the Quantity axis. Unlike the demand curve, though, MR goes right on through the axis into negative numbers. Again, our numerical example provides an illustration.

ELASTICITY, DISCRIMINATION, AND THE "WELFARE LOSS"

The "marginal revenue" of unit X is the change in your total sales revenue when you move from selling a quantity (X-1) to selling a quantity X. If a unit's marginal revenue is positive--like units one through five in our numerical example-- then selling that unit increases your total sales revenue. (A positive change in something means it's getting bigger.) Furthermore, to sell that extra unit (the X'th unit) a price searcher has to reduce the price he charges. In this case, then, a price cut produces an increase in total sales revenue. Remember the logic: If the marginal revenue of an extra unit is positive, total sales revenue increases. But the sale of that extra unit requires a price cut, so a price cut produces an increase in total sales revenue whenever marginal revenue is positive.

On the other hand, if we get down into units numbered six through ten in our numerical example, we find that the price cuts that were required to sell the larger quantities actually resulted in reductions of our sales revenue. To note that the total goes down is the same as saying that the <u>change</u> is negative, so for those units for which marginal revenue is negative, a price cut produces a decrease in total sales revenue.

Marginal revenue and elasticity of demand

Some time ago (Chapter 2), we examined the concept of elasticity of demand. Because marginal revenue describes the change in total revenue when "quantity" increases by "one," and elasticity has something to do with the relationship between the size of the increase in quantity and the size of the required price change, marginal revenue and elasticity are related in a rather interesting way.

Our current discussion of marginal revenue requires us to sell one additional unit, so we're primarily concerned with price reductions. How much of a <u>percentage</u> quantity increase <u>is</u> "one unit," anyway? And how large a <u>percentage</u> price cut is required to achieve it? If we're on the elastic portion of the demand curve, the percentage price cut required to sell one more unit will be smaller than the percentage increase in quantity demanded of which the "one unit" consists. If we're on the inelastic portion of the demand curve, selling one more unit will require a percentage price cut that's larger than the percentage change in quantity demanded attributable to the one extra unit.

Consider, as an example, the demand curve depicted in Figure 6.7. Each additional unit, whether we're referring to number 1 or number 986, requires a one-cent cut in price if it's to be sold. (Note that $10 is 1,000 cents so the slope of the demand curve is -$0.01 per unit.)

Near the upper end of the curve, say unit number 50 and a price of $9.50, a 1-unit increase is about 2% and a 1-cent cut is just a little larger than a tenth of a percent (0.001). Demand up there is very elastic, since -(2/-.1) is 20. A tenth-of-a-percent price cut produces a 2% increase in quantity demanded. (That's our one unit.)

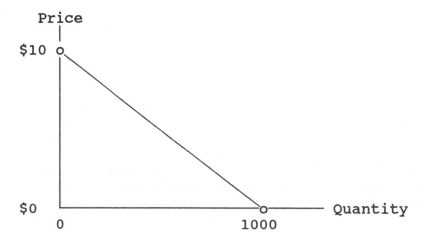

Figure 6.7: A simple linear demand curve

At the other end of the curve, say unit number 950 at a price of $0.50, things are reversed: The one-cent price cut is about 2% and it produces only about a tenth-of-a-percent increase (one in 950) in quantity demanded. Demand is extremely inelastic, equal to about -(0.1/-2) = 0.05. A 2% price cut produces only a tenth of a percent increase in quantity demanded (that's our one unit).

In the middle of the curve, a one-cent cut in a 500-cent price and a one-unit increase in a 500-unit quantity demanded produce the elasticity of "1" that defines "unit elastic."

When we reduce our price and demand is elastic, the "quantity demanded" increases by a larger percentage than our "price" decreased, so Price x Quantity, or total revenue, rises. But those are the prices and quantities on the upper half of the linear demand curve, and a rise in total revenue means that marginal revenue is positive. It follows that the marginal revenue of each of the units that lie on the elastic portion (the upper half) of the demand curve is <u>positive</u>.

When we reduce our price and demand is inelastic, our "quantity demanded" increases, but by a percentage that's smaller than the percentage price cut, so Price x Quantity, or total revenue, falls. Those prices and quantities are on the lower half of the linear demand curve, and a fall in total revenue means that marginal revenue is negative. The marginal revenue of the units that lie on the inelastic portion (the lower half) of the demand curve is <u>negative</u>.

These discoveries correspond to the results of our previous numerical example, and permit us to add some more information to our preceding graph. With all of our notes, it becomes Figure 6.8.

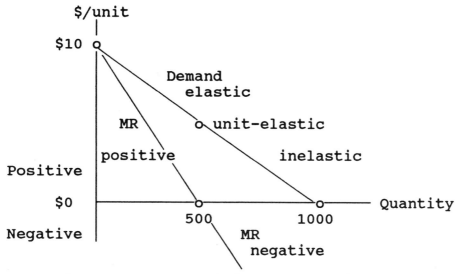

Figure 6.8: Elasticity and marginal revenue

If we imagine starting at a price of $10, each additional unit sold (requiring a one-cent price cut) would <u>add</u> to our total sales revenue until we reached a price of $5 and a quantity of 500. Further one-cent price cuts, each producing a one-unit increase in the quantity that we sell, would actually <u>reduce</u> our total revenue.

Figure 6.8 shows that the point at which MR intersects the Quantity axis (the quantity at which MR is zero) is directly under the middle of the demand curve. (People who like trigonometry--I hear that there are some--can prove that, if they wish.) We already noted that a straight-line demand curve is unit-elastic right in the middle, which makes sense: unit-elastic means no change in total revenue, which means that MR is zero.

The easiest way to think about the relationship between elasticity and marginal revenue is to remember that when we're trying to figure out marginal revenue, we only want to sell <u>one more unit</u>. If customers are very sensitive to price (demand is elastic), it won't take a very big price cut to sell that extra one. If they aren't sensitive (demand is inelastic), then the necessary price cut will be bigger.

"Say, boss, our marginal revenue is negative..."

Your first job, as a graduating economics major, turns out to be determining the demand for the only product produced by the small company that's hired you. We won't inquire too closely how you've come up with your conclusions. That falls into the category of sausage and legislation, for which it's joked that people are better off not knowing too much about how they're made. But you're absolutely certain that the demand for your company's product looks like Figure 6.9.

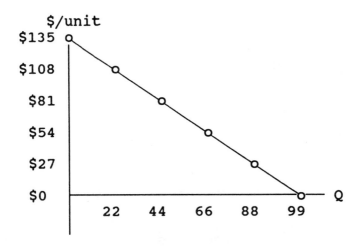

Figure 6.9: The demand for your company's product

You learn that the company is currently charging $27 and selling 88 per week, which is well out into the inelastic portion of the demand curve (and therefore way down on the negative portion of the corresponding marginal revenue curve).

Rather than rush to your new boss with this distressing information, perhaps you should think first about what it means. The company is selling some units that actually reduce its total sales receipts. The "benefit" (marginal revenue) of these units is negative, and we haven't even considered their costs yet! Cutting back on the quantity sold, by raising the price a bit, would actually <u>increase</u> sales revenue (by eliminating those units that subtract from it). Even if the reduction in quantity resulted in no cost savings at all (that is, even if the marginal cost of the offending units were zero), it would be a good idea to cut back.

In practice, of course, marginal costs are not zero. Any units for which marginal revenue is actually less than zero, therefore, are bound to have marginal revenue that's far less than marginal cost. Since we shouldn't produce any units for which MR is less than MC, we certainly shouldn't produce any for which MR is less than zero.

> A seller should never operate in the
> INELASTIC region of his demand curve.

If he ever discovers himself there, which can happen because demand curves shift around and price changes aren't always as rapid, he should immediately increase his price and reduce the quantity that he sells. Until he does, he's engaging in a charitable operation, underwriting out of his own pocket units that are bringing in less revenue from customers than they're costing him.

If you're right about what your company is doing, and can convince your boss of it, you may be in for a promotion soon. But don't forget that determining a demand schedule is risky business, and whether your marketing advice--raise the price--is a good idea hinges not only on the logic of marginal revenue and marginal cost, but also on whether you've guessed right about the shape of the demand curve. At least you can have confidence in the logic.

Any producer with positive marginal cost should also produce a quantity for which marginal revenue is positive (that follows from the MR=MC rule), and should therefore operate somewhere in the elastic range of his demand curve. Exactly where, though, depends on marginal cost. Imagine two businesses, in different industries, but with identical demand curves. Because of the nature of production in his industry, the first producer may have very high "fixed costs" and low variable and marginal costs. When he equates MR to MC, marginal revenue will, of course, be low also, so his price and quantity will place him on his demand curve only a little above the unit-elastic midpoint. With a different kind of product and production technique, the second business may have low "fixed" but high variable and marginal costs. He will, therefore, produce where MR is also high, and that's well up on the demand curve where demand is considerably more elastic. Figure 6.10 provides an illustration.

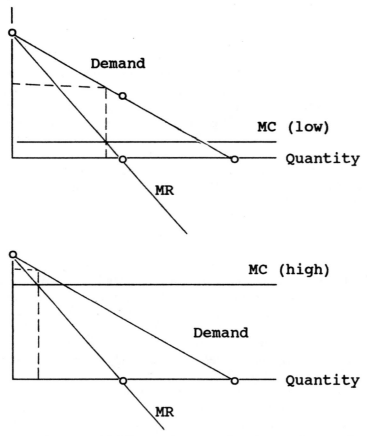

Figure 6.10: Different marginal costs and elasticity

In the rather interesting case in which marginal costs are zero (perhaps you charge people to look at a waterfall visible only from your property), the best quantity to produce is that for which marginal revenue is also zero. At that quantity, demand is unit-elastic and total sales revenue is maximized. Since our costs are zero here, maximizing our total revenue also maximizes our profit. It doesn't usually make sense for a seller to maximize his total sales revenue, but it does if his costs are zero.

And for the discriminating businessperson...

You're a price-searching wodget-seller, and from your perspective there are a couple of things wrong with this approach. If you can figure out how to fix them, you will.

Figure 6.11 provides a diagram of your situation. Setting MR=MC, you find that you should produce 20 and charge a price for each of $15. Your MR and MC of number 20 are each $5.

But look at Sally, whose demand price is $24 (she's way up near the top end of the curve, and is actually the buyer with the second-highest demand price). She's able to buy a wodget from you at the same $15 price as is everyone else, but her demand price--the maximum she would have been willing to pay rather than go without it--is $24. The difference between these two numbers is her <u>consumer's surplus</u>.

> An individual's CONSUMER'S SURPLUS is the amount of money by which his demand price exceeds the price that he actually pays.

Sally's consumer's surplus here is $9. She would be willing to pay you $24, she actually does pay you $15, and she enjoys the $9 surplus. Most of us are probably in Sally's position for most of the goods we buy. The price we actually pay is usually less than the maximum that we would have paid, rather than go without. That's just another way of saying that most buyers are <u>not</u> the marginal buyer.

It would really be nice if you could figure out a way to get Sally to pay that additional $9, or at least some of it. But raising the price that you charge to everyone is self-defeating; you would sell fewer units, and some of the ones you'd no longer sell have MR exceeding MC. So that's a bad idea. If only you could figure out how to charge Sally, oh, say, $23.95 (you don't want to be too greedy) while still selling to everyone else at $15, you would take in an extra $8.95 of revenue without affecting your costs at all.

Besides, look at Frank out there (the 25th most willing wodget buyer), and those other potential customers between numbers 21 and 30. Frank is willing to pay $12.50 for a wodget that would cost you only $7.50 to produce. He's on a part of the demand curve that lies <u>above</u> the marginal cost curve. Unfortunately, Frank's spot on the marginal revenue curve (zero) lies <u>below</u> the marginal cost curve. That illustrates that if you were to reduce to $12.50 the price charged to all of your customers, the increase in your sales revenue would be less than the increase in your costs. Frank himself is willing to pay, for his wodget, more than its cost of production.

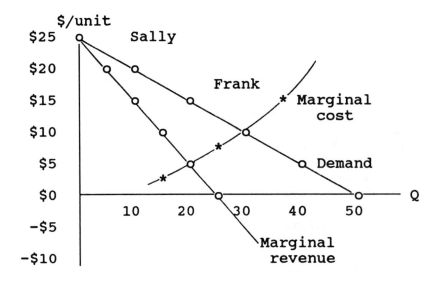

Figure 6.11: Why sellers would like to discriminate

The problem is that pesky need to reduce the price to everyone, even if they're willing (like Sally) to pay much more. That's what drives the marginal revenue down below marginal cost and makes the production of those units (numbers 21 through 30) undesirable, even though each of these wodgets could be sold at a price above its marginal cost.

"Could be sold, could be sold." How? That's the question. The ideal answer, from your viewpoint as a seller, is to figure out a scheme to charge each individual customer a different price. That way, you could raise the price to Sally, lower the price to Frank, and apply the same technique (though with different numbers) to each other individual customer. If you could pull this off, you might as well charge each customer the very maximum he would be willing to pay: his demand price. You'd charge Sally $24, Frank $12.50, and each other individual a price determined by his location on the demand curve.

This is perfect price discrimination:

> PERFECT PRICE DISCRIMINATION is the
> selling of each unit precisely for
> its demand price.

A little "social-science fiction" can demonstrate this idea.[4]

You've set up your wodget retail outlet, and every time a potential customer comes through the door something magical happens: a neon sign appears, hanging around his neck on a nylon cord. (He doesn't notice it, so I guess it must be weightless and invisible to him.) This sign is connected by small, discreet, wires to tiny sensors in the customer's brain. It immediately flashes the individual's exact demand price, the maximum price he would be willing to pay rather than go without the wodget.

As Sally approaches your counter with a wodget in her hand, she asks, "How much is this? It doesn't seem to be marked." Squinting slightly to read her flashing neon sign, you answer "That'll be twenty-four dollars, please." "$24! That's awfully expensive. I don't think...oh, all right." Then Frank strolls up. "That will be twelve fifty, sir." "No way," he bluffs. "I'll go $8 and not a penny more." You glance again at his sign, hold firm at $12.50, and he relents. And so it goes, for each customer a different price that's exactly the maximum he'd pay and still buy.

You've just pulled off "perfect price discrimination." The concept is an interesting economic curiosity for several reasons.

First, there's no more consumer's surplus. You have figured out a way to get it all for yourself. That doesn't mean you're doing anything wrong, immoral, or even illegal, because the exchange with each customer is still voluntary, but your scheme has made many of your customers (like Sally) worse off than they were with no discrimination, and you better off.

Second, the old "marginal revenue" curve is no longer relevant. You're still a price searcher, so you do indeed have to cut the price to sell an additional unit, but you charge the lower price only on that unit. You keep charging the "old" prices on the "old" units--a different price for each of them. The action necessary to sell wodget number 18 is "offer a lower price to customer number 18." Since the revenue obtained from the first 17 customers is absolutely unaffected, the marginal revenue of number 18 is identical to the price at which it is sold. But that's exactly its demand price. The marginal revenue curve for a perfectly discriminating price searcher is identical to the demand curve. They both slope down, and they lie right on top of each other.

A third interesting conclusion follows from the second. Like every seller, the perfectly discriminating price searcher produces each wodget for which MR exceeds MC, and none of those for which MC exceeds MR. Again, he follows the simple rule of producing that quantity for which MR=MC. But in a sense he's in the same position as the price taker: his MR curve is identical to his demand curve. (Of course the price taker's is flat, while the price searcher's slopes downward, but P=MR for each of them.) So when the perfectly discriminating price searcher produces and sells a quantity for which MR=MC, he automatically produces and sells that quantity at which price equals marginal cost. He produces and sells every wodget for which price exceeds marginal cost.

---

[4] Actually, a lot of science fiction--Heinlein is a good example--deals more with future relationships among humans than with rockets and asteroids.

Note the contrast with the price searcher who doesn't discriminate. Everyone produces and sells those units for which MR exceeds MC, but for the non-discriminating price searcher MR is less than price. That's why there are units (like numbers 21 through 30) for which MR is less than MC, but price is greater than MC. He won't produce and sell them.[5] The perfectly discriminating price searcher will, because for him the very idea that MC can lie somewhere in between MR and P makes no sense. MR and P are identical. You can see them in Figure 6.12.

As far as perfect price discrimination is concerned, most economists like the fact that every unit is produced that some individual values (as indicated by his demand price) more than its cost of production (as indicated by its marginal cost). They identify that property (specifically, P=MC) with an <u>efficient</u> economic system. But they don't care much for the fact that it's the producer, and not the consumers, who gets all of the surplus.

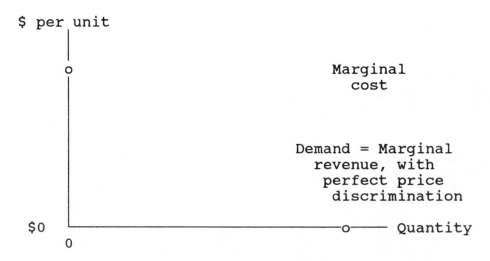

Figure 6.12: Perfect price discrimination

What economists think of this model isn't too relevant, anyway. There really are no neon signs. To make matters even tougher, individuals have incentive to conceal how high their demand prices really are. Because sellers can't even come close to obtaining the information they need to discriminate perfectly, and they certainly would if they could, the model has no practical significance.

---

[5] The existence of units which aren't produced even though price exceeds marginal cost, leads some economists to maintain that there's something <u>wrong</u>. This argument, that non-discriminating price-searching produces a "welfare loss," will be addressed in Chapter 7.

*Less-than-perfect price
discrimination: a common strategy*

The purpose of price discrimination is to charge a higher price to those who are willing to pay more, and offer a lower price only to those who aren't. Even if a seller can't do it "perfectly," he may be able to apply the principle.

The seller can't read his customers' minds, and they don't really have neon signs. But he can pretty much tell a middle-aged adult from a child, a teenager, or an elderly person. Perhaps he suspects that middle-aged adults have, in general, higher demand prices than these other groups of customer. A common type of price discrimination involves making use of this speculative "information" to try to extract more profit from those who aren't very sensitive to price, and also more from those who are. Cute trick--getting more profit from each of these subgroups of our customers.

First, imagine the price and quantity decision of a price searcher who doesn't discriminate at all. Figure 6.13 provides the illustration. He treats all of his customers as homogeneous, determines the quantity (Q_o, which is 160 in this example) at which MR and MC ($2) are equal, finds the corresponding price (P_o, which is $6 here) and charges it to everyone. His all-customers-together demand curve will have a specific elasticity (call it E_o), greater than one, at this price.

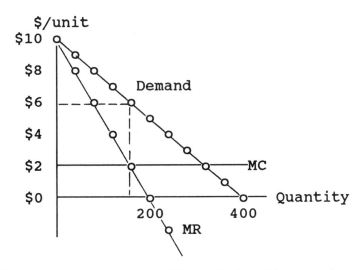

Figure 6.13: A non-discriminating price searcher

Now suppose that he can identify a subgroup (like adults at a movie theater) whose demand is likely to be less elastic than average (that is, it's less than E_o at the price P_o determined as above), as illustrated in Figure 6.14. His marginal costs may be the same for this less-elastic subgroup as for other customers, but their marginal revenue curve will be different. If we analyze this group of customers separately, we find that setting MR=MC produces a price ($8) that's above P_o ($6). The non-discriminatory price P_o, in other words, is too low and results in too many units sold to this particular subgroup. At P_o we're selling units (numbers 61 through 80) for which the MR from this subgroup is well below MC. Some of them (numbers 71-80), in fact, actually have negative marginal revenue. We are selling 20 tickets too many to this group, and should raise the price to them from $6 to $8.

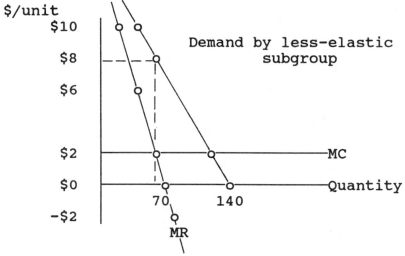

Figure 6.14: Too much, too cheap?

On the other hand, there must be another subgroup with a demand that's more elastic than average (greater than E_o at a price of P_o)--like children at the movie theater. Their situation is shown in Figure 6.15. Again this subgroup shares MC in common with the less-elastic folks, but the MR curve associated with their more-elastic demand curve will be different. If we set MR=MC for this subgroup, we'll find a price ($5) that's below P_o ($6). The non-discriminatory price P_o now is too high, resulting in too few sales to this subgroup. We should be selling them 98 at $5 each, but without discrimination we're selling them only 65 at $6 each. We're missing out on the sale of some units (numbers 66-98) for which MR exceeds MC.

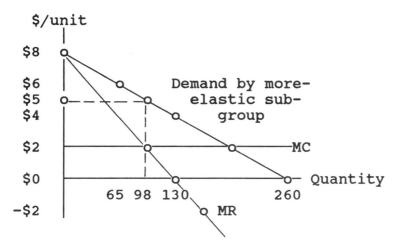

Figure 6.15: Too little, too expensive?

Compared to the price (P_o, $6 in our example) that would maximize our profit if we had (or could make use of) no information about different elasticities of identifiable subgroups of our customers, we should raise the price to the less-elastic subgroup and lower the price to the more-elastic subgroup. After all, the less-elastic group is less sensitive than average about price, and the more-elastic group is more sensitive than average. If we raise the price to those who don't care much about it, and lower the price to those who do, the profit that we obtain from each subgroup rises-- in one case because we quit producing some units for which MC exceeds MR, and in the other because we add some units (not previously sold) for which MR exceeds MC.

The information requirements here are much less severe than the unrealistic "perfect price discrimination." But there is one important condition: we must have some way to prevent the group to whom we offer the lower prices from <u>reselling</u> to the others. Imagine an entrepreneurial child buying an entire roll of movie tickets (at the child's price), then setting up shop in the adjacent alley, offering them to adults at a price somewhere between the theater's "child" and "adult" prices.

This less-than-perfect price discrimination is found at many places besides the movie theater. The key is the sale to different customers, or of different units of the good, at different prices. Have you ever had a fender-bender and had the body shop--before it quotes you an estimate--ask if you have collision insurance? Having insurance (of any kind) tends to make one rather insensitive to price, so people with it tend to get charged more than those who have to pay from their own pockets. Are people who rent cars on Tuesdays more likely to be business travellers (with expense accounts or other reasons for less-elastic demands), than people who rent the same cars on weekends?

Identifying price discrimination isn't always easy. Does the restaurant charge twice as much at dinner, for the same food it sells at lunch? Maybe the dinner demand is less elastic, but maybe it's just <u>greater</u>. The same goes for blocks of ice (to preserve food) and chain saws (to clear rubble) in the aftermath of a hurricane. A higher price doesn't necessarily indicate price discrimination. It's more likely simple price rationing in the face of surging demand.

Economists have a little tougher time deciding what to think about imperfect price discrimination. Since fewer units are sold to one group and more to the other, it isn't clear whether the total quantity that's sold goes up or down, compared to the case of no price discrimination. (Perfect discrimination clearly increases quantity.) This imperfect, elasticity-based discrimination makes the less-elastic group worse off, but the more-elastic group and the producer are made better off. No overall judgment of whether "we" are better or worse off is possible, because these changes affect different individuals and cannot be compared. But the use of whatever information he has justly acquired about his customers' demands is fully within the producer's rights.

YOU SHOULD REMEMBER...

1)   No customer of the imaginary PRICE-TAKING SELLER sees any reason whatsoever to prefer this seller's product over that of any other seller.

2)   The demand curve for the product of a seller who is a PRICE TAKER is a horizontal line, infinitely elastic at the market price of the good.

3)   The MARGINAL REVENUE of any particular unit is the amount that it adds to the seller's sales revenue.

4)   For a price taker, the PRICE at which a unit can be sold and the MARGINAL REVENUE of that unit are identical. The demand curve and the marginal revenue curve are the same horizontal line.

5)   The price taker's only decision is: What is the best quantity to produce?

6)   The price taker should produce that quantity for which marginal revenue equals marginal cost.

7)   If the quantity and price at which MR=MC will not permit him to cover his fixed costs, he should not go into the business at all.

8)   A PRICE SEARCHER is any seller the demand for whose product slopes downward.

9)   If there is ANYTHING that leads at least one customer to prefer a seller's product over those of his competitors, that seller is a PRICE SEARCHER.

10)   If the price searcher does not price-discriminate, a unit's marginal revenue is LESS THAN the price at which it can be sold.

11)   The easiest way to find the marginal revenue of, say, the 17th widget is to find the total revenue from the sale of 17 widgets and subtract from it the total revenue obtainable from the sale of 16 widgets.

12)   The price searcher, also, should produce that quantity for which marginal revenue equals marginal cost.

13)   He finds the PRICE for which he's searching by looking up to the demand curve, at the quantity at which MR=MC.

14)   If this quantity and this price will not permit him to cover his fixed costs, he should not enter the business at all.

15) Units for which demand is ELASTIC (the upper half of a linear demand curve) have POSITIVE marginal revenue. Units for which demand is INELASTIC (those on the lower half of the linear demand curve) have NEGATIVE marginal revenue.

16) No seller ever deliberately operates in the inelastic range of his demand curve.

17) An individual's CONSUMER'S SURPLUS is the amount of money by which his demand price exceeds the price that he actually pays.

18) PERFECT PRICE DISCRIMINATION requires the seller to sell each unit precisely at its demand price. Sellers would love it, but they can't get the necessary information.

19) LESS-THAN-PERFECT price discrimination is quite common. The seller RAISES the price to the group of customers who are less sensitive to price, and LOWERS the price to the group of customers who are more sensitive to price.

20) Neither the "price taker" model nor "perfect price discrimination" is a reasonable standard for judging the performance of real-world markets.

Problems

1. Bob is an enterprising 10-year-old who mows lawns. He mows Mr. Smith's for $10, but Mr. Jones (next door) will pay only $8. Since Mr. Smith and Mr. Jones are friends, Bob doesn't think he can charge them different amounts. If he mowed each lawn at a price that's low enough to attract Mr. Jones as a customer, what would be Bob's marginal revenue of Mr. Jones's lawn?

2. If the quantity demanded at a price of $100 is 50 units per week, but the price at which 51 would be demanded is only $99, what is the marginal revenue of that 51st unit?

3. Answer (2) again, but assume that the price would have to be reduced to $98 in order to sell that 51st unit. What happened?

4. If the amount by which MR exceeds MC gets smaller as you increase your output and sales, does such an increase make your profit fall? Why is the answer "No"?

5. Frank is considering the action "sell one more unit," and is smart enough to realize that he'll have to reduce the price a bit to be able to do that. If the demand for his product is shown below, fill in the table by finding the "marginal revenue" of each of the units.

Price	Quantity Demanded	Total Revenue	Marginal Revenue
$10	0		
9	1		
8	2		
7	3		
6	4		
5	5		
4	6		
3	7		
2	8		
1	9		
0	10		

6. As Frank imagines reducing the price from $10, what happens to his total sales revenue (increasing, decreasing, or unchanged)? Is marginal revenue positive, negative, or zero? Finally, what does all of this imply about <u>elasticity</u> (inelastic, elastic, or unit-elastic)? Fill in the following table:

	Total Revenue is...	Marginal Revenue is...	...and Elasticity is...
Above $5			
Below $5			

Based on what you know from the above numbers and from the concepts involved, what's going on exactly <u>at</u> a price of $5?

7.   If each unit of his product costs Frank $3 to produce and sell, what does our "MR MC" rule imply about the <u>quantity</u> that Frank should sell and the <u>price</u> that he should set for his good?

8.   How is your answer to (7) affected if you are informed that Frank spent $27.50 to get into this business?

9.   Here's a little more practice with marginal revenue. For each of the two demand curves below, find the marginal revenues of each of the units shown by filling in the following tables.

P	QD	Total rev	Marginal revenue		P	QD	Total rev	Marginal revenue
$50	0				$43	0		
48	1				43	1		
46	2				43	2		
44	3				43	3		
42	4				43	4		
40	5				43	5		

a)   Are we on the elastic or the inelastic portion of the first of these two demand curves? How do you know?

b)   What kind of market does the second demand curve represent? What does its marginal revenue curve look like, according to the numbers you obtained above?

10. Here are some demand and total cost data relevant to Sam's Widgets, Inc.

P	QD		Total Cost
$13	0		$25
$12	1		26
11	2		27
10	3		29
9	4		32
8	5		36
7	6		41
6	7		47
5	8		54
4	9		62
3	10		71
2	11		81
1	12		92

a) Using the space between the "QD" and "Total Cost" data, find the marginal revenue of each of the widgets. [Check: MR of #3 is $8, MR of #9 is -$4]

b) Using the space to the right of the "Total Cost" column, find the marginal cost of each of the widgets. [Check: MC of # 9 is $8]

c) If Sam believes that he should produce the quantity at which marginal revenue equals marginal cost, how many will he produce and what price will he charge per widget?

d) What will Sam's profit be, if he produces and prices as you determined in (c)?

e) What will Sam's profit be, if he were to produce one more than the quantity determined in (c)?

f) Explain exactly why Sam's profit declined by comparing the marginal revenue of that additional unit with its marginal cost.

g) If Sam has not already spent the $25 needed to get into this business, should he go ahead?

h) Suppose that "$25" were increased to "$35," so that each and every "Total cost" number above rises by $10. What effect does this have on your <u>marginal cost</u> numbers?

i) <u>Now</u> if Sam hasn't already invested in this business, should he go ahead? Why or why not?

j) What should Sam do if he has already spent the $35? Hint: Have either your marginal revenue or your marginal cost numbers changed?

CHAPTER 7

MONOPOLY AND COMPETITION

THE SPECTER OF MONOPOLY

"Monopoly!" It's the economic equivalent of Freddie Kreuger of the "Nightmare on Elm Street" movies, or Jason from "Friday the Thirteenth." Economics isn't known for being emotional, but the very word "monopoly" comes about as close as we get, provoking feelings of hatred, fear, and suspicion. A lot of people, including a lot of economists, don't believe that markets are really "free" if there are monopolies. Nobody--even an economist--likes being subjected to the will of another, and if "monopoly" really is a violation of individual freedom, then we ought to do something about it.

There's good reason for this suspicion. When there's only one seller (the technical definition of monopoly), the only alternatives are "pay his price" or "go without." If he knows that, and has some way of guessing your demand price (A neon sign around your neck? Maybe just a familiarity with your kind of life or business...), he may be able to set a price that you're just barely willing to pay. That leaves you with no consumer's surplus (if you're a consumer) or no profit (if you're a business).

The Central Pacific Railroad, during the late 1800s, offers an example. (It was the factual basis for Frank Norris's muckraking novel The Octopus.) Its founders (who included Leland Stanford, later to create the university) "succeeded, in the early '70s, in their effort to control the movement of freight to and from California and within the borders of the state..."[1] Historian Oscar Lewis reports:

> The degree of prosperity of every business or industry was directly dependent upon the officials...who fixed the railroad's freight rates... If merchants were found to be growing prosperous, rates were raised; if too many went bankrupt, rates were lowered. The manufacturer was allowed to earn enough to keep his plant in operation; freight rates on the farmer's products were nicely calculated to enable him to clear enough to plant and harvest his next year's crop and to support himself, not too extravagantly, in the meantime. (Lewis, pp. 365-6)

---

[1] Oscar Lewis, The Big Four (New York: Alfred A. Knopf, 1938), p. 365.

A monopoly that's like that is, indeed, something to be concerned about. But there's a highly pertinent fact about the manner in which the Central Pacific maintained its monopoly: the railroad substantially controlled the California legislature, which legally protected it from competition. Lewis reports that "efforts to remedy the situation were uniformly unsuccessful because of the railroad's control of the legislature, of state regulatory bodies, of city and county governments, and, in many cases, of the courts" (Lewis, p. 365). The violation of the merchants' and farmers' freedom and rights came not from the railroad itself, but from the California state government.

Whether "monopolies" that lack the assistance of legislation that suppresses competition deserve our hatred and fear is another question altogether. Before we get into that, we'd better step back a little and examine the meaning of the term "monopoly."

Single seller...but of what?

The word "monopoly" means "single seller," just as "monocle" is an eyeglass for one eye, a "monosyllable" is a word with one syllable (Huh?) and Johnny Carson's "monologue" has only one person talking. "Single seller" is simple enough, but the real start of your education into the problem of monopoly begins when you ask: "But of what?" ("Why" and "how" are pretty important, too; we'll get to them soon.)

```
MONOPOLY means "single seller"...
but OF WHAT?
```

Suppose there were only one convenience store, within a one-mile radius of your apartment, where you could get a cup of coffee. It's about a hundred yards down the road. Is that store a monopolist? That depends on how you define the good.

Coffee within a mile of your apartment? I guess that makes him a monopolist. But there's another little shop nearby that specializes in tea, and several places to get caffeinated soft drinks. If you just want to stay awake until you get your term paper finished, "some drink with caffeine in it" may be just fine, and our store is not a monopolist. Besides, there's another place that sells coffee just a little over a mile away; if we were to define the relevant good as "coffee within a mile and a quarter of your apartment," the nearby store again wouldn't be a monopolist.

These are the two problems faced by anyone attempting to determine whether a particular seller is a monopolist:

1) Product definition (Narrow or broad? Fresh-brewed coffee, or caffeinated drinks?)

and

2) Geographic market definition (Narrow or broad? Within walking distance, or a day's air-freight distance?)

As our example with the local convenience store suggests, any seller in the world can be identified as a monopolist if the product and geographic market are defined sufficiently narrowly. On the other hand, if we want monopolies to evaporate, all we have to do is define the product and geographic market very broadly. (Food, in the world? Goods, in the universe?)

> A sufficiently NARROW definition of product or geographic market can make ANY seller a "monopolist."

Am I a monopolist? Well, no. I'm certainly not the only college teacher in the Western world; I'm not even the only economics teacher at my university. On the other hand, I am the only one who teaches in a particular room at a particular time, waves his hand in a particular way at precisely 9:18 AM, and uses wodgets as a sunk-cost example. We're left with a typical economist's answer: On the one hand, yes; on the other hand, no.

Ah, but how significant are these characteristics that make me--or the nearby convenience store--unique? Some of the attributes I've listed above sound pretty trivial, and aren't likely to make my teaching <u>importantly</u> different from that of my colleagues.

This is an excellent question. There are, indeed, always distinctions of some kind among the products of different sellers. Since two stores can't occupy the same location, the one that's next door is geographically slightly different. The same people can't work in two stores at the same time, and perhaps the salesclerk in the closer store smiles as you make your purchase, while the one in the other store doesn't. How important are these distinctions to you? If they're absolutely vital, then you won't consider the store one door farther away, or the one with the somber salesclerks, to be offering even remotely similar goods. The smiling, nearby seller--as far as you're concerned--is a monopolist. If you really don't care about walking another twenty feet and whether the salesclerks smile, you'll consider them to be perfectly substitutable for each other, effective competitors, and you'll flip back and forth according to who's offering a price that's a couple of pennies lower at the moment.

Where does this leave us in our quest for a sensible concept of monopoly? Technically, no two sellers ever offer precisely the same good. If we insist on a strict definition that makes a seller a monopolist if no other seller offers precisely the same good, then every seller (including every worker, because every individual's work habits and personality are different) is a monopolist. It may be helpful to know this, if you're an anti-capitalistic radical and want to write newspaper editorials that attack the capitalist system as made up of millions of monopolies. As far as I'm concerned, though, if we insist on a concept of monopoly that makes the kid who mows the lawn every couple of weeks into one, that concept isn't very helpful. It just doesn't distinguish one seller from another.

Economists' terminology does us no favors

Economists have generally handled this whole issue of "monopoly" quite badly.

Remember the distinction between the "price taker" and the "price searcher"? A seller was a searcher if anyone perceived something unique and valuable about his product (including the seller's location or personality). If that's the case, the seller would not be likely to lose all of his customers if he raised his price a bit; his demand curve would slope downward.

To many economists, any unique attribute that makes a seller a price searcher is enough to make him a <u>monopolist</u> too.

> Most economists define a MONOPOLIST simply as any PRICE-SEARCHER, any seller whose demand curve slopes down.

This implicitly relies on the narrowest of product or market definitions. Here's an example, from the well-known economist Gary Becker's 1971 textbook <u>Economic Theory</u> (New York: Knopf, 1971: p. 94): "...a firm can be said to be in a monopolistic position when its demand curve is negatively inclined."

According to this use of language, the only seller who is <u>not</u> a monopolist is a <u>price taker</u>. Customers themselves consider his product to have no unique attributes whatsoever, nothing that distinguishes it from the products of other sellers, so if the seller asks even a very slightly higher price he'll lose all of his sales.

Look at the huge difficulty that this terminology creates. "Monopoly" is a word that provokes connotations of "evil," yet by the economists' identification of monopoly with price-searcher, <u>every</u> real-world seller of anything (including the kid who mows the lawn) is a "monopolist."

The only real ways out of this misleading and confusing situation are to train our emotions not to react negatively to the word "monopoly" (a long, slow, process), or to reject completely the economists' identification of it with the downward-sloping demand curve of the "price searcher."

I'd like to see the latter. It will come some day, but for now the equating of price searcher with monopoly is just too deeply entrenched in the economist's language. So we're stuck with trying to think clearly despite the fact that commonly accepted terminology hampers it. The key, as usual, is <u>understanding</u>.

First we'll learn that, even by their own narrow definition, economists recognize different degrees of "monopoly power," a notion that at least identifies some of our price-searcher/"monopolies" as less harmful than others. Second, and more importantly, we'll learn that although price-searcher/monopolies are all over the place, they pose a "monopoly problem" only when they are protected from competition by legislation that violates other individuals' rights.

Degrees of "monopoly power"

Since "monopoly" seems like a binary (all-or-none, zero-or-one) kind of word, economists sometimes use the term "monopoly power" (or "market power") to measure degrees. Although every price-searcher is, technically, a monopolist, their "monopoly powers" differ widely.

The nearby 7-11 store surely isn't <u>much</u> of a monopolist, and the fact that it <u>is</u> one is hardly very important. Most of its customers consider other stores to have excellent, though not perfect, substitutes. That implies that while the demand for this particular 7-11's merchandise is not infinitely elastic (perfectly flat), it will have high elasticity and a slight rise in price will cause a lot of lost sales. Just try to convince the store's manager that he has "no competition" because no other store sells products that are technically identical, and see how far you get. The local 7-11 may be a monopoly of sorts, but it certainly doesn't seem like anything to worry much about.

The seller of a product with fewer attractive substitutes, though, and therefore a demand curve that's less elastic, won't lose as many of his customers if he raises his price. He seems to be a bit <u>more</u> of a "monopolist," or a more serious or important kind of monopolist, than the 7-11. The extreme case, where consumers genuinely perceive "no choice," might be that of the only surgeon at an isolated rural hospital where you've landed in need of a life-saving operation within the next ten minutes. Your demand price is probably limited only by your wealth (including whatever you can borrow against your future lifetime earnings). Remembering that no real-world demand curve (including yours) is truly vertical over the entire range of prices, we can identify the imaginary purely vertical demand curve with the term "absolute monopoly."

Be a little careful here. Our analysis of the price-searching seller's determination of the best price to charge and quantity to sell illustrates that a seller doesn't just "raise his price" when he feels greedy. (He always feels greedy. So do you. So do I.) There are logical principles he has to follow, and we studied them. Think back to our "MR=MC" process by which a price searcher finds what he's searching for. What would happen if, in a sudden surge of extra greed, he decided to raise the price even more? There seem to be a lot of folks who think that a "monopolist" with "unbridled greed" would raise his price continually, and that we're just lucky that his

192

greed is bridled. Actually, of course, the more greedy a seller becomes, the more firmly he sticks to our MR=MC price-searcher strategy.

When the price searcher has determined the point at which marginal revenue and marginal cost are equal, he looks up to the demand curve to find his price. How far "up" he has to look--that is, the size of the gap between MR=MC and price--depends on the elasticity of demand. We saw this in our discussion of elasticity-based price discrimination, for example. Take a look at Figures 6.14 and 6.15 again, of the less-elastic and more-elastic subgroups of customer. Imagine, now, that the two graphs describe two different products (widgets and wodgets) whose production involves marginal costs that are each constant at $2 per unit. The seller of each will produce a quantity at which marginal <u>revenue</u> is also $2 per unit. But if the demand for widgets is very flat (corresponding to the more-elastic subgroup), the price that the widget seller charges will be only slightly above $2. If the demand for wodgets is much less elastic at the quantity at which MR=MC, the price of wodgets will be well above $2. Figures 7.1A and 7.1B provide some pictures.

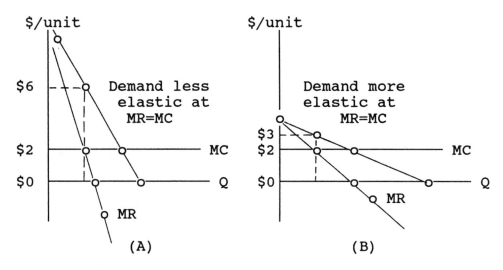

Figure 7.1: Elasticity and the "gap"

The size of the gap between price and marginal cost, expressed as a percentage of price, is often used as an index or measure of the degree of "monopoly power" or "market power." It's called the Lerner Index (after the famous economist Abba P. Lerner), and is defined as:

Lerner index of monopoly power = (P - MC)/P

evaluated at the proper price-searcher's quantity and price: MR=MC and P corresponding to the quantity at which this holds. With a little algebra and use of the fact that MC=MR, the formula above can be rewritten simply as

Lerner index of monopoly power = 1/E,

where E is the elasticity of demand at the quantity at which MR=MC. Either of these "monopoly power" formulas shows that a price taker (E is infinite, and MC = MR = P) has zero monopoly power.[2]

Imagine a perfectly horizontal demand curve developing a tiny downward tilt. It will sprout an MR curve with a downward slope that's twice as steep (still not very steep) and the quantity at which MR=MC will lie far to the left of the unit-elastic point (midpoint) of the demand curve, putting us way up in its elastic region. Elasticity is far greater than one, in fact nearly infinite. (That makes "monopoly power" a little greater than zero, but not much.) Now that you've exercised your mind by imagining all of this, you may look at Figure 7.2, where I've made an attempt to draw it.

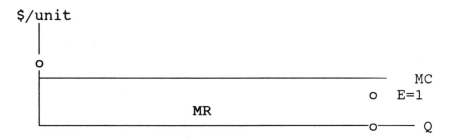

Figure 7.2: Way up in the elastic range

At the other extreme, as we imagine the demand for a seller's product becoming more and more vertical, marginal revenue becomes even more (twice as much) vertical. MR hits zero (the quantity axis) just beyond the quantity at which MR=MC, so this MR=MC quantity must lie just a hair above the unit-elastic (midpoint) of the demand curve. The gap between P and MR=MC becomes larger and larger. It's true that (P-MC) is always less than P, but as we imagine P becoming larger and larger (here's another "limit" problem) the Lerner Index approaches "1," or absolute monopoly.

---

[2] If you're trying to calculate the Lerner Index using discrete numbers like those of our problems, stick with the (P-MC)/P approach. The elasticity interpretation gives the same numerical answer only if elasticity is evaluated at a <u>point</u> on a smooth demand curve, using limits and calculus.

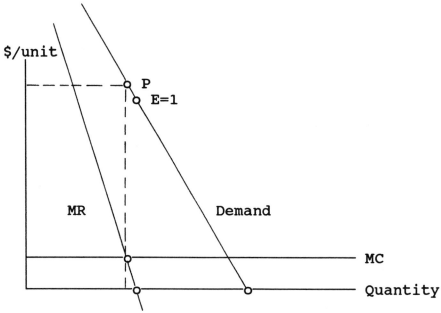

Figure 7.3: Barely into the elastic region

The Lerner Index of "monopoly power" therefore is zero for the price taker, and increases--as we imagine the elasticity of demand (at the quantity for which MR=MC) for the seller's product decreasing--up to "one." Every seller operates in the elastic portion of his demand curve (E > 1), but a nearly-absolute monopolist operates very close to the point of unit elasticity, while a near-"price taker" (perhaps like our local 7-11) operates at a point of much higher elasticity.

"So what?" and other relevant questions

"Waddyamean Dean" is a character in Joseph Wambaugh's 1975 police novel The Choirboys, an officer named Dean Pratt who doesn't seem too quick on the uptake and is always asking his partner what things mean. You might want to ask a related question about these "monopoly power" formulas: So what?

I've asked myself that question many times. Like you, I have other things to do with my life besides studying definitions of things like the Lerner Index. There are a couple of answers.

First, thinking about the concept helps us to understand more about the price-searcher's position. Reasoning--as we've done above--about the Lerner Index gives us valuable practice at thinking about the relationship between the elasticity of demand for his product and his marginal costs and revenue.

Second, and more importantly, it isn't unusual for economists to take this reasoning very seriously as support for recommendations about government economic policy. I warned you, earlier, about economists' tendency to believe that there's something wrong with the market if price doesn't equal marginal cost, as it would if every seller were a price taker (or could perfectly discriminate). The existence of a gap--any gap--between P and MC, and therefore the existence of a Lerner Index that's greater than zero, is often interpreted as a "market failure." It's a situation that many economists (not me!) describe either as "free markets don't work if sellers have monopoly power" or as "free markets don't <u>exist</u> if sellers have monopoly power," depending on how one defines "free markets." This is a sure sign, I'm afraid, of an economist who hasn't thought carefully about what capitalism and "free markets" are. Believe it or not, there are lots of them.

Does price-searching produce a "welfare loss"?

Perhaps the first thing that you should think of, when you see a question like this, is the punch line of our old vaudeville joke: <u>Compared to what?</u> What's the standard that establishes the "loss"?

I'll return to that basic question shortly. For now, let's consider the problem.

In Chapter 6, I noted that a situation in which certain units of a good--those for which marginal cost is less than price but greater than marginal revenue--are not produced is often identified as a "market failure." Remember units 21 through 30 in our Sally-and-Frank wodget example (Figure 6.11)? Here it is again, as Figure 7.4, with a new shaded area.

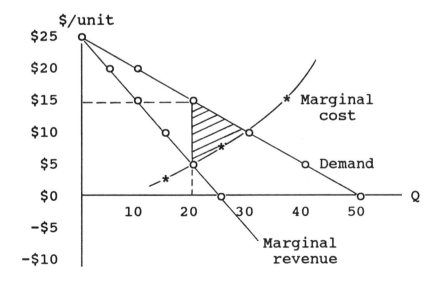

Figure 7.4: Welfare loss in the wodget market?

The shaded triangle in Figure 7.4, bounded by "marginal cost" on the bottom and "demand" on the top and the quantity at which MR=MC on the left, is often called a <u>welfare-loss</u> triangle. It is the consumer's surplus that demanders 21 through 30 would enjoy if we sold to them "at cost."

Such an area is present whenever a seller is a price searcher who cannot discriminate perfectly. There's no such area for either the price taker (see Figure 6.3), or for a price searcher who can perfectly discriminate (see Figure 6.12), because for each of these sellers price and marginal revenue are identical.

The size of this "welfare loss triangle" is inversely related to the elasticity of demand. If there are many excellent substitutes and a very elastic demand (like Figure 7.2), the seller has little "monopoly power" and the "welfare loss" will be small. With few or no attractive alternatives and a much less elastic demand (like Figure 7.3), the seller has much more "monopoly power" and the "welfare loss" is much larger.

But there is at least some "welfare loss" whenever a (non-discriminating) seller's demand curve slopes downward at all. Certainly "welfare loss" doesn't sound very good. Yet every price searcher seems to cause it. Hmmm. This recalls the practice of many economists of defining "monopoly" as any price searcher. When every real-world action or situation seems "bad," it's time to reconsider the <u>standard</u>.

"Compared to what?" It's finally time to revive that wonderful old gag. The triangle is a "loss" only compared to the situation in which it does not exist. But that's either when demand curves are horizontal (infinitely elastic) lines, or when the seller can perfectly discriminate at zero cost.

Neither of these is a fair standard against which to measure the success or failure of markets.

The elasticity of demand, as we shall see, depends on many things, but you're already aware that there's certainly no problem indicated when it isn't infinite. That just means the demand curve slopes downward.

So why don't we simply discriminate? After all, <u>not discriminating</u> has a pretty big cost: it's all of that revenue that we lose when we reduce the price to everyone. The simple fact that most sellers choose <u>not</u> to discriminate is evidence of the difficulty (high costs) of discriminating. You've seen some of those costs: The ticket clerk has to judge if the kid who says he's 13 really is, and the college administration tells you that it must process your family's financial statement before it can determine what to charge you to attend. Imagine a quick trip to the discount store, where you're told "Let's go into my office and discuss exactly how badly you need this package of athletic socks." No wonder that most sellers find it cheaper, more profitable, to put up with the universal price cuts than to try to discriminate.

The economist who decries the "inefficiency" of these sellers' "welfare-loss triangles" is telling us, in essence, that because they would produce more if they could perfectly discriminate at zero cost (the neon-sign approach), there is something wrong when they don't choose the same action when its costs are very high.

It is intriguing that there are unsold units for which price exceeds marginal cost, and they can stimulate us to think about why they exist. But it is absurd to identify them as some kind of "market failure" or "welfare loss." This terminology causes the same problem as the related--and equally ill-advised--practice of calling any price-searcher a "monopolist."

"Compared to what?" A world that could not exist. The less seriously we take this "welfare loss triangle," the better our understanding of the market is likely to be.

The relevant question: what limits the alternatives?

When the seller does not discriminate, both the Lerner Index of monopoly power and the size of the "welfare-loss triangle" depend on the elasticity of demand. To think further about the claim that they constitute market failure, we have to think about where the elasticity of demand for a particular seller's product comes from. What determines it? What makes it huge, or barely greater than one? Beyond that, is the "monopoly" and "monopoly power" terminology useful, harmlessly redundant, or is it--like the "welfare loss"--actually detrimental to careful thought about the operation of markets?

You'd love to purchase a hooey. It's just what you need to move forward in your career and have a great time on your upcoming vacation, besides. Your demand price is $100; obtaining one hooey is (barely) more valuable to you than the best alternative you could obtain for $100.

If there is only one seller (a shop called Hooey One) of hooeys, your demand price for one of his hooeys is clearly also $100, because there aren't any that aren't his. But suppose there are two sellers (Hooey One and Hooey Two), each offering hooeys for $55. The presence of Hooey Two will certainly affect your demand for the product of Hooey One. Perhaps the first shop is a little more convenient, so you'd be willing to pay a few extra bucks. But if One raises its price above, say, $58, your "quantity demanded" of his product drops off to zero and you begin to patronize Hooey Two.

The elasticity of the market demand for any seller's product, and therefore his monopoly power, depends on whether there are other sellers of products that we consumers consider to be substitutes. That depends partly on us: our subjective valuations of the slightly different attributes of different products. But it also depends on decisions made by individual businesspeople: whether to enter the hooey market at all, to install small wheels on it or make it glow in the dark, to package it in biodegradable materials, or to raise prices when the others do.

> Given the available alternatives, we CONSUMERS determine elasticities of demand by the VALUES that we attribute to them.

Given a range of different products offered to us, it is us individual consumers who determine the shape (including the elasticity) of our demand for the product of any one seller. If that range of alternatives is smaller, our demand for any one of them is likely to become less elastic.

If a particular seller has "monopoly power," then, it's either the fault of the individual consumers for perceiving and valuing some characteristic of his product that they don't find elsewhere, or the fault of businesspeople: others (for not choosing to produce a product that we consumers consider nearly identical) or the seller himself (for deliberately introducing attributes that consumers value and can find nowhere else).

The critic of the market system now has himself in somewhat of a bind. It's tough to blame individual consumers for valuing what they value, although this snobbish, elitist attitude is not uncommon among critics of capitalism. It's tough to accuse one producer of doing something wrong when he introduces a good that consumers love and--so far--haven't been able to get elsewhere. (This charge has been levelled, too, at successful entrepreneurs, on the grounds that they have done it to try to get rich and not out of charity). All that's left to blame are the other businesses, for not choosing to produce a highly substitutable product. (When they do, though, the critics are likely to call it "wasteful duplication.") Since any particular business presumably has sound cost/benefit reasoning for its actions, it's hard to accuse a particular producer for deciding to pursue the wodget rather than the hooey market. So the claim is left in general terms, that the "market system" doesn't produce enough close substitutes; it endows each seller with "monopoly power" by limiting the alternatives available to consumers.

The range of alternatives to anything, including the number of competitors offering a similar good, is never infinite.

> The range of available alternatives is always limited by <u>something</u>. That's an unavoidable implication of scarcity.

If that "something" is just the pattern of voluntary choices of all of the parties involved (consumers, sellers of the product and its close substitutes, and sellers who decided not to produce substitutes), then there is no fundamental problem with the market. In a free economy, there are millions of individuals hunting for the opportunity to make a profit. Whenever widget prices rise enough to make it seem as if a newcomer could more than cover his costs of producing and selling widgets, he's likely to give it a try. If there are only four, or eighteen, or even just one, producers of a particular good in a capitalist society, it's because no additional producers have yet decided that they can do any better.

The only monopoly problem: rights-violating legislation

When a producer is able to restrict the availability of attractive alternatives not by making his much more attractive but by successfully influencing the legislative process, however, our judgment changes considerably. This is not a free-market exchange. There's nothing "voluntary" about it. I would like to offer widgets for sale, and the current widget consumers would love to have me competing with their current supplier, but some form of legislation prohibits it.

Suppose that I would like to convert your wodget factory to producing widgets. But I can't afford to buy the factory, so I'm thinking about taking it over using bazookas and tear-gas grenades. Fortunately for all of us, legislation prohibits that, too. We have to differentiate between legislation that enforces individuals' rights and legislation that violates them.

If I do not enter the widget business because I don't think I can cover my costs, neither my rights nor yours are violated. When I stay out, it's because I don't think that my future widget customers will pay enough to permit me to outbid other uses for the resources I'd need.

But if I do not enter because I had to get a license, and the existing widget producers control the politicians who issue the licenses, the government has violated my rights. As a result, the alternatives available to you are restricted and your demand for one of them is less elastic than it would (and should) have been.

This legislative violation of rights is what happened with the Central Pacific case in California. As Ayn Rand puts it, in her "Notes on the History of American Free Enterprise" [Capitalism: The Unknown Ideal (New York: New American Library, 1966: p. 99)], the perpetrators

> were not free enterprisers; they were not businessmen who had achieved power by means of unregulated trade. They were typical representatives of what is now called a mixed economy. They achieved power by legislative intervention in business; none of their abuses would have been possible in a free, unregulated economy.

By "unregulated" she means that government's only function is the protection of individual rights. It emphatically does not mean that there are no rules or laws at all.

The monopolies we love to hate, the monopolies that give "monopoly" its bad name, are those that have managed to enlist the help of the government. They have connived legislation that prevents competitors from exercising their right to compete, restricting by law the alternatives available to individual consumers. As we've noted, the number of alternatives is always limited by something. If it's simply scarcity and the enforcement of individuals' rights to life and property, there's no problem. But if alternatives are limited by legislation that violates individuals' rights to voluntary exchange, then the operation of the market's coordinating forces is being thwarted.

> When the alternatives to a seller's good are limited by RIGHTS-VIOLATING LEGISLATION, then (and only then) there's a monopoly PROBLEM.

It follows that we can't simply determine whether there's anything wrong when, at the moment, there happens to be only one supplier of a good. We have to examine the <u>process</u> by which he obtained, and retains, his "monopoly" position. If it's been through superlative efficiency and competitive success, and he apparently retains his position only because he's doing it better than any other potential producer thinks he could, the market system is working just fine. If, on the other hand, it's apparently been retained by rights-violating legislation, such a "monopoly" deserves our hatred, fear, and disapproval.

Our attitude depends not on whether a producer happens to be a "single seller," in other words, but on the nature of the process by which he obtained and retains that position. Violations of individual rights--perhaps especially those undertaken with the support and assistance of the very institution (government) whose function it is to defend them--are to be disapproved, whatever form they take.

COMPETITION, ENTRY RESTRICTION, AND CARTELS

OK, brilliant and energetic businesspeople. You've just discovered a way to make a bundle. It's some new product that nobody else has thought of. Suppose that you can buy the resources needed to produce each unit for $6 (constant marginal costs, no fixed costs), and you've decided--never mind exactly how--to produce 2,000 each month and sell them for $11 each. For every one you make, you pocket five bucks profit. With thoughts of vast riches whipping through your head, you start scanning the Real Estate ads for large estates in exclusive suburbs.

Better proceed cautiously. Two different things are going to happen, and they're both going to squeeze that five buck per unit profit.

As soon as other entrepreneurial types see you producing this product, the thought is likely to occur to them to try it, too. They may not know your exact costs, but anyone who thinks he can produce the thing for less than $11 has incentive to do so. Your very success, in other words, attracts imitators who enter the market as your competitors.

The first of the detrimental effects--from your perspective--results from the increase in the supply of the product on the marketplace. Because the market demand curve slopes downward, that's likely to drive its price down: $11, $10.50, $10, $9, as more and more greedy imitators jump on board. Even if your costs were to stay at $6 each, the declining product price would gnaw away at your profit.

The second of the bad consequences of others' entry is that your costs will <u>not</u> stay at $6. After all, these new producers constitute a new source of demand for the resources that are used. The increase in the demand for inputs is likely to bid up their price.[3] Eventually, your--and everyone else's--costs are likely to be bid up (to, say, $8.25), and the price of the product is bid down (to $8.25), at which point your profit has disappeared.

A more realistic story would involve fixed costs with increasing marginal costs and a downward-sloping demand curve. The price searcher would discover that producing at MR=MC, and pricing accordingly, permits him to recoup his monthly fixed costs with thousands of dollars to spare. Entry by newcomers would reduce and make far more elastic the demand for his own output, and would raise both his marginal costs and his fixed costs. Net revenue would be eliminated.

Market restrictions for fun and profit

A dreadful state of affairs, you'll agree. There go the dreams of the horse farm in the Valley. Well, you could always come up with another idea for a new product that consumers value far more than it costs, and try to make a few more bucks before market competition sets in. But good ideas like that aren't easy to come by. Making it <u>economically</u> unattractive for newcomers requires you to do such a good job for consumers that none of your potential competitors believes he can do any better. It might be easier if you can figure out a way to make it <u>politically</u> unattractive.

If only there were some kind of law that makes it impossible, or at least costly, for someone else to produce and sell this product, the two competitive pressures that squeeze out your profit could be eliminated or limited. Now, how do we get such a law?

In a democracy our legislators have to be concerned with their reputation among the public; that's where the votes come from. A straightforward admission that "I'm proposing this bill to prevent anyone from starting up a new widget business in Baltimore, because I received a campaign contribution of $50,000 from the city's only existing widget seller" wouldn't go over too well. But if the bill can be made to appear to be good for "the public," if some carefully chosen legislator can--with the guidance of our highly paid lobbyist--word the bill to make it appear as if the future of civilized society depends on restricting competition in the Baltimore widget market,

---

[3] This rise of costs is not inevitable. If the resources are widely available and used in a great many other products, a doubling or ten-fold increase in the demand by your relatively tiny industry may have an insignificant impact on the total market demand for the resources. (Even ten small frogs may be pretty small in a big pond.) This would be known as a "constant cost industry," and all of the adjustment would be in the product price.

we've got it made. That's come to be known as "constituent service," though it's hardly a service to more than a few constituents.

"The public interest," or something like it, is always the advertised rationale for legislative restrictions that limit business activity and therefore consumer choice. Safety, quality, stability, jobs, fairness... all are words that are invoked by a legislature hopeful that we--the public--will accept the restrictions that they impose on our choice.

A few years ago, a man in a Baltimore suburb bought a new tow truck and planned to go into business for himself. Tow trucks are more expensive than the average new car, but the cost is low compared to many business fixed costs, so it's a good business for someone who "wants to be his own boss" and doesn't have much capital. Unfortunately, this man reckoned without the licensing process.

It turned out that he needed a special license to be able to operate a tow truck in his part of the county. To get it, he had to prove that there was a "need" for his services. Well, the licensing board didn't know, so guess who they consulted? The people who knew the most about the state of the tow-truck business in that area: existing tow-truck drivers. And guess what they said? (If only all questions were this easy!) Not only was there no "need" for another truck, but there wasn't enough business to go around as it was. According to these experts, if he were allowed to operate, none of the drivers--him included--would be able to cover their costs, a lot of them would go out of business, and stranded automobile drivers would be far worse off than they are now. The availability of towing services would actually decline, to the public's harm.

Needless to say, in the face of such dire predictions and tales of woe the license was denied, and--as far as I can remember--the fellow sold his tow truck. I'm not sure to whom. Must have been somebody from out of town. Or one of the companies that did have a license.

This kind of thing happens so often that economists have a name for it: the capture theory of regulation. The idea is that a government regulatory agency naturally has to call upon the expertise of, and work closely with, those who know the most about the industry they're regulating. Those with this knowledge, naturally, are the regulatees. Eventually a close relationship develops between the regulators and the regulated, with both looking out for the interests of the industry. There's give and take on both sides, partly to preserve appearances, but it evolves into a business-government partnership in which the agency has effectively been "captured" by the industry it regulates. Generally they wind up working together, protecting the firms that are already in the industry from the forces of free-market competition.

I do not wish to argue, here at least, that safety and health and educational requirements have no beneficial effects. Certainly we would want the restaurants that we patronize to be inspected and certified, by someone we trust, to be clean and healthy. Whether that "someone" must be, or even should be, a government agency is another matter entirely. When a seller claims that his product conforms to a certain standard of quality, enforcing that standard (and thereby preventing the seller from committing fraud) may be a legitimate part of government's protection of individual rights.

But I do want you to realize that many of the restrictions placed on new entrants into a business or a profession seem to have only the most flimsy claim to protecting genuine individual rights. They seem to be designed primarily to make it difficult and costly for new competitors to enter, and truly constitute a violation of the rights of the potential competitors.

These restrictions essentially constitute theft from would-be competitors, for the benefit of existing producers. The whole process also harms us consumers, leaving us with fewer alternatives (with higher prices and lower quality) than would have been available if legislation had not protected existing producers from the forces of competition.

Legislation that makes it difficult for individuals to enter a certain trade or profession, or to start up a particular kind of business, is everywhere and takes many different forms. Without a lengthy digression on the nature of individual rights, I'm going to have to leave it up to you to decide, for yourselves, when these restrictions are a natural consequence of the principle of individual rights and when they constitute one group's successful use of government to enrich itself by violating the rights of another group.

I raised an example of the first type earlier. You own a factory that I'd like to use to produce widgets, but I can't afford to buy it so I'm planning to take it over by force. When the police stop me and the courts jail me, they do indeed "restrict entry" into the widget industry. Of course they're justified, but it's because the process I've selected violates the rights of others.

Suppose, however, that an existing producer supports (and gets passed) legislation that requires me to compensate him for any loss in his revenue that my entry into the widget business might cause. (If you think this is unheard of, or only a remote possibility, you don't spend enough time reading The Wall Street Journal.) With such an addition to my costs, I'm unlikely to enter. Law or no law, though, there is no proper concept of rights that justifies his claim. When this law is enforced, the existing producer benefits by the entry restriction that violates my rights. Our case against such laws should have nothing to do with phrases like "entry restrictions" or "barriers to entry," but with the simple fact that they violate individuals' rights to voluntary exchange.

Let's get together

Perhaps we've been unsuccessful in our attempt to restrict entry, and find ourselves with one competitor. Our company (Alpha), and our competitor (Beta), make products that consumers consider to be close substitutes. It doesn't take us long to realize that open competition between the two of us will produce a result that neither of us likes much.

To make its product a little more appealing than ours, and attract a lot of our customers, Beta is likely to undercut our price a bit and incur additional costs of marketing or product improvement. To keep Beta from succeeding, and to outdo it at its own game, we'll shade the price a bit below Beta's and spend even more aggressively on advertising and improvement. Beta retaliates. We retaliate. Both of our profits are shriveling. The product's price is falling, and its quality and cost of production are rising. Our customers are delighted. When we both reach the point at which we're just covering our costs, the process of undercutting and outspending each other obviously has to stop, and we each learn to live with whatever share of the market we've achieved.

But we're both smart folks, and understand what the process of competition between us is almost sure to do. The idea may occur that we should get together, "colluding" to avoid competition between us. Collusion is generally illegal under the Sherman Antitrust Act (1890), but let's set that aside for now. We want to see how collusion would work if it were not illegal.

What we're doing is forming a voluntary cartel.

A CARTEL is an agreement not to compete.

A perfect one imitates the results of a monopoly. If we had two identical companies (Alpha and Beta), their executives would pretend that they were one company, the demand for whose product was the entire market demand. They'd determine the MR and MC of this "company," using price-searcher reasoning to find the quantity it should sell and price it should charge, just as if it were the only company serving the market. With this information, Alpha and Beta would each charge the monopoly price and sell half of the monopoly quantity.

Real-world cartels don't work like that, and never did. There are three problems:

1) The difficulty of setting up the cartel, reaching an acceptable agreement (principally the market shares allocated by the cartel to each firm; assumed to be 50-50 in our simple example);

2) The incentive for members to cheat on the terms of the agreement (violating both the price and the non-price aspects of the agreement); and

3) The difficulty of preventing entry into the industry by non-members (both domestic and foreign).

The first problem has frequently proved to be a hurdle that budding agreements simply couldn't overcome. With two firms of nearly equal size, each producing about half of the market total, 50-50 might be an acceptable agreement.

But what if one of the firms is a brash, up-and-coming newcomer with small market share but rapid growth, while the other has historically been the market leader but has become stodgy and recently suffered a declining market share? Since they've agreed to charge a price that's well above costs, each firm will want as large a share of the market as possible. One will argue for a share based on recent rate of growth, the other for a share based on an average of the past ten years' market shares. If they can't reach an agreement that seems fair to each of them, the deal's off. For a lot of attempted cartels, it was.

As for the third problem, the very purpose of the cartel is to drive the product price well above production costs. The more successful it is, the stronger the incentive for a newcomer to enter the industry. There's bound to be someone lurking around who never would have entered when the cartel members had been competing and charging $23, but who can produce the good himself for $25 and finds entry very appealing when the cartel charges $35. The cartel can invite him to join, but there are two problems with that: he's likely to refuse, because he knows where his bread is buttered (being able to undercut them), and if he accepts, the increasing number of members makes the cartel more difficult to maintain. With each new member the difficulty of keeping everybody in line increases by a much larger ratio than does the number of members. (A six-member cartel is much more than twice as difficult to maintain than a three-member cartel.) As for competition from abroad, about the only way to restrict that is by tariffs or quotas.

Members' incentive to break the cartel...

The principal problem with voluntary cartels, though, is the second: the members' own incentives to cheat on its terms. Remember that the mutually agreed-upon price is well above each member's cost. If firmly adhered to by each member, the cartel arrangement is likely to make each member better off than he would have been under open competition. That's the point of the cartel. But any particular firm will be <u>even better off</u> if he is able to substantially increase his market share, while still obtaining a price that is far above his costs. There is a way to do that: be the only member to cheat on its terms.

The effect is the same as if you went to your shop one morning and found that the three competitors on the adjacent street corners had each raised his price by 20 percent. You'd be delighted. You could either raise yours by 20 percent too, maintaining the same position relative to these other shops as before (the same market share). Or you could hold your prices steady, and draw away a large fraction of their customers. Or you could adopt some middle ground between these two, raising your price (but not by 20 percent) and increasing your market share.

Imagine joining with three other producers to form a voluntary cartel, which sets a price 20 percent above that determined under open competition. If you could figure out a way to raise your price by only 15 percent, say, you could draw customers from your competitors and be far better off than you were under open competition, and even than you would have been with the 20 percent increase but no rise in market share. But if the others discovered that you were raising only 15 percent, the cartel would quickly disintegrate. Open price cutting is the road to ruin, and secret price cutting (like rebates paid back to desirable customers who had to be "officially" charged the agreed-upon cartel price) usually doesn't remain secret for long.

Competition among cartel members for the customers' money, therefore, often takes a non-price form. Cartels attempt to restrict this kind of competition with careful, detailed specifications of the product to be offered, but cheating usually isn't difficult. Each seller charges the same price, but each begins to offer additional services. Some fairly blatant ones might include free delivery, no-interest financing, you buy this (for the standard price) and we'll give you that, any of the forms that competition routinely takes when competition by price is restricted. These efforts to outbid the other cartel members by offering a more attractive product naturally have their costs. This process of bidding up of costs eventually spells an end to cartel profits and to the cartel.

The principal problem with a voluntary cartel is that each member remains mainly interested in his own profit. He'll stick with it only as long as he identifies it as beneficial. But each fears the prospect that the cartel will promote new entry, and none of the members typically trusts the others not to cheat. (After all, they are mainly interested in their own profits, too.) As if this weren't enough, most of the benefits of cheating go to the first member who shades his price or improves his product: he's the one who draws market share from the others.

The consequence of these various pressures is summarized in a sentence common among economists:

> **Voluntary cartels are INHERENTLY UNSTABLE.**

Even if they can be successfully formed, they simply don't last very long. One business executive admitted that he used the meetings--ostensibly intended to form a cartel--mainly to gather information about his competitors, and that the "agreements" lasted only as long as it took the quickest of the participants to reach a telephone.

Despite the great fear that everyone seems to have that businesses would get together, colluding to raise prices and reduce quantities if it weren't for the antitrust laws, neither economic theory--which we have just been investigating--nor American economic history offers much support for the fear.

In our country's most famous price-fixing cases, Addyston Pipe (1899) and Trenton Potteries (1927), both trade associations were found to have violated the Sherman Act's prohibition of "restraint of trade." Both evidently tried to raise and stabilize the prices of their products by limiting competition among their members.

Neither succeeded. Dominick T. Armentano's pathbreaking <u>Antitrust and Monopoly</u> (New York: Holmes & Meier, 1990) describes prices actually paid by the customers of Addyston's and Trenton's member companies. Corporate buyers reported routinely throwing the published price lists in the wastebaskets, never having had to pay anything like the list price, playing one company's salesman against another's, obtaining discounts as great as 40 percent below list, and so forth.

It is highly provocative that in the most famous price-fixing cases in our nation's antitrust history, prices were not successfully "fixed." Nobody argues that the businessmen didn't <u>try</u>. But the forces of competition are--and were--just too strong.

COMPETITORS AND COMPETITION,
A "REVISIONIST" VIEW

Suppose that you were granted the powers of an economic dictator, able to use the force of government to order individuals and businesses to do anything you wish. But you want the economic system to make people as well off as possible, given the constraints of scarcity, and you have come to believe that <u>competition</u> achieves that goal. The trouble is, you're not sure exactly what competition is, and what kind of legislation permits it to function.

A simple kind of example can help to introduce us to the problem. There are two companies, Gamma and Delta, producing products that most people consider to be good substitutes. Competition between them has driven prices down and costs up, until each is just getting along. Suddenly the scientists or managers at Delta discover a way to cut costs in half. They successfully shield this knowledge from the prying eyes of Gamma, and reduce the price of their product by 20 percent. Although this price is well above Delta's new improved cost of production, it is well below Gamma's. As customers flock to Delta, Gamma goes out of business.

Now: should legislation that's consistent with competition permit this, or prohibit it?

This simple question has been the source of fundamental disagreement about government policy toward competition and antitrust for many years.

On the one hand, of course, Delta is now a "monopoly." Because its former competitor is no longer around, its demand curve looks more like Figure 7.3 than Figure 7.2, and it can charge a price well above its marginal cost. Consumers no longer have the alternative of patronizing Gamma. Some law should have prevented Delta from driving Gamma out of business, because now it has no competitors. The exact form of such a law isn't important. Maybe Delta should be legally required to show Gamma how to achieve the cost savings. Maybe Delta shouldn't be allowed to cut its price below Gamma's costs, even though that leaves its price well above its own.

On the other hand, of course, the <u>reason</u> that Gamma isn't around is that Delta out-competed it by offering consumers a choice that most of them found more attractive than that offered by Gamma. Gamma isn't around because, basically, consumers don't <u>want</u> it around. This kind of activity, continually trying to discover a better way to satisfy the consumer and earn his patronage, is the essence of the competitive process. A law that tries to maintain "competition" by protecting the inefficient Gamma, making it illegal for Delta to offer a product that individual consumers prefer, has things precisely backwards. Such a law restricts, and to some extent even prohibits, competition.

So which is it? Would legislation that prevents Delta from doing this promote competition, or destroy it? If we want to devise a legal structure that promotes and preserves competition, do we want to encourage--or, at least, not stand in the way of--actions like Delta's, or prohibit them?

Competitors, or competition?
It's one or the other...

It seems pretty evident that we can't have competition unless there are competitors. But a particular seller "competes" for consumers' scarce money by trying to offer them a better deal than they're getting elsewhere, and the better he does it the more likely it is that some of his competitors go out of business. Should pro-competition legislation protect the innovative seller's right to try to offer consumers a better deal, or should it protect less-efficient competitors from the consequences of such actions?

A competitor is one who competes. "To compete" is a verb, and competition is a kind of action. Certainly two producers of a similar good (our Delta and Gamma, for example) <u>might</u> behave intensely competitively, each continually experimenting with product improvements and cost-saving production techniques and marketing strategy in an effort to outdo the other, but they might not, either. The same can be said if there are ten, or fifty, firms producing similar goods. The industry can be innovative, creative and lively, or it can be dull and stodgy, with everyone doing things the way they always have and nobody stirring up the water. The number of firms producing similar products is no gauge whatsoever of competitive activity.

Besides, even the "single seller" of a particular good--perhaps our Delta--faces competitors. Not actual ones who are already in the business, of course; our example precludes that. But unless restrictive legislation prevents entry, Delta will always face <u>potential</u> competitors. In a free, capitalistic, society, anyone who sees advantage in a particular line of business or work--and can enter it without violating other individuals' rights--is free to do so. These ghostly creatures are constantly peering over the shoulder of "monopolists" like Delta, and if Delta is tries too hard to profit from its single-seller position it will suddenly find itself with a bunch of <u>actual</u> competitors.

> A free market permits anyone to try
> to do better. A wise "monopolist" is
> always competing with these non-
> existent but "potential" competitors.

A wise "monopolist" knows that a free market offers others the opportunity to do better, and that they're continually trying. Offering consumers a better deal than your actual competitors is no special trick if you don't have any actual competitors. But it's a lot tougher, and requires continual cost-saving innovation and product improvement and price cutting, to continue to offer consumers a better deal than anyone else in the society thinks that he could. There may be nobody on your heels at the moment, but if you try to use that situation to relax and slack off a bit, they'll appear out of nowhere.

Once we realize that competition is a kind of activity, any necessary link between the intensity of competition and the number of actual competitors in a market evaporates. Even a "monopolist," the single actual seller in a market, retains his position only by perceiving potential competitors around every corner and outcompeting them.

A couple of interesting conclusions follow. First, if we identify "monopolist" as a single actual seller, and "competition" as a particular form of action, there's no contradiction between monopoly and competition. The conflict arises only when the single seller is protected from competition by legislation that violates the rights of those would-be competitors. A second interesting implication is:

> Legislation that attempts to preserve
> "competition" by protecting "competitors" is
> logically INCONSISTENT.

After all, what it's trying to protect them from are the effects of competition. To preserve "competitors," the legislation must prevent the very competitive actions that it's supposedly trying to protect by preserving the competitors!

Competition: process, or state?

A strong tradition in economics interprets competition as a state of the economy, not as an active process. According to the state (sometimes also called an "end-state") interpretation, one can simply take some kind of snapshot, a still photograph, of the economy at an instant of time, sit down at a desk with it and a magnifying glass, and by a thorough examination of the state of the economy at that instant determine the extent to which competition is present.

The alternative process view, which I strongly prefer, argues essentially that one must use a movie camera or camcorder, capable of tracing action through time. Like our views on the fairness of a particular income distribution, one determines nothing of significance by a simple examination of an instantaneous state; one must judge according to the process that produced it.

The "state" approach derives its inspiration from the price-taker model, actually identifying it as "perfect competition." From a particular consumer's viewpoint, the term seems appropriate. He has thousands of sellers from which to choose, each offering him the very same product. No one of them has any ability whatsoever to raise the price he charges without losing all of his customers; no customer is ever in the position of feeling that he's better off tolerating any seller's even slightest price increase.

No economist is so "ivory tower" that he believes any real-world good can actually be produced by thousands of identical, tiny firms, but many consider as some kind of ideal the results that would follow from such a situation. "Infinitely many tiny firms" is obviously impractical, but any particular industry should have as many firms as "economies of scale" permit. Ideally, too, they should all be of pretty much the same size--one big one and a bunch of tiny ones wouldn't be good.

The number, and size distribution, of firms in an industry determine the industry's market structure. A larger number of producers, and more nearly equal market shares, are considered desirable; concentration is to be reluctantly tolerated only if it seems justified by the economies of large-scale production.[4]

From the "state" view of competition, Delta would probably be required to show Gamma how it effected the cost savings. (Again, antitrust decisions have actually required an innovator to share his discovery with his competitors.) This approach emphasizes the importance of the number of competitors, so legislation based on this theory of competition naturally aims at protecting existing competitors from market forces that might prove detrimental to them. Activities that tend to reduce the number of competitors, and to increase concentration, are disapproved--no matter how they're achieved.

In the process perspective, competition is a type of action that requires no specific number of competitors. According to the adherents of this approach, one cannot look at an industry's market structure (number and size distribution of firms) and determine anything whatsoever about competition from it. One has to examine the manner in which the industry acquired and maintains its present shape. If one

---

[4] A famous antitrust case in which economies took a back seat was the denial of the proposed merger of Brown Shoe with Kinney. Here are the words of Mr. Chief Justice Warren, of the United States Supreme Court, delivering the opinion in 1962: "But we cannot fail to recognize Congress' desire to promote competition through the protection of viable, small, locally owned businesses. Congress appreciated that occasional higher costs and prices might result from the maintenance of fragmented industries and markets. It resolved these competing considerations in favor of decentralization. We must give effect to that decision." Richard A. Posner, Antitrust (St. Paul: West Publishing Co., 1974), p. 395.

producer is dominant, but it's entirely because he has been innovative and adept at offering consumers better deals than others have been able to, the process of competition is strongly at work.

There are many reasons why the "state" perspective has been popular among economists for decades. Apparently a process view was dominant until the 1920s or 1930s, though, and there are indications that it is becoming more popular today.

A "revisionist" view of regulation

If this notion of protecting competition by protecting competitors from competition sounds a little strange to you, you aren't alone. Historians and economists have begun to wonder, in the past few decades, if the main purpose of government regulation of business has _ever_ been to preserve the competitive process by protecting the public from businesses' violations of their rights.

The story has always been that the big businesses that emerged during the late 1800s--the railroads, Standard Oil, and U. S. Steel among them--were "monopolies" that ran roughshod over the public until they were reined in by the formation of the Interstate Commerce Commission (to regulate railroads) in 1887 and the Sherman Antitrust Act in 1890. The Federal Trade Commission Act (1914), the Clayton Antitrust Act (1914, much tougher than Sherman), and other regulatory legislation followed during the so-called "Progressive Era" (roughly 1900-1917).

The first thing that might make us wonder about this story is a contradiction that Armentano (cited above) notes between American economic history and the implications of the price-searcher "monopoly" theory that we've discussed. That theory shows that an "industry" that consists of one monopolist with no competition produces less, and charges a higher price, than an industry in which producers face strong competition.

Well, during the late 1800s, real output in the United States was growing strongly, and prices in general were gently falling. (I don't mean the rate of inflation was diminishing; the "rate of inflation" was negative.) And the industrial sectors in which output was rising most spectacularly, and prices falling much faster than average, were precisely those that were supposedly "monopolized"!

This is going to be a puzzle only to those who believe that the degree of competition is directly proportional to the number of producers in an industry. In fact, though, the late 1800s was a period of intense competition. The increasing concentration in a number of important industries resulted from the competitive innovation and success of business geniuses like John D. Rockefeller (Standard Oil) and Andrew Carnegie (U. S. Steel). Characteristically, as other firms imitated their successful methods, their market shares declined significantly in the early 1900s.

When you're an eager and self-confident youth out to turn the business world upside down, competition is a wonderful opportunity to put your ideas into practice and get rich if you're right (which, of course, you're sure you will be). When you've succeeded and are now a middle-aged owner and Chief Executive Officer of an established business with a good reputation and solid market share, competition can begin to look a little different. Even though you, yourself, used its freedom to achieve success, it now offers the same freedom to innovators who may challenge your position. You can't rely much on your customers' loyalty if some upstart offers them a superior product. From the (relative) top of the mountain, competition now may seem more of a threat than an opportunity. (It's an opportunity to your potential challengers; that's the threat to you.)

Voluntary cartels--agreements among producers of similar goods not to compete with each other--were tried, and they repeatedly failed; members' self-interested cheating and entry into the industry by new non-members proved time and time again that simple, voluntary, agreements to limit competition didn't and couldn't work. There was only one recourse: Big business turned, for help, to the government.

Those of you who may identify, in your minds, big business with laissez-faire capitalism, with their leaders fighting government tooth and nail, may find these "revisionist" views surprising. It is still generally believed that business regulation was staunchly opposed by big business, but was forced on them unwillingly by government to protect the public. But large, established, firms not only did not oppose the government regulation that developed since, say, 1880; they demanded it. Unable to restrict competition among themselves by voluntary cartels, they asked the government to establish what amounts to involuntary cartels, with government legislation and the police force doing what they never could: limit "cheating" and entry by newcomers.

Some of the earliest work on this revisionist interpretation of regulation was historian Gabriel Kolko's Railroads and Regulation 1877-1916 (Princeton: Princeton University Press, 1965), which recounted the railroads' repeated failures to restrict competition among themselves and their avid support for the formation of the Interstate Commerce Commission to regulate rates, standardize services, and limit entry. Historian and economist Murray N. Rothbard [Egalitarianism as a Revolt Against Nature (Washington DC: Libertarian Review Press, 1974: p. 25)] cites a famous industrialist's wish for similar protection:

> A typical view was that of Andrew Carnegie; deeply concerned about competition in the steel industry, which neither the formation of U. S. Steel nor the famous "Gary Dinners" sponsored by that Morgan company could dampen, Carnegie declared in 1908 that "it always comes back to me that government control, and that alone, will properly solve the problem." There is nothing alarming about government regulation per se, announced Carnegie, "capital is perfectly safe in the gas company, although it is under court control. So will all capital be, although under government control..."

Perhaps what happens is that when the eager and creative entrepreneur becomes successful, he finds himself subtly transformed into a manager. In any case, he becomes <u>conservative</u> in the sense of focusing increasingly on conserving or preserving that which he already has. There is, of course, nothing wrong with this <u>per se;</u> it is natural for a person who has accumulated some assets through a lifetime of saving to shift his focus toward less-risky investments. Without a principled devotion to individual rights, however, the attempt to "conserve" one's own position can--all too often--lead one to advocate the violation of others' rights. The conflict between this kind of "conservatism" and support for genuinely free markets and open competition is suggested by the title of a more-general Kolko study of this period (1900-1916) of increasing regulation: <u>The Triumph of Conservatism</u> (Glencoe IL: The Free Press, 1963). Other studies that recount big-business support for regulation include James Weinstein's <u>The Corporate Ideal in the Liberal State 1900-1918</u> (Boston: Beacon Press, 1968) and Arthur A. Ekirch, Jr.'s <u>The Decline of American Liberalism</u> (New York: Antheneum, 1969).

If we interpret "conservative" as seeking to <u>preserve</u> an existing pattern of wealth and power, then there is nothing "conservative" about a free market.

Success in the marketplace requires continual innovation, more clever anticipation of consumers' tastes than one's competitors have achieved, active and lively out-competing of others who may not even be in the industry yet.

> There is nothing "conservative"
> about the free market.

It's no place for a producer who simply wants to be comfortable, and it's no wonder that such a producer is likely to promote legislation that makes it more costly and difficult for others to challenge him. (Established firms are almost always willing to incur some additional costs, as long as the regulation is even more burdensome to their competitors.) Indeed, because regulations and rights-violating restrictions on competitive behavior make the economy much more rigid, protecting established positions from competitive challenge, the term "conservative" is much more appropriate to a system of extensive government regulation of business--like fascism--than to the "free markets" of capitalism. How's <u>that</u> for "revisionist" thinking?

How to protect the competitive process

Protecting "competitors" means protecting them <u>from</u> competition. The whole history of government's effort to protect the forces of competition by protecting specific competitors from those very forces, is therefore a fundamentally mistaken and misconceived task from the word "go."

There are a couple of possibilities for making sense of the government's regulatory and antitrust efforts to promote and protect "competition." First, policymakers may not understand that competition is an active process that requires no more than one actual competitor. This is a distinct possibility, since many economists still accept a "state" view that strongly associates the degree of competition in an industry with the number of its actual producers. A second possibility is that the preservation of the competitive process may not be, and perhaps <u>never was</u>, the true goal of regulation and antitrust. It may have been, instead, a thinly disguised partnership between our country's most successful big businesses and government, a conspiracy against the public to deny them the benefits of the competitive process and to protect the established businesses from that process.

In any case, all that's really necessary to protect the competitive process is the protection of individuals' natural rights to life and property. Any legislation that tacks something onto this, specifically focused on competition, inevitably both violates individuals' rights and restricts the competitive process.

YOU SHOULD REMEMBER...

1)   Monopoly means "single seller," but determining "of what" (the proper product and geographic market definitions) will always be a matter of judgment.

2)   A sufficiently NARROW interpretation of product and geography makes every seller a monopolist; very BROAD definitions can leave no monopolies at all.

3)   Many economists have adopted the unfortunate terminology that any PRICE SEARCHER is a MONOPOLIST.

4)   The degree of a seller's MONOPOLY POWER is inversely related to the attractiveness of the available alternatives.

5)   The LERNER INDEX of monopoly power is (P-MC)/P, or 1/E, with all evaluated at the price and quantity at which MR=MC. It varies between zero (price taker, horizontal demand curve) and one (absolute monopoly, vertical demand curve).

6)   To determine whether there is a "monopoly PROBLEM," we must determine what limits the availability of alternatives.

7)   If alternatives are limited simply be SCARCITY (as in the case of large capital requirements), there's NO PROBLEM; the market is doing its job.

8)   Only if a "monopoly" is protected from competition by RIGHTS-VIOLATING LEGISLATION is there a "monopoly problem."

9)   Legal restrictions can protect established producers from competition that drives prices down and costs up.

10) These restrictions are always advertised as in "the public interest," as if the future of civilization requires that consumers be protected from alternatives to our product.

11) The "capture theory of regulation" states that a government regulating agency often winds up protecting from competition the existing producers in the industry it regulates.

12) A CARTEL is an agreement among sellers (or sometimes buyers) not to compete.

13) Cartels are illegal, but even if they weren't, they would be unlikely to pose a problem.

14) Voluntary cartels are INHERENTLY UNSTABLE. They are difficult to form, promote entry into the industry by new producers, and provide great incentive for members' cheating.

15) In America's most famous price-fixing antitrust cases, the businesses tried BUT WERE NOT SUCCESSFUL at raising and stabilizing prices.

16) Legislation can protect either competition or competitors, but to do both is a contradiction: what it protects competitors from is competition.

17) Revisionist historians have argued that businesses around 1900 demanded government regulation as a government-enforced cartel, to protect themselves from competition.

18) Young, small, entrepreneurial businesses tend to view competition as an OPPORTUNITY; old, large, established businesses may view it as a THREAT.

19) If "conservative" means seeking to preserve existing patterns of wealth and power, there is NOTHING CONSERVATIVE about the free market.

20) Legislation that protects competition is identical to that which protects individual rights to life and property.

Problems

1. For the price-searcher example on p. 164, in Chapter 6, use the Lerner Index to calculate this seller's "monopoly power." (Your answer will be one number, although you should show how you obtained it. Don't forget that the Lerner Index is evaluated only where MR=MC. It's best NOT to use the elasticity formulation.)

2. For the seller described in the numerical example on page 155, use the Lerner Index to calculate this seller's "monopoly power."

3. How would you go about determining whether the seller in problem #1 above is somehow violating the principles of the capitalist system, interfering with the way free markets should work?

4. "This book claims that businesspeople never try to fix prices and restrain competition among themselves." Is this right? If not, what does it claim about this?

5. Is competition an opportunity or a threat? If "it depends," on what? What is the significance of this question, anyway?

6. Suppose that the market demand curve for acmes is a steep downward-sloping line, and that there's only one current producer (the Acme Corporation). But the company fears that if it raises its price very much above its costs, to take advantage of that near-vertical demand curve, new competitors will enter the industry and its sales will drop significantly. Although the current demand for its product is nearly vertical, Acme will act as if the demand for its product looks like what? Why?

7. To compete effectively in the widget business, you would have to spend $2,000,000 on specialized equipment. Is this capital requirement a "barrier to entry" into the widget industry? Should a "free market" have such things?

8. Is there a difference between political and economic meanings of the word "free"? What does the word mean, in each of these senses? Can markets be "free" in the political sense, even if goods aren't "free" in the economic sense?

9. Can entry into an industry be "free" in the political sense, without being "free" in the economic sense? Is entry into the widget industry (Problem 7) "free" if it costs two million dollars?

10. Think about the massive political and economic changes in Eastern Europe and the former Soviet Union. What does the term "conservative" mean in those societies? Is that consistent with what this chapter says about the meaning of "conservative"?

CHAPTER 8

EFFICIENCY, EXCHANGE AND COMPARATIVE ADVANTAGE

THE CONCEPT OF "EFFICIENCY" IN ECONOMICS

Everyone likes efficiency. The hero of the romance novel opens the champagne with a smooth, efficient motion. After the homeowner has fumbled around for three hours, the master plumber solves the problem quickly and efficiently. Modern electrical equipment--from air conditioners to televisions--and modern automobiles are more efficient than old ones.

What do we normally mean by "efficiency"? How about getting the job done with minimum waste, no unnecessary motion, using up fewest resources? I think that's about what people usually mean, and it's also pretty close to the economist's concept of efficiency. If either method A or method B can be used to achieve a particular goal, the efficient method is the one that requires the smaller sacrifice.

When we claim that a new air conditioner is more efficient than one that's fifteen years old, we mean that it provides us with the same cooling with far less electricity. To travel 100 miles the new car uses less gasoline (and creates fewer pollutants) than does the old one. The master plumber gets the same job done, but in many hours less time.

These uses of the term "efficiency" are all right for casual conversation, but they're not sufficiently precise for careful analysis. To get a little closer to the economist's perspective, think about why anyone <u>cares</u> how much electricity a refrigerator uses, or how long it takes to fix a split water pipe.

We care because we have other things to do with our time, things that must be sacrificed while we fiddle with the propane torch and solder. Electricity costs money because it has alternative uses that we must outbid (as do the resources needed to produce it), and paying the bill requires us to work more hours or go without a new exercise machine. Using an air conditioner that makes the electric bill higher, or using more time to fix the pipe, requires us to sacrifice a larger number of other things that we value. The value of the most desirable alternative that we must sacrifice to use the air conditioner or fix the pipe is our <u>cost</u> of taking that action. If we're considering two alternative means of reaching the same goal, the <u>efficient</u> method is the lower-cost one.

A better way of putting it is that it is efficient to choose the lower-cost method of achieving a goal, and inefficient to choose a higher-cost method. This is close enough to the economist's perspective that we're going to take the plunge. We'll back up to some more applications later.

The efficient action

Efficiency means simply that benefit exceeds cost.

Some time ago, I emphasized that benefit and cost always refer to actions, not to things. (When we speak of "the cost of a chair," we always refer to some kind of chair-related action--like manufacturing it, or purchasing it from the furniture store.) It follows, then, that efficiency is also property of <u>actions</u>, not of things.

> EFFICIENCY means "benefit exceeds cost." It applies only to <u>actions</u>.

When we speak of an "efficient air conditioner," we mean that if we are trying to choose between using either it, or a creaky ancient one, our efficient action (our lower-cost alternative) is to use the new one. When you hear the word "efficient" or "efficiency," you should think immediately of <u>action</u>. What <u>action</u> is someone claiming to be efficient or inefficient?

A lower-cost alternative is, automatically, a higher-benefit alternative. Picking the lower-cost way of cooling your apartment means you get the same cool air that you would have had with either choice, but you can afford more <u>other</u> things that you'd like.

Now we can see how the comments about efficiency with which I began this chapter could be a little off base. If your choice is between a new and an old air conditioner, is your efficient action to choose the new? If your only cost is the electricity, sure--pick the one that uses the less electricity. Maybe you've rented an air-conditioned apartment (you pay utilities) and the landlord has offered you either of these two window units. If they're equally quiet and cool equally well, the obvious choice is the one that uses less electricity.

But what if you have to buy the air conditioner, and the new one is $700 while the old one is $50? Your decision is a lot more complicated now, having to weigh the monthly electric-bill saving against the far greater purchase price. It isn't obvious. There are plenty of people who seem to believe, in this age of environmentalism, that the only thing that matters is using less electricity. But then, it's <u>your</u> $650 they're waving away, not theirs. (Even on their own grounds, the problem is more complex. If recycling is good, why isn't keeping an old air conditioner alive? It saves on solid waste disposal and, more importantly, on the resources needed to produce the new air conditioner. Looking only at the electricity consumed in use is not only bad economics, it's bad environmentalism.)

If you have the choice of using either a brand-new or an old car, your gasoline cost is almost sure to be lower if you choose the new car. Most drivers have more than gasoline to consider, however, and their decision sensibly involves far more than the simple cost of gas. If you've got to choose between a cheap ($500) old car (20 miles per gallon) and a nice ($13,000) new car (30 miles per gallon), even if you don't care about differences in comfort, safety, or noise you have a complex problem deciding which is preferable, which is efficient. We'll learn techniques for balancing the gas savings against the higher purchase price later, in Chapter 10, but for now you should realize that it's just too simplistic to assert that "efficiency" is determined solely by gasoline usage. (Again, those environmentalists who rail against old cars seldom consider the solid-waste problems of disposing of them, or the energy and resource costs of manufacturing--and repairing--the new car that would replace it.)

This discussion is quite similar to our observations on cost. Given the definition of efficiency, of course, that's no coincidence. What is the cost of using a new air conditioner? The answer depends on whether you already own it (and can't sell it), or have yet to purchase it. If your "cost of using a new air conditioner" includes its purchase price, it is quite possible that continuing to use that "energy-inefficient" old one is the efficient choice. The lower-cost choice is always the efficient choice. The people who don't think so are usually looking at only part of the costs (like judging automobiles solely on their gas mileage).

An inherently subjective concept

Because it is determined by judgments of cost and benefit, efficiency is a subjective, personal concept. It's something that can be judged only by the individual actor.

Think back to our discussions about the nature of the benefit and cost of a particular action. They're based on how well-off the acting individual anticipates that he would be, in the future, if he chose the considered action or chose its best alternative. If you and I anticipate the future differently, or have attitudes or values that are different in any respect, an action that you interpret as efficient I might well consider inefficient. You'll take the action and I won't, because of our different judgments of its benefit and cost.

An efficient action is one for which the benefit exceeds the cost, judged by the actor at the moment of his decision.

> Efficiency is a judgment of VALUE, made by the actor at the moment of his choice.

Acting efficiently simply consists of picking the highest-valued of the alternatives that are available to you. But it's one of our "Principles of Choice" that individuals always select the highest-valued alternative. Another way of expressing that Principle, therefore, is that individuals always take efficient actions, and never inefficient ones. An efficient action is any simply any action that is actually taken; we never observe inefficient actions, because the actor rejected them and chose something else.

When someone else's action clearly seems inefficient to you, you're almost certainly making one of the mistakes about which you were warned in our discussions of cost and benefit. You're probably judging _his_ action by _your_ values and knowledge. It's mostly to help you to recognize these errors in others' arguments, and to avoid them in your own, that this discussion of efficiency is presented.

Judging the efficiency of another's action

It's a bright Saturday morning in the Fall, and the leaves, knowing the name of the season, are falling. You go out into the front yard and see your neighbor, Sam, engaged in some very strange behavior. He's lying on his front lawn, with his arms at his sides, and he's crawling around picking up leaves in his mouth and dropping them into a plastic lawn bag. "How ridiculously inefficient," you think, heading back in for another cup of coffee with thoughts of how you're going to get your own leaves cleaned up in about five minutes with your new super-turbo three-horsepower leaf blower.

You might want to use a little of what we now know about the concept of efficiency to rethink your snap judgment. What you've really asserted is that the cost of Sam's action is greater than the benefit of Sam's action.

Two powerful arguments work against you.

First (the less powerful): You can't know what _Sam's_ perceived costs and benefits are. You can try to imagine yourself taking that action, and guess at how you would view its costs and benefits, but that doesn't mean that Sam has to view things in the same way.

Second (the more powerful): You can't know his benefit, or his cost, but you _do_ know something about the relationship between them. Your knowledge comes from the simple fact that Sam is taking the action. As silly as it seems to you, he would not have done so unless he had judged its benefit to exceed its cost.

This is a pretty wierd example, and I made it so on purpose to dramatize the point. To judge another's action to be inefficient, you must have some way to determine _his_ cost and benefit. Where do you get this knowledge? All that you can actually infer from observing his action is that _he_ believed it to be efficient.

> The simple fact that an individual
> took an action VOLUNTARILY is
> indisputable evidence that he
> considered it to be EFFICIENT.

If you want to claim that he's wrong, you must have some standard that permits you to judge that he misperceived his own costs and benefits. These costs and benefits are in his own mind. Good luck.

What goal is Sam trying to achieve? You're figuring that he just wants to get his leaves cleaned up. But what if he's combining this task with training for some kind of competition, developing certain muscles, trying to win a $1,000 bet, savoring the smell (and taste) of the grass and leaves, or testing the stain-resistant properties of his new shirt? You aren't trying to do any of these things, but that doesn't mean that he isn't. In fact, a more sensible conclusion--if you know Sam and believe him to be of sound mind and body--is that he's definitely trying to achieve some kind of goal that you don't understand or know about.

Actually, this is the way that most people already think. If our neighbor seems to be doing something strange, we try to understand it by thinking of what we would probably be trying to achieve, if we had found that action to be efficient.

Is it efficient to take your car, or your bicycle, to the grocery store? Consider the alternative actions "driving the car to the grocery store" or "riding the bike to the grocery store." You determine the cost of (say) driving the car, and its benefit. If the cost exceeds the benefit, riding the bike is efficient and driving the car isn't. You must consider, for yourself, what the costs and benefits are. A cost of driving is the advantage of the exercise that you could have had with the bike, for example. If your planned purchases are small, the store isn't too far away, and the streets aren't too dangerous, you may judge riding the bicycle to be efficient and driving the car inefficient. Another individual, who has already worked out for two hours today and is terrified of automobile drivers' attitudes toward bicyclists, may well make the opposite judgment.

Why would a person practice the piano for hours a day, when she can buy a compact disk and effortlessly hear the world's greatest performance? Why does one individual laboriously and dangerously inch his way up the rock face of a mountain, when a hundred yards to his left a Lincoln Town Car full of tourists cruises effortlessly up the toll road to the summit? Why does someone build a barn using only hundred-year-old hand tools, when electric drills and staple guns are cheaply available just down the road at the hardware store?

Clearly these individuals' goals are not simply to hear the music, get to the top, or obtain a completed barn. That may be all that you would be interested in, but your goals (costs and benefits) are inappropriate standards for judging others' behavior.

> The subjective (value) nature of costs and benefits means that we have no standard that permits us to judge the voluntarily chosen action of another to be inefficient.

Indeed, the very fact that he chose it offers proof that he judged its benefit to exceed its cost. If we judge that we wouldn't take such an action, all that we can conclude is that it would be inefficient for us. We can't conclude that it is--therefore--inefficient for him.

*"Efficiency" depends on the
availability of alternatives*

It is common to hear that "automobiles are a terribly inefficient means of transportation," that "recycling is efficient" or that "cardboard hamburger boxes are more efficient than styrofoam." Perhaps. At least to some people, in some situations. Everything that we've said about efficiency, cost, and benefit should make you a little suspicious of blanket assertions like these.

Consider the claim about automobiles. It's 7:30 AM, you're dressed for work in your business suit, ready to head out the door of your suburban home for your office 12 miles away. Whether driving your car is "efficient" or "inefficient" depends on your own costs and benefits. What's the best alternative? Walking five blocks, paying $1.50 to ride a crowded and noisy and dirty bus for forty-five minutes, and having to rely on similar transportation for any unexpected errands during the day? Even if the bus came to your doorstep and were clean and fast, you might prefer to be alone in your car. Some people are hardly ever alone except when they're driving back and forth to work.

If the alternatives confronting you had been different, you might well have judged "driving your own car" to be inefficient. Imagine some things that are likely to increase the cost of driving your own car. The gas tax has just been raised, triple-trailer trucks have just been allowed on the Beltway with their own speed limit of 85 miles per hour, and a clean and fast light rail system has just been completed with a station a block and a half from your house.

> There is no sensible interpretation of
> sweeping claims that, regardless of the
> individual or his circumstances or
> alternatives, "X is more efficient than Y."

Efficiency is determined by costs and benefits, each of which is determined by each individual in a particular context of values and available alternatives. Any concept of efficiency that is divorced from the choice and valuation process of particular individuals should be dismissed; it can only harm our effort to understand economic society.

In our discussion of competition, we found that it was very important exactly what limited the range of available alternatives. If it was simply scarcity and the enforcement of legitimate property rights, competition and the market system worked fine; if some kind of legislation prevented market adjustments (like entry into an industry, or price competition among its producers) by violating individuals' natural rights, then this legislation prevented competition from working.

A similar question arises in our discussion of efficiency. Given the available alternatives, for example, many people in many circumstances will find it efficient to use their private automobiles. But what is it that determines those available alternatives? Why, in short, aren't there some available that many people consider superior to the use of their own cars? Then using the cars would be inefficient, and they wouldn't be driven.

In an ideal free society that defines pure capitalism, in which individual property rights are clearly defined and enforced, there is only one reason that superior alternatives wouldn't be available: entrepreneurs do not believe that they would be able to cover their costs. Remember what that means. A potential builder doesn't believe that customers of, say, a light-rail system will be willing to pay enough for its services to enable him to bid away (from alternative uses) the resources necessary to construct it. Under laissez-faire capitalism, the only way for him to obtain the resources he needs is to buy them from their owners, offering more than their value in their best alternative use. If the entrepreneur doesn't think that individuals will find "riding the trolley and paying its full cost" to be an efficient action, then his own efficient action is to <u>not build it</u>.

The world in which we live is, of course, far from one in which individual property rights are understood and enforced. When legislation alters individuals' costs and benefits by violating individual rights, the kind of actions that people judge to be efficient can deviate dramatically from that which would prevail under a system of strictly voluntary exchange.

Consider, for example, governments' use of tax receipts to pay for the construction and maintenance of highways and expressways for which the automobile driver makes no explicit payment ("user fee"). The reason potential light-rail riders are likely to find driving efficient relative to full-cost trolley-riding is that using the highways has zero monetary cost. (Like everyone else, the commuter is a taxpayer. But his "marginal tax" of driving downtown on the expressway is zero.) This process makes the cost of driving one's automobile far less, and therefore leads many more individuals to decide that it's the efficient thing to do, than in the absence of this government involvement.

There are many similar situations in which governments use their power to tax and spend in ways that take property and wealth from some individuals and use it to pay part or most of the costs of particular actions that other individuals would have to incur in a free market. Take solid waste disposal. (Please.)

A private entrepreneur will open a landfill only if he expects to receive from his customers enough money to more than cover his costs. His costs become, in effect, their costs, and they'll deposit solid waste only if the disposal is worth more to them than the cost of disposing of it. If a government creates and operates the landfill, however, it can cover its costs through taxation and allow anyone to throw junk in at no charge. Now the individual's cost of using the landfill is approximately zero, and the landfill is likely to be filled quickly.

Similar problems abound. Government-financed logging, provision of costly water to Southern California farms at a very low price to the farmers, municipally owned airports. When governments seize some individuals' resources through taxation and use them to make other individuals' costs and benefits different from what they would be under a system of strictly enforced individual rights, resource use no longer reflects people's genuine values. The actions that are chosen (because, given the distortions resulting from government involvement, they are efficient) would not have been chosen (and would not have been efficient) in a legislative system that recognizes and enforces individuals' rights.

It's really a little tricky to say that the problem with government-subsidized activities is that they produce "inefficient" actions. That's because, given the presence of the taxation and subsidization, the actions that individuals choose (filling the landfill, irrigating the desert, driving their cars everywhere) <u>are</u> efficient. Of course some of them would be inefficient, and therefore not taken, if legislation respected and enforced individuals' rights instead of violating them. These actions that are efficient (and therefore taken) only under a legislative system of taxation and subsidization would not be efficient (and therefore wouldn't be taken) under laissez-faire capitalism.

As we found with competition, however, there is no need to drag "efficiency" arguments into determination of proper legislation. It is true, as economists like to point out, that legislation that taxes some activities and subsidizes others promotes actions that would, indeed, be "inefficient" under a legal system that protected individual rights. But the real problem with such legislation is simply that it violates individuals' rights.

THE EFFICIENCY OF EXCHANGE

"Shop 'til you drop" may not describe us all with perfect accuracy, but we all obtain a great many of the goods (a new shirt?) and services (having a new muffler installed?) by <u>shopping</u>. We exchange something that we have and that the seller wants (money), for something that he has but we want (the shirt or muffler-installing services).

A moment's thought will convince you how widespread and important this process is. When you get up in the morning and fumble for a cup of instant coffee, think about the process that placed that jar of coffee in your kitchen. (If you're like me, the very word "think" has little meaning until after a couple of cups.) You exchanged money for it at the store. (You got the money by exchanging your labor services--waitressing?--for it.) The store obtained it by exchanging money with its distributor and truck driver and stockboys and sales clerks (who provide the jar of coffee, and various associated services, in return). By the time this story has stretched back through the ship that transported the coffee beans to the Colombian workers who planted them, there are thousands of individuals involved. And that's just your coffee. How about your cereal, your toothpaste, and your shirt?

Any modern economy functions by an overwhelming number of trades, going on constantly, that are interrelated in a manner too complicated for any one individual to know or understand. The reason the whole system works is that while no individual knows the whole picture, particular individuals know a lot about their own tiny pieces of the action. Furthermore, each of them has the <u>incentive</u> to respond to changes in demand or supply, and the information about changes in others' relative valuations, that are conveyed by prices. (These are the "functions of price" that we discussed in Chapter 4.)

The process of voluntary exchange works, on a scale and with detail that no one individual could possibly grasp, because individuals are free to express their preferences by demanding and supplying. This process generates prices that reflect these preferences, and provides incentive for others to respond.

You engage in the process of exchange to get things that you couldn't make, or that would be too hard to make, for yourself. This common-sense explanation is OK as far as it goes, but to truly understand how the process of exchange works, we have to be more careful and precise in our use of language.

An efficient exchange

An efficient action, as you know, is one for which the benefit exceeds the cost. The only trick to extending this concept to an exchange or trade between two people is that each person has to consider the action "giving up what I've got for what this other guy is offering" to be efficient. We saw that back in the early pages of Chapter 4, where we hunted for a price that one party was willing to pay and the other accept.

We can get down to basics by considering a simple two-person trade. Sam has always been an avid bicyclist, but recently the in-line skate has caught his eye and he'd love to try it. As far as he's concerned, a little piece of his value scale looks like this:

In-line skates

(Bicycle)

with the circle depicting the good that he actually owns. This value scale shows that, if the opportunity were available, it would be efficient for Sam to exchange the bicycle for the skates. The cost of obtaining the skates is the satisfaction he anticipates from his future use of the bicycle, and that's less than the satisfaction that he expects from the skates.

Suppose now that Frank has been trying out a fine, nearly-new, pair of in-line skates and has decided that he doesn't care for them. He wants to go back to bicycling. Frank's value scale looks like this:

Bicycle

(In-line skates)

with the circle, again, indicating which good Frank currently owns. If he had the chance, he'd give up the in-line skates (lower valued) in return for a bicycle (higher valued). The benefit (value) of the bicycle exceeds its cost (the value of the skates), so the exchange would be an efficient action.

If Sam and Frank get together and begin to discuss these two sports, it's likely that they'll discover the possibility of a small trade between them. The exchange looks like this:

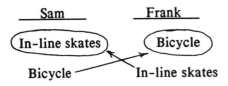

with the circles depicting the new owners of the two goods, and the arrows showing the transfers of ownership. Each of the two individuals moves to a higher point on his value scale, each valuing the good that he <u>obtains</u> in the trade more than the good that he <u>gives up</u> in the trade.

This is a bare-bones example of a mutually beneficial exchange. If Sam is to benefit, he must value the skates more than he values the bicycle. If Frank is to benefit, he must value the bicycle more than he values the skates. It is this pattern of <u>opposite relative valuation</u> that makes the exchange possible. (Consider, as a counterexample, what would happen if both Frank and Sam valued the bicycle more than the skates. The exchange that we've been discussing would benefit Frank, but it would harm Sam, so he wouldn't do it.)

> Each individual involved in an exchange must value the good that he <u>receives</u> more than he values the good that he <u>gives up</u>.

This can't hold for just one of the individuals--it must be true for <u>each</u> (that is, both) of them. It's not enough for Sam to value something that he doesn't have, more than he values something that he does have. That would make the exchange efficient for Sam. But there must be someone else around (like Frank), who owns the good Sam prefers and prefers the good Sam owns. That pattern of valuation makes the exchange efficient for Frank. Since each of them, individually, perceives the trade as efficient (creating value, benefit exceeding cost, moving up on each party's value scale), it will take place. It's a voluntary exchange.

Every voluntary exchange benefits both parties, or it would not take place. (At least each thought it would be beneficial, at the moment of decision. We all revise our estimates of cost and benefit as we learn more, but it's our evaluation at the time that matters.) And since we cannot read others' minds, the only real source of our knowledge about others' values and preferences is our observation of their actions.

When we see someone buying a necktie for $25, we obtain a little glimpse at his values. It sure isn't much, but it's the best we can do.

The perils of judging others' exchanges

Here's a fairly common attitude: "Exchange and trade are OK as long as everyone benefits, but it's pretty obvious that there are some trades in which the value of one of the goods is a lot greater than the value of the one that's exchanged for it. In such a trade, one trader gets all the benefit, and the other trader is harmed."

Maybe that's obvious to you, but if it were obvious to him why would he carry out the trade? About all that's truly obvious here is that the "harmed" party valued what he received more than what he gave up, and you don't think he should have! Everyone acts in the context of his own knowledge, each of us has only limited knowledge, and each of us knows different things.

Perhaps you simply can't believe that he would have made the trade if he had known what you know about the goods' properties. There are, indeed, trades in which it is difficult to believe that each buyer has much knowledge of the alternatives that are available. Tales of shady home-repair outfits charging elderly customers thousands of dollars for services available elsewhere much cheaper spring to mind. If they promised and didn't deliver, that's fraud. But if they simply charged more than you think is fair, the best remedy is probably exactly what's being done: publicity, so that elderly people who face the decision in the future will not consider the exchange beneficial.

The "zero-sum game" or "objective value" fallacy

It's important that you understand that the trade made the buyer "worse off" only by some standard other than the one that he actually used in his decision. In the early stages of the development of economics, there was another error associated with trade: the use of some concept of "objective" value.

Try to imagine that the value of a bicycle, and of a pair of in-line skates, is a strictly physical property of the goods. Pretend that these values have nothing to do with Sam's and Frank's desires, satisfaction, and utility; they are objective properties of the goods, independent of what anyone thinks about them. Maybe these values are determined by the goods' weights, the kind of materials of which they're made, or the number of labor-hours it took to produce each of them. According to this "objective" fallacy, value is not something imputed or attributed to goods by individuals who perceived some benefit to them; it's a physical property of the goods themselves.

If this were, indeed, the proper concept of value, then each trade would be a "zero-sum game." If the bicycle's value is greater than that of the in-line skates, then the exchange would make Frank better off, but it would make Sam worse off by exactly the same amount. Any trade that benefits one party (what he gets has more value than what he gives up) must harm the other party (what he gets is less valuable than what he gives up). The only trade that wouldn't harm either party would be one of equal values--but then neither party would benefit, either.[1]

The brilliant French economist Frederic Bastiat (1801-1850) lampooned this "objective value" concept in a number of delightful satires. In one, Robinson Crusoe and Friday were thrilled to see a canoe pull up, loaded with foods that were unavailable on their island. When the stranger proposed to trade for some of the fruit that was plentiful to Crusoe and Friday, Friday was all for it. But Robinson asked the stranger if the trade would benefit him. When he replied, "Of course!," Robinson reasoned that the trade must, therefore, make himself and Friday worse off, and he sent the fellow paddling.

Once the principle of subjective value was understood, the problem disappeared. Good X can be more valuable than good Y to person A, while good Y is more valuable than good X to person B. That was, indeed, exactly the case of Sam and Frank's trade.

The principle of subjective value helps us to avoid another error. Quick, answer this: When Sam gives up the bike for the skates, and Frank does the reverse, is this evidence that Sam values the bike more than Frank does, and that Frank values the skates more than Sam does?

It's tempting to answer "Yes." But all that we really can know is that Sam values the skates more than Sam values the bike (that's why he's willing to make the trade), while Frank values the bike more than Frank values the skates (that's why he trades). This is all that we need to explain trade and its benefits. We don't have to compare how much Sam values the bike with how much Frank values the bike. It's a good thing, too, because there's no way to do it. <u>Interpersonal utility comparisons are impossible</u>, in this chapter just as in earlier ones.

> Interpersonal utility comparisons are impossible. We have no way to compare the value of a good to one individual with the value of that good to another individual.

It follows that it's a bit of an error to explain that the process of voluntary exchange that characterizes the free-market system "allocates goods to those individuals who value them the most." This terminology suggests that it's possible to compare Sam's value of the skates with Frank's. That's not accurate. The free-market system permits each individual to engage in trades that are efficient, make him better off, have benefit exceeding cost, for which the individual values the sacrificed good less than he values the received good. (As you've probably noticed, these are all ways of expressing the same point.) The free market offers each individual the maximum

---

[1] Aristotle, for one, believed that only the exchange of equal values was a fair trade.

ability to exchange lesser-valued for greater-valued situations. That's about all we can accurately say. It's plenty.

Exchange creates value

Since voluntary exchange makes each party to the trade better off, it can be referred to as a positive-sum game, not zero-sum. Trade creates value, in the sense that each individual gives up a smaller value in return for a larger one. (Remember that this is possible only because value is subjective, attributed to goods by the individuals involved.)

It follows that someone who helps to make trading opportunities available, who makes it easier and cheaper for us to learn of alternatives, makes an important contribution to this value-creating process. These are middlemen or merchants or traders. They may not change the physical nature of the goods in which they deal, but if they make it easier for the rest of us to learn of beneficial opportunities that we might never have discovered otherwise, they create value.

What if you don't already own the good?

The story of Sam and Frank, and the bike and the skates, forms the basis for all of our discussion of exchange, so if you have any problems with it, this is the time to get them straight. That said, it's time to move on to the next step: what if Sam doesn't already have a bicycle to trade?

Let's make the example more general--it's a little tough to imagine Sam manufacturing either a bicycle or set of in-line skates for himself. Let's just make it goods X and Y. Sam doesn't have either of them, but he really wants to obtain an X for himself. The question is, how should he go about it?

This would be a pretty silly question if Sam lived by himself in a cave somewhere--he'd have to make it himself, or go without it. But in a society, there's usually the possibility of trading for what you want. Perhaps Sam can obtain the X by purchasing it from Frank. Frank, it turns out, is willing to exchange an X for a Y. Sam's only problem now is that he doesn't have a Y, and if he's going to be able to trade with Frank, the first thing he'll have to do is build a Y.

Sam's alternatives, then, are to obtain the X simply by building it himself, or to obtain it by building a Y (for which he has no personal use) and exchanging it for an X (which he does want). Which of these two alternatives is efficient, obtaining the desired X for Sam at lower cost?

Figure 8.1 provides a little diagram of the choice that Sam faces. Which path to the X is the efficient one? Direct self-production, or the indirect path that involves first producing Y and then exchanging it for X?

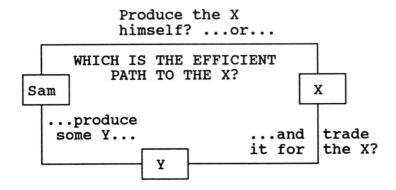

Figure 8.1: Is trade or self-production efficient?

Note that if Sam knows that he can instantly exchange one Y for one X, then producing a Y is just another way to produce an X, and the decision hinges on whether Sam can produce X or Y at lower cost.

At this point, we're going to make an important simplifying assumption that has the effect of wiping out certain subjective preferences for the sake of simplicity. We also did this when we were discussing business costs and production: businesspeople definitely do consider the morality of their actions, but if we assume that the alternative that makes more money is just as moral as the one that makes less, the one that makes more will be preferred. We followed the ceteris paribus method and assumed "equally moral," and figured that if the alternatives really were of different moral standing we could account for that later.

Here, our ceteris paribus "one thing at a time" assumption is that Sam has no preference for one kind of production activity rather than the other. He doesn't care whether he produces X or Y, but only wants to obtain the X in minimum time.

Cost, as you know, is a subjective value, a hypothetical feeling of "well-offness." Because different actions are involved, if Sam enjoyed working on X and hated working on Y it is quite possible for him to decide that "producing X directly, in 1 hour" has a lower (subjective-value) cost than "producing X indirectly, in 30 minutes." Our assumption eliminates that possibility. By temporarily assuming away all considerations except time, we are able to use simple cardinal numbers (like 3 or 4.7) to indicate the size of each individual's cost. We'll drop this assumption a bit later, and see what can happen if Sam actually prefers working on one good or on the other. As usual, the analysis becomes more realistic and interesting, but more complex. But for now, all that either Sam or Frank cares about is "minimum time."

If it takes Sam 1 hour of labor to produce an X himself, and 30 minutes of labor to produce a Y himself, then if he can exchange one Y for one X it is efficient (under our "only time matters" assumption) to produce Y and trade for X. He sacrifices 30 minutes of leisure to obtain the X in this way, while if he'd produced it himself it would have taken him twice as long.

Suppose that Frank's price for an X is now 3Y: he'll still sell Sam the X that Sam wants, but now Sam has to pay him three Y's for it. That means that if Sam wants to obtain the X in trade, he first has to build three Y's, which takes him an hour and a half. But he could have produced the X himself in one hour. If he has no personal preference about which good he works on, he'd clearly be better off building his own X. Obtaining the X by building the 3Y and trading for the X is the higher-cost, inefficient, way to go and Sam won't do it.

It depends on price and comparative cost

An interesting way to explain this conclusion requires us to use a slightly different way of expressing Sam's cost of producing his own X. Instead of measuring his costs by the amount of time the production of the two goods takes (1 hour for X, 30 minutes for Y), consider how many units of good Y Sam could have produced in the time that it takes him to produce one X. This is sometimes called a "comparative cost":

> The COMPARATIVE COST of producing a unit of one good is the number of units of some OTHER good that must be foregone.

Comparative cost accurately indicates genuine costs only under the simplifying assumption described above: The individual has no preference for working on one good or the other. Here, Sam's (comparative) cost of producing one X himself is 2Y: in the one hour it would take him to produce his own X, he could have produced two Y's. We could equally well say that his (comparative) cost of producing one Y is one-half of an X.

If Frank is willing to give Sam one X in return for one Y, Sam's cost of obtaining one X through trade can be expressed simply as one Y. If he were to produce the X himself, though, obtaining the X would cost him 2Y (the number that he could have produced in the time it takes him to produce his own X). Exchange is clearly the lower-cost method for obtaining the X.

When Frank sets the selling price of his X at 3Y, however, the cost to Sam of obtaining one X through trade is now 3Y (the price that Frank's charging). Since Sam can produce the X himself at a cost of 2Y, self-production is a lower-cost method than is trade. He's better off as a do-it-yourself'er.

If Frank were to set a price of 2Y for 1X, it wouldn't matter to Sam which method he used. It would cost him 2Y to produce the X himself, but to get it in trade he'd have to actually produce 2Y and then give them up. Either way, the cost is 2Y. Sam would obtain no benefit from exchanging, no "gains from trade."

Figure 8.2 is a table that shows the cost to Sam of obtaining an X in various ways.

COST TO SAM OF OBTAINING ONE "X"

Self-Production	Exchange		
	Price of X = 1Y	Price of X = 2Y	Price of X = 3Y
2Y	1Y	2Y	3Y

Figure 8.2: The costs of obtaining a good

Whether trade is efficient for Sam depends upon the relationship between the price that he has to pay, and his own cost of producing the good for himself. If the price that he has to pay is lower than his own cost of producing the good himself, then buying it is efficient. (That's when Frank charged 1Y but Sam's own cost of production was 2Y.) If the price is higher than the potential buyer's own cost of producing the good himself, he's better off ignoring the market and playing "do-it-yourself." (That's when Frank charged 3Y, but Sam could produce the X for himself at a cost of 2Y.) The point can be expressed fairly simply:

> A BUYER will find exchange to be efficient only if the price of the good is <u>less than</u> his own cost of producing it.

You can think about how this works with some of the things that you do yourself. When do you pay for someone else's services, and when do you "do it yourself"? Do you change your own car's oil? Do your own laundry? Mow your own lawn? Pull your own wisdom tooth? In each case, we compare the price that we'd have to pay with the cost of producing the service for ourselves. Sometimes, like the tooth, the decision is pretty obvious.

EXCHANGE AND COMPARATIVE ADVANTAGE

If an exchange is going to benefit the buyer, he must be able to obtain the good through trade at a lower cost than that of producing it himself. This works fine if--as in our simplified example--we're just talking about two goods, but it also works if we're talking about the use of money in normal real-world exchanges. If a mechanic says it'll cost you $150 to have him fix your car, and you don't have $150, you compare "fixing the car yourself" to "earning $150." Maybe that spells more than a full 40-hour week at a terrible minimum-wage job, while you think that (with the help of a couple of library books and a new pair of locking pliers) you could probably do the job yourself in about 6 hours. You be the judge. The individual actor always is.

The seller is in exactly the same position. After all, he's the <u>buyer</u> of the other good. Sam buys X and sells Y, Frank buys Y and sells X. Everything that we've said about the buyer (Sam) applies equally well to the seller (Frank), with a few things properly flipped around.

We've found that exchange is beneficial to Sam when the price of an X is less than 2Y (which is his own cost of producing an X). Apparently Frank wants some Y, and to find out the conditions under which exchange will be beneficial to him we have to make some assumption about his cost of producing the Y himself. Perhaps it would take him 1 hour to produce an X, or 1 hour to produce a Y. Frank's cost of obtaining each Y through self-production, then, is simply 1X: in the time it takes him to produce one Y for himself, he could have produced one unit of X.

If trade is going to benefit Frank, he must be able to obtain each Y at a cost of less than one X. Maybe X isn't divisible, though, so it doesn't make sense to talk about 0.87 of an X. Our problem is a little easier to handle if we imagine that at least one of these goods is divisible. Let's make it Y. Then "getting a Y for less than one X" can't really be done (X isn't divisible into fractions), but it's equivalent to "getting more than one Y in return for exactly one X." A ratio of "one Y for 80 percent of an X" should be interpreted as "one-and-a-quarter Y for one X." So a trade that benefits Frank has to provide him with <u>more than one</u> Y for each X that he gives up. If it doesn't, he'll just build the Y's that he wants for himself.

Price must be greater than the seller's
cost, and less than the buyer's cost...

Frank is selling X here, and there's a simple principle, known to every seller, that can help us to understand what's going on:

> A SELLER will find exchange to be efficient only if the price of the good is <u>greater than</u> his own cost of producing it.

A seller benefits by trade only if the price that he receives is greater than his own cost of production. Frank's cost of producing an X is 1Y, so as long as he can get more than one Y in exchange, the trade is efficient for him. The price of 1X, in other words, must be greater than 1Y (perhaps 1.5 Y?) if Frank is to choose exchange over self-production.

But we also determined that if Sam is to find the trade beneficial, the price of an X has to be less than 2Y. The price of an X has to be greater than the seller's cost of production (1Y) if he's to benefit, but it must be less than the buyer's cost of production (2Y) if _he's_ to benefit.

> The only range of prices at which
> voluntary exchange is mutually
> beneficial lies BETWEEN the two
> parties' COSTS OF PRODUCTION of the
> good that is being exchanged.

Exchange is efficient and will take place only if a price is established that is between the two parties' costs of production. Figure 8.3 depicts these price ranges.

Frank would like the price of each X to be as high as possible; after all, he's the guy who's selling the X. But it can't go above 2Y, or Sam won't exchange. (Self-producing the X would be his lower-cost option.) If the price actually were 2Y per X, the price is as far above Frank's cost of production as it can possibly be and still permit exchange to take place. At this price, Sam is indifferent between trading and self-production. In this case, Frank is said to obtain all of the "gains from trade," and Sam none.

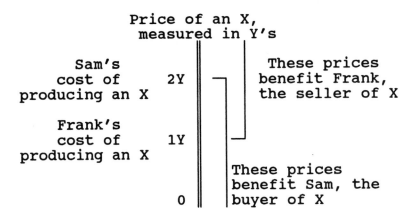

Figure 8.3: The mutually beneficial range of prices

Sam, of course, would like the price of an X to be as low as possible; after all, he's the buyer. But it can't be less than 1Y, or Frank won't exchange. If it actually were 1Y for 1X, Sam would enjoy all of the "gains from trade" and Frank none. When the price is nearly equal to one of the party's cost of production, the other party enjoys nearly all of the "gains from trade." Voluntary exchange, efficient exchange, requires that the parties _share_ the gains. Exactly how they're shared (50-50, 10-90, or whatever) depends on their bargaining abilities. Frank and Sam will each try to convince the other to accept a price closer to 2Y or 1Y per X. You've all probably been to yard or garage sales; you know some of the strategies they'll try. I described a couple of bargaining ploys in Chapter 4.

*Comparative advantage: the basis
for all trade*

Since we've found that exchange is mutually beneficial only at prices that are between the two parties' costs of production, it follows that those two comparative costs have to be different. The seller's cost has to be less than the buyer's cost, because a mutually beneficial price has to be greater than the former and less than the latter. Imagine Frank's cost of producing an X to be not 1Y, but 2Y. That's the same as Sam's. Then a price that benefits Frank would have to be greater than 2Y, and one that benefits Sam would (still) have to be less than 2Y. Sorry, guys: there aren't any prices that meet both of those conditions!

Whenever comparative costs (the cost of producing one good, measured by the number of units of the other good than must be foregone) differ between two individuals, there is the possibility of mutual benefit through exchange. There will be a set of prices (between their two costs) at which each party finds exchange to be efficient. Each prefers to produce a good he doesn't want, and then trade it for the good he does want, rather than simply producing for himself the good that he wants. When someone else can produce it far cheaper than you can, you'll be better off paying him a price that may be well above his cost of production as long as it's below your own cost of producing the good. You both benefit: you get the good that you want cheaper than you could have produced it yourself, and he gets the good that he wants cheaper than he could have produced it for himself.

If the parties have no particular preference for producing one good or the other, then the party with the lower comparative cost of producing a good is said to have a comparative advantage in that good.

Individual A is said to have a comparative
advantage in good X rather than good Y,
relative to individual B, if A's cost of
producing an X rather than a Y is lower than
B's cost of producing an X rather than a Y.

Sorry about that; I would have made it less awkward if I could have figured out how to. But there are two individuals and two goods... well, once you think you understand it, try to find a simpler expression if you wish.

When neither party prefers either task, the "cost of producing an X rather than a Y" is just the individual's "comparative cost." In this case, the party with the lower comparative cost of producing a good has the comparative advantage in that good.

Remember that "comparative cost" measures cost by the number of units of another good that must be foregone. It's based on a ceteris paribus assumption like our "only time matters." If there are relative preferences for the different tasks, the "cost of producing an X rather than a Y" will include some subjective considerations that make a clear conclusion less obvious. Comparative advantage follows from "lower comparative cost" only when our assumption about "no preference" is valid.

In our example, neither Frank nor Sam found producing X or Y more unpleasant or undesirable in any way than producing the other good. Since Frank's comparative cost of producing 1X was 1Y, while Sam's was 2Y, Frank has the lower comparative cost and, therefore, the comparative advantage in good X. Not coincidentally, we found that in mutually beneficial exchanges, Frank would be the producer and seller of X (the good in which he has the comparative advantage). On the other hand, Frank's cost of producing 1Y was 1X, while Sam's was only 1/2 X. It follows that Sam has the comparative advantage in good Y, because his comparative cost of producing Y is considerably lower than Frank's. In our exchange, Sam produced and sold Y, the good in which he had the comparative advantage.

It's no coincidence that when Frank has the comparative advantage in one of the goods, Sam has it in the other. That's a logical property of the way we're measuring costs.

> If one party has a COMPARATIVE ADVANTAGE in one of the goods, the other party has a COMPARATIVE ADVANTAGE in the other good.

Compared to the other person, if you sacrifice more Y to produce an X, then you necessarily would sacrifice less X to produce a Y. The comparative cost of producing one good is the reciprocal of the comparative cost of producing the other: 2Y per X, (1/2)X per Y. If Sam's cost of producing an X had been 3Y, or 87Y, then his cost of producing a Y would have been (1/3)X, or (1/87)X. It also follows (it's just algebra) that if Sam's comparative cost of producing good X (say, 2Y) is greater than Frank's (1Y), then his comparative cost of producing good Y (the reciprocal: (1/2)X) will be less than Frank's (the reciprocal: 1X).

If comparative costs differ, then one party has the comparative advantage (lower comparative cost) in one of the goods, and the other party necessarily has the comparative advantage (lower comparative cost) in the other good. If comparative costs don't differ, as in our hypothetical case of it costing both Sam and Frank 2Y to produce an X, then neither party has a comparative advantage and there is no possibility of mutually beneficial exchange.

> If the two parties' comparative costs
> are identical, then neither has a
> comparative advantage and mutually
> beneficial exchange is impossible.

If it looks as if one party has the comparative advantage in <u>both</u> goods, you're doing something wrong somewhere, because that isn't logically possible. You've probably slipped in some measure of cost other than the comparative costs of the two goods.

Better at both?

In the Sam and Frank example that I used to introduce this concept, it took Sam longer to produce an X than it took Frank--twice as long. It took them equally long (one hour) to produce a Y. It's tempting to conclude that they're equally good at producing Y, but Frank is better than Sam at producing X.

This terminology is misleading, though, and it's best avoided. It suggests that time has the same value to Frank as it does to Sam, so that an hour's sacrifice by one of them is the same as an hour's sacrifice by the other. No such comparison is possible; it requires "interpersonal utility comparison." But it isn't necessary anyway. (It's always satisfying to assert that something that isn't <u>possible</u> isn't <u>necessary</u>!) We found that we didn't have to compare the two individuals' values of the in-line skates, or their values of the bicycle, to explain the benefits of exchange. The same principle applies here: all we need are different <u>comparative</u> costs.

Here's an example in which one individual--Mary--is apparently smarter, or has greater dexterity or concentration, than the other (Mike).

<u>Daily production capabilities</u>

	<u>Blodgets</u>	or	<u>Hooeys</u>
Mary	12	or	8
Mike	6	or	3

This table shows how much of each good each person could produce in one day if that's all he worked on. Either of them could split his day between the two goods; if Mary worked half a day on each, for example, she could produce 6 blodgets <u>and</u> 4 hooeys.

To determine who--if anyone--has a comparative advantage in what, we'd better calculate some comparative costs. That means measuring each individual's cost of producing one unit of one of the goods as the number of units of the other good that could have been produced instead. Here's a table of comparative costs:

	Cost of producing one blodget	Cost of producing one hooey
Mary	8/12 = 2/3 hooey	12/8 = 1.5 blodgets
Mike	3/6 = 1/2 hooey	6/3 = 2 blodgets

It's easy to get confused by the algebra, and the fact that we have to deal both with a fraction and its reciprocal (like the 8/12 and the 12/8). Here's an easy--well, relatively--way to think about it. Which good takes Mary more time to produce? (If production abilities are described in "units per time," as here, it's the good with the smaller number. If abilities are described as "time per unit," as with Frank and Joe, it's the good with the larger number.) If it takes Mary longer to produce a hooey than a blodget, then in the time that she would need to produce one hooey, she could have produced <u>more than one</u> blodget. (If your calculation shows less than one, you probably just have your fraction upside down.) The comparative cost of producing one unit of the "slower" good must be <u>more than one</u> unit of the "faster" good.

Here's a case in which Mary looks better at both, but their comparative costs tell a different story. Mary is the lower-cost producer of hooeys (her cost is 1.5 versus Mike's 2 blodgets). As for Mike, we know automatically that if Mary is the lower-cost producer of hooeys, he <u>must be</u> the lower-cost producer of blodgets. And sure enough, Mike's comparative cost of producing one blodget is 1/2 hooey, while Mary's is 2/3 hooey. Mary has the comparative advantage in hooeys, and Mike has it in blodgets.

This should mean that mutually beneficial exchange is possible. Let's look at hooeys. Mary has the comparative advantage, so she should be the seller, and the price that she receives must exceed her cost of production (1.5 blodgets). But the price that Mike pays can't exceed his cost of producing a hooey himself (2 blodgets), so one hooey must be priced between 1.5 and 2 blodgets for exchange to be mutually beneficial. Let's try 1.75, which in fractions is 7/4, and see what happens. The H and the B stand for "hooey" and "blodget."

	<u>Self-production</u>		<u>Trade at 1.75 B per H</u>	
	Cost of one blodget	Cost of one hooey	Cost of one blodget	Cost of one hooey
Mary	2/3 H		4/7 H	
Mike		2 B		1.75 B

(It's a lot easier to see the relationship between 2/3 and 4/7 by using their decimal equivalents: approximately 0.67 and 0.57.) We could fill in the whole table, if we wish. Some of it already appears above, but we could fill in the "trade" columns. It's rather interesting to see, for example, that if Mary were unwise enough to obtain a hooey through trade, it would cost her 1.75 blodgets when she can produce one herself at a cost of only 1.5 blodgets. But the purpose of the table is to show that at this price (half-way between their costs of production), each party--Mary and Mike--obtains the good in which s/he lacks the comparative advantage at lower cost through trade than through self-production. That's shown by the fact that 4/7 is less than 2/3 (for Mary), and 1.75 is less than 2 (for Mike).

If it seems as if Mary has nothing to gain by exchanging, because she's "better at both" than Mike, you should rethink the meaning of "better." The fact is that Mike's comparative cost of producing a blodget is smaller than hers. That's why she can offer him a price (0.57 hooey) that's above his cost (0.50 hooey), but still below her own (0.67 hooey), and both individuals benefit by such a trade. She gets the blodgets cheaper than she could have produced them herself, and he gets the hooeys cheaper than he could have produced them for himself.

Despite all of the fractions and decimals, and ratios and their reciprocals, the principal point is that:

> When two individuals have different comparative costs of producing two goods, it pays each of them to <u>specialize</u> in the good for which he has the comparative advantage, and to obtain the other good by trade.

Any price that lies between the two parties' comparative costs allows them to share in the "gains from trade." Exchange at such prices is efficient, and would be voluntarily chosen.

We'll go into some of the implications of the principle of comparative advantage shortly. For now, you should get plenty of practice determining it; problems are provided at the end of the chapter. You must be given some information about the two parties' production capabilities of the two goods. That allows you to find each party's comparative cost of producing each of the goods (measured as a number of units of the other good production of which has to be foregone). As long as neither party has a preference for working on the production of either good, the comparative costs tell you not only who has the comparative advantage in what, but the upper and lower limits to the prices at which they share in the gains from trade and therefore find exchange mutually beneficial.

A CLOSER LOOK AT COMPARATIVE ADVANTAGE

Comparative advantage is the foundation of all exchange, whether the individuals involved live in the same house or in different countries. You've thought about the extent to which the way that you live your life depends on exchange-- buying from, and selling to, other individuals (including businesses). Even on days that we don't buy or sell anything, which are fairly rare, we rely on previous sales and purchases.

The number of exchanges in which you're directly involved is relatively limited: the grocery store, the gas station, the landlord, the fast-food place where you sell your labor services. The number and specific type of exchanges in which you're involved indirectly is something no individual can really know. It might include such things as a meager payment to a laborer who helped to dig an irrigation ditch, in some distant country, to grow a crop whose chemical derivative is an ingredient in the chewing gum that you just bought.

Every one of these exchanges exists because each trader--the buyer and the seller--finds the trade to be efficient. It's a lower-cost way to obtain a good that he wants than by producing it himself.

Consider again the example of your broken water pipe. If you've never tried to fix such a thing, the very idea that it's possible might strike you as absurd. Usually all that means is that you attribute a very high cost to "fixing it yourself." You may imagine having to enroll in a plumbing trade school, and so forth; meanwhile, water is spraying all over your kitchen. The very idea is ridiculous, and you "automatically" grab the telephone for the plumber with the biggest ad in the Yellow Pages.

If you think to ask for an estimate, and it's high enough, you might begin to examine alternatives more carefully. Try calling the plumbing department of a local full-service hardware store, and explaining your problem. They might tell you about a patch that's lined with rubber and clamps onto the outside of the pipe with four little screws. It costs about three bucks.

When the plumber says he wants $100, and the only alternatives that you know of are to let it leak (extremely undesirable) or repair it yourself, you make a quick informal comparison of costs. If it would take time, and get you dirty and otherwise cause trouble that you'd be willing to pay at least $100 to avoid, the exchange is efficient. If you have a high-paying job, working three extra hours at that job (to earn the hundred bucks) may be preferable to working five hours, yourself, on the pipe.

But I hate plumbing...
or: dropping that ceteris paribus assumption

It's time to see what happens when we introduce a little complication that we've been assuming away. Suppose you're not indifferent between working at your job as a certified public accountant (CPA) and lying under your sink with dirty water dripping in your face. You'd not only choose to work <u>three</u> hours CPA'ing to avoid five hours of plumbing; you'd rather work <u>six</u> hours as an accountant than five as a plumber.

If the plumber were to charge $200, then, you'd rather work at your own profession long enough to earn this (6 hours) than spend 5 hours (at the sacrifice of $167 accounting income) doing the work yourself. The loss of the extra $33 (one hour's accounting income) is more than worth the difference between doing accounting work and doing plumbing work.

Measured in money, it costs you $200 to have the plumber do the work, and $167 to do it yourself (5 hours' sacrificed accounting earnings, at $33 per hour). That's another way of calculating comparative costs: fixing the pipe indirectly (by accounting, and trade) costs 1.2 times as much (time <u>or</u> money) as fixing it yourself. (That's either 6/5 hours or 200/167 dollars.) If time or money were all that mattered, you'd "do it yourself" because you can provide your own plumbing services cheaper than the plumber can. You'd have the comparative advantage in plumbing, in this situation, and--despite his profession--he wouldn't. You wouldn't trade.

If you have a strong preference for one kind of work over the other, though, the comparative costs (like 1.2 "pipes fixed myself" per "pipe fixed professionally") convey an incomplete and inaccurate picture of comparative advantage.

Remember our initial assumption that Sam and Frank didn't care whether they worked at producing X or Y, they just wanted to get as much as they could in a given period of time, or spend as little time as possible to get a given amount. Now we're dropping that assumption, making the matter simultaneously more complicated and realistic.

In our plumbing example, your strong distaste for plumbing work (compared to accounting) may mean that it is <u>efficient</u> for you to pay $200 for services that you could have produced yourself for $167. The concept of <u>cost</u> is a <u>value</u> or <u>utility</u> concept, the value (to you) of the best alternative that must be sacrificed. Given that you're going to get the pipe fixed in one of these two ways, should you choose "working five hours as a bumbling, inept, dirty, greasy, uncomfortable amateur plumber and sacrificing $167" or "working six hours in clean, quiet comfort in my chosen profession at work that promotes my career, and sacrificing $200"? The decision hinges on how you weigh the $33 monetary saving against the differences in the kinds of work.

Raw, easily calculated (well, relatively) numbers--like those of our previous examples--do not accurately demonstrate comparative advantage when the individuals have a preference for one activity over the other.

> Objective "comparative costs" do NOT
> suffice to demonstrate COMPARATIVE
> ADVANTAGE if either party prefers one
> productive activity over the other.

If you check back with my awkwardly worded definition of comparative advantage, you'll see that I used the phrase "cost of producing an X rather than a Y." That phrase--unlike "comparative cost"--leaves room for subjective elements. While in <u>time</u> a fixed pipe (5 hours) may cost less than 6 hours of accounting, in subjective value it may cost much more.

Using such data (simple "hours it takes," "this many in a day," or "money it costs" measures), we may calculate comparative costs and conclude that Phil has the comparative advantage in changing cars' oil and Sally has it in weeding flower beds. But if Phil hates working on cars and loves flowers, all bets are off. His preferences oppose the story told by the comparative-cost numbers, and we don't know--without further information--which effect is stronger.

If you prefer accounting work to plumbing work, but not strongly enough to justify the extra $33, then you still have the comparative advantage in plumbing because you prefer five hours of slightly more distasteful work (and the sacrifice of $167) to six hours of slightly preferable work (and the sacrifice of $200). If Phil actually prefers working on cars, and you actually prefer plumbing to accounting, these preferences reinforce the tales of the comparative costs and make his comparative advantage in changing oil, and yours in your own plumbing, even greater.

This has a somewhat unfortunate effect on our calculations of comparative advantage. As confusing and difficult as the calculation of comparative costs may seem at first, with fractions like "47/31" and "4/7" flying around, our introduction to the subject made it seem, basically, like just a matter of algebra. As we introduced the concept, if an oil change costs Phil 1.52 flower beds, while an oil change costs Sally 1.63 flower beds, then he's the lower-cost oil-change producer and she's (therefore) the lower-cost flower-bed producer, those are the tasks in which they have their comparative advantages, and that's all there was to it.

Suppose that we're observing Phil and Sally, and trying to determine whether their actions are consistent with the principle of comparative advantage. That means that we must have some way of <u>determining</u> comparative advantage before we actually know how they act. Perhaps we know their comparative costs of 1.52 and 1.63. But that's not enough to determine comparative advantage. And we have no way of knowing whether they are indifferent between these two tasks, or any way of knowing the strength of their relative preferences for them. This additional information that we need, if we're going to determine comparative advantage, is something that we have no way of obtaining: their own relative <u>feelings</u> about the two kinds of activity.

We ran into this same problem when we were discussing efficiency, and it's not surprising. Having a comparative advantage in one activity means that it's efficient to attain other goals by offering that activity in exchange for them, and "efficient" means that benefit exceeds cost. But both benefit and cost are subjective concepts of value, and neither can be perceived or measured by some individual other than the person taking the action.

There's only one way to "determine" either comparative advantage or efficiency: establish a legal system of fully defined and enforced individual rights, and see what happens.

> Because costs are subjective, the only way that ONE individual can determine OTHERS' comparative advantages is to <u>infer</u> them from the observation of their <u>voluntary exchanges</u>.

Individuals will demonstrate their own comparative advantages, based both on how skillful they are at different tasks and their own subjective preferences for different kinds of activity.

How do individuals get comparative advantages?

Phil can change a car's oil at the cost of 1.52 flower-bed weedings, while Sally's comparative cost of an oil change is 1.63 flower beds. If neither has any preference for one activity or the other, these numbers indicate that Phil has the comparative advantage in changing oil, while Sally has it in weeding. If Phil actually <u>likes</u> working on cars, and Sally actually likes digging in the dirt, their subjective preferences make the "comparative advantage" story that is told by the comparative cost numbers even stronger.

Actually, it wouldn't be surprising if there were a correlation between what they like and what they're relatively good at. Phil has probably been fiddling with cars for years, spending many enjoyable hours with them, and has learned a lot. He can now rely on that knowledge, having become relatively skillful at mechanical work. Furthermore, as many a young man has discovered (sometimes to his regret), hours spent learning about cars are hours <u>not</u> spent studying and doing homework. The very acts that produce skill as a mechanic are likely to make one <u>less</u> skillful at other tasks.

As we specialize because of our particular interests and personalities, we accumulate knowledge and experience, and tend to become relatively better at our specialty and relatively worse at other things.

> Each of us tends to develop a
> COMPARATIVE ADVANTAGE in activities
> in which we are interested and enjoy.

In a free society, many of us are able to specialize in the kind of work that we enjoy (and, therefore, are likely to be relatively good at), exchanging that work (through the use of money) for goods and services produced by others who prefer to specialize in (and are relatively good at) producing them.

Even two perfectly ordinary individuals, then, are likely to develop comparative advantages based on slight differences in relative interests. Even if they began with "equal abilities" (however one might determine that), as they make different choices about how to live their lives they learn about different things. Each is likely to find that he benefits by selling the service in which he has become relatively expert, and buying the service in which the other has become the expert.

It's hard to know what those phrases "perfectly ordinary" and "equal abilities" even mean, though, because every individual is different. Different physiques, eyesight, hearing, "intelligence," abilities at various types of reasoning, artistic expression--these "inherited" traits surely have some relationship to the kind of interests we develop. A seven-footer has a certain inherent advantage in basketball, while individuals with extremely sensitive palates may be drawn to cooking or careers as tasters at food companies or wineries.

One of the most delightful characteristics of a free society is that it imposes no barriers to each individual's pursuit of his own comparative advantage.

> A wonderful advantage of a FREE
> society is that each individual is
> able to develop and pursue his own
> "comparative advantage."

An individual who thinks he can more pleasantly "produce" his food and shelter by building complex model trains and selling them to others, is free to give it a try. Modern communication and transportation facilities may make it possible for him to succeed with only a few customers in each state. The widespread pursuit of comparative advantage, with each individual tending to specialize in the productive tasks that he enjoys and is relatively good at, contributes tremendously to our standards of living. We are likely not only to have more goods, but to be happier about how we produce them.

If the individuals live in different countries...

Many economists use the concept of comparative advantage <u>only</u> when they're discussing international trade. The British economist David Ricardo (1772-1823) first clarified the concept by discussing trade in wine and cloth between Portugal and England. It is frequently said, today, that "Japan has a comparative advantage in consumer electronics, while the United States has it in agricultural products."

Consider, though, the foundation on which comparative advantage is based. It's the economic concept of value, applied both to a considered action (benefit) and its best alternative (cost). Value is a sense of well-being or satisfaction that is formulated in the mind of the individual by imagining what his future will be like if he selects the action he's evaluating. Only individuals can do that, and each can only do it for himself.

A "country" can never do such a thing. Neither can a society, a group within society, or even a <u>pair</u> of individuals. The determination of cost and benefit are inherently subjective, individualistic, acts of valuation.

When someone says that "Country X has a comparative advantage in the production of good A" (relative to other countries and other goods), he probably means that many or most of the <u>individuals</u> who live in country X prefer to obtain the other goods that they want by producing and selling A than by producing these other goods for themselves.

Of course it isn't just chance that a lot of people in the mountains of Peru or Colombia prefer to obtain the goods they want by producing something they don't much want--coffee beans--and then selling it to individuals in other countries, and that individuals in Canada prefer to obtain their coffee in this manner rather than try to grow it themselves. Climactic conditions--combinations of rainfall and temperature, for example--differ throughout the world, as do endowments of natural resources. These differences are a big help in explaining why many of the individuals who live in a particular region find it efficient to specialize in the production of goods that are especially well suited to their locations.

Geographic differences may, ultimately, explain a lot more than you might suspect. Countries and regions of the world differ in culture, economic development, and history, too, and at least some of these differences may arise from geographic considerations. It is likely, for example, that changes of season--with reasonably harsh winters--stimulate human endeavor. Philosophical differences that affect societies' respect for individual achievement and their legal protection of private property help to determine the amount of investment and capital. (Who would save, and invest in a factory full of machinery, when a slight shift in the political wind could easily lead the government to seize it?) An individual with few productive alternatives, with capital goods scarce and expensive, will find it efficient to specialize in tasks which require a lot of labor and can be performed with little capital. He's likely to import (buy from individuals who live in other countries) goods that are best made by techniques that use a lot of capital.

So there are reasons that individuals living in particular places, under particular governments and cultures, tend to have comparative advantages in particular activities. It's still inadvisable to say that a particular country has a comparative advantage in something, or even perhaps that tropical regions have a comparative advantage in growing papayas and bananas. Only individuals can determine costs and benefits, so only individuals have comparative advantages.

By the same token, the notion of "international trade" must be used carefully. All that it means is exchange between individuals who live in different countries. Shaking the habit of speaking and thinking as if "nations trade with each other" is an important step toward thinking like an economist.

Free trade and the pursuit of comparative advantage

In the perennial debates between "free trade" and "protectionism," the term "free trade" simply means that a nation's government establishes no legislation that prohibits or hinders voluntary exchange between its citizens and individuals who happen to live in a different country. "Protectionism" is the policy of establishing legislation that deliberately makes it more costly, perhaps illegal, to exchange with individuals who live in other nations.

The case for free trade is simply that it permits individuals to conduct exchanges that they consider to be mutually beneficial; it permits each individual to pursue his own comparative advantage.

> The case for international "free trade" is simply that it permits the pursuit of comparative advantage between individuals who live in different countries.

No special reasoning is required if the individual with whom one perceives a beneficial exchange lives in Taiwan rather than Nebraska or down the block. All of the principles of comparative advantage apply, regardless of where Sam and Frank happen to live.

Some time ago, I stated that capitalism is inherently peaceful. This is an important reason why. It respects the process of voluntary exchange and accords no weight whatsoever to political boundaries and "nationalism." There's an old saying that sounds pretty radical but contains considerable wisdom: "Where goods don't cross borders, armies will."

The case for protectionism generally is based on the possibility that when you shift from buying your neighbor's product to buying the one from Taiwan, your neighbor might lose his job. (The fact that the party in Taiwan is likely to use his dollars to buy some different American good, stimulating its demand and production and employment, is seldom recognized.) But your neighbor would lose his job just as surely if you had simply decided to buy some different American product. Should we pass a law that requires you to buy the same amount from him, year after year, so that he will never have to switch jobs or learn a new trade? This question will be addressed briefly in the next chapter. For now, it's enough to note that the fact that the individuals who are involved live in different countries plays no fundamental role in the arguments.

> The real case for "free trade" is that it respects the rights of individuals. The case against "protectionism" is that it violates individual rights.

Although protectionists often claim that the workers "have a right to their jobs" while domestic consumers have "no right to foreign imports," this has things precisely backwards. Individuals do have the right of voluntary, mutually beneficial, exchange wherever they live (even in different countries), and no seller of anything (including productive services like labor) can claim a "right" to have someone buy them (whether or not that someone finds it beneficial).

But what about "fair trade"?

A confusing--at least to me--issue arises when we drop our implicit assumption that both traders live in societies in which individual rights are defined and enforced. Suppose that it costs $3.50 to grow a dozen mangoes on island B and only $3.00 to grow them on island A. Island B's government, wishing for some reason to stimulate its mango industry, taxes the island's citizens and uses the tax revenue to pay $1.50 of the mango-growers' costs. These growers understandably act as if their costs were only $2, eagerly exporting them to island A and finding eager buyers at $2.50.

Who's got the comparative advantage here? If individual rights were enforced on each island, A would have the advantage in mangoes and would export them to B. Since B's government is violating its citizens' rights in a particular way, it appears as if B has the advantage (though I would say that A still really does), and mangoes flow from B to A. Island A's mango growers go out of business, though other businesses on the island thrive because of the increased demand from island B and from A's citizens who have more to spend on goods other than mangoes.

Now, what should be the policy of the government of island A? A policy of non-interference is often identified as "free trade, but not fair trade." Is it free? Is it unfair? The workers will argue that their "right to a job" is violated. That argument is not valid. But should A's mango consumers be permitted, under a consistent stand on individual rights, essentially to trade in stolen goods? The government of island B is stealing from its own citizens, and some of the loot is being passed along to residents of island A in the form of cheap mangoes.

I'm afraid that matters of philosophy and political theory are involved that are--as yet--beyond me. Would a properly conceived government insist on free trade and individual rights within its national boundaries, and butt out of other countries' internal politics? (That would allow citizens to buy cheap goods from abroad, even if they were produced in slave labor camps.) Or would it refuse to allow its citizens to benefit from oppression abroad, on the grounds that the trade would also benefit the oppressors? (This may require a complex system of tariffs on imported goods, based on an impossible calculation of what the goods might have cost if free markets had obtained in the producing countries.)

My own inclination is toward the former. I would encourage humanitarian groups to widely publicize oppressive conditions abroad, encouraging voluntary boycotts. To those who know the goods' origin and are sensitive to it, the subjective costs of using these inexpensive imports are likely to rise above the subjective costs of the higher-priced domestic alternatives. For our government to become involved-- and therefore to involve us citizens--in the internal politics of other countries in this way is probably unwise. My tentative conclusion is subject to change as I learn more or think better about the problem. Whether (and how strongly) we consider such matters in our purchase decisions is the business of each of us. It should not be forced on us by our government.

YOU SHOULD REMEMBER...

1. EFFICIENCY means simply that benefit exceeds cost.

2. Every VOLUNTARY action is efficient.

3. Exchange will be efficient if, and only if, each party values what he receives more than he values what he gives up.

4. Voluntary exchange creates value; it is a "positive-sum game."

5. It is NOT CORRECT to assert that, in a voluntary exchange, one individual values one of the goods more than the other individual values that good. Such "interpersonal utility comparisons" are impossible.

6. The COMPARATIVE COST of producing one good is the number of units of ANOTHER good the production of which must be foregone.

7. If the parties are indifferent between producing one good or the other, the party with the lower comparative cost has the COMPARATIVE ADVANTAGE.

8. Mutually beneficial exchange is possible at any PRICE that is between these two producers' COMPARATIVE COSTS.

9. The price must be GREATER than the SELLER'S, and LESS than the BUYER'S, own cost of production.

10. If their costs of production (comparative costs) are identical, there is no possibility of mutually beneficial exchange.

11. If one or both of the parties is NOT INDIFFERENT between the tasks, COMPARATIVE ADVANTAGE cannot be determined from comparative cost information alone.

12. Subjective preferences may REINFORCE or WEAKEN the "comparative advantage" story told by comparative costs.

13. The only real way for one individual (even an economist!) to determine another's "comparative advantage" is to establish a free society, and see what happens.

14. Each of us largely creates his own "comparative advantage" by his choices and interests.

15. One of the greatest advantages of FREEDOM is that each of us is able to pursue his own "comparative advantage."

16. The possibility that traders may live in different countries alters NONE of the principles of comparative advantage and mutually beneficial exchange.

17. The case for "free trade" is that it respects individuals' rights by permitting voluntary exchange among individuals who live in different countries.

18. One reason that capitalism is inherently peaceful is that it permits trade with absolutely no attention to national boundaries.

19. "Protectionism" does not protect, but rather violates, individuals' rights to mutually beneficial, voluntary, exchange.

20. Should a free government permit open trade with citizens of a nation whose own government systematically violates their rights? My answer is a tentative "yes"; what's yours?

Problems

1. Henry can build five birdhouses in a day, while Henrietta can build only four. If Henry spent his time, instead, on building mailboxes, he could build eight. In one day, Henrietta could build only five mailboxes. Neither prefers either task.

   a) What is Henry's cost of building a birdhouse (in mailboxes foregone)? [Don't get your fractions flipped over! See my advice following the table of Mary and Mike's costs of blodgets and hooeys.]

   b) What is Henrietta's cost of building a birdhouse (in mailboxes foregone)?

   c) Who has the lower comparative cost of producing birdhouses? Who has the lower comparative cost of producing mailboxes?

2. Fred can make 100 widgets in a day if he does nothing but work on widgets, or 110 wodgets if he does nothing but them. Joe can make 100 widgets in a day too, or 105 wodgets. Neither of them has any preference for one task or the other. Which of them has the lower comparative cost of producing wodgets? How do you know?

3. Harper can install a row of roof shingles in 20 minutes or build three square feet of a new deck in 30 minutes. It takes her friend Sandy 30 minutes to install a row of shingles or 45 minutes to build three square feet of deck. Neither woman has a particular preference for either task. They just want to get the roof reshingled and the deck finished before it rains.

[Warning: (d) and (e) take some algebra. Don't let yourself get bogged down on them and take all of your time. They do illustrate an economic point, but it isn't worth hours of working with algebra.]

   a) What is the cost to Harper (in rows of shingles foregone) of constructing three square feet of deck? [Hint: which can she do faster? That should help you decide whether your answer should be less than one row, or greater than one row.]

   b) What is Sandy's cost of the same action, measured in the same way?

   c) It is apparent that Harper is stronger or more clever or has more dexterity or confidence or experience at each task than Sandy. Does Harper have a comparative advantage in one of the tasks? If so, which one?

d) They're friends, and they'll both work until both jobs are finished. (If Harper finishes one of the jobs, she'll work with Sandy on the other one until it, too, is done.) The deck they want to build is 60 square feet, and they need to install 10 rows of roof shingles. If Harper begins on the deck and Sandy on the roof, how much time will they work?

HINT: One of them will finish the job at which she began (how much time did that take?), then join the other (who hasn't finished the task at which she began). How much of the second task remains for them to work on together, and how long will it take them--working together--to finish it? [This problem takes a bit of algebra.]

e) How much time will they work if Sandy begins on the deck and Harper on the roof?

f) Do your answers to (d) and (e) seem consistent with your answer to (c)? Comment.

4. Sam and Sally each has a garden and a lawn. Each wants his/her garden to be weeded, and her/his lawn to be mowed. [Note that, please! At the end of their work, Sam wants his lawn to be mowed and his garden to be weeded. Sally wants the same for her own property.] Sam takes 2 hours to weed and 1 hour to mow, while Sally takes 3 hours to weed and 2 hours to mow. Neither of them has any greater dislike for either task, and each simply wants to get the goal accomplished in minimum time.

a) What is Sam's cost of mowing one lawn himself, measured in the number of gardens that he could have weeded in the same time?

b) What is Sally's cost of mowing one lawn herself, measured in the number of gardens that she could have weeded in the same time?

c) Which of the two of them, when we measure costs in this way, is the lower-cost lawn-mower?

d) Who, of the two of them, is the efficient (lower comparative-cost) garden-weeder?

e) Who has the comparative advantage in weeding, and who in mowing?

f) Can you tell, simply from what's stated in the problem and what we've already done, whether mutually beneficial exchange is possible between Sally and Sam? If so, is it?

g) How much time would each of them spend, if each did both of his/her jobs alone?

h) Suppose they agree that Sally will weed half of Sam's garden in return for Sam's mowing Sally's whole lawn.

    1) How much time will Sam spend mowing? Weeding? Total? [Hint: the "weeding" answer is 1 hour.]

    2) How much time will Sally spend weeding? Mowing? Total?

    3) Who gets the "gains from trade"? Can you explain why?

i) Suppose they agree that Sally will weed 2/3 of Sam's garden in return for Sam's mowing Sally's whole lawn.

    1) How much time will Sam spend mowing? Weeding? Total?

    2) How much time will Sally spend weeding? Mowing? Total?

    3) Who gets the "gains from trade"? Can you explain why?

j) What can you conclude about the "price" that Sally can pay to Sam in order to get him to mow her lawn, if the exchange of services is to benefit both of them? Could you have determined this without going through the time calculations in (h) and (i)?

5. A careful calculation of comparative costs, based on the two individuals' amounts of time, shows that Shirley has a comparative advantage in sewing drapes while Charlie has a comparative advantage in changing cars' oil. Yet the two make a mutually beneficial trade, fully voluntary, in which Charlie sews Shirley's drapes in return for Shirley's changing his oil.

a) How is this possible? What's going on?

b)   Who really has the comparative advantage in each task?

6.   It takes Ethan 80 minutes to wax a floor and 40 minutes to wash dishes. Nancy can wax the floor in 60 minutes and wash the dishes in 20 minutes. If neither prefers either task, and each wants both tasks completed with minimum sacrifice of his own time, find a mutually agreeable "price," describe what happens, and demonstrate that each of them saves time over "working alone."

7.   What would happen in Problem #6 if it were to take Nancy, instead, 30 minutes to wash the dishes? Try a couple of "prices" to demonstrate your answer.

8.   A well-meaning friend looks at your Problem #6 and notes that Nancy is faster at each of the two tasks.

a)   "It's obvious that her comparative costs of doing each of the two tasks are lower than his," he helpfully observes. Evaluate his assistance.

b)   "It's perfectly clear that she has the comparative advantage in both of the tasks," he helpfully continues. Evaluate.

c)   Based on this example, does it look as if you, or your friend, has the comparative advantage in explaining economics?

9.   You probably have a particular talent at which you believe you're relatively good. (That's relative to most other people and other activities.) Maybe it's horseback riding, reading news on a radio station, or handling special effects for stage productions. How did you get that "comparative advantage"?

10.   When "the United States runs a trade deficit," that means (roughly) that the dollar value of consumer goods that its residents buy from people who live in other countries (say, $10 billion) exceeds the dollar value of the consumer goods that people who live in the US sell to the residents of other countries (say, $7 billion).

a)   What happens to the difference (here, the $3 billion)? [Hint: What happens if you sell $100 worth of labor services, but only spend $80?]

b)   Suppose the folks who are selling us the consumer goods decide to use that $3 billion to buy real estate, factories, and office buildings from individuals who live in the US. Would these appear to be voluntary, mutually beneficial exchanges?

c)   Your neighbor tells you that he's planning to sell his land or corporate stock to someone who lives in a foreign country, so that he can afford a new wall-sized television and power boat. You don't think this is a good idea.

    (i)   What is a <u>legitimate</u> action that you can take (consistent with the principles of capitalism) to try to stop it?

    (ii)   What is an <u>illegitimate</u> action (violating the principles of voluntary exchange) that might stop your neighbor's planned exchange?

CHAPTER 9

INCOME—WHO GETS HOW MUCH, AND WHY

AN INTRODUCTION TO THE DETERMINATION
OF INCOME

How much money do you make, or your parents, or your professor? How about the other people who live in your neighborhood? Donald Trump or Axl Rose? Is it fair? Do these people deserve more, considering how hard they work, or are they overpaid for what they do?

It's curious that so many people who think that economics is dry and boring suddenly become intently interested, emotional, agitated, sometimes even furious when the matter of their incomes is raised. No wonder. A person's income has a big effect on how he can live. Maybe "the best things in life are free," but a lot of runners-up aren't: safe and comfortable shelter, medical care, healthy food, instruction by professional teachers. Then there are things like stereo systems and bookcases that, while they aren't required for artistic and cultural enrichment, make it a lot easier and convenient.

Perhaps the importance of income is overemphasized. You may have personal experience with a parent or spouse whose pursuit of monetary income conflicted with other important aspects of family life. If you don't, you probably know a little about it anyway because plenty of TV shows are built on this plot. The hard-driving business executive has no time for his family but gives them any material thing they want...you can fill in the rest. He (she) almost always is firmly convinced that this is the best thing that he can do for them.

There are individuals who identify monetary income with "self worth" or "self esteem," and even judge others according to the apparent size of their incomes. (It's pretty hard to determine this, so easily observed proxies like the kind of car they drive, or the size and location of their house, are used instead.) This phenomenon may be especially prevalent among "yuppies"--young urban professionals--and is an attitude that's widely identified with the decade of the 1980s.[1]

Identifying the "worth" of an individual human being--whether it's you or someone else--with the size of his monetary income is a tragic mistake. One way to guard against it is to think about someone who makes a huge amount of money, but who you are convinced is an absolute creep. (In my case, certain rock stars with annual incomes upwards of $30 million come to mind. Feel free to think of some

---

[1] The contention that the 1980s was one of narrowly selfish "me-ism" has been disputed by Richard B. McKenzie ("Decade of Greed? Far From It," Wall Street Journal, July 24, 1991: p. A10), who based his discussion on rising charitable contributions.

antidote for this "money equals value as an individual" poison.) Don't make the opposite mistake, though: attributes that we normally consider virtuous, like honesty and respect for others, are certainly no more common among the poor than among the wealthy. A more solid way to guard against misinterpretation of what income means is to understand what it is, where it comes from, and why it's as big (or small) as it is.

The sale of your productive services

An individual earns income by selling his productive services. People who don't have many services to offer, or who have a lot but find that others don't value them, or who have them but don't want to sell them, have low incomes. People who have services for sale on which others place a high value earn high incomes. That is-- just about--all there is to it. (Ah, the dreaded "just about" that signals pages of further analysis!)

What about morality, ethics, hard work, honesty, courtesy, respect for other human beings, being nice to stray cats, being a loving spouse, and going to your kids' school play? How are these characteristics, normally considered desirable and virtuous, related to "selling productive services that others value highly"? Many "self-help" writers (Napoleon Hill, whose Think and Grow Rich was mentioned in a Chapter 1 problem, is one of many) agree that there <u>are</u> positive correlations: individuals who work hard, are scrupulously honest and ethical in their business life, and treat others (customers and associates as well as family and stray cats) with respect <u>do</u> tend to earn higher incomes than they would have without these traits. (There's <u>ceteris paribus</u> again.)[2]

But don't forget:

> Income is earned from the sale of productive services, and depends on the VALUE that other individuals attribute to those services.

Ultimately, any linkage between hard work and income, or courtesy and income, or education and income, must function by affecting the value that others attribute to the services you offer for sale.

If you spend years (and a fortune in explicit monetary outlays) learning neurosurgery, but decide instead to offer for sale your services as a basket-weaver, nobody is going to pay you for the neurosurgery services that you aren't offering. While you may think you work "harder" weaving baskets than you would have in neurosurgery (the kinds of work are so different that it's not clear what "working

---

[2] Making this claim in class sometimes reminds me how emotional the concept of income is. Occasionally someone takes great personal offense, believing that because he has a low income I am accusing him of moral turpitude. Is that a correct interpretation of the text? When emotions rule, logic takes a hike.

harder" means), and you make more than a neighboring basket-weaver who doesn't work as hard, strenuous effort and long hours almost surely won't produce what you could have earned as a surgeon.

If you're interested in thinking more about the specific causes of incomes, there's almost no limit. As a salesperson, should you be courteous to potential customers? Well, sure; customers prefer to deal with a pleasant salesperson. But to some extent courtesy takes time away from other productive tasks. Listening to the life story of someone who's a poor sales prospect probably isn't a good idea. Where's the balance? Businesspeople shun colleagues they don't believe are trustworthy, but perhaps your return from a shady real-estate deal or the breaking of a promise on a recording contract is so great that you're willing to sacrifice the possibility of ever dealing with reputable people again.

Here's the point again: an individual earns his income by selling productive services to others, and the amount they pay depends on their perception of the value of the services. Once you realize this, and think a bit about how it's related to morality and respect, it's a lot easier to resist the temptation to associate monetary income with "worth as an individual." The two aren't completely unrelated, but the connection is complex enough that you can't come anywhere near properly inferring one from the other.

The three faces of income (or maybe four)

Since the earliest days of the science of economics (which most economists date from Adam Smith's The Wealth of Nations in 1776), economists have identified three or four sources of income, depending on the kind of productive service that you're selling.

First and foremost, to most of us, is our wage income. We sell our labor services, and earn a wage. (The differences between wages and salary can be interesting--who's paid by the hour or by the piece, and who's paid by the month-- but in general it's all just called "wage income.") Our wage income is determined by multiplying our hourly wage rate (w) by the number of hours that we work (L); if you worked 31.5 hours last week at $5.75 per hour, your wage income is $181.13 for that week.

Second, as you begin to save, and invest your savings in a savings account or stocks and bonds or mutual funds, you begin to earn interest income from the sale of the services of your financial capital. Of course nobody expects the average college undergraduate to be a heavy saver; your earnings are low because so much of your effort is directed at your education, and your expenses are high for the same reason. Believe it or not, this changes eventually, and as you begin to earn more than you spend on consumption you begin to earn interest income. It's the product of the interest rate and the number of dollars you have invested. If you put $1,500 in a savings account that earns 5.5 percent per year interest, your interest income this year will be $82.50. It may not sound like much, but the amazing discovery that he could earn income without laboring for it sounded so good to the young John D. Rockefeller (who, from a boyhood of rural poverty became the founder of Standard Oil, now called Exxon) that he embarked on a career as a great capitalist.

Third, you may find it desirable to own nonfinancial capital of one form or another, but to sell its services to others. Your income from this source is called <u>rent</u>. This kind of activity doesn't appeal to everyone, but according to books with titles like "How I Made a Million Dollars in Real Estate," many people have found it a means to wealth. It's sometimes possible to buy a duplex or small apartment building with very little down payment, relying on the rental receipts to cover your own loan payments. In any case, whatever's left can be interpreted as the product of a rental rate per unit and the number of units rented out. If your apartment building has five apartments, and each rents for $400 per month but normally has expenses (repairs, utilities that you provide) of $225 per month, then your rental income would be 5 x $175, or $875 per month.

The fourth source of income is more controversial: it's economic <u>profit</u>. It arises from a new discovery, from entrepreneurship, and it can't be broken down into the product of a "price per unit" and a "number of units sold." If you discover that you can buy an exercise machine from one individual for $300 and sell it to another for $400, you've made $100. Now let's see...how many units of "entrepreneurship" did you sell, and at what price? Economic profit may be considered a source of income, arising from entrepreneurship, but it's significantly different from wage, interest, and rental income. We'll be discussing it in Chapter 11.

We can write out a little equation that illustrates these various sources of income:

$$I = (w \times L) + (i \times K) + (rr \times N) + profit$$

where w, i, and rr are the <u>prices</u> at which each unit of labor service, the service of a dollar of financial capital, and the service of a unit of nonfinancial capital, are sold ("rr" stands for "rental rate"). L, K, and N are the quantities of labor service, dollars of financial capital services, and number of units of nonfinancial capital services that are sold.

Each of the first three terms of this equation is the product of a <u>price</u> and a <u>quantity</u>. How many units did you sell, and how much did you get for each of them?

Prices and quantities, prices and quantities. Haven't we been discussing these since day one? We've been using supply and demand to analyze the market-clearing levels of price and quantity, to discuss what happens if price is above or below equilibrium, and to analyze the effects of changes in demands or supplies of other goods, the effects of changes in cost, and so forth.

This approach is exactly what we need for an economic analysis of income. The income that each person earns from each source is determined by supply and demand, which--in turn--determine the quantity and price of each service that he sells. I know that doesn't sound quite as exciting as the emotional discussions of income or the lack of it, but a logical, thoughtful analysis is just what we need if we're truly going to <u>understand</u> why some people are poor and some aren't, and what's likely to put us in one of these groups rather than the other.

The "distribution" of income

Before we get specifically into a discussion of the supply of and the demand for each of the three types of productive service (and a discussion of entrepreneurship and economic profit), there's a matter that we ought to address because it gets a lot of publicity. That's the pattern of "income distribution" in our country.

Suppose we break the country's families into quintiles: the lowest-income 20 percent of the families, the next-to-lowest 20 percent, and so forth, until we finally reach the 20 percent of the families who had the highest income. If there were 80 million families, for example, we would identify the 16 million poorest, the 16 million richest, the 16 million next-to-poorest and next-to-richest, and the 16 million in the middle. Now we examine the actual incomes of the families in each of these quintiles (fifths). Although the poorest quintile contains 20 percent of the families (that's why it's called a quintile), those families may--all together--only earn 5 percent of the total income earned in the nation. The sixteen million highest-income families may earn 40 percent, with the intermediate quintiles earning decreasing fractions of national income as we move from the richest to the poorest.[3]

The publicity surrounding these data is usually something to the effect that "How terrible it is that income is so unequal in this country!" or "The rich take too much and don't leave a fair share for the poor." If you haven't seen commentary like this, keep an eye out for it; I guarantee that you will.

Its hidden implication is that the goods that individuals produce, the incomes that they earn, are really the property of "the nation," which then bears the responsibility of doling it out ("distributing" it) to individuals on some "fair" basis. Ayn Rand [Capitalism: The Unknown Ideal, p. 4], who is sharply critical of this attitude, calls it "the tribal premise": that individuals have no rights, even to their own lives, and that everything (individuals' lives and incomes included) belongs to "society" or "the nation." Watch for it whenever you hear phrases like "society's resources" or "the national income."

> The "tribal premise" is the incorrect belief that everything, including individuals' lives, belongs to SOCIETY, the "nation," or the "tribe."

It's unfortunate that some people are poor, and some people make far more money than any reasonable person could use sensibly. These are commonly held value judgments, and I agree with each. But before we decide that there's something wrong

---

[3] Bruce Bartlett, "A Class Structure That Won't Stay Put," Wall Street Journal November 20, 1991, p. A16: "The 1990 Census data show that the lowest quintile of families received 4.6% of America's aggregate money income, while the highest quintile received 44.3%. These numbers change only very slightly from year to year." This aggregate stability, Bartlett goes on to explain, hides the fact that many individuals move from one quintile to another.

with "the distribution of income," we have to think about the process that produced it. Many of those who use the phrase "distribution of income" would like you to believe that all income properly belongs to "the nation," and the only reason that some people are rich is that they grabbed more of it than did others. Neither of these propositions, of course, is true.

Voluntary exchange determines incomes

In a free-market capitalistic society, there is a specific process that produces individuals' incomes. If you wish to find fault with the pattern of incomes (an end-state), you must identify a problem with the process. That process is simply <u>voluntary exchange</u>.

You sell productive services, and someone else buys them; the price is one at which you both benefit. It will not be as high as you (the seller) would prefer, nor as low as the buyer (your employer, borrower, or tenant) would prefer, but it's a wage or interest rate or rental fee at which you each perceive benefit.

It seems to appeal to some kind of emotion for people to believe that their employer pays them whatever he feels like, and if it's not as much as they wish then it's just because he's greedy and unfair. But it should make sense (we'll actually investigate the economics of it shortly) that an employer can't pay you any <u>more</u> than the value actually created by your services; if he does, then he's simply engaging in charity, gradually giving away to you the capital invested in the business by its owners. On the other hand, he can't pay you less than what you perceive as the value of your next-best alternative (probably working elsewhere), or he wouldn't be able to keep you.

When you buy a jar of instant coffee, you contribute to the incomes of thousands of individuals of whom you have no knowledge at all. Some of them, you probably wouldn't personally like, and you might regret contributing a penny or two to their incomes. Others are fine family breadwinners. But you have no way of even knowing who they are, where they live, what they do, and which quintile of the "income distribution" they're in. All you know is that you value the coffee more than the best alternative use of $3.49. It's your expenditure that makes the supermarket willing to order more, the supplier to continue to employ his delivery person, and so forth.

Simple decisions like yours ultimately determine the pattern of incomes in a free society. If you decide to buy a mountain bike instead of a drop-handlebar road-racing style bicycle, your decision adds to the income of people with skills specific to mountain bikes, doesn't much affect bicycle workers who can work on either type, and makes a bit poorer the workers with skills that apply only to road-racing bikes. You didn't <u>intend</u> for these folks' incomes to be affected, because they're probably all nice people with families to support, but some of them produce a good that you value and the others don't.

How does a popular rock star or actor make so much money? The latest fad rock group, talk-show host, television or movie actor, probably makes $50 to $100 million annually. Incomes like those are nothing that you <u>intend</u>, or perhaps even <u>like;</u> it just seems like too much. So how'd it happen? Well, the recording contract may call for the artist to receive a dime for each single sold, or fifty cents for each cassette or compact disk. You buy a cassette because you like the music and it's worth more than $7.95 to you, and you neither know nor care that the artist's income just went up by half a buck. When millions of other music fans feel the same way and take the same action, there's the artist's $20 million a year income.

Is there anything wrong with the process? The talent is the artist's; if she sets a reserve price of fifty cents per album, that would seem to be her right. You surely have the right and freedom to decide whether or not to buy it. So does each of the other music fans. None of you, individually, <u>intends</u> or deliberately tries to cause the artist's income to be that high, but among all of you it's your voluntary action that causes it.

On a smaller scale, the same process determines the relationship between how much you and your neighbors like to shop at the nearby discount store, and the salary of its manager.

The income earned by each individual in a free society is the result of an exceedingly complex set of decisions by unknown thousands of other individuals. As consumers, they decide whether or not to buy products that your efforts directly or indirectly produce; as producers themselves, they decide whether to help to produce products that compete with yours (which tends to reduce your income), or to produce goods that may require your product as an input (which tends to increase your income).

No one individual can ever hope to know the ever-changing details of this process. That's why I always wonder at the people who seem so ready to conclude that there's something <u>wrong</u> with the income distribution determined on a free market. Where do they get their standard of comparison? Everyone <u>would</u> earn equal incomes if every individual were equally adept at creating value for other individuals. Since they aren't, and the process of voluntary exchange pays people according to the value they create, unequal incomes are inevitable.

Watch out for writers who treat "unequal" and "inequitable" as if they were interchangeable. They aren't. "Unequal" doesn't mean "unfair" or "inequitable." Indeed, if individuals create different values, a process that forced equal rewards would have to violate individual rights, and would therefore be unfair and inequitable.

To assert that the market system does something <u>wrong</u> in its determination of the pattern of incomes implies that there is something wrong with the process of <u>voluntary exchange</u>. If some individuals earn little because they have little value to offer, the problem is a lack of skills and not any defect in the market.

> The proper response to a handwringing complaint about our country's "income distribution" is simply to ask the critic what it should be, and how he knows that.

The critic of the market is almost certain to advance some claim that incomes should have nothing to do with voluntary exchange, or that voluntary exchange should have nothing to do with the values that individuals attribute to alternatives. Either is a sign of someone who may be well-meaning (though I've learned to not necessarily grant that), but is simply too ignorant of elementary economics to be taken seriously.[4]

Although we have no way of judging that incomes determined on a free market should be different from what individuals' actions make them, we are right to criticize a pattern of income that results from systematic violations of the principle of voluntary exchange and protection of individual rights. Whether we're talking about a Savings and Loan executive who paid for his Ferrari by defrauding shareholders, or a barely-making-it farmer whose lower-middle income arises solely from the government's restrictions on crop prices, these individuals have not earned their incomes through voluntary exchange. The problem, as we've argued before in other contexts, is not primarily what private or governmentally-enforced theft does to income distribution. The problem is simply that individuals' rights are violated, the property and part of the lives of some individuals are taken from them by force.

DERIVED DEMAND AND
MARGINAL PRODUCTIVITY

If you know the price of a pair of roller skates, and the quantity of them that is exchanged, you can find the total money spent on roller skates by multiplying price by quantity. And if you know the demand and supply of roller skates, you can determine price and quantity. It all comes down to demand and supply.

Your labor income is the product of price and quantity too: your wage rate and the number of hours that you work. (We'll discuss interest in Chapter 10, and rental income (cursorily) and profit (more thoroughly) in Chapter 11. You're most concerned about labor income anyway.) To analyze that income, we must investigate the demand for labor of the kind that you're willing and able to sell. After that, we'll investigate its supply.

---

[4] Of course neither our nor any other country is fully capitalistic (protecting individual rights). If the critic is able to point to systematic violations of rights, we can agree with him wholeheartedly.

The principle of derived demand

One of the most fundamental principles in the analysis of income is also one of the most simple and common-sense:

> A producer's demand for any productive input is DERIVED FROM the consumers' demand for the product that it is used to produce.

This is known as the "principle of derived demand," and it's an application of the general law that people impute value to <u>means</u> according to the value of the <u>ends</u> that those means help them to attain. (We first came across it in Chapter 3, explaining your demand for a Veggie Whacker that you knew someone else was willing to pay $7 for.)

The easiest way to convince yourself of the validity of the principle is to ask yourself why any producer is willing to spend good money to purchase a productive service (like an hour of your labor). What's in it for him? It's fairly clear that he plans to sell something to customers, and his eagerness to purchase your labor depends in some way on how eager his customers are to purchase his product. His demand for your services is <u>derived from</u> his customers' demand for his product. What's likely to happen to your job at the car wash (the owner's demand for your labor services) if people suddenly decide they don't really mind having dirty cars?

Usually, there's a direct relationship between changes in the demand for a business's product and its own demand for any one productive input (like labor). Sometimes an increase in demand that's expected to be permanent will lead a business to engage in capital investment that actually results in a reduction of its workforce. We're going to leave that case to a more advanced course in microeconomics. In the meantime, there's never any reason to be concerned about net "job destruction." For one thing, somebody has to build those new machines.

Marginal productivity theory

To discuss a producer's demand for any input with more precision, we should think again about his reasons for buying inputs. He's in business to make money, and he does that by selling products to his customers. The <u>causal connection</u> between you (his employee) and "making money" can be separated usefully into two parts: how much you contribute to the business's output, and how much that contributes to the business's sales receipts.

Here's an example. Without you, the firm is able to produce 100 blodgets each week, selling each for $150. (That's $15,000 per week of sales receipts.) If the firm were to add you to its 20-person work force, output would rise to 102 blodgets per week. To sell this larger quantity, suppose the price would have to be cut to $149 each. Total sales receipts would rise to $15,198 (that's 102 x $149). The very most that the firm would be willing to spend for the additional inputs required to produce these extra two units is a little less than $198, because $198 is the amount added to the firm's sales receipts.

The change in the number of units of output, arising from the addition of one unit of any particular input, is called the marginal product of that unit of that input.

> The MARGINAL PRODUCT of a particular unit of an input is the change in the quantity of OUTPUT arising from the addition of that unit of input.

In the example above, the marginal product of the 21st unit of labor (that's you) is "2 blodgets per week." We can imagine, at first, that the quantities of all other inputs (like raw materials, electricity, and machines) remain the same. This strains the imagination a little, when some inputs (like raw materials) almost necessarily have to change with the level of output. We'll take care of them at a later stage in the argument.

The firm then has to consider how much additional money it can get for these extra units of output. We've already studied in some detail the concept of marginal revenue: the change in sales revenue arising from the production and sale of one more unit of the output. Now we're interested in the change in sales revenue that arises from the sale of however many more units of output are added by the new unit of input. In this example, we want the marginal revenue of another two units of output. In general, what we're after is the marginal revenue of the marginal product. Not surprisingly, that's called the "marginal revenue product."

> The MARGINAL REVENUE PRODUCT of a unit of an input is the change in sales revenue arising from the purchase and use of that unit of input.

It's the marginal revenue of that unit's marginal product. In our example, the MRP of the 21st unit of labor (that's you) is $198 per week.

(Want more realism--at the usual cost of complexity? Let's admit that some extra raw materials and electricity would probably be needed, in addition to your labor. Then the $198 is the MRP of this collection of additional inputs--not of your labor alone. Dividing it up among them isn't always easy, or even possible. If we know, however, that the other inputs can be obtained for $26, then we can attribute the difference ($172) to your labor, and consider it your MRP. A rise in the price of these complementary inputs (say to $30) would reduce your MRP (to $168).)

If you consider the business's action whether or not to hire you, the firm's decisionmaker is likely to interpret the "benefit" of the alternative "hire him" as your MRP: the extra sales revenue that will probably result. Against this, of course, he must weigh the costs of his action; we'll discuss them shortly. For now, let's look a little more closely into this "marginal revenue product."

If you learn to think of it as "the marginal revenue of the marginal product," that will help you to understand how MRP is related to the quantity of labor that is employed. If the MRP of unit number 21 was $198, what can we say about what unit 22's MRP is likely to be, or what number 20's was? Well, think about the causal link between employment and revenue: first the new worker adds output, then that output gets sold.

In general, each new unit of labor adds less output than did preceding units.

> The principle that each successive
> unit of an input adds less output
> than did preceding units of input is
> the LAW of DIMINISHING MARGINAL
> PRODUCTIVITY.

Total output usually rises with each additional unit of labor, but at a declining rate. Total output with 9 workers may be 1000 units per week, with 10 workers 1050, and with 11 workers 1095. The MP of worker number 10 is 50 units, and that of worker number 11 is 45 units. It's not hard to think of exceptions (like so many workers packed into a small building that nobody can move), but--again, as you'll learn in a later course--no sensible producer uses a quantity of any input for which "diminishing marginal productivity" does not apply. As a result, marginal product declines with the quantity of the input. Figure 9.1 gives us a picture.

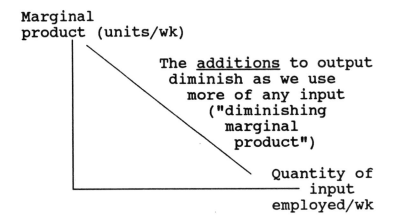

Figure 9.1: Diminishing marginal product, and...

On top of that is something that you already know: marginal revenue diminishes as the quantity sold increases. (The marginal revenue curve slopes downward.) Even if marginal product were to remain constant (suppose that each new unit of labor that you hire were to add five units of output, no matter how many you hire), the sales revenue added by that constant number of extra units would diminish because of the downward-sloping demand and marginal revenue curves. Figure 9.2, which omits demand, reminds you of this.

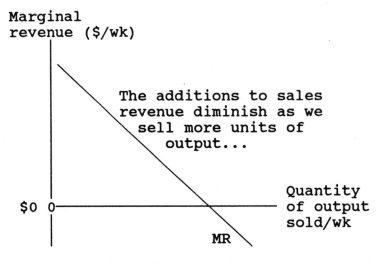

Figure 9.2: Diminishing marginal revenue, give us...

Either of these considerations (diminishing marginal product, and decreasing marginal revenue) taken alone would be enough to assure us of a downward-sloping marginal revenue product curve. Together, they reinforce each other and make the MRP curve's downward slope especially certain and dramatic. A typical MRP curve is shown in Figure 9.3.

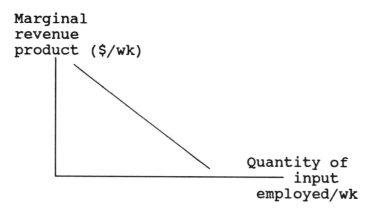

Figure 9.3: Diminishing marginal revenue product.

Remember the double-whammy: first, additional units of input add a diminishing number of units of output; second, additional units of output add a decreasing amount of additional sales revenue. MRP is the MR of the MP, and both MP and MR decline with increasing quantities of the input.

Marginal revenue product as the demand for labor

If we're trying to investigate the firm's hiring decision, we have to think about more than the benefit side of its choice. The simplest--and, unfortunately, not too realistic--assumption to make about the cost side of its decision is simply that the only cost involved is the payment of money wages. The monetary benefit from hiring a particular unit of labor (like the 21st: you) is its MRP, and the monetary cost of hiring that unit of labor is the wage that the business must pay.

Suppose that the business is a price taker in the relevant labor market: there's a "going wage rate," like $4.50 per hour, at which the firm can hire as many or as few unskilled and inexperienced workers as it wishes without its own decision having any effect on that wage rate. This isn't always very realistic--for the same reason that horizontal demand curves aren't either--but it certainly makes our analysis easier. We can consider complications later.

This assumption makes the cost of hiring each additional worker simply "the wage rate." Figure 9.4 gives us a picture.

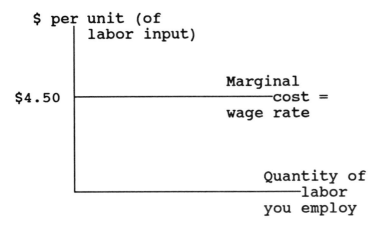

Figure 9.4: Wage as marginal cost of hiring

Now we have what we need to analyze the employer's decision. His monetary cost of each worker is the wage rate, and his monetary benefit of each worker is that worker's MRP, so he should hire each unit of labor for which MRP (benefit) is greater than the wage rate (cost). If, to continue our previous example, the wage rate for labor like yours is $175 per week, while your MRP to the blodget producer is $198 per week, he's $23 better off each week by hiring you than by not doing so. You add $175 to his weekly costs, and $198 to his weekly revenue. Your productivity covers your own wage and leaves a bit for your employer.

This principle is exactly the same as that which we used to analyze the quantity of <u>output</u> that a price-searcher should produce: sell every unit of output for which benefit (marginal revenue) exceeded cost (marginal cost of the output). In its present application, that rule tells us to hire every unit of <u>input</u> for which benefit (marginal revenue product) exceeds cost (the marginal cost of the <u>input</u>: the wage rate).

Picking a particular wage rate (w_o) and drawing a particular MRP curve, as in Figure 9.5, illustrates the point.

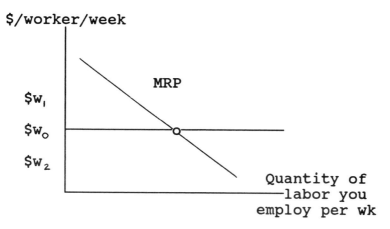

$/worker/week

$w_1

$w_0

$w_2

MRP

Quantity of labor you employ per wk

Figure 9.5: MRP as the demand for labor

The producer should hire every unit for which MRP > w_0, and none of the units of input for which MRP < w_0. The easy way to describe the proper quantity of input is simply to tell the producer to select that quantity at which MRP = w_0: the marginal revenue product is equal to the wage rate. As in our price-searcher analysis, the real point of this rule is to make sure that he hires each and every unit for which MRP <u>exceeds</u> the wage, and none of the units for which MRP falls short of the wage. If there actually <u>is</u> a unit for which the two are precisely equal, we don't care if he hires that particular unit or not, and neither does he: its benefit (MRP) precisely equals its cost (wage).

The quantity at which the wage rate (w_0) line (it's really the supply curve of labor to this employer, under price-taker conditions) intersects the MRP curve therefore is the quantity that the firm will choose to buy at this wage rate. If we imagine a couple of different wage rates (w_1 higher and w_2 lower than w_0) and follow through the same logic, we find that whatever particular wage rate we wish to hypothesize, the point on the MRP curve that corresponds to that wage rate shows us the <u>quantity</u> that the producer will choose to hire.

A curve that relates the <u>price</u> of something to the <u>quantity demanded</u> of it is, as you know, a <u>demand</u> curve. That's exactly what our MRP curve has become, under these conditions.

> For an employer who is a "price taker" in the labor market, the MARGINAL REVENUE PRODUCT curve is his DEMAND for LABOR.

As long as his own decision about how much to hire does not itself affect the market-clearing price of labor, then his marginal revenue product of labor is also his <u>demand</u> for labor.

Prodding at this analysis a little...

Now we're in a better position to understand the principle of derived demand in the market for labor--the principle that, one way or another, determines your income.

Think about a change in the consumer's demand for the product that your employer produces. It feeds through to the labor market by affecting the sales revenue that your employer can get for any particular quantity of output.

An increase in demand (a parallel shift to the right of the demand curve) also increases the marginal revenue of each unit of output (the MR curve shifts to the right, too). That means a rightward shift in the MRP curve: an increase in the employer's demand for labor. A reduction in the demand for his product (a leftward shift in the product's demand curve) will, similarly, cause a reduction in his demand for labor (a leftward shift in his MRP of labor curve).

With normal upward-sloping supply curves, when a demand curve shifts to the right both the price and the quantity exchanged (supplied and demanded at equilibrium) increase. If a particular producer really is a price taker in the labor market, though, his increase in demand will result only in a larger quantity: he hires more labor. A reduction in demand results only in layoffs: no reduction in the wage rate.

In the real world, firms are not as quick to hire and fire as this analysis suggests. That's largely because of <u>transaction costs</u>, which include record-keeping hassles (a lot of them caused by government requirements of one sort or another), interviews, and other problems involved with changes in personnel.[5] No business casually dismisses part of an experienced work force whose capabilities it well knows, unless it believes the future looks pretty bleak. Most businesses want to be quite sure that an increase or decrease in demand is going to last for a while before they hire or fire.

If a business is <u>not</u> a price-taker in the labor market, then we aren't justified in treating the wage rate as the relevant marginal cost. Just as a non-discriminating price searcher must reduce the price to sell extra units of output, a non-discriminating buyer of labor must generally raise the wage he offers if he wishes to hire more labor. The relevant cost curve (called "marginal resource cost") bears the same relationship to the upward-sloping supply-of-labor curve that the marginal revenue curve bears to the downward-sloping demand curve: it slopes upward too, but much more steeply

---

[5] "The cost of replacing departing help can run from $500 for an hourly worker to $5,000 for a manager, a survey of 577 companies by temporary personnel firm Olsten Corp. shows..." (<u>Wall Street Journal</u>, July 30, 1991: p. A1)

because hiring one new unit at its higher wage requires that the higher wage be paid to all preceding units of labor also.

If you have 25 workers each paid $300 per week, but it would take $305 to hire a 26th worker, then--with no discrimination, remember!--you'll have to pay $305 to the new worker plus an extra $5 to each of the 25 others, for a "marginal resource cost" of $430 per week (that's the $305 paid to worker number 26 plus the additional $125 paid to the other 25 workers). That 26th worker had better have a MRP that's greater than $430 per week, or you're better off not hiring him.

If you can figure out a way to keep his wage a secret, or believe that it doesn't matter whether the first 25 workers feel that they've been treated fairly, you might try paying $305 only to the new guy. Then you'll hire him if his MRP is as low as $305. In fact, if wages are absolute secrets at your company, you might be able to pay each worker exactly the minimum that would induce him to work for you. In this case, each worker would be paid a different wage, precisely his "supply wage," corresponding to his point on the labor-supply curve. This is the precise analog of the perfectly-discriminating seller, and just as marginal revenue and demand were identical for that seller, marginal resource cost and supply will be the same for the buyer. Figures 9.6A and 9.6B show what's going on.

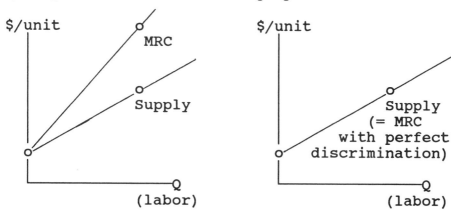

A: No discrimination B: Perfect discrimination

Figure 9.6: When the employer is not a "wage taker"

Although a truly proper theory of marginal productivity must rely on the concepts of marginal revenue product and marginal resource cost, the result is a theory that's a little deeper and more complex than we really need. You'll see it in later courses, but the main issues of employment and income can be understood pretty well with a less complex theory. So let's treat the "marginal revenue product" of an input, to a particular producer, as that producer's demand for the input, and see how

276

the principle of "derived demand" works to shift resources around in response to changes in consumer demands.

How consumer demands determine resource allocation

Consider (yet again) the widget industry. Also consider the wodget industry. Each uses similar labor, neither is in a geographic location that's more or less desirable than the other's location, neither involves work that is more dangerous or unpleasant or morally objectionable than the other. As a result, the wage rates in these two industries are about the same, w_1. The graphs in Figure 9.7 show the initial story:

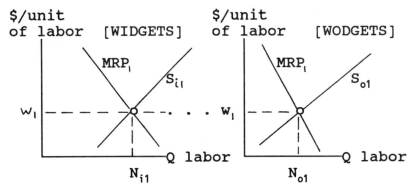

Figure 9.7: Widget and wodget labor markets...

There are N_{i1} workers in the widget industry (the "i" comes from "widget"...) and N_{o1} workers in the wodget industry (...and the "o" from "wodget").

Each set of producers is tooling along in this happy state of affairs when people suddenly decide that widgets aren't so great but wodgets are wonderful. These shifts in consumer demands produce a decrease in labor's marginal revenue product in the widget industry and an increase in labor's marginal revenue product in the wodget industry, as the graphs of Figure 9.8 show.

The short-term response is a fall in wages and employment in the widget industry (as we slide back down the supply curve), and a rise in the wage rate and in employment in the wodget industry (as we slide up the supply curve there).

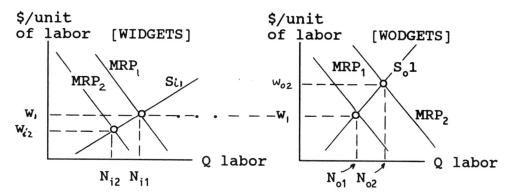

Figure 9.8: Initial response to consumer demands

Someone in the depressed widget industry is bound to notice that things are booming over in wodgets, and to decide that working for high wages producing wodgets is better than working for low wages in the widget job. (Remember that we have assumed that there are no other reasons why people would prefer working in one of the industries to working in the other.) As this happens, workers begin to leave widgets and enter the wodget industry. That shifts the labor supply curves, as Figure 9.9 shows. The original MRP curves and the intermediate levels of employment (the N_2's) are omitted to keep these graphs from being even messier than they are already.

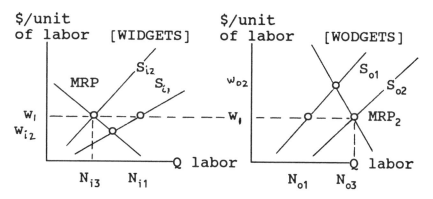

Figure 9.9: Supply response completes the example

The final result is simply a shift of labor from widgets (the good that consumers now value less) to wodgets (the good that consumers now value more). This is, in fact, the only effect (thanks to all of our assumptions): the wage rate is back to its original level, and the only difference is that employment has shifted from widgets to wodgets, following the shift in consumer demand.

Although this is a highly simplified example, it accurately captures the process by which the uses of productive resources (including labor) are determined in a market economy. No government economic czar had to notice that people liked widgets less and wodgets more, and he didn't have to order workers to stop producing one and start producing the other. This shift of resources--away from goods that individuals decided they valued less, and into goods that individuals decided that they valued more--takes place simply because such a shift is in the self-interest of the individuals who are involved.

If the producers consider maintaining their initial levels of production and employment, despite the demand shift, the widget producers will find that they are producing widgets that cost more than they bring in, and that they're hiring workers who can't cover their own wages. The wodget producers will discover that units of output that bring in far more than they cost are going unproduced, and workers whose MRPs far exceed their wage rates have not yet been hired. As the two groups of producers respond to their incentives, the wage differential between the two industries emerges. Workers respond to this incentive, switching from work in the widget to work in the wodget industry. The final result, an increase in the production of the product that consumers have decided that they value more and a decrease in the production of the product that they have decided that they value less, was not planned or intended by any one individual.

The process of voluntary exchange, with its market prices and the incentives and information that they contain, allocates resources in a manner that is far more responsive to individuals' preferences than that which could be attained by the central economic control that defines socialism.

THE SUPPLY OF LABOR

The maximum amount that an employer can profitably pay for your services is determined by the value that you are able to create, measured by how much his customers are willing to pay for the stuff that you produce. That's your "marginal revenue product" to this particular employer, and it determines his demand price, the maximum wage that he would be willing to pay rather than go without your services. (If he can get you for less, of course, so much the better. Better for him, that is!)

The minimum that he has to pay to obtain your services, the minimum that you would be willing to accept and still take the job, is your supply price for this type of labor to this particular employer. Any wage that the employer actually pays, and that you actually accept, must be greater than your "supply wage" and less than his "demand wage." To better understand the employer's process of choice, let's put you into his shoes. What would you think about, if you were considering hiring someone? Some of you will actually be in this position someday. Some of you may already have been.

You have to outbid his best alternative...

If you want someone to take a particular action, you have to make it worth his while. You must make sure that he perceives that action as the best of the alternatives that are available to him.

If you want him to come to work for you, you have to outbid his best alternative. This is the simple principle behind the concept of the "supply of labor."

Let's dispose of "leisure" right away. It usually isn't the best alternative that you have to outbid, but it might be. If the options that Jim perceives are "relaxing around the house" or "working for you," he will anticipate the pleasure of lounging around, the pleasure of whatever he thinks he would be able to buy with the money he might earn, and compare them.

If it would take $100 per day to buy things that offer Jim as much satisfaction as a day of relaxing at home, it will take a wage of at least $100 per day to bid him away from his leisure. If he's already worked five 14-hour days this week and has more money than he's ever seen before, it's going to take a lot more to bid him away from the next two days of leisure than if he's been unemployed for six months and just ate the last of his savings. (If anything sounds familiar about this example, it should: you constructed a "supply of labor" curve in the estate-cleaning problem of Chapter 3.)

In many cases, though, the best alternative to "working for a particular employer" is "working for some other employer." If Jim is in this situation, either having a job already, having a job offer, or perhaps just believing that he could earn a certain wage elsewhere, the alternative that you must outbid is not simply the value that Jim places on his leisure. Others have (or could have) already bid him away from that. It's the attractiveness of the best of these other jobs that now determines the supply price of Jim's labor to you.

Suppose you run a plumbing company and Jim has plumbing skills that you believe would add $350 per week to your sales revenue. That's your guess at his MRP to you, your demand price for his services. Do you have to offer that much? Will even that be enough to get him? Well, we have to investigate his alternatives.

Unfortunately for you, another plumbing company knows Jim too, and estimates that his MRP working for them is $340 per week. Since that's the "benefit" they perceive from hiring Jim, they'll be willing to offer him nearly that much rather than go without him. If Jim is indifferent between working for you and working for them (neither company has a less desirable location, worse trucks, more obnoxious other employees, etc.), then it's this other offer that you must outbid. The minimum that you can offer--Jim's supply price of labor to you--is determined by his highest MRP elsewhere, since that determines the maximum that someone else would be willing to pay him rather than go without his services. Here's a graph that tells the story (Figure 9.10), with Jim's leisure shown at $75 per week (and his corresponding supply curve shown in dots) just to emphasize that leisure is often far from the alternative that really determines the supply to any particular employer.

If it were just between you and Jim's leisure, you'd be willing to pay as much as $350 per week but it would take only $75 per week to snag him, so there's a wide range for negotiation--a big range of prices at which the supply and demand curves overlap. With the other potential employer in the picture, however, Jim requires at least $340 from you and your maximum is $350, so the overlap (the range of prices at which "quantity supplied" and "quantity demanded" are both equal to "one") is only $10. You'll have to pay at least $340 and he's worth only $350 to you.

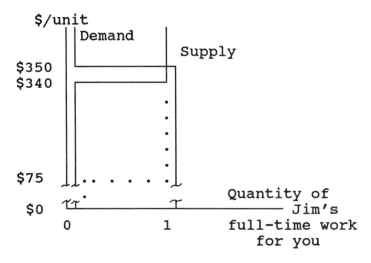

Figure 9.10: Jim's supply of labor to you

(If something looks a little familiar about that supply curve, look back--way back, Chapter 3--at the supply of Adirondack chairs to you, before and after your neighbor put in a bid for a deck. The graph looks the same because the principle is the same!)

In general, the supply of labor to any one employer is determined by the highest marginal revenue product of that labor used elsewhere. What you must pay (at minimum) is determined by what he can earn elsewhere, which is--in turn-- determined by the marginal revenue product of his labor in other uses. That, as we've discussed, is determined by the value that consumers attribute to the goods that the labor produces in those occupations.

Ultimately, then, one employer must outbid the consumers who value the alternative goods that the worker could produce working elsewhere. He'll be able and willing to do so only if consumers value the product that the worker can produce working for <u>him</u> more than they value the goods that he can produce working for someone else.

This is really a remarkable and wonderful conclusion. It implies that any particular worker tends to be employed in that occupation at which he has the greatest marginal revenue product; at which consumers place a value on his production that is higher than the value they would place on anything else that he could produce.

> Each worker tends to be employed in that
> occupation at which his marginal revenue
> product is greatest.

We've been focusing on labor, because that makes up the lion's share of most of our incomes. But every other resource obeys the same principle. Each machine, each piece of real estate, each dollar of "working capital." There's nothing about this analysis that is unique to labor.

There's many a slip 'twixt the cup and the lip, of course. We'll consider some of those slips soon. But don't let your recognition of human fallibility and human ignorance get in the way here. This process of individual incentive, involving voluntary exchange from the consumers' choices to the employers' incentives to the workers' motivations, "automatically" encourages individuals to do the best for themselves by doing the best for others.

The lower-cost qualified worker is preferred

Another intriguing implication involves the matter in which an employer is considering two prospective workers for the same job. In many settings the nature of "the job" pretty much sets the MRP, and slightly superior and slightly inferior performances by particular individuals are hard to detect. When this is the case, the employer believes that each applicant has the same MRP, and must decide which to hire.

His decision hinges on which worker has the <u>lower</u> marginal revenue product elsewhere. He's the one who will be the easiest (cheapest) to bid away from his best alternative. If Pat and Paul each has an MRP of $350 per week with us, but Pat's best alternative MRP is $320 while Paul's is $310, we will hire Paul at a wage above $310 but below $320. We get our job done for, say, $315, while Pat produces $320 elsewhere. With our demand for labor still identified by a quantity demanded of "1" below $350 and "0" above, the effect of being able to choose between Pat and Paul is shown in the supply-and-demand graph of Figure 9.11. The equilibrium wage is somewhere between $310 and $320; at any other level, "quantity supplied" and "demanded" are unequal.

Among those who can do the job, every position tends to be filled by those who have the <u>lowest</u>-valued best alternative. They're the qualified applicants who can be obtained most cheaply, which is--of course--the employer's motivation. In the broader view, which neither the employer nor the employee has any particular motivation to care about, their self-interested actions mean that consumers manage to get the product with the smallest sacrifice of other valued goods. This is another way of making a point that has been made much earlier: producers try to find and use the lowest-cost means of producing a good, that technique which requires consumers to sacrifice other goods with the least value. It's this applicant (Paul) who has the comparative advantage: although each produces $350 of output, Paul does so at the sacrifice of only $310 of "input" (sacrificed production elsewhere), ten bucks less than Pat.

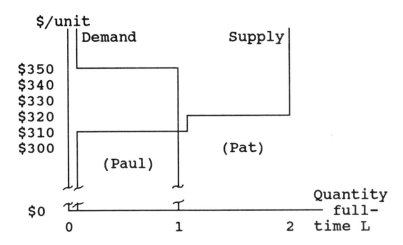

Figure 9.11: Outbidding the lower alternative MRP

Any particular worker, then, tends to be employed where his MRP is greatest; he is paid a wage that is below this MRP but greater than his MRP in his next-best occupation. (These two MRPs may be only a few dollars per week apart.) Any particular job tends to be held by that qualified worker who could earn the least in his next-best occupation. He's the efficient, lower-cost, alternative.

Try to apply this reasoning to other productive inputs, like real estate. Your private business office could be located either on a quiet side street somewhere, or on a busy corner inside a popular shopping mall. (That might be rather convenient, assuming the proper noiseproofing.) A shoe retailer faces the same alternative locations. While you might slightly prefer the mall, no doubt the shoe retailer strongly prefers it. If the strength of his relative preference is greater than yours, he will outbid you; the mall location goes to the business to which it offers the higher MRP.

If we look at the same issue just from your perspective, you're trying to decide where to locate your office. If you find the mall and side street just about equally attractive, you'll wind up on the side street--a location with fewer people bidding for it and, therefore, that you can get cheaper.

All of this happens simply through the process of voluntary exchange, individuals attempting to make the choices that make their future lives as pleasant as possible.

Garbage collectors, blizzards,
and "compensating differentials"

If you could earn the same wage being a lifeguard at a beautiful beach or by slinging garbage into trucks at six in the morning in the middle of a blizzard, which would you prefer? Although I'm a "mountain," not a "beach," person, I can understand how most people would answer this one.

Think about what your answer implies about the relative supplies of lifeguard vs. garbageman labor. Because the latter's working conditions are so much less attractive, the wage required to induce folks to put up with them is greater than for similar-skilled jobs with pleasant working conditions. The effect of these relative preferences on labor supply is depicted in Figure 9.12.

Working conditions that people perceive as unappealing (hot, cold, wet, smelly, dangerous, inconvenient) make the supply of labor lower than it would otherwise be. Since they'd rather receive a little less in return for a nicer work environment, the supply of labor to occupations perceived to be pleasant (or high-status, safe, comfortable) is greater than it would be in the absence of these perceptions.

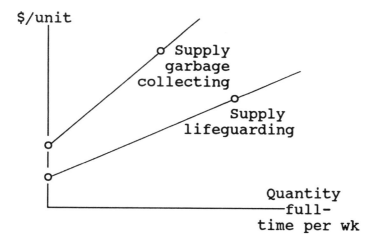

Figure 9.12: "Baywatch" or the garbage truck?

These effects on the relative supplies of labor to these types of occupation give rise to something that economists have labelled "compensating differentials," differences in wage rates arising from different perceptions of the attractiveness of the jobs. The effects on the supplies of labor result in equilibrium wage rates that are higher in the unpleasant occupations and lower in the appealing ones. Although you may interpret this as compensation for accepting risk and uncomfortable working conditions, don't forget that it all works through the supply and demand of labor. Nobody gets paid simply for being uncomfortable or taking risks.

So here's a clue to earning a high wage: develop a liking for climbing high-voltage transmission towers in the middle of snowstorms, a positive preference for the smell of garbage, or a tolerance for crawling around in cramped spaces, getting dirty, and looking like the scum of the earth. Other things the same (specifically, the demand for labor), the fewer people who are willing to tolerate what you are, the smaller the supply of the type of labor that you offer and the higher your wage rate.

Get a good education, make lots of money?

The supply of labor of any particular type is a little more complicated than our "blizzard and garbage" discussion suggests. What if different skills are required? (I know that lifeguarding and garbage collecting are not really equivalently skilled occupations, for example.) In particular, how do the costs of entering a particular occupation affect the labor supply (and, hence, wage rates)?

The answer might be pretty straightforward, but it's best approached by considering your own case. Imagine two occupations that you believe you would find equally attractive, once you were established in them. But one of them--say, being a medical doctor--requires eight years of extremely expensive training, while the other--getting an MBA from a prestigious university--requires only a couple of years of very expensive training. There is no doubt that the relative costs of entering these two occupations affect labor supplies: it's lower in medicine and higher in business than would be the case if training costs were the same. As a result, wage rates have the opposite pattern: generally lower in business than in medicine.

Are garbagemen really paid a lot more (because their unappealing working conditions reduce supply) than a secretary (in a pleasant, air-conditioned office)? To my knowledge, the education required of individuals who load garbage is not particularly great; it's an easy occupation to enter. Low entry costs, ceteris paribus, increase the supply of labor and make wage rates lower than they otherwise would be. When this is balanced against the effect of the poor working conditions (which, ceteris paribus, tended to reduce labor supply and raise wages), we have two opposing forces. Maybe they just about cancel each other out and leave garbagemen earning an average wage.

So here's my second clue for earning a high wage: be willing to pick an occupation with severe training or other entry costs. That will discourage lots of other people, leaving a small labor supply. Before you actually decide to do this, remember to weigh your (future) high income against your (current) high costs, using techniques of comparison that we'll discuss in the next chapter. All things considered, a lower-income but much-lower-cost career could be a better choice.

Amid all of this concern with labor supply, and my advice that you can boost your wage by finding a dangerous unpleasant job with fierce educational requirements because those characteristics reduce the labor supply, don't forget labor <u>demand</u>. At any particular time, the pattern of wage rates and the amount of employment in different occupations tends to be pretty well adjusted to all of these risk/unpleasantness/education considerations. If two occupations have similar working conditions and entry costs, but the demand for labor (arising from consumer demand for the product) is much higher in one than in the other, the two occupations will pay about the same wage but the amount of employment in the two fields will reflect the difference in demand (like the final position in our widget-wodget example). No employer can pay you more than your MRP, the value that consumers attribute to your productive service. Before you decide to earn big bucks selling some kind of dangerous, high-skilled labor (weaving macrame baskets while hanging upside-down over a cliff?), try to make sure there will be a <u>demand</u> for it. What will your entry do to the existing market (if there is such a thing) for baskets made in this fashion? Don't forget that your employer must perceive some benefit to hiring you, and that means he must expect to get big bucks from customers for your baskets.

Unemployment

Contrary to popular belief, you're not necessarily "unemployed" if you don't have a job. You also have to want one (not everyone does) and be actively trying to get one (not everyone who says he wants one actually is trying). In the official government statistics, people who aren't trying to find a job are simply considered not to be in the "labor force," which consists of those who are employed or actively trying to become so. The "unemployment rate" is the fraction of the labor force (employed plus looking) that is looking.

Unemployment results from the fact that people do not know, automatically and costlessly, what their best alternatives are. Economists sometimes distinguish between "frictional" and "structural" unemployment. An individual is "frictionally" unemployed if there is demand <u>somewhere</u> for his services, at a wage rate that he would accept, but neither he nor his potential employer knows it (yet). He is "structurally" unemployed if the demand for his skill has disappeared or fallen sharply, so that--although he may not know this (yet)--<u>nowhere</u> is there demand for this skill at a wage that he would accept.

Our hypothetical omniscient economist might know whether Joe Blow is frictionally or structurally unemployed. Joe himself probably doesn't. When he is laid off, he hopes and expects that it's frictional, that a little hunting will turn up another employer who will buy the same skills from him at about the same wage rate. While he is <u>searching</u> for this hoped-for employer, Joe is unemployed.

> Unemployment denotes a process of
> SEARCH. If an individual isn't
> searching, he isn't "unemployed."

After some time--weeks or months--Joe may decide that there is no such employer lurking around the corner waiting to be discovered, and that his unemployment is structural. At this point he decides either to retrain in a new skill, or accept a lower-paying job using some other skill that he already possesses.

Either of these economic classifications of unemployment results from changes in the pattern of demands and supplies throughout the economy. By now, you can appreciate that there could well be some way that an increase in consumer demands for Earl Grey tea in Anchorage could reduce the marginal revenue product of labor in the South Carolina textile industry. (No, I don't know exactly how either. Maybe the Anchorage cafe owners, becoming wealthier, decide they can afford Scottish wool now...) The textile producers may be unwilling to offer, or the workers to accept, lower wages, so layoffs arise. They probably don't know, and surely wouldn't much care, that there are now jobs to be had selling tea in Anchorage. They also probably don't know of other desirable jobs close to home. Sometimes there's a minimum-wage fast-food job available, but if they had been earning twice that before, perhaps something better can be found. While they hunt, they're unemployed.

This kind of unemployment is inevitable in a free society. After all, the consumer calls the shots and can change his mind at any time. Although the processes that we've described in this chapter explain the incentives (through demands to marginal revenue products to wage rates) that encourage the owners of resources (including labor) to use them to best satisfy consumer demands, nobody knows the details of these demands instantaneously and costlessly. If you run a little shop and nobody buys anything for two days, is it just chance or does it indicate a drop in demand that calls for reducing your prices? It's very unlikely that anyone else--even economic forecasters with big computers--knows more about that than you do.

A dynamic free market is always changing, always adjusting, as consumers change their minds and entrepreneurs offer them new alternatives. These changes inevitably give rise to frictional and structural unemployment, inescapable consequences of the process of voluntary exchange. It can be lamented, just as our inability to know everything is regrettable, and each of us can expect and prepare for it.

Unemployment arises from the very nature of human action and voluntary exchange, and unrestricted markets themselves provide the best information and the strongest incentive to resolve it. An ideal government policy toward unemployment would help individuals to discover the new pattern of consumer demands and, therefore, the new job opportunities and wage rates. But implementing such a policy would require the government to know, first, exactly what that new pattern of consumer demands is. There is no way that a government agency could obtain better information about new consumer demands than that which individuals discover, themselves, in the process of searching for mutually beneficial, voluntary, exchanges.

YOU SHOULD REMEMBER...

1. Income is earned from the sale of productive services, and depends on the value that other individuals attribute to those services.

2. Income is classified by the kind of productive service that is sold: wages (labor services), interest (the services of financial capital), rent (the services of nonfinancial capital), and profit.

3. The "distribution of income" refers to the fraction of total national income that is received by the wealthiest fifth of families, the next wealthiest fifth, etc., and the poorest fifth.

4. Much of the concern about "income distribution" reflects the TRIBAL PREMISE that everything belongs to <u>society</u> or the <u>nation</u>, rather than to individuals.

5. In a capitalist economy, "income distribution" is an <u>unintended consequence</u>, resulting from complex patterns of voluntary exchange.

6. A producer's demand for any productive input is DERIVED FROM the consumers' demand for the product that it is used to produce.

7. An employer benefits from your work by (a) obtaining more units of output, and (b) obtaining more sales revenue when he sells them.

8. The MARGINAL PRODUCT of a unit of input is the number of units of OUTPUT that it adds.

9. The addition to sales revenue when the marginal product is sold is the MARGINAL REVENUE PRODUCT of that unit of input.

10. Marginal Revenue Product is "the marginal revenue OF THE marginal product."

11. If the employer is a price-taker in the labor market, the MRP of labor is his DEMAND for labor.

12. A change in CONSUMER DEMAND changes marginal revenue; MRP, and therefore the DEMAND FOR LABOR, usually change in the same direction.

13. MRP is an essential link in the explanation of how changes in consumer demand result in a change in the way that productive resources (like labor) are used.

14. The SUPPLY OF LABOR to a particular business or industry is based on the principle that "you must outbid his best alternative."

15. Most workers' "best alternative" is the best they could earn elsewhere, and that is their greatest MRP elsewhere.

16. Every worker tends to work where his MRP is highest.

17. Every <u>job</u> tends to be filled by the qualified worker whose next-best MRP is the <u>lowest</u>.

18. As a result, the pattern of employment tends to produce maximum value at minimum cost.

19. Unappealing working conditions produce "compensating differentials," higher wages, resulting from a smaller labor supply.

20. Unemployment is inevitable in a free society where consumers can change their minds, and exists during the process of SEARCH for new employment opportunities.

Problems

1. The Acme Corporation currently produces 1,000 acmes per week with a work force of 63 identical persons. It is considering adding a few more and wants to use "marginal productivity theory" to help it decide. With no increases in any other input (even raw materials), its output per week is related in the following way to the number of workers:

Number of workers	Output per week (acmes)	Marginal (Physical) Product (acmes per week)	Marginal Revenue Product (P=$8) ($ per week)
63	1000	----------	----------
64	1050		
65	1095		
66	1138		
67	1177		
68	1212		

a) Fill in the remainder of the table above. For MRP, assume that Acme is a price taker in its output market (its demand curve is horizontal) and that each acme, no matter how many the company offers, can be sold for $8.

b) If any number of new workers can be obtained for a wage of $315 per week, how many new (that is, in addition to the original 63) should Acme hire? Why?

c) We are just about to act when a surge in consumer demand for acmes raises the market price to $10. How many new workers will our company want to hire now? Why?

d) Suppose, on the other hand, that during our planning stage consumer demand falls so that the market price of each acme drops to $6. What should our new-hire plans be now?

e) To make this problem a little more realistic, suppose we want to take into account the fact that each additional acme requires $0.37 of new raw materials, electricity, and packaging. How might we do it? Or does the whole marginal productivity theory have to be discarded because of the existence of costs like these?

2. Consider unemployment compensation, the weekly check that one can get, under certain conditions, if he's unemployed.

a) Does it provide incentive for the unemployed person to search more vigorously, or less vigorously, for a new job?

b) Does it make a longer search, with greater probability of finding a better and more productive job, more feasible or less feasible?

c) Can you think of any advantages of replacing the system of compulsory unemployment insurance with a voluntary system that would, in effect, mean that people would have to rely on their own savings while they are unemployed? (The tax that pays for the current compulsory system would be eliminated, and this plan would be announced years in advance, so that people could build up their savings if they wished to.)

d) How about some disadvantages?

3. If a great many bright young people develop the attitude that "white collar" office jobs have more prestige and "class" than blue-collar skilled-trades work, what is this new attitude likely to do to (a) supplies of labor, and (b) average wage rates, in these two types of employment? Do you think that this has really happened?

4. There is great emotional appeal to having one's printed words read, or one's music heard, and appreciated by thousands of others. What might this suggest about the supply of labor to "free-lance writing" or to "performance arts"? What, in turn, would that suggest about the average monetary incomes earned in these fields? Do you know anything about these averages? (Stephen King and Michael Jackson are the exceptions!)

5. Suppose that you discover that Joe Smith cheated your great-great-grandfather out of $100 in a card game in 1874, and used it to buy a vegetable cart which grew into the Smith grocery empire that's now worth billions. (Your ancestor became a hobo, riding freight cars and doing seasonal fruit-picking work.) Smith's heirs are sailing off Martha's Vineyard while you're

struggling to pay the rent. How could we (or could we?) correct this injustice now? Can you trace what would have happened in the past 120 years if Joe had not cheated your great-great-grandfather?

6. With 100 workers, we can produce 1,000 units per week and sell each of them for $59.95. If we had 101 workers, we could produce 1,004 units per week.

   a)   If we are a price taker in our product market, what will be the MRP of worker #101?

   b)   If we are a price searcher, we may find that to sell 1,004 per week we must cut the price to $59.85 per unit. What will be the MRP of worker #101 in this case?

7. In a recent radio interview, the owner of a custom printing shop with eleven employees explained that the health insurance that she provides costs as much as would a twelfth worker. Explain, using MRPs and costs of hiring, what "mandated benefit" legislation (it requires many employers to provide such benefits to any full-time employee) is likely to do to the demand for full-time labor.

8. Your neighbor, a third-generation steelworker, had planned to spend his working life at the local steel plant. But decisions by you and thousands of others to buy steel elsewhere have caused him to lose his job. Is that fair? Would you like to try to explain it to him, rather than to me?

9. In the widget industry, a new worker is useless without a new hydraulic stamping machine. The machine can be leased for $100 per week, and the new worker plus the new machine can add $450 per week to the firm's sales receipts.

   a)   What is the maximum that the widget firm could pay to the new worker?

   b)   What would happen to that maximum if the lease fee for the machine were to rise to $130 per week?

10. Other executives at Tracy's company made some bad decisions, the company went bankrupt, and she's unemployed. Can you make an argument that it may be more "productive" for Tracy to use some time searching for an employment opportunity that uses her skills than to immediately accept a job that doesn't? Could she even be said to be working productively while she's searching?

CHAPTER 10

THE RATE OF INTEREST AND ITS SIGNIFICANCE

INTEREST, TIME PREFERENCE, AND MARKET RATES

Interest is one of the most fascinating and unusual concepts in economics, and it has important effects on how each of us lives. Many books have been written on the theory of interest alone, and many more on the history and specific determinants of actual interest rates. We're just going into the basics here. As with the other material in this book, my goal is to provide a solid foundation. Those of you who, like me, find the concept of interest intriguing can build on it later.

We all know that interest has something to do with time, and it seems to have something to do with money also. We receive some money from someone at one point in time, then later we give it back--plus a little extra. That "extra" is the amount of interest that we pay.

Why does the person who provided us with the money (the lender) ask for some extra? Is it necessary to cover some kind of opportunity cost that lending the money to us imposes upon him? And what makes us willing to pay it? Once we've figured these things out, we can address the issue of the size of the "extra"--the rate of interest. To borrow $100 for a year we might be willing to pay $108 back (an 8 percent interest rate) but not $150 (a 50 percent interest rate). Under what circumstances will he be willing to lend to us at an interest rate that we're willing to pay?

Because businesses borrow for capital investments, the rate of interest affects their interest costs. A higher rate of interest, ceteris paribus, makes capital investment (new production lines, factory and office buildings, highly specialized farming machinery) more costly without affecting its benefits, so producers tend to retain production methods that are less capital-intensive. That, in turn, means that any given amount of human labor and raw materials produces a smaller output of consumer goods. If the higher rate of interest is truly the result of voluntarily expressed individuals' preferences, it's hard to say that it lowers the "standard of living." But it does produce fewer material goods.

Time preference: the foundation of interest

The very phenomenon of interest arises from a characteristic of human behavior that economists have labelled "time preference."

> TIME PREFERENCE is the individual's preference (<u>ceteris paribus</u>) for "sooner" rather than "later."

There is some controversy over the exact nature of this concept--whether it's a logical necessity (based on the notion that a person wouldn't act at all if he didn't prefer acting <u>now</u> over acting <u>later</u>) or simply an empirically observed (though not logically necessary) feature of nearly everyone's behavior. I'm going to sidestep that debate and rely on the fact that "time preference" is not only very helpful to understanding interest, but that interest cannot be understood without it.

Some of the debates about time preference require us to dig into exactly what it is that comes along either "sooner" or "later," which is an examination of the meaning of that phrase <u>ceteris paribus</u> in this context. A supposed counterexample to the axiom of time preference involves a block of ice: If it's the middle of February and there's ice coating your sidewalk and windshield every morning and your apartment won't get above sixty degrees, you may think ahead six months to hundred-degree, 97-percent humidity, August days and strongly prefer "a block of ice six months hence" to "a block of ice now." The response of the "time preference" theorists is that the comparison isn't fair, because <u>ceteris</u> aren't <u>paribus</u>. The two imaginary blocks of ice (one very scarce in the summer heat, the other oversupplied by nature in frigid winter) are <u>economically</u> different. They're perceived as different goods. The "time preference" axiom requires us to imagine the <u>very same satisfaction</u> to be available either sooner or later, and maintains that people will universally prefer "sooner."

It sometimes requires considerable mental stretching to conceive of the very same satisfaction being available at different points of time, since the passage of time necessarily involves change of one sort or another.[1] I have a little trouble, myself, when I get deeper into "time preference" than this. So let's back out a little and see how the concept is useful. After all, few of us possess mathematics doctorates in number theory, but we don't mind making use of the fact that 2+2=4.

The <u>strength</u> of this preference differs among individuals. Individuals for whom the preference is <u>strong</u> for "sooner" rather than "later" are said to have "high time preference." The timing of a satisfaction means a great deal to them. If we can somehow imagine a specific satisfaction being moved farther and farther into the future, the value that such an individual attributes to it drops off rapidly the farther out it gets.

"High time preference" (HTP) always makes me think of the beer ads that encourage us to "grab for the gusto" because "you only go around once." The advice

---

[1] "For Aristotle, time is essentially connected with change, indeed, it is what measures change. Or, as it is frequently stated, time is the number of change." Max Alter, <u>Carl Menger and the Origins of Austrian Economics</u> (Boulder CO: Westview Press, 1990), p. 119.

from various literary figures and biker-gang members to "live fast, die young" reflects a similar short-run hedonism. (Fortunately, most people who try what they mean by "living fast" quickly learn, without harming themselves permanently, that it really isn't that much fun.) "If it feels good, do it," Jerry Rubin's quaint remnant from the '60s, similarly urges us to ignore future consequences. Such a person has little or no interest in saving, which requires the postponement of satisfaction until a later date. He's far more likely, in fact, to out-consume his own income, borrowing the difference--"max'd out" on each of his credit cards, for example.

The "low time preference" (LTP) person also prefers "sooner" to "later," but not nearly as strongly. If we imagine grabbing a specific satisfaction and gradually pushing it farther and farther out into the future, the value that the LTP individual attributes to it drops off relatively slowly as the satisfaction recedes into the future. The timing of a satisfaction affects its value, but not nearly as significantly as for the HTP person.

> If we imagine pushing a particular satisfaction farther and farther into the future, its value drops off very RAPIDLY for a "high time preference" individual and SLOWLY for a "low time preference" person.

Needless to say, low time preference isn't glorified in television ads that urge us to ignore our budgets and enjoy ourselves. An extreme of LTP may be the "Puritan Ethic," a set of attitudes that held consumption (even the wearing of colored clothing) to be at best a necessary evil and glorified work and production. This belief, grounded in religion and instrumental in the survival of early European immigrants to America, resulted in high saving and provision for the future.

Today, an individual with low time preference simply pays more attention to the future than most people do. He saves, although if his income is low he may not save very much. He may even lend to--and earn interest from--his gusto-grabbing HTP neighbors. He consumes less than he produces, saving the difference for the future.

Exactly how we develop our attitudes about time preference is a complex matter. Each of us forms his own, based on values learned from parents, religious leaders, and other influential forces in our lives. Time preferences normally seem to decline with maturity; children have not yet learned the advantages of paying close attention to the future. This is, of course, understandable and natural with genuine children; it's hardly the same when some middle-aged '60s throwback demonstrates the same attitudes. It often seems to me that the very process of maturing is largely a process of reducing one's time preference.

The simplest example that illustrates the basic nature of interest is a little artificial, but--as usual--once we understand it, we can tack on more realism (at the cost of complication) later.

Sally has $100 that she could either spend on her own current consumption or lend. She also imagines some advantage in borrowing--and spending, also, on her own current consumption--another $100. In her own current situation, she has a <u>rate of time preference</u> of 10 percent per year: she considers "$100 now" and "$110 in a year" to be of the very same subjective value. If a hundred dollars' worth of current satisfaction were postponed for a year, the strength of Sally's time preference would reduce the value of each dollar's worth by 10 percent; she therefore requires 10 percent more dollars just to break even. Waiting imposes a subjective cost of 10 percent per year on Sally, and the extra $10 merely covers that cost.

Frank, on the other hand, also has $100 that he could lend, and can imagine uses for a second $100 that he might be able to borrow, but his rate of time preference is 13 percent per year. He values "$100 now" the same as "$113 in a year," with the extra $13 just compensating him for the unpleasantness of having to wait. He has higher time preference than does Sally. We don't know why. We don't have to know why.

These two individuals meet in a field somewhere, get to talking about current consumption, and each obtains some information about the other's time preference. Let's see what might happen.

Sally learns that Frank values "$113 in a year" the same as he values "$100 now." But she herself values "$113 in a year" considerably <u>more</u> than she values "$100 now." If she could get Frank to give her "$113 in a year" in exchange for "$100 now," she would be considerably better off and he would be no worse off. She would get all of the gains from trade, but he wouldn't be hurt.

Frank, HTP person though he may be, is a quick thinker too, and discovers that while Sally values "$110 in a year" the same as she values "$100 now," he values "$110 in a year" considerably <u>less</u> than he values "$100 now." (Remember that $113 is the in-a-year value equivalent for him.) If he could get her to give him "$100 now" in return for "$110 in a year," she would be no worse off and he would obtain all of the gains from trade. He would obtain something ($100 now) with a value equivalent of "$113 in a year," in return for "$110 in a year."

If Sally were to lend $100 to Frank at an interest rate of 13% per year, she would obtain all of the gains from trade and he would break even. If she were to lend at 10% per year, he would obtain all of the gains and she would break even. A rate below 10% would delight Frank but harm Sally (she'd be giving up something ($100 now) with a value equivalent of "$110 in a year" in exchange for, say, "$109 in a year"); a rate above 13% would delight Sally but harm Frank (he'd be obtaining something ($100 now) with a value equivalent of "$113 in a year," but giving up, say, "$114 in a year" in exchange for it).

You may notice that somehow I've slipped in the assumption that Sally is the lender and Frank is the borrower. It's no mere assumption. Sally has the lower time preference, and if exchange is to be possible at all she will have to be the lender. It's an interesting exercise to imagine Frank lending to Sally; is there any interest rate (given their two time preference rates) at which such an exchange could be mutually beneficial? It'll do you some good to try to find one, but the answer is "no."

Only an interest rate that's above 10% (Sally's time preference) but below 13% (Frank's time preference) permits each to share in the gains from trade, making each party better off. This is the same principle that we found earlier: in a mutually beneficial exchange, the price must exceed the seller's cost of production and be less than the buyer's cost of producing the good himself. Here, "$110 in a year" is Sally's cost of producing "$100 now," while "$113 in a year" is Frank's cost of producing "$100 now." If Frank can buy "$100 now" for less than "$113 in a year," the purchase benefits him; if Sally can sell "$100 now" for more than "$110 in a year," the sale benefits her. Any borrowing/lending transaction at an interest rate between 10% and 13% meets this criterion. Figure 10.1 illustrates the point with a diagram like that which we used to illustrate comparative advantage and the gains from trade.

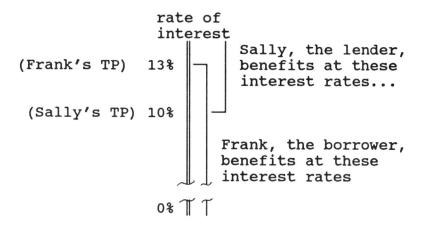

Figure 10.1: Mutually beneficial lending and borrowing

Let's try 12%. Sally gives up "$100 now," which--as far as she's concerned--is equivalent to giving up "$110 in a year." She gets back "$112 in a year." Since this is (obviously) greater than "$110 in a year," the trade makes her better off to the tune of "$2 in a year." Frank gets "$100 now," which is equivalent--according to his own values--to "$113 in a year," and pays only "$112 in a year" for it, benefiting to the tune of "$1 in a year."

We have witnessed the emergence of a loan transaction, with borrower and lender, and discovered the principle that determines the market-clearing (equilibrium) rate of interest. All that was necessary was the existence of two parties with different subjective valuations of time, different "time preferences."

It's no coincidence that the same kind of diagram that we used to illustrate comparative advantage, with the price at which mutually beneficial exchange occurs lying somewhere between the two parties' costs of production, can also illustrate the mutual benefit of a loan exchange when the parties have different time preferences. The party with the lower time preference can be said to have a comparative advantage in "present goods," and the higher-time-preference individual a comparative advantage in the provision of "future goods."

There are interest theories that discuss "capital productivity" and other concepts that can be important in particular cases, but this simple example properly conveys that time preference is the fundamental source of interest and "intertemporal exchange" (lending and borrowing).

The supply and demand of "loanable funds"

Although Sally and Frank exchanged present and future <u>money</u>, there was nothing fundamentally monetary about the transaction. We could have used corn or notebooks just as well. The fact that individuals in a modern economy frequently borrow and lend <u>money</u> must not blind us to the fact that interest is fundamentally a <u>non-monetary</u> concept.

Still, money is normally used and it's interesting to rephrase Sally and Frank's situation in terms of demands and supplies of "present money" and "future money."

At an interest rate between 10% and 13%, Sally wants to <u>supply</u> "loanable funds" (that is, to lend) and Frank wants to <u>demand</u> loanable funds (to borrow).

> LOANABLE FUNDS are just amounts of money
> that can be loaned and borrowed.

Since it has to be diverted from current consumption, the "quantity supplied" of loanable funds depends on the rate of interest and increases with higher interest rates. The "quantity demanded" depends on the rate of interest too, but decreases with a higher interest rate.

In our simple problem, Sally wants to lend at any rate above 10%, and to borrow at any rate below 10%. (If the unrealism here bothers you, you can introduce some kind of hassle or transaction cost, or a preference for following Shakespeare's advice to "neither borrower nor lender be." Then perhaps Sally would lend at any rate above 10% but wouldn't be willing to borrow unless the rate fell below, say, 6%.) Frank wants to lend at any rate above 13% and to borrow at any rate below that. If we plot their planned actions on a graph with "present dollars" along the horizontal, with "borrowed" in the positive and "lent" in the negative directions, we can describe Sally and Frank with Figure 10.2:

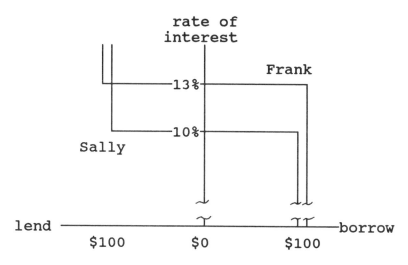

Figure 10.2: Lending and borrowing

Figure 10.2 illustrates that the amount that one of the parties wants to lend is equal to the amount that the other wants to borrow only for interest rates between 10% and 13%. Below 10%, they each want to borrow (sorry, that won't work if there are only the two of them) and above 13% they each want to lend (that won't either, for the same reason).

A more conventional diagram would show "borrowing" as the <u>demand</u> for loanable funds, and "lending" as the <u>supply</u> of loanable funds. Below 10%, the quantity demanded is $200 and the quantity supplied is zero; above 13% the quantity supplied is $200 and the quantity demanded is zero; between them, quantity demanded and supplied of loanable funds are each $100.

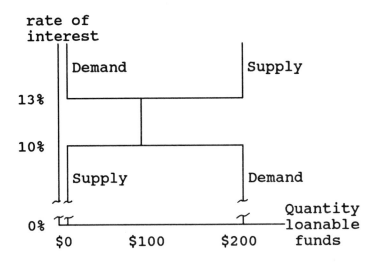

Figure 10.3: Two people supply and demand

If you think back to the way that we developed smooth supply and demand curves in Chapters 2 and 3, after starting with discrete step-type curves describing one person, you'll understand what happens in this market when we add dozens of other individuals. Each has his own rate of time preference. The range of interest rates at which supply and demand overlap becomes smaller and smaller, and when there are so many potential borrowers and lenders that smooth curves work pretty well, they overlap only at one rate of interest. Figure 10.4, which appears late in this chapter, shows the result.

Some notes on actual market rates of interest

Although this Frank-and-Sally example provides the fundamentals of interest, a brief look at your <u>Wall Street Journal</u> illustrates that the problems of real-world interest rates are much more complex. There are two basic reasons.

First, there's risk. That was brushed aside in our example, but the future is inherently uncertain so no lender is ever absolutely <u>sure</u> of being repaid. Some borrowers are more credit-worthy than others, of course, and since lenders don't like risk they prefer to supply funds to "safe" borrowers. That increase in the supply of loanable funds reduces the rate of interest that these borrowers have to pay, and (by reducing the supply to riskier borrowers) raises the rate that less credit-worthy borrowers must promise.

A <u>risk premium</u> thus arises, like the "compensating differential" in dangerous jobs, compensating the lender for undertaking risk. It differs among borrowers, of course, and is the main reason that the corporate bond yields in your financial section differ so widely among companies.

There's a second consideration, though, if the government--as it has been, for decades--is deliberately reducing the value of the dollar through a policy of inflation. If you expect each dollar's purchasing power to fall by 6 percent during the next year, you'd have to get 6 percent more dollars simply to have the same purchasing power at the end as at the beginning. If you also need 7 percent to cover your time preference, you're going to break even only if you receive back (in one year) at least 13% more dollars than you lent. Expected inflation reduces the supply of loanable funds (lenders prefer to buy real goods, at relatively low prices, now) and increases the demand for them (borrowers want to be able to buy the real goods now, too, and repay with devalued dollars later). These effects raise the rate of interest by a price premium, the expected rate of inflation.

The market rate of interest on a particular loan (to a particular borrower) can be expressed as the sum:

```
Market loan rate = TP rate + risk
premium + price premium
```

where the risk premium depends primarily on the credit-worthiness of the borrower and the price premium (the expected rate of inflation) on the government's monetary policy.

I read somewhere that the famous turn-of-the-century Austrian economist Eugen von Bohm-Bawerk (pronounced OYgen von Bome-BaVAIRK), whose works are amply rewarding even today, made a curious and interesting comment about the rate of interest. (Though I'm fairly familiar with Bohm-Bawerk's writings, I've never come across this comment myself.) He is said to have stated that the degree of civilization in any society is inversely related to that society's general level of rates of interest.

That sounds pretty strange, but pick apart a market rate of interest. Low time preference indicates a future-oriented, high-saving, attitude--generally considered civilized. Low risk premium suggests that borrowers are highly credit worthy and that a legal structure enforces property rights and contracts, again consistent with civilization. As for inflation, eliminating it (and its resulting "price premium") is a hallmark of a wise and civilized government. This strange-sounding statement, attributed to Bohm-Bawerk, actually seems to me to make a fair amount of sense, and it might help you to think about the principal determinants of a market rate of interest.

PRESENT AND FUTURE VALUES

The simple fact that time matters to people, that the time at which a particular satisfaction becomes available affects its value, has an interesting implication.

> An individual cannot compare directly two alternatives that provide their satisfaction at different times.

If you're trying to decide between option A that would provide almost immediate satisfaction, and option B that would provide its satisfaction only in six months, you have to reckon somehow with that timing difference.

In our discussion of valuation earlier in this book, I didn't separate the time element explicitly. Obviously we do form judgments of the relative values of A and B, and we take timing into account when we do that. It's not that we ignored timing earlier in our analysis; it was built into the valuation process. Now we're trying to separate its effect. In a context of individual choice and valuation, this separation seems somewhat artificial: if the satisfaction of A is available now, we try to imagine how valuable the satisfaction provided by B will be at the time that it becomes available. We then take into account the strength of our time preference, shrinking that value down a little (if we're LTP) or a lot (if we're HTP) to determine its present value equivalent. Although A is available now and B is available only later, we have now taken the significance of this timing difference into account, and can make the choice by comparing the value of A (available now) with the value equivalent of B (also available now).

Although this process of adjusting for the value of time is perfectly general, it's a lot easier to understand if actual money figures are attached. Many of our choices in this world involve "money now" or "money later."

The savings account and its compound interest

Perhaps the most straightforward way to introduce this issue is to ask you to imagine a savings account of some kind that pays 6% per year. It may not be realistic to expect this rate, but we're making up this problem and can pick any rate we want.

You put $100 into this account at the start of year 1, earn $6 interest, and wind up the year with $106. If you leave it there, you start year 2 with $106 and earn 6% of that during the second year: $6.36 interest. You wind up year 2 with $112.36 in the account: your $100 principal, the $6 you earned on it in year 1, the $6 you earned on it in year 2, and the $0.36 that you earned during year 2 on the $6 interest that you had earned during year 1.

This "earning interest on the interest," as it's been called, involves the process known as <u>compounding</u>, and it can produce some quite remarkable results if you're willing to wait long enough. But let's return to our example for the addition of one more year.

You start year 3 with $112.36 in the account, earn interest that year of 6% of that amount ($6.74), and wind up year 3 with $119.10. The $19.10 is made up of three years' $6 on your original $100 (that accounts for $18 of it), two years of interest on your first year's $6, and one year of interest on your second year's $6. We could dig into this a little farther, but perhaps this is enough. It's time to generalize, using some algebra.

The amount in your account at the end of year 1 is $106, which is ($100 + $6) or $100x(1.06), principal plus interest. You start year 2 with $106 and earn 6% interest on <u>that</u> during year 2, winding up with $106x(1.06) = $112.36. But that $106 that you started the year with is, itself, equal to $100x(1.06), so we can rewrite your end-of-year-two balance as [$100x(1.06)]x(1.06), or

$$\$100x(1.06)^2.$$

(Anyone who doesn't believe that this works should actually multiply 1.06 by 1.06. I guarantee that you'll get 1.1236, which when multiplied by $100 gives you the $112.36 that we're after.)

You begin year three with $112.36, and during the year that sum gets multiplied again by (1.06), producing $119.10 at year end. If we use our work of the preceding paragraph, we know that $112.36x(1.06) is the same as [$100x(1.06)^2]x(1.06), but that's identical to

$$\$100x(1.06)^3.$$

(Again, please do the algebra if that will help you to believe this story. (1.06)x(1.06)x(1.06) is 1.191016, which is rounded off to 1.1910.)

Now, take a look at the powers to which (1.06) is raised in the various years. At the end of 2 years, we had $100x(1.06)^2, at the end of 3 years we had $100x(1.06)^3, and--since anything raised to the first power is just itself--at the end of year 1 we had $100x(1.06)^1. I'm picking up a pattern here. During each year, what you started with gets multiplied again by (1.06), so that at the end of n years you'll have

$$\$100x(1.06)^n.$$

Here is a brief table summarizing this example. (We could easily figure out some formulas that could go in the blank spots under "year n," but there's not much point to it.)

Year	Start of yr	Interest earned	End of year	Formula
1	$100	$6	$106	$100(1.06)^1
2	$106	$6.36	$112.36	$100(1.06)^2
3	$112.36	$6.74	$119.10	$100(1.06)^3
n	----	----	-----	$100(1.06)^n

Future and present values

To make our results more general, we should be able to handle initial amounts different from $100 and interest rates other than 6%. Suppose that we denote the interest rate as "r," measured in decimal form (that is, 6% means that r = 0.06), and P as your original principal (here, $100). Then our general formula can be written as:

$$F = P \times (1+r)^n,$$

which tells us the "future value" of $P invested now for n years at an interest rate of r per year.

If we should happen to know "F," and want to find P, that's just a matter of algebra again. Assume that P is now the unknown in the above equation, and solve for it:

$$P = F/(1+r)^n,$$

or

$$P = F(1+r)^{-n}.$$

The "present value" P of a future sum $F to be received n years in the future, if the annual interest rate is r, is $F(1+r)^{-n}$. (I'm making use of the fact that "principal" and "present value" both start with the letter P, but there's no problem. At the time that the principal is invested, it is its own "present value.") For those of you who are uncomfortable with negative exponents, note that $(1+r)^{-n}$ is the same as $1/(1+r)^n$.

Enough of this algebra. Let's apply it to the bank account.

We've already gone forward in time: the "future value" in 2 years of $100 invested now at 6% per year is $112.36, and so forth. More interesting is the matter of moving <u>back</u> in time, from the future to the present.

When we attempt to find the present value of a future sum, we seek an answer to the question: How much would I have to invest now to be able to have $F at a time n years in the future, if I can earn r interest per year? Now...if you know that you want to have $112.36 in 2 years, and can earn 6% on your savings, how much do you have to put in the bank right now? Since we already know that $112.36 is the future value (in 2 years, at 6%) of $100 now, it follows that "$100" is the present value of "$112.36 in 2 years" (at 6%). It also follows that $100 is the present value, at 6%, of "$106 in 1 year" and of "$119.10 in 3 years." Whatever you invest for 3 years at 6% gets multiplied by 1.1910, as we've already seen, so if we're trying to find out how much we must invest now to have $119.10 in 3 years, we divide $119.10 by 1.1910 and--presto!--we get $100. (No surprise, since we got the $119.10 by multiplying $100 by 1.1910 in the first place.)

These conclusions can be generalized if we begin to move away from the specifics of the bank-account example. Suppose you would like to have $1000 in 3 years, can earn 6% per year on your savings, and want to know how much you have to invest now. The answer is $1000/1.1910, or about $840. If you would like to have the $1000 in only 2 years, you must invest $1000/1.1236, or about $890, right now. The former figure, $840, is the "present value of $1000 to be received in 3 years, discounted at 6%," and the latter, $890, is the "present value of $1000 to be received in 2 years, discounted at 6%." The process of using the rate of interest, and the period of time involved, to find the present value of a future sum is called discounting.

When we go the other way, using the rate of interest and the time period involved to find the future value of a present sum, the procedure is called compounding.

Well...so what?

If there's anything more annoying than some economist playing with mathematics just to show off, I don't know what it is. Two comments: First, this mathematics isn't very advanced. If you find it so, please consider that there is a deficiency in your education, and consider using your college's resources to correct it. It's never too late. Second, there is a proper economic use for all of this stuff. It isn't just showing off.

Remember our caution at the start of this section. You can't compare directly alternatives that occur at different points in time. Suppose you're offered either "$100 now" or "$118 in 3 years," and have to decide between them. Clearly $118 is greater than $100, and that's good. But "in 3 years" is later than "now," and that's bad. You cannot simply base your choice on either of these properties alone; you wouldn't prefer "$100.01 in 80 years" to "$100 now" just because it's more money, and you wouldn't turn down "$1,000 in 2 minutes" in preference for "$100 now" just because it comes later. We have to find some way to balance these opposing effects: more (that's good) but later (that's bad).

We do it by taking into account the value of time, using what we know about the relevant rate of interest. It's either your rate of time preference, or the interest rate that you could earn if you invested the $100 elsewhere, whichever is larger. By the way...

> Your rate of time preference can be interpreted as the rate of return that you earn on your own current consumption.

Our reasoning is to calculate the value equivalent of one of the alternatives, at the same point in time as the other alternative. To compare the "$118 in 3 years" to the "$100 now," we must either project the "$100 now" three years into the future (so that we can compare its "future value" with $118) or pull the "$118 in 3 years" back to the present (so that we can compare its "present value" with $100). In either case, we are eliminating the time element from consideration. Using the information that we have about the value of time (information contained in the interest rate), we have transformed our problem into a choice between two alternatives available at the same point in time. Which one is bigger? Take it.

If the rate of interest at which you could invest is 6% per year, the "future value" in 3 years of the "$100 now" is $119.10. Since this sum and the $118 occur at the same point in time (three years down the road), you can compare them directly. Better stick with the "$119.10 in three years," which is actually the "$100 now." The other way to do this is to determine how much you would have to invest now, to have $118 in 3 years, if you can earn 6% per year. The answer, the present value at 6% of $118 to be received in 3 years, is $118/1.1910 or $99.08. What you're really being offered, then, is the choice between "$100 now" and "$99.08 now," and again the numbers can be directly compared because they occur at the same time. Better stick with the "$100 now."

This is the way that Sally and Frank made their decisions, too. Should Sally give up "$100 now" in exchange for "$112 in a year"? We can't simply say, "Sure--she makes twelve bucks on the deal," since she has to go without other uses of that $100 for a whole year. How important is that to her? What we did, what she has to do, is either find the "future value" in 1 year of the "$100 now" and compare it to the $112 (we did that; it was $110 which isn't as good as $112), or find the "present value" of the $112 to be received in one year and compare that to the $100 (we haven't done that; it's $112/1.10 or $101.82, which is better than $100). Whichever time frame we choose for analysis, present ("now") or future ("in one year"), lending at 12% comes out looking good.

The goal: identifying the alternatives accurately

This discussion is all part of the general proposition that if an individual is to choose among alternatives, it's advisable to identify those alternatives properly. If you misidentify one of the options that's open to you, unintentionally pretending that you have an alternative that you don't really have, you're likely to make a mistake. You're likely to pick an alternative that makes you less well off than you could have been.

Perhaps you know, for example, that your two alternatives are "invest $100 for 3 years at 6% per year" and "give up the $100 now in exchange for $118 in 3 years." (Devoting the $100 to current consumption, you've already decided, lies lower on your value scale; your rate of time preference is, say, only 4 percent.) You have to have some process for determining which of these is more advantageous. It isn't obvious.

To make it more convenient to work out analyses like the ones discussed above, I've included a few tables at the end of this chapter.

Table I shows the "future value," in n years at r per year interest, of $1 invested now. (You should find our familiar numbers--1.06, 1.1236, and 1.1910--to begin to learn about the table.) It's really just a table of

$$(1+r)^n.$$

If you want to find the future value of $100 (or $83 or $98,000), just multiply the number that you obtain from the table by 100 (or 83 or 98,000).

Table II shows the "present value," at r interest per year, of $1 to be received n years in the future. It's really just a table of

$$(1+r)^{-n},$$

or

$$1/(1+r)^n,$$

which makes each of its entries the reciprocal of the corresponding entry in Table I. For example, Table I's entry for 3 years and 9 percent is 1.1910; Table II's is 0.890 (another number that we've seen before in this chapter). If you wish to find the present value of $60,000--not of $1--to be received in 3 years if the interest rate is 6%, just multiply the $1 present equivalent (89 cents) by 60,000.

Table III is derived from Table II (and, therefore, indirectly from Table I). It's called an annuity table, and shows the present value of "$1 to be received at the end of each year, for n years, discounted at an interest rate of r per year." Each entry in Table III is the sum of the years' entries in Table II. Try $1 per year for 3 years, at 6%: that stream of three bucks has, according to Table III, a present value of about $2.67. If you add the present values of each of the three years' individual dollars, from Table II, you get about 94 cents + 89 cents + 84 cents, which adds up to $2.67-- exactly the figure in Table III.

You can use Table III to easily find the true present value of a "$1,000,000" lottery prize that actually pays you $50,000 per year for 20 years. If the proper rate of interest is 9%, then the Table shows that "$1 per year for 20 years" has a present value of about $9.13 (actually $9.129). Fifty thousand of them, then, would have a present value of $456,450. Your "million dollar" prize (strung out over the next 20 years), and $456,450 right now, are exactly equivalent. For more practice using Table III, see the problems at the end of the chapter.

If someone convinces you that you'd better have $150,000 in 20 years to pay for your own child's college education, and you think you can earn 6% on your savings, Table II allows you to determine that you'd need to invest "only" $150,000 x 0.312 = $46,800 right now. Table II doesn't tell you where to get the forty-seven grand.

Suppose that you think that having a college education yourself will permit you to earn $8,000 per year more, for forty years, than you otherwise could have.[2] (Remember that if you're sharp and motivated enough to get your degree you probably could have done better-than-average without it.) But college will cost $80,000 right now...well, pick an interest rate and give it a try. What's the present value of a 40-year, $8,000 annuity? (Be sure to use Table III.) If money is all that you see in college, it's barely worth it at 9% ($8,000 x 10.757) and not worth it at 12% ($8,000 x 8.244).

"Double your money!"...and other
deceptive terminology

A few years ago, before the Savings and Loan crisis, newspapers carried dramatic ads (mostly from S&Ls seeking deposits) blaring that they would "Double Your Money!"

A look into the fine print usually revealed that if you deposited $10,000 now, and left it in the institution for 12 years, they'd give you $20,000 back then. Now there's no disputing that 20,000 is double 10,000. But these dollars occur at different points of time, so a direct comparison between them is absolutely meaningless. Timing makes a difference to people; it affects values. You must take it into account whenever there's a difference in the timing of the returns from two alternatives.

In this case, we can either enjoy the current use of our $10,000 (now) or enjoy the use of $20,000 in 12 years. To make the choice, to compare values, we must incorporate our knowledge of the significance of time (in the form of an interest rate).

---

[2] "Education pays. And here's proof: High school dropouts earn an average of $485 a month, while high school graduates average $967, according to the U.S. Census Bureau.

People with four-year college degrees earn an average of $1,804, and those with master's degrees pull down about $2,317." Glenn Burkins, "Put 2 credit cards to work and save money over time," Baltimore Sun, October 27, 1991: p. 7C.

One interesting way to proceed is to scan through Table I to find the interest rate that would double (multiply by 2) a present sum in 12 years. Looking across the "12 years" row, we come to "2.012" at an interest rate of 6%. Apparently, then, simply investing for 12 years at 6% would also "double your money." What the S&L is so dramatically offering is simply a 6% rate of return.

Can you earn a higher rate elsewhere (without incurring more risk)? Is your own time preference (which you can consider the "rate of return" that you earn on your own current consumption) higher than that? Then stay away!

It's actually interesting to scan through Table I for numbers that are close to 2, unearthing combinations of interest rates and time periods that permit you to "double your money." Five years at 15% comes close, as does 25 years at 3%. (Obviously, the lower the rate that you can earn, the longer it takes.) For some years, nothing really close to the "2" appears. At 10 years, for example, it looks as if "2" is about halfway between the figures for 6% and 9%; perhaps a rate of 7.5% would do it. There's actually a quick rule of thumb...

> The "rule of 72" states that the
> product of the interest rate and the
> number of years that it takes to
> double your money is about 72.

This rule doesn't work too well for way-out interest rates, but for 6% (12 years) and 4% (18 years) and 9% (about 8 years) it works fine.

Other misleading advice also encourages you to compare dollar amounts that occur at different points of time. Watch for it, and guard against it. Dollar sums that occur at different points of time are simply not the same dollars. They don't have the same value, and they can't be added up without producing <u>nonsense</u>. You must use either a discounting process (to bring the future dollars back to their present value equivalent) or a compounding process (to push your present dollars out to their future value equivalent), using the proper rate of interest, before you can do any comparing.

"Save $78,000 in interest payments by paying off your mortgage early!" Sounds good. (For those of you without the dubious experience, the total number of dollars paid in interest, over the years, on even an average home mortgage can be staggering.) But some of that $78,000 would have been paid next month, some of it in 11 years, some of it in 27 years, etc. Adding up these differently-timed payments produces a number with no meaning whatever. Besides, you'd have to "pay it off early" with "money now," or at least "money earlier than otherwise." What else could you have done with that money? The early payoff may or may not be a good idea, but the "$78,000" has nothing to do with it. It's just meaningless and confusing.

DISCOUNTING AND INTEREST:
ADDITIONAL OBSERVATIONS

Now that we have examined the fundamental origin of interest--the differing subjective time preferences of individuals in the society--and explored some of the mechanical details of how the rate of interest is actually used, it's time to leap on our horse and dash wildly off in all directions at once. In a sense, anyway.

I'd like to both step back a little from our preceding discussion to examine in another way the meaning of the discounting and compounding processes, and move forward from it to further applications of the processes. Finally, because the market rates of interest that we read and hear about are much more complex than "Frank and Sally in a field," we'll conclude with a few observations about market interest rates and some of the ways that the government's actions affect them.

Discounting and compounding--a reexamination
of their functions

Discounting permits us to compare an alternative which offers its satisfaction now with an alternative which offers its satisfaction later. Using our knowledge of the value of time, we construct an imaginary alternative that has the same value as the later one but whose satisfaction is available now. We then can treat this present value of the future option as if it were a currently available choice, and compare it to the other presently-available option. I've cautioned you against "imaginary alternatives" before, but this one is necessary to help us to make an informed choice. And we've been careful to make sure that it has the same value as the option for which it's substituting.

Compounding achieves the same goal by permitting us to transform the present alternative into another future one, offering its satisfaction at the same point in time as the genuine future alternative. We construct an imaginary alternative that has the same value as the present one, but doesn't offer its satisfactions until the same (future) time at which the other option offers its benefits. Since the future alternative and the "future value of the present alternative" offer their satisfactions at the same point in time, they can be directly compared.

Suppose that, like Sally, you could spend $100 on your own current consumption, or sacrifice consumption for a year in return for $112 then. Your rate of time preference is 10%. Let's do some compounding and discounting and see what they accomplish.

Compounding that $100 one year into the future, we find its "future value," $110. That's the future (one year out) sum with the same value as the present alternative ($100 now). It consists of your principal (the $100) and the interest that is required just to compensate you for the waiting ($10). If you had received only $110, you'd have earned $10 of interest income, but in a <u>value</u> or utility sense you would have just broken even. That $10 has really just compensated you for one of your costs. Of the $112 that you actually receive, only the other $2 actually makes you better off.

Projecting a present sum into the future, at the proper rate of interest, is a way of determining how much interest income you have to sacrifice if you give up the opportunity to invest that sum at that rate of interest.

> Projecting a present sum into the future allows us to find the <u>implicit interest cost</u> of giving up that sum now.

That sacrificed interest income is properly viewed as the <u>implicit interest cost</u> of choosing the alternative. Let's take the $100 for 3 years at 6% again. Its "future value" was $119.10, made up of $100 principal and $19.10 of interest income. That must be sacrificed to pursue other alternatives, so they're going to have to do better than that. The alternative in our example only offered $118 in three years. That's enough to repay our $100 principal, but it doesn't quite meet our implicit interest costs--the $19.10 interest that we would have earned by investing at 6%. The "$118" option is a loser by $1.10 (in three years).

Discounting, rather than put our interest earnings explicitly into the present alternative by projecting it into the future, pulls them out of the future alternative by projecting it back to the present.

> Discounting a sum to be received in the future PULLS OUT the <u>implicit interest cost</u>, leaving the principal that can be covered.

If the option of receiving $118 in three years were actually to offer us a 6 percent rate of return, we could obtain it for a present investment of only $99.08 (its present value: $118/1.1910). This process consists of pulling the interest portion out of the $118, leaving us with the principal that could be covered. Unfortunately, it's $0.92 less than the $100 that we're being asked to spend on this project, so the "$118" option is a loser by $0.92 (now, at the present).

If you've noticed that I identified the loss both as $1.10 and as $0.92, please also note that one of these figures is "at the end of three years," and the other one is "now." Needless to say, that makes a difference. Actually, if you find the present value of the "$1.10 in three years" by dividing it by 1.1910, you'll obtain $0.92. The loss can be evaluated at either point in time.

Discounting and "capital budgeting"

You can save big bucks on your heating and air-conditioning bills by purchasing a complete set of new high-tech triple-paned windows. Or so the ads tell us. Good idea? Should you spend $3,000 on new windows to be able to save $200 per year on your gas and electric bill? Golly, in only 15 years your savings has paid for the windows (15 x $200 = $3,000), and after that it's pure gravy.[3]

This is how the window salespeople--but not economists--want you to think. The $3,000 goes out now, while the stream of $200's trickles in a year at a time: $200 at the end of year 1, $200 at the end of year 2, etc. We cannot simply add up (or multiply) these $200's; they occur at different points of time, and are not comparable in value terms. We have to go through some kind of process that adjusts for the value of time. We must either discount the future stream of $200's back to the present for comparison with the $3,000 present outflow, or somehow project the present $3,000 into each and every future year, getting something that we can compare with those years' $200's.

It's interesting to imagine the $200 annual savings as permanent, and compare it to the annual interest income that you could receive every year if you invested the $3,000 and never touched the principal. If you can earn 9% per year, investing the $3,000 permits you to consume $270 per year (your interest income) while leaving the $3,000 undepleted. That's $70 per year better than the savings from the windows. The windows' $200 annual utility-bill savings is $70 short of covering your annual implicit interest cost.

The more common approach is to discount that expected future stream of savings back to the present, finding its "present value." The present value of the stream of annual $200's is just the sum of the present values of each of them. The present value (at 9%) of the $200 saving received at the end of year 1 is about $183; year 2's is $168; year 3's is $154; and so forth. If these savings go on forever, and we were able to compute all of the rest of them and add them together (which is OK because they all occur at the same point in time--right now), we'd get $2,222. This is the present value, at 9%, of our permanent stream of $200 annual utility-bill savings. (Note that if we invested $2,222 right now at 9%, our annual interest income would be $200. Needless to say, that's no coincidence. Note also that 2,222 = 200/0.09, which is how I computed it. If you know about the mathematical concept of the limit of an infinite series, that's what this is.)

Instead of the intractable problem of comparing $3,000 now with $200 each year forever, we have converted our problem into something that we can handle. We have found the present value equivalent of that future stream of savings. Your choice

---

[3] The fifteen years is often called the investment's "payback period." A businessman's rule of thumb is that the shorter the payback period, the better. It's easy to find fault with it, but on the whole it's not bad.

is effectively between $2,222 and $3,000 now, or between $200 and $270 per year forever. The windows don't save you money; they make you $778 poorer than if you just kept paying the higher utility bills.

This is just an example, of course. New windows often <u>are</u> a good idea, especially if they actually make a house more comfortable. Real dealings with window salespeople are more complex, and while our <u>method</u> is correct, you'll have to doctor up the details to make a sensible decision in your own case. Maybe they save more than $200 per year. If you expect utility bills to be rising sharply in future years (many people do), you'll want to adjust your savings upward as time goes on. Even if they still come out a money-loser, perhaps you're willing to make that sacrifice to help the environment. (But don't forget the resource use and pollution caused by manufacture of the new windows, and the solid-waste disposal of the old ones.)

Business planners face problems like this every day. A typical capital investment decision requires a fairly large current outlay (like buying a machine), but promises a stream of future net cash inflows (lower costs of other inputs, greater sales revenues from customers, or some combination of both). In Finance, these matters are called "capital budgeting." The business planner has to estimate the future effects of the machine or other capital investment: $6,241 net outflow in year 1 (not using it efficiently yet), $10,766 net inflow in year 2, $13,428 net inflow in year 3, $4,021 net outflow in year 4 (the machine will need rebuilding), and so forth. He must then determine the proper interest rate to use--this is often quite a problem in itself, and it can have a big effect on the decision--and find the <u>present value</u> of this projected future stream of effects. This is the "benefit" side of the decision to go with the investment; the "cost" side is just the current required outlay. The difference (and they <u>can</u> be subtracted, because they both occur at the same point of time) is called "net present value," or NPV, and it's a commonly used procedure in business planning. If NPV is positive, the project is a good deal and you go ahead; if it's negative, the project doesn't cover its costs and you stay away.

What's the maximum that you could pay for a small apartment building that looks as if it will yield net rents (that is, after utilities and taxes and maintenance expenses are paid) of $10,000 per year? Well, suppose you think the ten grand will go on forever, but it's a little risky so you establish a rate of return of 15% as the minimum that would let you believe the purchase is advantageous. The maximum purchase price is equal to that amount which, if invested at 15%, would produce $10,000 per year interest. It's $10,000/0.15 or $66,667. If the price were, say, $80,000, your minimum-required 15% rate of return would call for $12,000 annual net rents, and you can't get them. But if you can obtain the property for only $53,000, your annual implicit risk-adjusted interest costs (15% of this, or $7,950) are more than covered by the $10,000 annual net rent, and the deal is quite beneficial.

These examples provide just a taste of the procedures that permit us to compare alternatives that provide their benefits at different points of time. I always found capital budgeting to be the most interesting subject in the study of finance.

Further observations on the rate of interest

Time preference is the foundation of interest, the concept that explains the existence of interest and--in a general way--the level or height of interest rates. But an understanding of observed market interest rates probably best makes use of the apparatus of the "supply and demand of loanable funds." There's no real conflict between these views. As our Frank-and-Sally example suggested, individuals' time preferences provide the most important explanation of the supply of and demand for loanable funds. In the truly free market of laissez-faire capitalism, it is likely that the only sources of supply and demand of loanable funds would be individuals' voluntarily expressed time preferences.

Figure 10.4 shows the general shape of these supply and demand curves when there are many demanders and many suppliers. (It's just a smoothed-out Figure 10.3.) A widespread increase in individuals' time preferences is likely to both reduce the supply of loanable funds (as people save less) and increase the demand for them (as they, or others, borrow more); the effect is a higher rate of interest. Although the amount borrowed and lent may stay about the same, more of it will be used for consumption and less for investment. That higher interest rate will turn investment projects that previously covered their implicit interest costs into losers that can no longer be economically justified.

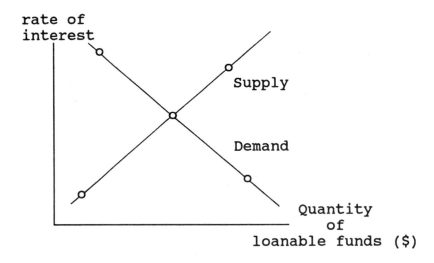

Figure 10.4: Supply and demand of loanable funds

The federal government exercises a major effect on the "credit markets," as the markets for loanable funds are usually called. When politicians decide to spend more than the federal government's tax receipts, the difference ("the deficit") has to be borrowed and adds to the demand for loanable funds. Other things the same, that drives up the market interest rate as the government--which doesn't seem to be very sensitive to interest costs--outbids private businesses seeking funds for investment. This process is called "crowding out," and it's just one of the ways in which the government alters the pattern of resource use, making it different from that which would be voluntarily selected by the individuals who properly own the resources.

The government often enters the market on the other side, too. When it looks as if Treasury borrowing to finance the deficit (adding to the demand for loanable funds) might drive the rate of interest up "too much," the Federal Reserve System can essentially just print up some new money and buy the Treasury's new bonds. This new money adds to the <u>supply</u> of loanable funds and--temporarily, at least--helps to keep the rate of interest down. (By the way, how much of a rise is "too much" is a political decision, based mostly on how upset voters might be.)

The reason that monetary expansion holds the level of market interest rates down only temporarily originates partly in that <u>price premium</u> that we discussed earlier. The additional money creates inflation, a general decline in the purchasing power of the monetary unit (dollar), and as soon as individuals begin to experience or even <u>expect</u> that, they reduce their supply and increase their demand of loanable funds. Picture the process on the above graph: monetary expansion shifts the Supply curve to the right, but the public's expectations of inflation shift both Supply (back to the left) and Demand (to the right), leaving a market rate of interest that's higher than before.

The financial markets have become so sensitive to this effect of monetary expansion that they react very quickly to reports of "easier Fed policy." Years ago, an increase in the rate of monetary expansion seemed to do little but <u>reduce</u> market interest rates; now, they seem just about as likely to rise as borrowers and lenders have learned to look beyond the immediate impact to the probable later inflation.

Think back, for a moment, to our discussion of capital budgeting. It described how business planners use the rate of interest to find present values, and thereby determine which investment projects are desirable and which aren't. That, in turn, determines <u>how</u> different goods get produced (with or without the machinery, say) and perhaps even <u>which</u> goods are produced. The marginal revenue products of different labor skills are affected; a high rate of interest may make interest costs so high that the MRP of the skilled labor that is complementary to the capital good is reduced to zero. These workers will have to find employment elsewhere. (Ask a construction heavy-equipment operator how this works.)

The rate of interest has such a great impact on the way that we all live that it is especially important for it to accurately reflect individuals' genuine time preferences. "High interest rates" are often criticized. But there's no problem with what the market is doing as long as the process that <u>made</u> them high involves nothing but the voluntary choices of individuals, exercising their legitimate property rights and their own subjective beliefs about time preference. (If you want to criticize them for having high time preferences, that's another story. It's not a problem with the market.)

Although it's true that greater capital investment would produce a greater output of consumer goods with the same inputs of labor and raw materials, that greater output would come along only <u>later</u>. A high rate of interest, which makes this investment unprofitable, means that individuals value time so highly that they prefer "less, sooner" to "more, later." Similarly, a <u>low</u> market rate of interest is fine if it genuinely reflects individuals' low time preferences. It is nothing to applaud if it has been achieved only by government policy that has made it a distorted picture of individuals' true preferences.

It was a dark day in the history of economics when the notion was developed that "the rate of interest" was something that the government could <u>and should</u> determine. The rate of interest, like any other price, "has work to do." It does its job best when it is left alone to accurately reflect the time preferences of the individuals in the society.

TABLE I

The "future value" of $1 invested now, at the end of n years, at an interest rate of r per year. (The table expresses "r" as a percent.) It is actually a table of

$$(1+r)^n$$

where r is expressed in its decimal (e.g. 0.06) form. Asterisks denote a number too large to fit in the table.

Year	0%	2%	4%	6%	9%	12%	15%	24%
1	1.000	1.020	1.040	1.060	1.090	1.120	1.150	1.240
2	1.000	1.040	1.082	1.124	1.188	1.254	1.323	1.538
3	1.000	1.061	1.125	1.191	1.295	1.405	1.521	1.907
4	1.000	1.082	1.170	1.262	1.412	1.574	1.749	2.364
5	1.000	1.104	1.217	1.338	1.539	1.762	2.011	2.932
6	1.000	1.126	1.265	1.419	1.677	1.974	2.313	3.635
7	1.000	1.149	1.316	1.504	1.828	2.211	2.660	4.508
8	1.000	1.172	1.369	1.594	1.993	2.476	3.059	5.590
9	1.000	1.195	1.423	1.689	2.172	2.773	3.518	6.931
10	1.000	1.219	1.480	1.791	2.367	3.106	4.046	8.594
11	1.000	1.243	1.539	1.898	2.580	3.479	4.652	10.657
12	1.000	1.268	1.601	2.012	2.813	3.896	5.350	13.215
13	1.000	1.294	1.665	2.133	3.066	4.363	6.153	16.386
14	1.000	1.319	1.732	2.261	3.342	4.887	7.076	20.319
15	1.000	1.346	1.801	2.397	3.642	5.474	8.137	25.196
16	1.000	1.373	1.873	2.540	3.970	6.130	9.358	31.243
17	1.000	1.400	1.948	2.693	4.328	6.866	10.761	38.741
18	1.000	1.428	2.026	2.854	4.717	7.690	12.375	48.039
19	1.000	1.457	2.107	3.026	5.142	8.613	14.232	59.568
20	1.000	1.486	2.191	3.207	5.604	9.646	16.367	73.864
25	1.000	1.641	2.666	4.292	8.623	17.000	32.919	216.54
30	1.000	1.811	3.243	5.743	13.268	29.960	66.212	634.82
40	1.000	2.208	4.801	10.286	31.409	93.051	267.86	5455.9
50	1.000	2.692	7.107	18.420	74.358	289.00	1083.7	46890
60	1.000	3.281	10.520	32.988	176.03	897.60	4384	402996
70	1.000	4.000	15.572	59.076	416.73	2787.8	17736	****
80	1.000	4.875	23.050	105.80	986.55	8658.5	71750	****
90	1.000	5.943	34.119	189.47	2335.5	26891	290272	****
100	1.000	7.245	50.505	339.30	5529.0	83522	****	****
infinite	1.000	infinite	............................infinite					

318

TABLE II

The "present value" of \$1 to be received at the end of n years, discounted at an interest rate of r per year. This is a table of

$$(1+r)^{-n}$$

where r is expressed as a decimal.

Year	0%	2%	4%	6%	9%	12%	15%	24%
1	1.000	0.980	0.962	0.943	0.917	0.893	0.870	0.806
2	1.000	0.961	0.925	0.890	0.842	0.797	0.756	0.650
3	1.000	0.942	0.889	0.840	0.772	0.712	0.658	0.524
4	1.000	0.924	0.855	0.792	0.708	0.636	0.572	0.423
5	1.000	0.906	0.822	0.747	0.650	0.567	0.497	0.341
6	1.000	0.888	0.790	0.705	0.596	0.507	0.432	0.275
7	1.000	0.871	0.760	0.665	0.547	0.452	0.376	0.222
8	1.000	0.853	0.731	0.627	0.502	0.404	0.327	0.179
9	1.000	0.837	0.703	0.592	0.460	0.361	0.284	0.144
10	1.000	0.820	0.676	0.558	0.422	0.322	0.247	0.116
11	1.000	0.804	0.650	0.527	0.388	0.287	0.215	0.094
12	1.000	0.788	0.625	0.497	0.356	0.257	0.187	0.076
13	1.000	0.773	0.601	0.469	0.326	0.229	0.163	0.061
14	1.000	0.758	0.577	0.442	0.299	0.205	0.141	0.049
15	1.000	0.743	0.555	0.417	0.275	0.183	0.123	0.040
16	1.000	0.728	0.534	0.394	0.252	0.163	0.107	0.032
17	1.000	0.714	0.513	0.371	0.231	0.146	0.093	0.026
18	1.000	0.700	0.494	0.350	0.212	0.130	0.081	0.021
19	1.000	0.686	0.475	0.331	0.194	0.116	0.070	0.017
20	1.000	0.673	0.456	0.312	0.178	0.104	0.061	0.014
25	1.000	0.610	0.375	0.233	0.116	0.059	0.030	0.005
30	1.000	0.552	0.308	0.174	0.075	0.033	0.015	0.002
40	1.000	0.453	0.208	0.097	0.032	0.011	0.004	0.000
50	1.000	0.372	0.141	0.054	0.013	0.003	0.001	0.000
60	1.000	0.305	0.095	0.030	0.006	0.001	0.000	0.000
70	1.000	0.250	0.064	0.017	0.002	0.000	0.000	0.000
80	1.000	0.205	0.043	0.009	0.001	0.000	0.000	0.000
90	1.000	0.168	0.029	0.005	0.000	0.000	0.000	0.000
100	1.000	0.138	0.020	0.003	0.000	0.000	0.000	0.000
infinity	1.00	0	0	0	0	0	0	0

TABLE III

The "present value" of a $1 <u>annuity</u>, $1 to be received at the end
of <u>each of</u> the next n years, discounted at an interest rate of r
per year. This is a table of

$$\sum_{i=1}^{n} (1+r)^{-i}$$

where r is expressed as a decimal. (Each number in this table is
the sum of all of the numbers at and above its location in Table
II. Try it with, say, 9% and 2 years.) The "inf" stands for an
infinite number.

Year	0%	2%	4%	6%	9%	12%	15%	24%
1	1.000	0.980	0.962	0.943	0.917	0.893	0.870	0.806
2	2.000	1.942	1.886	1.833	1.759	1.690	1.626	1.457
3	3.000	2.884	2.775	2.673	2.531	2.402	2.283	1.981
4	4.000	3.808	3.630	3.465	3.240	3.037	2.855	2.404
5	5.000	4.713	4.452	4.212	3.890	3.605	3.352	2.745
6	6.000	5.601	5.242	4.917	4.486	4.111	3.784	3.020
7	7.000	6.472	6.002	5.582	5.033	4.564	4.160	3.242
8	8.000	7.325	6.733	6.210	5.535	4.968	4.487	3.421
9	9.000	8.162	7.435	6.802	5.995	5.328	4.772	3.566
10	10.000	8.983	8.111	7.360	6.418	5.650	5.019	3.682
11	11.000	9.787	8.760	7.887	6.805	5.938	5.234	3.776
12	12.000	10.575	9.385	8.384	7.161	6.194	5.421	3.851
13	13.000	11.348	9.986	8.853	7.487	6.424	5.583	3.912
14	14.000	12.106	10.563	9.295	7.786	6.628	5.724	3.962
15	15.000	12.849	11.118	9.712	8.061	6.811	5.847	4.001
16	16.000	13.578	11.652	10.106	8.313	6.974	5.954	4.033
17	17.000	14.292	12.166	10.477	8.544	7.120	6.047	4.059
18	18.000	14.992	12.659	10.828	8.756	7.250	6.128	4.080
19	19.000	15.678	13.134	11.158	8.950	7.366	6.198	4.097
20	20.000	16.351	13.590	11.470	9.129	7.469	6.259	4.110
25	25.000	19.523	15.622	12.783	9.823	7.843	6.464	4.147
30	30.000	22.396	17.292	13.765	10.274	8.055	6.566	4.160
40	40.000	27.355	19.793	15.046	10.757	8.244	6.642	4.166
50	50.000	31.424	21.482	15.762	10.962	8.304	6.661	4.167
60	60.000	34.761	22.623	16.161	11.048	8.324	6.665	4.167
70	70.000	37.499	23.395	16.385	11.084	8.330	6.666	4.167
80	80.000	39.745	23.915	16.509	11.100	8.332	6.667	4.167
90	90.000	41.587	24.267	16.579	11.106	8.333	6.667	4.167
100	100.00	43.098	24.505	16.618	11.109	8.333	6.667	4.167
inf	inf	50.000	25.000	16.667	11.111	8.333	6.667	4.167

1.   TIME PREFERENCE is the individuals's preference for "sooner" rather than "later."

2.   Individuals with HIGH time preference have a stronger preference for current consumption over future consumption than do people with LOW time preference.

3.   Different time preferences make lending and borrowing MUTUALLY BENEFICIAL, at an interest rate between the two individuals' rates of time preference.

4.   Lending and borrowing money can be called "supplying" and "demanding" LOANABLE FUNDS.

5.   The market interest rate on a particular loan is the SUM of the "time preference rate," the RISK PREMIUM, and the PRICE PREMIUM.

6.   Real-world interest rates are complex, but TIME PREFERENCE is the essence or basic nature of interest.

7.   Because the timing of events affects their VALUE, one cannot DIRECTLY compare two alternatives that offer satisfaction at different times.

8.   The process of finding the FUTURE VALUE of a present alternative is called COMPOUNDING, like "compound interest" on a savings account.

9.   The process of finding the PRESENT VALUE of a future alternative is called DISCOUNTING.

10. Your rate of time preference can be interpreted as the rate of interest that you earn on your own CURRENT CONSUMPTION.

11. The PURPOSE of discounting and compounding is to ACCURATELY IDENTIFY your alternatives.

12. Adding together sums of money that are to be received or paid at different times produces a number that is MEANINGLESS.

13. COMPOUNDING a sum that you are considering giving up now is a way of finding your action's IMPLICIT INTEREST COST.

14. DISCOUNTING a sum to be received in the future is a way of EXTRACTING from it your implicit interest cost.

15. Business capital investments always provide returns and involve costs at different times, so DISCOUNTING is vital to CAPITAL BUDGETING.

16. The federal government's "deficit spending" adds to the DEMAND for loanable funds.

17. The Federal Reserve System's process of creating new money often adds to the SUPPLY of loanable funds.

18. But monetary expansion raises expectations of INFLATION, and therefore increases the PRICE PREMIUM.

19. Market rates of interest are very important PRICES. They "have work to do," and should "be free to tell the truth" about people's time preferences.

Problems

These start out pretty slowly, but pick up the pace as we go along. It might help to begin to use the Tables right away, even for those that are easy to determine without recourse to the Tables' help. [I have provided a few answers to guide you along.]

1. How much money would you have in 1 year if you invest $1,000 now at an annual interest rate of (a) 6%, (b) 9%, (c) 15% ?

2. How much money would you have in 7 years if you invest $1,000 now at an annual interest rate of (a) 4%, (b) 24%, (c) 9% ?

3. Approximately what interest rate would allow you to "double your money" in 7 years? How did you determine it?

4. If you want to have $1,090 one year from now, and can earn 9% on your savings, how much will you have to invest now?

5. What is the "present value" of $1,090 to be received in one year, discounted at 9%?

6. Find the present value of $1,000 to be received in one year, discounted at 9%. [Answer: $917]

7. How much money would you have to invest now, if you can earn 6 percent on it and want to have $1,000 in one year?

8. Find the present value of $1,316 to be received in seven years, discounted at four percent.

9. Find the present value of $1,316 to be received in seven years, discounted at six percent. [Answer: $875]

10. Please infer, from (8) and (9), something about the present value of $1,316 to be received in seven years, discounted at five percent.

11. If you have $1,000 that you know you can invest at five percent, would you be better off lend it instead to an absolutely trustworthy person who promises to pay you $1,316 in seven years? Why or why not?

12. Would you rather invest $5,000 at nine percent, or exchange it for the right to receive $3,000 three years from today and another $4,000 five years from today? Explain, using present values. [Partial answer: there's a $2600 involved...]

13.   If the best investments (in the traditional sense--lending, or buying capital goods yourself) that you can find pay only 6% but your own personal subjective rate of time preference is 8%, how should you "invest" (that is, use) your money to get the best return (in satisfaction)?

14.   You invest $10,000 in a small business. Two years later, the somewhat successful operation is sold, and your share is $13,220. If you could have earned 12 percent on your money invested in the best alternative way, did you more than cover your implicit interest costs? What annual rate of return did you actually earn on your investment in the business? [Hint: I'd use Table I.]

15.   An investment alternative promises to pay you $10,000 per year at the end of each of the next 20 years. What is the present value of this stream of future inflows, if the relevant interest rate is 9 percent? [Hint: This is a Table III problem.]

16.   If you happened to have sufficient cash sitting around at the moment, and you could indeed earn 9 percent in the best alternative, would you be willing to pay $100,000 for the annuity contract described in #15? How about $85,000? Why or why not?

17.   What is the present value, discounting at 9 percent, of a contract that will pay you $100 per year for 30 years and $1,000 at the end of year 30? [Hint: Use Table III and Table II, and add the results together. Partial answer: There's a $1,027 involved...]

(Note: This will be the current market price--you can find it in your Wall Street Journals--of a newly issued 30-year bond with "par value" of $1,000 and a "coupon rate" of 10 percent, that has a "yield to maturity" of 9 percent.)

18.   Find the market price of the bond above if its yield to maturity (the rate that was 9% in #17) rises to 12 percent. What happened to it? Can you explain this in common, everyday, English?

19.   You are convinced that if your small business had a certain machine, your net revenues would increase by $3,000 per year for each of the next 8 years. Your relevant "cost of capital" or interest rate is 15 percent. What is the maximum that you could pay for this machine and still profit from the investment? [Hint: another Table III problem.]

20.   Let's make #19 a little more realistic. Suppose that the machine above requires a $7,000 overhaul at the end of year four, and can be sold for $2,000 to a used-equipment dealer at the end of year eight. (Don't bother evaluating whether the thing should be scrapped after four years to avoid the overhaul.

Of course a real-world business planner would.) <u>Now</u> what's the maximum you could offer for it? [Hint: Start from your answer to #19 and adjust it, as required. Don't forget the <u>timing</u> of the overhaul payment and the salvage receipt. Partial answer: There's a -$4,004 involved.]

CHAPTER 11

PROFIT AND ENTREPRENEURSHIP

PROFIT AND IMPLICIT COSTS

For once, a word's common, everyday definition and that which is just fine for economic analysis turn out to be the same.

> Profit is revenue minus cost.

If you're suspicious, though, because you don't believe that things can be that simple in an economics book, I'm afraid you're right. Profit really isn't that simple. The definition above works just fine; the problems and debates arise as soon as one tries to define with precision revenue and cost.

Actually, we've been dealing with profit since Chapter 1. In its general sense, revenue is nothing other than benefit, or the value of the alternative you're considering. Cost, of course, is the value of the best alternative to the one that you're considering. Profit, then, in this very general sense, is the amount by which you benefit by choosing the action you're considering rather than the best alternative to it. It's "net benefit."

In this sense, individuals take only those actions that are profitable; "profitable" and "efficient" are synonyms for actions with benefits that exceed costs; no individual ever takes an action that, at the time of his choice, he evaluated as unprofitable. Your "profit" from eating at the Snack Bar rather than at the Student Union is how much better off you think you are, than you think you would have been in the Union.

A more narrow interpretation: business and money

Although it's important to understand the general nature of profit, the word profit is usually restricted to business activities that are designed to "make money." Revenue and cost are interpreted as sums of money. If revenue exceeds cost there's profit; if it doesn't, we use the term "loss" to identify a negative profit.

Think back, for a moment, to the concept of comparative advantage. We began our investigation by assuming away any subjective preference for either kind of work.

That allowed us to learn what the comparative costs had to say, who would have which comparative advantage under this assumption.

Then we relaxed the assumption ("But I hate plumbing..."), admitting that individuals really base their choices on subjective benefits and costs which involve their attitudes toward the different tasks. Since we can't <u>know</u> what these preferences are, we can't determine their comparative advantages. We economists may be able to help a person to understand how many extra minutes he'll have to work, or how many wodgets he'll sacrifice, but only he can determine if it's worth it. If our goal is his well-being, we must recognize the limitations of our knowledge, and leave the choice up to him.

We adopt a similar procedure with profit. Ultimately, any decision reflects the subjective judgments of the actor. Nothing that we say, no matter how "businessy" we get about our calculations of monetary receipts and expenditures, changes that.

Suppose that we are able to show, conclusively, that Shirley could make $85,000 per year more by writing advertising in New York City than by running a small country inn somewhere in central New Hampshire. Does it follow that we economists have scientifically "proven" that she should write advertising rather than keep tabs on the stew planned for her guests' dinner? Of course not.

It might be very important to her decision, however, to realize exactly how big a pay cut a move to New Hampshire would involve. This computation is somewhat like our comparative costs: a relatively concrete, objective calculation of numbers. (Widgets, minutes, or dollars.) Such numbers are never enough to determine the proper action. But they often provide helpful information about the nature of the alternatives. Value the alternatives as you wish, but you must know what they are, first.

Our goal in this chapter is only to provide the actor with better information about the nature of his alternatives. It's his obligation to attribute subjective value to them. The world is full of people who are deliberately choosing to make less money than they could. Our calculations of profit provide us with no basis for judging that they should act in some way other than that which they've voluntarily chosen.

Economists don't usually pay much attention to the revenue from business activity. For a thorough elucidation of the difficulties of determining revenue, you should consult an accounting textbook. If revenue seems pretty straightforward (the money that you receive from your customers), consider some of these situations. You receive $300 cash in late July for a service contract that starts in August and lasts for a year: is that a $300 revenue for July, $25 revenue in August and each of the 11 following months, or something else? On July 30 a man signs a contract to buy a refrigerator ($700), paying $35 per month for two years. Should that full $700 be labelled "July revenue," or should we try to allow for the possibility that he won't make his payments? Calling the whole $700 definite revenue might be overoptimistic, and we want our accounts to tell the truth.

Accountants have to allocate revenues and costs among different time periods, and it poses many of their most vexing problems. Economists simply aren't much concerned with these difficulties. I'll return soon to some of the differences between economics and accounting; suffice it to say that both are valuable, but because they have different functions their concepts and methods are a little different.

The problem of implicit costs

If the economist treats revenue rather cavalierly, as simply money taken in from customers (PxQ for a non-discriminating seller), he takes the matter of the determination of cost seriously.

Most importantly, we insist on an "opportunity cost" concept, that the cost of producing the revenue be properly identified as the value of most-attractive opportunity that has to be foregone.

Evaluating the profitability of an action taken in the past, like the last month's operation of our business, requires us to evaluate the value of the best opportunities that we actually passed up during the past month. We can then decide if, knowing what we know now about what happened on the 18th and the 29th, the decisions that we made on the first were good.

That's interesting and important information, but we must always remind ourselves that decisions that our business managers made on the first of the month could be based only the information available to them on the 1st. As I cautioned you earlier about judging others' actions, we have to base any criticism of their performance on some judgment that they <u>should have foreseen</u> on the first of the month, better than they apparently did, what was likely to happen later. Financial markets are generally very fair about this; a report of disastrous quarterly earnings that arose from events nobody could reasonably have been expected to foresee is not taken as representative of the quality of management, and has little effect on the price of the corporation's stock.

To judge the profitability of a currently considered action, the decision maker follows the procedures that we described in Chapter 2. He imagines the future cash inflows attributable to his decision, the future cash inflows that might have arisen (or outflows that could have been avoided) from the best alternative, and compares them. Timing differences must, of course, be considered, using techniques that we examined in the last chapter. This decision process--evaluating the profitability of a currently considered action--is no different from the process of choice that we've been considering all throughout this book.

One of the important contributions that economists have to make is their emphasis on the nature of cost as the value of the best foregone opportunity. That raises the matter of explicit and implicit costs, which is perhaps best illustrated with an example.

Explicit and implicit costs: an example

A couple in their sixties operates a "Mom'n'Pop" grocery store on the first floor of their row house in a large city. We are trying to evaluate the profitability of their business operation. Interpreting "profit" narrowly in terms of money, we must determine whether they are making more money by operating the business than they would make if they pursued a realistic alternative.

We aren't interested in whether they're making more money than they would if they both simply watched television all day, or if they were running a trapline along a Yukon river (or pursuing some other alternative that they, themselves, would never consider). No matter how our calculations turn out, we can't show whether they should, or should not, operate the store, because that depends on their subjective values. But it's interesting and important whether "operating the grocery store" is likely to provide them with greater monetary income than they would receive if they pursued a carefully specified alternative.

Alternative? What alternative? I haven't been very specific about that. Actually, it depends on the individuals who confront the choices. Profit is a way to compare two alternatives (or, at least, to determine how much extra money one of them will bring in than the other), and specifying them is really the privilege of the actor. Economists often use <u>market prices</u> as the universal alternative, as we'll see in our example. In some circumstances, the sale or purchase of something at "the market price" isn't the actor's second-best option. But it's a good place to start.

Each month this couple takes in $5,000 from their customers. This is their sales revenue or "total revenue." The goods that they sell cost them $2,500 (and restocking the shelves for next month will, also) and utilities and business-related insurance add another $500, so their explicit monthly outlay of cash comes to $3,000. There are businesspeople who will figure like this:

Revenue:	$5,000
-Cost:	<u>$3,000</u>
= Profit:	$2,000.

Not bad, for a couple of their age owning and operating their own business in their own building. They're likely to congratulate themselves on the business's profitability.

But they may also comment that "It's a good thing we work here ourselves, because if we had labor expenses the store wouldn't be nearly so profitable." They are evidently treating their own labor services as costless. From an economist's perspective, that is hardly likely to be the case. If they can properly run their own grocery store, for example, they can certainly do the same for someone else's. When they work in their own store, they're sacrificing the opportunity to do similar work elsewhere. It is true that they do not have any <u>explicit</u> wage bill, or payroll. But they have <u>implicit</u> labor costs: the wage income that they could have been earning, doing similar work elsewhere, that they must forego to operate their own store.

Let's say they are open for 20 hours a week, and the owner of a similar store nearby (we don't want to complicate the problem with transportation and other inconvenience) would pay them $5/hour each to do identical work for him. With 4 weeks per month (another economist's simplification), the couple could be receiving $800 per month of explicit wage income by doing identical work under nearly identical circumstances. Because they must sacrifice this wage income to devote the same labor to their own store, it's an <u>implicit</u> labor cost: not wages that must be paid, but wage income that can't be received.

Whenever the owner of a business provides his own labor services, and is not properly compensated by an explicit wage payment, an accurate measure of the profitability of the operation of the business must consider his implicit labor cost. The effect that it has here is to increase "costs" by $800 per month, reducing "profit" by that much:

Revenue:	$5,000
-Explicit costs:	$3,000
-Implicit labor cost:	$ 800
= Profit:	$1,200

The operation of the business still looks pretty good; the couple could actually pay themselves the same wage that they could be earning elsewhere ($800 for the two of them, for month of half-time work) and still show a net monetary benefit from operating their own store of $1,200 per month. It's not as good as $2,000, but it's closer to the truth and it's still OK.

But it's time to consider another implicit cost. They're running the shop in their own building, probably living in a few rooms upstairs, and are likely to explain, "It's a good thing we own the building, because we could never afford rent expenses." But the couple could probably have rented the space to another individual, perhaps even to operate his grocery store. (Maybe he's the guy who hires them to run the store at a wage of $800 per month.) What rental income could they have earned, if they had rented the property for a use similar to their own retail grocery store? (We don't want to consider a wildly different use, like rehearsal space for a heavy-metal band; that would introduce additional complications.) Perhaps $1,000 per month?

Taking into account this new implicit cost reduces our apparent profit even further. Of course we aren't really reducing the business's profit. We're just making the numbers tell a more accurate story. The profit really is less than $1,200; incorporating the $1,000 of foregone explicit rental income as a cost of using the property themselves simply gets us closer to the truth about the overall benefit of operating the grocery store. Compared to the alternative of renting out the property for a similar use, and working at a similar job for the same hours, these folks are only $200 per month better off by operating their own store.

Revenue:	$5,000
-Explicit monetary costs:	$3,000
-Implicit labor costs:	$ 800
-Implicit rental costs:	$1,000
= Profit:	$ 200

A neglected implicit cost: interest

And we're not done yet. (That's what this pleasant couple was afraid of. They probably think we economists are robbing them of money every time we grab for our calculators.) One of the most important implicit costs is so frequently overlooked that I thought it deserved its own heading: the implicit cost that consists of the explicit interest income that the owner of a business must sacrifice if he finances the business with his own capital.

Every business has to have various kinds of assets: inventory, cash register, shelves, cabinets, signs. Suppose that the regular, ongoing operation of our little grocery store requires the use of $10,000 in capital (for the assets listed above), and that the owners could recover this sum if the business were ever sold. The $10,000 must be invested to operate the business, in other words, but it can be recovered whenever the business ceases operation.

Our couple puts up the $10,000 themselves, withdrawing it from a mutual-fund account in which they had spent many years accumulating it, and comment: "It's a good thing we didn't have to borrow that money. The interest costs would eat up our profits."

By now you're aware that they do not avoid interest costs by using their own money. If the mutual fund in which they had been investing was somewhat risky, they may have earned 10 percent per year on their money. That means that they have to sacrifice $1,000 of explicit interest income each year, if they withdraw the money for use in their own business. It's an <u>implicit</u> interest cost.

That $1,000 per year works out to about $83 per month, so our little income statement now becomes:

Revenue:	$5,000
-Explicit monetary costs:	$3,000
-Implicit labor costs:	$ 800
-Implicit rental costs:	$1,000
-Implicit interest costs:	$ 83
= Profit:	$ 117

This sum, while still positive, is vastly different from the $2,000 "profit" that ignored all of the implicit costs. A slight change in assumptions--perhaps the space could have been rented out for $1,200 per month--could easily have turned it into a loss.

To see what's going on, it's interesting to imagine the couple actually pursuing that "next-best alternative." Their $10,000 would still be earning them $83 per month interest, they'd be collecting a rent check of $1,000 from the proprietors, and they'd be collecting paychecks totalling $800 from their bosses. That's $1,883 of explicit, actual, monetary income. This is exactly $117 per month less money than if they had operated the store. (Of course they don't have to pay the $3,000 explicit monetary costs, and if you want to add that in as one of the benefits of <u>not</u> operating the store, it looks as if they're $4,883 ahead. But then you can't forget that they also miss out on the $5,000 of revenue; that's a cost of <u>not</u> operating, and when it's considered it again shows that they'd be $117 in the hole by "not operating" rather than "operating.")

If the couple actually had borrowed the $10,000 at 10% per year, they would have had to make an explicit monetary payment of $83 per month just to cover the interest. (Unlike your car loan, some financial institutions are willing to extend businesses' credit arrangements indefinitely, as long as they continue to make regular interest payments. That's because the business is expected to live forever. Your car isn't.) It's unlikely that, having to write out a check every month for $83, they would have neglected to consider interest costs. But that's because they would then be <u>explicit</u>, actually requiring the payment of money. It's a lot easier to ignore a cost when it consists simply of the foregoing of the opportunity to receive something.

Economic versus accounting "profits"

The economist's insistence that all genuine opportunity costs, the monetary value of the best foregone alternative, be included among "cost" and therefore subtracted from revenue when calculating profit, leads to a somewhat different perspective than that which is reflected in businesses' "profit and loss" or "income" statements.

One of the principal differences arises from the matter of implicit interest costs. Consider a business corporation in which stockholders have purchased $1,000,000 of common stock. All that means is that individual investors have given the corporation a million dollars, cash, in return for pieces of paper symbolizing the ownership of a fraction of the corporation.

If the corporation's business operation is successful, its value will rise and so will the value of each fractional share of ownership: its stock price goes up. That's one way that the stockholder benefits. The other way that the initial investor can get a return on his investment is from <u>dividends</u>, periodic payments from the corporation to its stockholders. Although an individual stockholder who wants cash can get it by selling to another individual, the only flow of money from the corporation to its stockholders is its payment of dividends.

The payment of dividends on common stock is not <u>legally</u> required. That's why accountants do not consider dividends to be a cost of doing business. They view common-stock dividends as a "distribution of profits." Here's a very crude corporate income statement, including only the minimum needed to illustrate the point in which we're interested.

```
            Revenue:   ------
   - Cost of goods sold:   ------
 - Explicit interest cost:   ------
          - Depreciation:   ------

               = Profit:   ------
            - Dividends:   ------
    = Retained Earnings:   ------
```

From this perspective, a portion of profits are paid out to stockholders (e.g., the monthly dividend check that many retirees count on for income) or are retained by the corporation, to be reinvested in new assets. The analysis of a corporation's best dividend policy (What determines the fraction of profits that should be retained? What's the importance of a reputation for "never cutting the dividend," even in the face of declining profits?) is a fascinating topic addressed in the study of corporate finance.

But don't those common-stock investors have alternative uses for their money? An old lesson might usefully be dredged up from earlier in this book: If you want someone to take a particular action, you must outbid his best alternative. Maybe the corporation has no legal obligation to pay interest to those stockholders, but it surely has an economic obligation. If it doesn't offer something that they perceive as better than their best alternative, they're going to take their money and run.

From the economist's perspective, in other words, something else has to be subtracted before we identify the result as profit: implicit interest on the stockholders' equity. If our dividend payment exceeded the economically-required payment for "implicit interest on stockholders' equity," then the rest of it really does constitute a payout of some of the corporation's genuine economic profit to the stockholders. If our dividend payment is not as large as the economically necessary compensation to stockholders, then--if they leave their money invested with us--they must be expecting a larger return in the future, and it's our (economic, not legal) obligation to see that they get it.

```
            Revenue:   ------
   - Cost of goods sold:   ------
 - Explicit interest cost:   ------
          - Depreciation:   ------
 -Implicit interest on
      stockholders' equity:   ------
               = Profit:   ------
```

There is no obvious connection between the size of the dividend payment and the size of the economically required "implicit interest cost" on stockholders' equity. It is also not obvious just what this "implicit interest cost on stockholders' equity" is. But it's determined by the return that the investors believe that they could obtain on an equivalently risky investment elsewhere. Because it depends on judgments of risk, that's not an interest rate that can simply be read from a financial table somewhere. (This whole problem takes us back into the issue of the determination of the "corporate cost of capital," which I identified in the last chapter as another fascinating study within corporate finance.)

Huge corporate profits?

The "corporate profits" that make the headlines are those reported in the accounting statements. The legal community and tax authorities (governments at all levels) impose obligations on the accounting profession to report numbers that can be proven with invoices and other evidence of past payments actually incurred. This explains a past-oriented perspective that is quite contrary to the economist's future-oriented outlook. And no tax collector is likely to accept the argument that, although there's no legal obligation to pay common stockholders, it's an implicit interest cost.

(Just for the record, it's not clear that even "future-oriented" economists would prefer to see our current historical financial statements replaced by costs and revenues that consisted of the corporation's executives' anticipations of future alternatives.)

Accountants and economists simply have different functions, different roles to play, in the understanding of human action. It should not be surprising that they look at things a little differently. While accounting concepts of cost and profit do not satisfy the economist's requirement of relevance for current action, the economist's "anticipations of the future" don't meet the accountant's requirements for objective verifiability--something that would convince skeptical financial analysts and could be proven in a court of law.

Here's an imaginary headline:

XYZ REPORTS RECORD PROFITS
$10,000,000 for the year

Well, that's very interesting, and it certainly sounds impressive. It's better than $9,000,000. But what was the corporation's implicit interest cost on stockholders' equity?

Perhaps XYZ uses a hundred million dollars of investors' money in its pipelines, factory buildings, real estate, and chemical testing laboratories. Now, what interest rate should we assume that stockholders implicitly require? If we assume 10%, then XYZ's annual implicit interest cost is ten million and its economic profit is zero. That "spectacular" profit was actually no profit at all, just large enough to cover the corporation's costs.

Perhaps that required return is 12%. Then our headline ought to read:

XYZ SUFFERS LOSS FOR YEAR
Fails to cover costs by $2,000,000

Please think about these implicit interest costs the next time you hear about "huge corporate profits." You can't really know if they're profits or not, or the size of them, without knowing how large the stockholders' equity is, and making some guess at the required rate of return on that investment. There is no doubt that the true, economic, profits--that is, the degree to which the business operation has more than covered its genuine costs--are generally much smaller than reported corporate accounting profits. Many reported "multimillion-dollar profits" are, in fact, negative.

Staying in business on zero profits?

Defenders of the American business system can often be heard to say that people shouldn't be so critical of profits, because profits are required if a business is to survive. It must have profits to be able to pay its stockholders, to compensate them for investing in a productive future.

They're right, if they're talking about <u>accounting</u> profits. After all, accountants consider payments to stockholders to be a "distribution of profit," and if there's no profit there's no distribution. (Well, there can still be a dividend payment, but it has to come out of the corporation's capital.)

But the economist considers those economically-required payments to which the individual above refers as one of the business's legitimate <u>costs</u>. It's already been covered by the time we calculate profits. In fact, economic profits can be precisely <u>zero</u> and still offer a competitive rate of return to the corporate stockholders.

When accounting profit is zero, there are implicit costs (especially interest to common stockholders) that cannot be covered, and continuation of the business is not feasible for long. But an economic profit of zero means that <u>all</u> genuine costs (including implicit costs of all kinds, especially interest to common stockholders) are covered. There's nothing left over, but all resource owners are being paid exactly the minimum necessary to retain their services.

A business with zero economic profit can go on forever, since all of its costs are covered. Whenever you hear someone claim that "profits are unnecessary" because businesses don't need them to survive, find out whether he means accounting or economic profit. (People who say things like this usually don't know.) If he means economic profit, he's right; if accounting profit, he's wrong. Sometimes he'll explain why <u>economic</u> profit is unnecessary, then conclude that <u>accounting</u> profit isn't needed either. It takes some sharp thinking to keep things straight when the same word ("profit" or "cost") is used with two different--but related--meanings.[1]

---

[1] For a <u>real</u> misunderstanding of "profit," take the case of a television show that I saw recently. The protagonist announced happily that the owner of a hamburger stand had donated "one day's profits" of $500 to a certain charity. He surely meant total sales revenue. Annual <u>profits</u> of $180,000 (about $500 per day) would make that stand worth perhaps $2 million, as we'll see later.

DISCOUNTING AND ECONOMIC PROFIT

Back in Chapter 7, I asked you to imagine discovering a way to combine $6 worth of resources (at their current market prices) to produce a product for which people will pay $11. You plan to produce and sell 2,000 of them each month, and to retire to your own horse farm in the Valley before you're 30.

Here's your (hoped-for) monthly income statement:

Revenue:	$22,000
-Cost:	$12,000
= Profit:	$10,000

As you learned--to your dismay--a few chapters ago, two market responses are likely to interfere with your plans: new entrants into the industry (trying to imitate your success) will increase the supply of the good and reduce its price (down from $11), and they'll also bid up the costs (up from $6) by adding to the demand for the resources. In principle, this process is likely to continue until something like this depicts your monthly profit-and-loss picture:

Revenue:	$16,500
-Cost:	$16,500
= Profit:	$0

As long as there remains any gap whatsoever between revenue and costs (as accurately defined in economics), there is _incentive_ for existing producers to expand or new producers to enter. The incentive disappears only when there is no longer any (economic) profit.

If we try to draw out some of the implications of this little story, the concept of profit becomes a particularly intriguing one.

Profit emerges from a new discovery, some way of creating value that had not previously been known. The attempt to make such a discovery is known as _entrepreneurship_, and the discoverer as an _entrepreneur_.

```
ENTREPRENEURSHIP is the attempt to discover
a previously unknown way to create value.
```

(It's French; the English equivalent is "undertaker," which is evidently why we keep using the French.)

The discovery can be a new product, more valuable than the best of the known alternative uses for the resources (like this example), or it can be the same old product produced with a new combination of (less-valued) resources, like our Delta and Gamma "competition" example. In either case, value is created. Of course the entrepreneur would like to capture for himself as much as he can of the value that he has created. But exchanges must be mutually beneficial, and--in practice--entrepreneurs often receive only a small portion of the gains from trade. For one thing, people with the temperament to be good entrepreneurs--creative, innovative, independent, courageous--don't always excel at business management and legal affairs.

Just as soon as others begin to learn of the product or technique, however, their own self-interested action begins to chip away at that profit. The more widely the opportunity becomes known, the more vigorous the attempts to cash in on it, and the more quickly it disappears.

There is no such thing as a widely-known opportunity for profit. There are always, in free-market capitalism, opportunities for profit, but they require discovery, innovation, and risk-taking. Anyone who feels obliged to wait around until everyone agrees, is going to find himself with zero profit.

We'll get back this general nature of profit, and what it takes to earn income in the form of economic profit, after some examples.

Even if entry is impossible...

In the example above, apparently there were no legal restrictions (including legitimate property rights) that prevented others from producing an identical--or at least similar--product. Your idea either wasn't patentable or you simply didn't bother (many companies don't), and the production didn't require the use of unique resources of which you were the sole owner. Let's introduce the latter situation into our discussion.

You bought a few acres of land outside of town. You paid a market price determined solely by the location and the view, and were happy to get it. One morning you discover, in the corner of your property right down by the road, a mineral spring that produces the most delightful water you've ever tasted. You put up a little paper sign (essentially zero cost) announcing the spring, and people immediately begin to purchase your water. They bring their own cups, drop their money in a cigar box, and trample only a couple of feet of your grass. (These conditions are supposed to establish that providing the water has no costs at all to you.) Using proper price-searcher techniques, you set a price to sell that quantity at which marginal revenue equals marginal cost (both are zero, in this problem). You discover that you will sell exactly $10,000 per year of this water, and believe that it can go on forever.

Here's what you anticipate for your first-year income statement:

Revenue:	$10,000
- Cost:	$ 0
= Profit:	$10,000

Since it isn't possible for anyone else to offer water like this, you have no fears of competition. It looks as if that profit can go on forever. Well, let's reconsider that.

If the relevant rate of interest is 10%, in your own judgment the present value of the spring is the present value of an annuity of $10,000 per year forever, discounted at 10%. That's the amount of money that, if you had it now and invested it at 10%, would earn you $10,000 per year forever. It's $100,000. As far as you're concerned, owning the spring and having $100,000 invested at 10% are equivalent. You'd get $10,000 per year either way.

As others begin to learn of the spring's marvelous economic productivity, you're likely to begin to receive offers. The first one comes along: "I happen to know that you bought this land for the location and view, and paid nothing for the spring. I'll give you $30,000 for it--just the few square feet that includes it. What a deal! You paid essentially nothing for it."

If you've already perceived that the spring is worth $100,000, of course, you're not going to consider it such a deal. But look what the very offer does to your profit. Instead of producing the $10,000 annual revenue with an asset that has no market value, you are now using an asset (it's the same asset, of course: the spring) with a market value of $30,000. If you sold the spring for that price and invested your money at 10%, you would earn $3,000 per year interest. By not selling, you sacrifice that interest. Of course you're happy to do so, but here's what it does to your annual operating profit:

Revenue:	$10,000
-Implicit interest cost:	$ 3,000
= Profit:	$ 7,000

There's no denying that you still receive $10,000 per year. But you could have had $3,000 if you had sold. Your $10,000 revenue is comprised of $3,000 interest income that you earn as the owner of a $30,000 asset (at 10%), plus $7,000 that you receive in economic profit as the operator of the spring.

Others, particularly if they saw this clever fellow try to get the spring for thirty grand, will offer more; after all, any price less than a hundred thousand offers a profit opportunity. Suppose the price is bid up to $85,000. As the operator of the spring business, your annual implicit interest cost is now $8,500 and your business shows only a $1,500 profit. (As the owner of the spring, however, you now enjoy $8,500 interest income.) Anyone successfully purchasing the spring with $85,000 borrowed at 10% would bear an explicit interest cost of $8,500 per year, but that cost would be more than covered by his $10,000 revenue.

This process comes to an end only when the market price of the spring has been bid up to $100,000. At that point, nobody will offer more; if the price were to fall a bit, eager buyers would appear from nowhere. At this price, you're now using assets (only one of them, actually) worth $100,000 to produce annual revenues of $10,000, and your income statement looks like this:

Revenue:	$10,000
-Implicit interest cost:	$10,000
= Profit:	$ 0

Of course since you happen to be the <u>owner</u> of the asset, you receive interest income of $10,000 per year. But that's exactly what you would receive if you sold the spring and invested the $100,000 proceeds. Remaining the owner and operator of the spring makes you no better off than your best alternative: no profit.

It's not likely that you'll be invited to elicit tears of sympathy on television's "Oprah" because the cruel operation of the market has reduced your economic profit to zero. After all, the very process that reduced your profits to zero did so by making you the owner of an asset that, though worth nothing when you bought it, is now worth a hundred grand.

You are $100,000 wealthier than you used to be--whether you sell the spring or not--and we should call that "profit." But it arose from the <u>discovery</u>, not from the exploitation of an opportunity already discovered. In your own judgment, the spring was worth $100,000 as soon as you discovered it.

But the sum that you could obtain for the spring is limited to its <u>market price</u>. During the process in which that price is bid up, a portion of your $10,000 revenue is still economic profit from operating. When the price of the spring has risen to $70,000, for example, your $10,000 revenue contains $3,000 profit. If that were to be received forever, its present value would be $30,000. When added to the $70,000 rise in the value of the asset, we obtain our $100,000 profit. However we look at it, your discovery produced a profit of $100,000 for you.

> As others discover and BID UP the market
> price of your unique resource, the <u>economic
> nature</u> of your "net revenue" changes from
> PROFIT to IMPLICIT INTEREST INCOME.

There's no taking that away (barring force and the violation of individuals' property rights), but the market process will quickly eliminate your <u>operating</u> profit. It quickly pulls your implicit interest costs up to the level of your revenue by bidding up the market value of your unique asset.

If you want to earn economic profit, you're going to have to discover another spring--or something economically like it. Entrepreneurship, the attempt to discover a previously unknown means of creating value, is the only source of profit.

The protection offered by a patent

A patent is legal recognition of some kind of new idea, a new discovery. It identifies the idea as the property of the holder of the patent, permitting him to benefit from his creativity for a period of seventeen years. There is a certain amount of controversy over the patent process: If the "idea" really is the individual's property, why not forever instead of only 17 years? If it isn't, then why 17 years rather than zero? And what about the property rights of the guy who discovers the same thing, independently, three weeks later?

The goal, I think, in picking this strange number of years was to strike a balance between encouraging innovation and invention, and establishing a legal monopoly by legislatively restricting competition.

In any case, the holder of a valuable monopoly is in much the same position as the owner of our spring. Rather than develop an example completely from scratch, let's endow our widget producer with patent protection. Through his own creative powers of entrepreneurship, he's discovered a way to turn $6 worth of inputs into $11 worth of outputs, and has a patent to prevent anyone else from doing it.

With his $10,000 per month net revenue (this is a considerably bigger operation than the spring), he realizes that his patent is responsible for $120,000 per year of net revenue. If the appropriate rate of interest is 12% (an interest-rate selection dictated partly by those included in Table III at the end of Chapter 10), a 17-year annuity consisting of $120,000 at the end of each year has a present value of (120,000 x $7.120 =) $854,400. (That "$7.120" is the present value of $1 to be received at the end of each of the next 17 years, discounted at 12%; see the 17-year row and 12% column of Table III.)

Because the value of the patent diminishes each year, reaching zero at the end of year 17, identifying the "implicit interest" component of his net revenue is not as simple as it was with the infinite-lived spring. Suppose the value of his patent has become known, and he is now receiving offers of $854,400 for it. During the first year, he uses an asset with a market value of $854,400 and therefore incurs $102,528 implicit interest cost. (That's what he could earn, in interest, if he sold the patent, went out of business, and invested the $854,400 at 12%.) But the other $17,472 of his $120,000 net revenue isn't profit.

At the end of that first year, his patent only has 16 years left. Like a machine that's now partly worn out, we have to find the reduction in its value. If we again use Table III, but the 16-year row this time, we find that the value of a $120,000 16-year annuity is only (120,000 x $6.974 =) $836,880. This is a reduction in value of $17,520 from the original $854,400. If we add this "depreciation" to his implicit interest costs, we obtain $120,048. The extra forty-eight bucks just comes from round-off errors; this is about as close to $120,000 as one normally gets using multiple figures from tables like ours.

Revenue:	$264,000/yr
-Explicit costs:	$144,000/yr
= Net revenue:	$120,000/yr

-Implicit interest cost:	$102,528
-Depreciation:	$ 17,520

= Profit: $ 0 (rounded off)

Although the details may seem perplexing, the main point is that the same mechanism operates here as with the permanent spring.

As the value of the patent becomes known, its market price rises to the PRESENT VALUE of its expected future returns. At this point, the PROFIT from USING it has disappeared.

The market value of the unique asset (here, it's the patent) is bid up until the individual who uses it receives enough net revenue only to cover his implicit costs. The economic profit from using the asset is eliminated by the bidding up of the asset's market value.

If our entrepreneur sells the patent to someone else and goes out of production himself, he certainly wouldn't be the first inventor to do so.[2] As I mentioned earlier, the talents required to manage a business that successfully uses the patent or asset are quite different from those that characterize entrepreneurs who discover and innovate. (Steve Wozniak, co-founder of Apple Computers, comes to mind.) Many of them welcome the opportunity to capitalize on their discovery without having to endure what they perceive as the day-to-day grind of business operations. (Fortunately, other individuals find that "day-to-day grind" fascinating and have a comparative advantage in it, relative to innovating!)

PROFIT, ENTREPRENEURSHIP, AND THE DYNAMIC MARKET

Profit (in its economic sense) arises only from the discovery of value, and as knowledge of the particular opportunity to create value becomes more widely known, the opportunity disappears. It's like discovering gold on a remote river: as soon as word gets widely publicized, the likelihood that any particular newcomer (say, the

---

[2] Here's an example, from the Baltimore Sun (August 7, 1991: p. 1D): "If you watch TV, surely you've seen the ubiquitous Vittorio--a dark-haired young man who holds a pizza as he and his off-screen Italian mama gush about what a great discovery Boboli is. 'Eight minutes in the oven,' he says cheerfully. 'You never taste such a good pizza.'...A California entrepreneur sold the Boboli formula to General Foods in 1985 for $3.6 million."

8,439th hopeful Alaska gold-rusher to struggle over Chilkoot Pass in 1898) will strike it rich becomes smaller and smaller. And even if the original discoverer's claim is legally protected, he's likely to find that he could be just as rich, and subjectively happier, by selling it to the highest bidder as by continuing to operate it himself. (Many of them did.)

Profit and Disequilibrium

An opportunity for profit is an opportunity to make one's self better off, and it has to refer to an action that has not yet been taken. If your demand price for a notebook is $2.83, and the store's supply price is $2.69, there's a profit opportunity. After you've bought the notebook, you <u>realize</u> the profit (it's indicated by your consumer surplus, showing that you actually are better off), but the very act of doing so erases this particular opportunity. Now that you already have a notebook, you no longer perceive a way to make yourself better off by buying one (that is, another one): the store's supply price is still $2.69, but your demand price is now zero.

Profit works that way, too, in the monetary world of business and market exchange. A businesswoman perceives a profit opportunity as a gap between price and cost, between demand price and supply price, between the demand curve (as she perceives it) and the supply curve. Nobody else has noticed it yet, but we're somewhere over to the left of the equilibrium quantity on those "market adjustment" curves of Chapter 4. People are willing to pay more for this good than it costs to produce--that is, than what they're willing to pay for other goods that can be produced with the same resources.

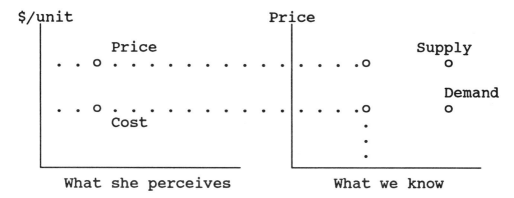

Figure 11.1: Profit opportunity signals disequilibrium

When she acts on this perception, beginning or increasing production of the good in an attempt to <u>realize</u> (to make real, to turn into cash) some of those perceived profits, her very action tends to reduce the size of the gap between the demand price and the supply price. She moves the market a bit, down along its demand curve, and up along its supply curve. And as other entrepreneurs catch on, she's going to find the price falling and her costs rising until the profit from producing this good has disappeared.

There's only one point, on conventional supply-and-demand diagrams, at which profit is zero: equilibrium. If we're off to the left, price exceeds cost and profits are positive; off to the right, cost exceeds price and they're negative (losses). It's the very act of attempting to capture profits, in fact, that drives a left-of-equilibrium market to the right, and it's the natural desire to avoid losses that pulls a right-of-equilibrium market back toward the left.

Profit is a sign of disequilibrium, of markets that have not fully adjusted.

Be cautious about making value judgments about whether this is "bad" or "good," about whether markets are "working" or "failing," though. (I'm afraid I might have encouraged this, back in Chapter 4, by identifying the equilibrium quantity as the amount that "ought" to be produced.) Don't forget that we economists can know about all of these profit opportunities and equilibrium points simply by glancing at the graphs of supply and demand that we've constructed. A real-world business decision maker doesn't have this data. He has to act on the basis of what he can infer about other people's values.

> If it looks as if a market free of legislative restrictions is persistently in disequilibrium, we should ask why nobody (including US!) is pursuing this "obvious" opportunity for profit.

Apparently those with the courage to <u>act</u> don't agree with what we think we know about demand and supply.

The incentives and information provided by market prices and the exchange of money provide strong motivation for people to identify and act on gaps between demand and supply. That's what explains the "tendency," to which we've referred so often, for markets to move toward equilibrium. As long as demand and supply curves are moving around--that is, as long as consumers are free to change their minds and suppliers to create new products or discover new cost-saving technology--markets will be in disequilibrium. But the process of adjustment is always at work.

A world without profit is either a world with no change or a world of instantaneous, perfect knowledge of everything. The latter is unimaginable, and the former, if not unimaginable too, is undesirable.

Even a "monopolist" loses his profit...

Some time ago, we had an extended discussion of the price searcher. Even before that, we discussed about 87 different kinds of "cost." (Well, six or seven, maybe.) If you think back to those complexities, it may seem a little glib or superficial to now be talking simply about "price" being greater than "cost." It's time to consider how the subject of profit fits into those previous discussions.

Profit--in its most general sense--simply means that the benefit of the considered action exceeds its cost. Exactly what the benefit and cost are, depends on the specific situation. The profitability of the action "produce and sell 40 instead of 39" depends on the marginal revenue of unit number 40 and the marginal cost of unit number 40, and if MR is greater than MC then the action is a profitable one. The profitability of the action "enter this business and produce and sell 40" depends, again, on the "marginal revenue" and "marginal costs" of this action--that is, "MR" and "MC" in their most general sense, the change in revenue and cost that the choice would produce. In this particular situation, we normally would call them the "total revenue from the sale of 40" and the "total cost of producing 40." If we've already incurred our "fixed costs" (license or rental fees that don't vary with the level of output) then they're now "sunk" and not costs at all; the only relevant, true costs are the "variable" ones.

A "price taker," a frog so small in a pond so big that his decisions have no effect on the market price of his product, may find himself earning profits if the market demand increases. But it's easy (to the point of being costless) for anyone to enter this imaginary kind of business, so prices and costs are quickly driven back to equality. (That's why you might want to think twice, as we suggested back in Chapter 6, before you entered such an industry...if you can even find one!)

The more interesting case is that of a price searcher. Suppose that we've found one, Joe, who determines the quantity (1,200 per week) at which MR = MC, finds the corresponding price ($75 each) by looking up to the demand curve, and determines that his total revenue ($90,000 per week) at this price and quantity (PxQ) far exceeds his total cost. If we express that "total cost" on a per-unit or average basis, we find that it's much less than $75. Apparently Joe has discovered some new product or lower-cost production technique that is, as yet, unknown to others.

In a thriving, entrepreneurial society, though, situations like Joe's don't go unnoticed for long. As others perceive this profit, arising from the gap between revenue and cost (or, equivalently, between price and average cost), they're likely to enter the market. That will reduce the demand for Joe's product and make it more elastic, since his customers now have an attractive alternative. Each of these changes has the effect of reducing both Joe's best quantity and the price that he should charge. If that weren't bad enough (from Joe's, not the consumers', point of view), the new source of demand for inputs may also raise Joe's costs. His profit takes a nosedive.

Perhaps, though, no other producer decides to compete with Joe. Many others may be fully aware of his profit, but whether they view it as a profit opportunity for themselves depends on their anticipation of what would happen if they entered the market. Everyone has heard the old Western movie line, "This town isn't big enough for both of us." A potential entrant may decide that while there's more than enough demand to support one, there's not enough to support two or more competing producers. Sometimes an aggressive competitor will enter the market anyway, planning to out-compete Joe and become the sole producer himself. But if none does, Joe goes on, earning permanent profit--right?

> The very phrase "permanent profit" should set off a RED FLAG: there just isn't such a thing.

The correct response to our "right?" is: "Wrong!"

If Joe owns some unique resource (like the spring, or the patent) that prevents others from producing the same product, the mechanism by which the market reduces Joe's profit to zero is easy; we've already discussed it. The market value of the unique resource is bid up, until it equals the present value of the future stream of net revenue (like the spring's annual $10,000) that Joe is able to earn by possessing it. When the implicit interest cost of retaining the ownership and use of that asset are included among Joe's costs, his profits become zero. He could do just as well for himself by selling out, investing the proceeds, and living on the interest income.

This same economic process, however, operates to eliminate profit even if there's no physical asset like a spring, or legal asset like a patent. If no upstart newcomer believes that he could draw enough of Joe's customers away to make a go of it, it's clear that Joe has something that he doesn't. It's probably an established reputation, consumer loyalty, that Joe has created by being the first to offer the product and by treating his customers well. (As many an innovator has learned, simply being the first doesn't work for long.) Joe's entrepreneurship and record of customer satisfaction have produced an intangible asset, often called "good will" on accounting statements, that others don't believe they can get along without.

> A producer's "unique asset" may be simply the established reputation he earned by "being first."

If a gap persists, year after year, between Joe's explicit costs and his revenues, and it cannot be explained by the ownership of a unique physical or legal asset, it will and must be attributed to an intangible asset like "reputation" or "good will." Such an asset usually can be sold--often consumers don't even know who owns a company or a brand name--and if Joe doesn't sell it he's foregoing interest income. If the reputation is inseparable from Joe himself, that stream of future net revenues attributable to his reputation can't be capitalized and sold (Joe isn't a machine). Perhaps others can buy the business and hire him at a wage that includes the annual net revenue attributable to his reputation. If even this isn't possible because customers--for some reason--consider it vital that Joe actually <u>own</u> the operation, each year's net revenue should be considered the business's implicit wage expense (and Joe's wage income). He has made his services unique, and they have a very high marginal revenue product.

As far as our little tables of "cost" figures go, or our graphs illustrating them, the effect of identifying this net revenue with the use of a valuable asset is to increase each period's "fixed costs." Those costs rise by the implicit interest cost that we incur by using the asset, which--because of the way we found the asset's value--is the same as the period's net revenue. None of this affects either demand, marginal revenue, or marginal cost, so the price-searcher's proper quantity nor price don't change, either. But it makes the "average cost" of producing that quantity equal to the price at which it can be sold. Profit is gone.

> The producer's implicit interest cost is part
> of his "fixed cost," which rises until it
> precisely equals the sum of all of the
> differences between "marginal revenue" and
> "marginal cost." Profit is zero.

Where'd it go? Don't feel sorry for Joe; he's still raking in big bucks. But the economic (the real) nature of that income has changed. The entry of new competitors would have snipped off his stream of incoming money, if Joe hadn't possessed some uniquely productive asset unavailable to them. At first, before people understood how valuable and important and unique this asset was, it had little market value and Joe's net revenue was mostly profit. As others tried to enter and failed, or simply examined Joe's operation more carefully, they learned of the significance and value of his asset and bid its market price up. As this happens, Joe earns the same stream of net revenue as before, but the value of the asset that he's using to do it is increasing. Fortunately for him, he's also the owner of that asset. Joe's income is unchanged, but he's earning a larger and larger fraction of it as implicit interest, from his role as capitalist (resource owner), and a correspondingly smaller fraction as profit, from his role as entrepreneur.

Profit is an ephemeral, ghostly sort of thing. It exists at any particular time, but market forces--that is, the actions of self-interested, alert, individuals--are always tending to eliminate it. Gaps between revenue and cost last only to the extent that they aren't generally known. If it looks to you as if genuine economic profit is persisting over time, you'd better look again. There's an asset of some kind--perhaps even an intangible one--whose costs of retention and use you haven't adequately considered.

Profit, interest, and rent

You're thinking of buying a duplex (a two-apartment building) for $100,000 and renting it out. You fully expect the market value of the building to remain at this figure forever. If the relevant risk-adjusted interest rate is 12%, then your implicit interest cost of buying and owning the building is $12,000 per year.

Perhaps you are able to obtain $15,000 per year (forever) in net rents. That rental receipt, like all rents, can be separated into interest and profit components: it's $12,000 interest, and $3,000 profit.

RENT is made up of an "implicit interest" and a "profit" component, with their sizes determined by the market price of the asset and the rate of interest.

From your perspective, the previous market was in disequilibrium: you could "buy" $15,000 per year for a price of $12,000 per year. Or an asset with a present value of $125,000 (that's the present value of a permanent $15,000 annuity, discounted at 12%) can be purchased for $100,000.

Others either did not agree with your risk estimate (their risk-adjusted required rate of return was 15%), or they had been able to obtain only $12,000 in net rents. Your discovery that $15,000 could be obtained, or that the investment was less risky than believed, has produced an annual stream of $3,000 profits (or its equivalent, a lump-sum profit of $25,000).

If you own a piece of land that you could sell for $50,000, but lease it instead for $5,000, that rent is the sum of your implicit interest cost and profit. The profit portion can be negative: if the rate of interest is 12%, a rent of $6,000 would be required simply to cover your implicit interest costs, and you aren't getting it. You're suffering a $1,000 loss (negative profit) each year.

In our example of the mineral spring, as the spring's market value was bid up the interest component of the rent (the $10,000) rose, and its profit component diminished. Once the "spring market" reached equilibrium, when it was no longer possible to purchase a future revenue stream with present value of $100,000 for less than that, the annual rent contained no profit component.

"Windfall" profits

The term "windfall profits" is usually used without a clear definition. It seems to refer to economic profit that was not anticipated even by the individual who receives it.

> WINDFALL PROFIT is economic profit that was
> not anticipated EVEN BY ITS RECIPIENT.

Economic profit that <u>most</u> people didn't anticipate is just plain economic profit. If it had been widely anticipated, it wouldn't have existed. But the subcategory of economic profit identified as "windfall" seems to include the recipient among those non-anticipators.

I asked, some time ago, how good you are at reading others' minds. That issue has arisen time and time again in this book, since it's the only way that we could hope to determine someone else's costs and benefits, efficient actions, and comparative advantage (among other things) apart from what we are able to discern from simply observing his own voluntary choices. If you--prudently--have only limited confidence in your own ability to read others' minds, you should be rather modest about drawing conclusions that require knowledge of others' values. Apart from the logical principles we've been discussing in this book, our only trustworthy knowledge of others' values is limited to what we can infer by observing their voluntary choices.

But mind-reading is exactly what is required to determine that a realized economic profit was not anticipated even by its recipient. You may know that <u>you</u> didn't anticipate it, and you know that most people didn't (or it wouldn't have existed). But how about him?

As far as I can see, if there were some way that we could know, for sure, that a particular profit was entirely the result of pure chance and blind luck, a "windfall profits tax" that took it away would have no detrimental effect on individuals' incentives. But how can that ever be known? Even if you were to ask the recipient and knew for sure that he would tell the truth, he's likely to modestly maintain that he had no idea that the good with which he's filled his warehouse was going to become so much more scarce. If you press him, though, he may admit to a "feeling" or sense that "something was up"; nothing he could prove or that would meet tests of scientific knowledge, and he may not even be able to say where his feeling originated. Nonetheless, his act of supplying the good after its price has risen makes the good less scarce--and its price a little less high--than it would otherwise have been.

Since there is no way to determine whether or not the recipient of profit anticipated it, there is no way to distinguish "windfall" from other economic profit. The great danger is that the public's sense that there's something "unfair" about windfalls will lead to legislation that permits politicians to determine which profits are windfalls and, therefore, not deserved.

> Since there is no way for an external observer
> to distinguish a "windfall" from an ordinary
> profit, a tax on "windfalls" would discourage
> the pursuit of <u>any</u> profit.

Remember that profit, by its very nature, is something that most individuals did not expect. When we threaten any recipient of profit with an after-the-fact determination that he couldn't have anticipated it, we discourage entrepreneurs from seeking any economic profit whatsoever.

The pursuit of profit

In a free society, individuals are largely able to pursue their own values. In their role as consumers, they can change their minds, demanding goods that differ from those they had in the past. As producers, they can decide to switch careers and supply an entirely different kind of labor, or adopt new methods of production that require inputs entirely different from those used before.

Consumers are often fickle and demanding, even ruthless, in search of better ways to satisfy themselves and their families. No wonder. If a shopper can save a few dollars by clipping grocery coupons or by purchasing generic or "house" brand products, she may be able to buy her child a new pair of shoes. Everyone has a paycheck that he has to try to stretch. Can the family handyman get drill bits two bucks cheaper at the new discount home-repair superstore than at the friendly old neighborhood hardware store? As much as he might miss dealing with his old friends, that two dollars may have important other uses for the family. The consumer's unpredictability would keep a free economy hopping even if entrepreneurs were not constantly searching for lower-cost production techniques. Combined, they produce a dynamic economic system in which supplies and demands are always shifting in response to changes in individuals' values and in technology.[3]

These changes are constantly producing opportunities for profit, incentives for everyone--consumers and producers and resource owners alike--to alter their behavior so that the new patterns of consumer preferences are better satisfied.

It's the pursuit of profit that makes an economic society a dynamic and responsive place. The pursuit of profit just describes other individuals' responses to something that each of us values and appreciates: the freedom to change our minds.

---

[3] Actually, when the consumer is searching for a better deal or a way to attain certain goals at lower cost (and thereby be able to afford to attain other goals too), he is acting entrepreneurially. He is attempting to create value.

YOU SHOULD REMEMBER...

1. PROFIT is revenue minus cost. If that sounds too simple, remember how careful the economist must be about the concept of cost.

2. The cost of operating a business must include the <u>implicit</u> costs of owner-provided services: the wages, rent, and/or interest that he could have earned elsewhere.

3. PROFIT will show how much "better off" <u>operating the business</u> makes the businessperson, in a monetary sense, than if he had pursued his best alternative instead.

4. Because ACCOUNTANTS perform different functions than do ECONOMISTS, their concept of cost generally EXCLUDES "implicit costs."

5. A business can operate indefinitely on ZERO economic profit, but if it has zero <u>accounting</u> profit it is not covering some of its costs.

6. ENTREPRENEURSHIP is the attempt to discover a previously unknown way to CREATE VALUE.

7. Successful entrepreneurship produces profit, but as it is observed by others, the subsequent market process eliminates the profit.

8. If a UNIQUE RESOURCE is involved, its PRICE is bid up until the implicit interest cost of using it equals what <u>used to be</u> "profit."

9. Once the price of an asset has risen to the PRESENT VALUE of its future returns, there is no longer any PROFIT in using it.

10. PROFIT exists only during the time between the INITIAL discovery of a new way to create value, and the time at which it is widely known.

11. The "unique resource" may be something <u>intangible</u>, like REPUTATION or GOODWILL.

12. RENT is the sum of its "implicit interest income" and its "profit" components. The size of the two parts depends on the market price of the asset (and, of course, the rate of interest).

13. WINDFALL PROFIT is economic profit that was not anticipated, EVEN BY ITS RECIPIENT.

14. Unless we have finally learned how to READ MINDS, we cannot know whether someone else's profit was "windfall" or not.

15. An attempt to TAX windfall profits is, therefore, likely to discourage ENTREPRENEURSHIP.

16. Entrepreneurship, the pursuit of profit, is responsible for the dynamic and responsive nature of our economic system.

Problems

1. "Profit leads a ghostly sort of life. It exists only as long as most people don't see it, and when they do, it disappears." Discuss.

2. You decide to start your own business, working at home.

    (a) If you take in $17,000 revenue and had only $9,000 of cash expenses in your first year, does it look as if the operation of your business was profitable?

    (b) Now, please take into account that the monetary value that you place on the best alternative use of the room that your business takes up is $2,000, and that you could have earned $12,000 per year doing similar work for someone else. How does the profit look now?

3. You are considering the purchase of a bond that costs $900 now and will return $1000 to you in one year. If you believe that you could earn 9 percent per year on an equivalently risky investment, how much profit will you have at the end of the year if you buy the bond and it pays off as expected?

4. You and a number of competitors each sell a good and receive $700,000 per year revenue from the sales. Each of your competitors incurs annual costs of $700,000. But you just discovered that if you use a peculiar and unique resource that you happen to own, which has absolutely zero value on the market, your annual costs would be only $628,000.

    a) Do your competitors earn profits? Do you? (In either case, if so, how much?)

    b) How do the self-interested actions of individuals in the marketplace change the situation you described in (a)?

    c) Using the Tables from Chapter 10 and a 6% rate of interest, assume that your revenues and other costs remain constant forever, and give a number that spells the end of the process you described in (b).

5. Explain the connection, emphasized in this chapter, between the concept of "windfall profits" and the ability to read another individual's mind. What's the point, anyway? Why is this observation important?

6. You have $10,000 to invest in your business, and it would be very costly to get any additional funds. You know of two alternative ways to use this money. One of them returns $11,000 (in present value), and the other $10,700 (in

present value). Is the profit from the first alternative $1,000, or is it only $300? Discuss. [I'm not sure there is a right answer to this, but examining it will help you to appreciate meanings.]

7. If a radical "tenants' rights" group convinces more and more renters to bring lawsuits against landlords and, in other ways, increase the landlord's annual costs of operating apartment buildings, what will happen to the market value of those buildings? Have you read any evidence--perhaps in <u>The Wall Street Journal</u>--that this is actually happening?

8. Explain why the operation of the market system makes it impossible for a "monopolist" to earn profit forever, even if he owns a unique resource that he refuses to sell or license for others' use.

9. Dorothy just bought a small office building for $200,000. An equivalently risky investment could have earned her 12% per year interest. If she expects the building and the rents to last forever, how much annual profit and how much implicit interest income is she receiving if her annual net rental receipts are $25,000?

10. Consider #9 again. Do <u>other</u> people consider 12% appropriate, and/or expect the building and the $25,000 to last forever? You can't read their minds, of course... but you <u>can</u> infer an answer from the numbers in #9.

$$
\begin{bmatrix}
\text{A} \\
\text{A-\$10} \\
\text{B} \\
\text{A-\$11} \\
\text{C}
\end{bmatrix}
$$

Figure 12.3: Some new alternatives become available

Of course the "A" at the top is unavailable, because you don't know how to get it. "A-$10" is immediately above B on your value scale, and "A-$11" is the first alternative below B.

Alternatives A and B may be completely different kinds of things, or A may be simply "buying the same good as under alternative B, but $10.01 cheaper." In any case, although you'd prefer to simply know about A automatically, you're still better off paying $10 for the information than by choosing B.

A comparative advantage in information?

One of the difficulties in treating information as a scarce good is that you must know something about it before you can even place a tentative value on it. In the above example, Harry told you just enough to permit you to assign a value, but not enough to give away important details.

Any time you decide to incur costs to obtain information, you're in a similar position. Before you can decide that it's worth driving to the library to look something up, you must have some "information" about what your search is likely to discover. But your existing knowledge can't include the specific details that you hope to find, or the whole exercise would be pointless: you would already know everything that the library trip would turn up.

Knowledge that we already possess is obviously costless to acquire. (It wasn't, once, but those costs are now sunk.) "Knowledge" of which we truly know nothing, that we have no inkling even exists, can't be a scarce good either. It simply can't appear on our value scales because we're unaware of its existence. If an individual is to treat information as a scarce good, he has to know something--but not too much--about it already.

> For an individual to identify a particular
> kind of INFORMATION as a scarce good, he must
> know SOMETHING about it... but not TOO MUCH.

He must be able to imagine what specific details he would find if he invested some resources in investigation, and to assign value to those details.

Often individuals have the alternative of hunting down certain information by themselves, or paying someone else to provide it to them. Unfortunately, doing one's own searching has costs, so it isn't necessarily preferable to simply purchasing the information from someone else. Let's try a couple of examples.

You're looking for a new car, and you know exactly the model, color, and optional equipment that you want. Your problem is to find the lowest price in a 30-mile radius. An auto buying service offers to arrange the lowest-price deal, for $100. To find that information yourself would require hours of telephoning, driving many miles to obscure dealerships, money and time. You're confident that you could duplicate the findings of the buying service, but can you do it at a lower cost than $100? Your problem can be illustrated with the "which path to choose?" illustration of Figure 12.4. (Of course the purchase price of the car is common to either alternative. Your choice is simply between methods of obtaining the information.)

This diagram will look familiar, because I used it in Chapter 8 to illustrate comparative advantage. As in any comparative advantage problem, your lowest-cost route to the car depends on your relative abilities (and preferences) at producing the information for yourself and earning money, and on the money price of the information. If you believe that it might take you two full workdays to discover that lowest price yourself, and--considering your lost pay or vacation days and the resulting small setback in your quest for a promotion--you figure your monetary loss at $250, then at any price below that the buying service is preferable. At $100, it's a great deal.[1]

---

[1] For a similar but genuine, non-made-up, example, see the Wall Street Journal, August 9, 1991: p. B1. "Worried that the used car you want to buy is a lemon in disguise? Car Checkers of America will inspect everything from air bags to ashtrays for about $80."

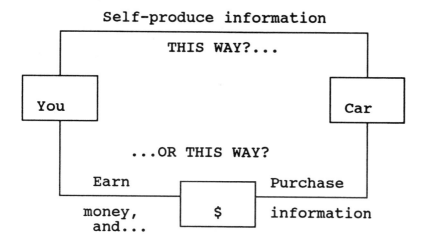

Figure 12.4: The efficient path?

Should you dig through library card catalogs and display terminals, climb up and down stairs to musty stacks of old academic journals, and spend hours poring through them to locate some particular research finding from fifty years ago? Or should you pay fifteen bucks to a computerized search service that can do the job for you cleanly and instantly? (Well, the search itself is clean. If you're comparing the overall cleanliness of the two options, be sure to think about how you would earn the $15--maybe as a garbage handler?) All things considered, which is likely to be a lower-cost way of achieving your goal?

Once we appreciate that information is a scarce good with costs of production, we can treat it--in some respects, anyway--like any other good. X and Y? Widgets and wodgets? If two individuals have different comparative costs of producing it, there will be a price at which exchange is mutually beneficial. It will lie between their comparative costs of production: greater than the seller's, and less than the buyer's.

Individuals with the lowest comparative costs of producing information are likely to be those who have it already. Their marginal cost of <u>obtaining it for themselves</u> is now zero.

If an individual already KNOWS something, his cost of acquiring that information is NOW ZERO.

They'll try to price it using our price-searcher techniques, determining the quantity at which marginal revenue is also zero and selecting the appropriate price by looking up to the demand curve. If they can't or don't discriminate, this will be at the unit-elastic midpoint of a linear demand curve.

Our earlier examples of comparative advantage, based--for pedagogic reasons with which you're now familiar--on simple exchange between individuals, treated each person's cost of "obtaining the good for himself" as identical to his cost of "providing it to another individual." When one of the traders is a price searcher supplying many units of the good to a market, however, the costs of these two actions are not the same. Even though the information costs him nothing to produce (he already has it), to sell it to another individual requires a price reduction that would actually reduce his sales revenue.

In this case, it may be appropriate to identify the seller's "cost of providing the information to any particular customer" as simply this revenue-maximizing (MR=MC=0) price. Any lower price would make him worse off, and any higher price would, too.

If you find that his price is below your own cost of producing the information yourself, you're going to be one of his buyers. Obtaining the information through exchange, rather than self-production, is your efficient action. If he finds that he would have to cut the price below this level to sell to you, then "not selling" is his efficient action.

When you begin to look at many of your everyday trades from an "information" perspective, it pops up everywhere. When you pay several hundred dollars to have your car fixed, aren't you paying primarily for the mechanic's knowledge? Knowing which wrench to pull on, and how hard, is far more valuable than the pure brute force of doing the pulling. Many other professionals, including medical doctors, lawyers, and college professors, are primarily in the business of selling information.

Middlemen specialize in services

The individuals with a comparative advantage in providing information about markets, about the availability and nature of alternatives, are usually the people who spend their lives in those markets. If you spend half of your waking hours working in a shop that rents out videotapes, you're very likely to know a lot more about videotapes than someone who spends his life selling corporate bonds.

> A middleman is a businessman who purchases a good and resells it, making little if any physical change in it.

The middlemen we know best are retailers, who buy from wholesalers (other middlemen, who buy from manufacturers) and resell to consumers. (There are frequently several levels of middlemen: the study of marketing will provide further details.) Another is the broker, such as a real-estate or stock broker; the broker doesn't even take legal title to the good. He never becomes the owner. He simply hooks a buyer up with a seller, and charges a fee for the service.

Before value was understood as a subjective concept imputed to goods by individuals, it was considered some kind of objective property of the goods themselves. (See Chapter 8.) To anyone holding such a view, the middleman could hardly create value, since he seldom changes the physical nature of the good at all. Who really made the jeans that you can get at Jeans West in the mall? Certainly not the retailer.

The very existence of middlemen must be quite a puzzle to someone who tries, consistently, to hold an objective theory of value. Middlemen would seem to create no value, because they don't change the physical nature of the good, yet they have wedged themselves into the chain of distribution, somehow, making customers pay more than the goods are worth (that is, than the manufacturer receives). Quite a trick. I wonder how they did it, and why the consumer puts up with it.

There's no real problem once we throw off that archaic mistake, the objective theory of value. The fact is that middlemen provide a wide variety of services related to the process of getting the jeans from the manufacturer into the hands of the consumer. The consumer values those services, and is willing to pay for them.

Among those services are transportation (you don't have to fly to the factory in Taiwan or Mexico) and financing (you can use your Visa). Those services alone-- especially transportation--are worth a lot; surely a pair of jeans at $30 right up the street is much more attractive than a pair at $12 in a foreign country thousands of miles away.

> Middlemen provide services. One of the most important of them is simply INFORMATION.

Among the major services that the middleman provides, and earns his living by selling, is information.

This is most clear with the broker, who never even possesses the good with which she's involved. Any time you're inclined to sell your house yourself, to save the 7% (or so) broker's commission, ask yourself what the knowledge of the market that she has acquired (and the other services she and her firm provide) are worth to you, and whether you can self-produce them cheaper. The simple error of either underpricing or overpricing your house, because you don't know the market, could easily cost you more than that commission. I have no special interest in real-estate brokers, but I've seen more than one sign "For Sale by Owner" stand forlornly for three months, finally to be replaced by the sign of a brokerage firm.

It's not that real-estate or stock brokers are any smarter or hard-working than you. But we develop our comparative advantages by the way we choose to live our lives. You've devoted yours to the subjects of your own interest, and they've devoted theirs to "house prices and sales in the extreme northwest Baltimore County area" or "the immediate past, present, and future of low-priced non-computer technology stocks." It's no wonder that they know more about these narrow little issues than you do. It wouldn't be at all surprising if you'd prefer to buy the information from them rather than either produce it yourself or go without it.

But the retailer, too, provides his customers with a great deal of information. Who ever knows exactly how a suit or dress or pair of jeans will fit before he or she tries them on? Simply being able to see an appliance "in person," rather than merely its photograph, is very informative, and if you can lift it, turn the knobs, and push it around a little, so much the better. No catalog description could ever provide the same information that seeing and grabbing a product, before buying it, can convey. And it's the retailer who provides his customers with this opportunity.

His action has costs--the implicit interest cost of maintaining his inventory, his rent, utilities, and labor--that make his cost of providing you with the good (and these services) considerably more than his cost of obtaining the good himself (its wholesale price, probably). If you want him to incur those costs, you have to make it worth his while--by paying a price above wholesale. Of course you would prefer to have the information and other services at zero cost to you, just as you preferred alternative "A" in Figure 12.3 to "A-$10." But "A-$10" is available (thanks to Harry), while "A" is not, and even "A-$10" is superior to your best other available alternative ("B").

The difference between the wholesale and the retail price is what you're paying for the information and other services that the retailer provides. Although many customers could produce these services for themselves, they have other uses for their time and money, so they find the purchase of the services from a retailer to be a worthwhile exchange.

"You can eliminate the middleman...
but you can't eliminate his function"

Long ago, I was studying for a business degree at night school and was obliged to take a marketing course. Everyone has different interests and mine definitely did not (and do not) lie in marketing, but catalog requirements are catalog requirements. The one thing that I remember from that course is the phrase that I've used above.

Like any catch-phrase, it has to be interpreted properly. ("MR=MC," "sunk costs are irrelevant," and "profit is revenue minus cost" have to be used with similar caution.) It's intended to remind you that middlemen are not simply aggressive robbers who have somehow managed to stuff themselves into the channel of distribution and seize an unearned tribute every time you buy something. They provide a significant list of valuable services, at a price that typically makes the purchase of them attractive.

As our discussion above indicates, though, it is often possible to "eliminate the middleman." Not in the gangster-movie sense of "eliminate," but in the sense that one can often bypass his place in the channel of distribution by purchasing directly from wholesalers. The explicit price one pays will be lower, but few of the services that retail customers expect will be provided.

The phrase "you can't eliminate his function" reminds us that middlemen provide services. If you want to "eliminate" him, you must either (1) provide those services, at some cost, for yourself, or (2) get along without them.

> If you want to "ELIMINATE THE MIDDLEMAN," you must either provide his services for yourself, or get along without them.

Which of your three alternatives--buying the services from the middleman, producing them for yourself, or going without them entirely--is preferable depends, obviously, on the specific circumstances. If information services are valuable, but not as valuable as the alternatives you'd have to sacrifice if you either purchased them or produced them yourself, you'll get along without them. Often they're more valuable than what the middleman is charging, but less valuable than what you'd have to give up to produce them yourself. If you're a computer expert, and the only service that the computer retailer up the road offers that a mail-order outfit ($700 cheaper) doesn't is plugging the components together, showing the neophyte how to boot up WordPerfect, and general hand-holding, your better alternative is pretty clear. If you really are a computer neophyte, your best option may be to purchase those services at the price that the retailer is asking for them.

The practical lesson in all of this is to be wary about advice that you can

SAVE BIG BUCKS! ELIMINATE THE MIDDLEMAN!

Usually it's a promotion for some kind of co-op or non-profit group that refers to the middleman's "profits" and how you can avoid paying them. Having been through the last chapter, you might genuinely wonder "What profits?" (I'm sure that's what most middlemen, especially most small retailers, would like to know!)

Invariably, though, the "savings" arise either from sacrificing services routinely provided by commercial retailers or by the members' producing at least a semblance of those services for themselves. The money that you save doesn't come from the middleman's "profit." It arises because you are no longer making an explicit monetary payment for the services that he sells. It can be fun to belong to a natural-foods or environmentally-pure kind of co-op, donating one's time and labor, and the services of one's car and computer, to "the cause." But a careful accounting of opportunity costs usually reveals the activity to be a money-<u>loser</u>. That doesn't mean it's a bad idea, but it should be considered a consumption activity, a deliberate sacrifice of money in exchange for the fun involved.

SEARCH AND SPECULATION

Information is a scarce good with its own costs of production and market prices. Economists have devised a technique for analyzing individuals' decisions about information that uses their standard concepts of cost and benefit. It's called "search theory."

Search theory

Ideally, an analysis of individuals' choices regarding information would relate the "quantity of information" to its "price." We'll look first at why this is a little tough to achieve, then explain the approximations developed in "search theory."

To place a value on information, as we discussed above, you have to know something about it--but not too much. Normal supply and demand curves for oranges imply that the suppliers and demanders know about oranges. If we are going to treat information like these oranges, the "information" that we can permit the individual already to have must be very general. He must know only enough to know that details exist, likely to be discovered by a process of search, and enough about them to make an estimate of their value.

We also run into the difficulty of defining "units" of information. What do we put on the Quantity axis? How does one tell the difference between three and four units of information? Does a person who knows the principal exports of Bhutan know 3.7 times as much as someone who just knows where the country is?

Engineers who work in the field of communication theory have borrowed the thermodynamic concept of <u>entropy</u> to measure information. (One implication is that the letter "U" following a "Q" conveys no information in the English language, since Q is <u>always</u> followed by a U.) The concept of entropy has been applied in economics, but a famous economist, writing recently about the state of his subject, said that one sure sign of bad economics is the mention of the word "entropy." (Yipes.) I'm inclined to agree (present paragraph excepted).

So we're left without a real measure of the "quantity of information." The theory of search uses, as a proxy, some measure of the amount of time spent searching. Any of you who have actually hunted for information know that this isn't always a very good measure, but it's the best we can do.

Now that we've dug up something to put on the horizontal ("Quantity") axis, we have to think about the vertical ("Price" or "$/unit") axis. Rather than attempt to use money measures, the usual approach is simply to denote the height along the vertical axis as <u>symbolic</u> of the size of the individual's anticipated benefit and cost associated with the information expected from each "unit" of search. There is no need for cardinal numbers (like 3, 87, and 16.4) to measure these benefits and costs, as long as our graph indicates which is larger than which.

With all of these qualifications, Figure 12.5 presents a graph that depicts the main point of "search theory."

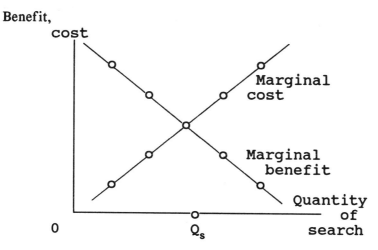

Figure 12.5: The benefit and cost of search

If we apply our by-now-familiar reasoning that each unit should be obtained for which benefit exceeds cost (or just use "Egger's Law of Economic Graphs"), we conclude that we should "purchase" a quantity Q_s of search for information. The crossing point indicates our "optimum search time," the number of hours or days or months of search that we've decided is best for us.

> According to SEARCH THEORY, an individual estimates the benefits and costs of additional search for information, and stops the search when the MARGINAL BENEFIT falls below the MARGINAL COST of continued search.

This whole exercise is filled with approximations and glossings-over of fundamental difficulties (like the problems of measuring quantities and benefits and costs). Nonetheless, it conveys an impression of how we all act that is, in many ways, insightful and accurate. That's all it's supposed to do.

We don't always learn the single most important fact about something first, but often we do, and if we had our choice we'd rank the order in which we learn facts about a subject in the order of their importance. (The "marginal benefit" curve slopes downward.) And while it's usually pretty easy to learn major, significant facts about something, since everyone else already knows them, finer details require more extensive hunting--bigger libraries in other cities, dealerships in more-distant suburbs. (The "marginal cost" curve slopes upward.)

We all reach some point at which we decide that we've satisfied our curiosity and we're going to act on the basis of the knowledge we have already acquired, partial though it is. Further search, we judge, just isn't likely to be worth its cost. At this stage, we're at Q_s on the graph; we've used up our "optimum search time" and already obtained every unit of information (or used every day of search) that we think is likely to prove more valuable than its cost.

One interesting and important application of search theory is to unemployment. During the process of hunting for a job, one normally discovers openings that don't seem particularly desirable and are passed by. (Career opportunities as fast-food flippers offer a perennial example.)

> SEARCH THEORY is especially useful to explain
> UNEMPLOYMENT.

It's the individual's judgment of the costs and likely benefits of further search that determines how long he remains unemployed. You might consider how the existence of unemployment insurance affects his costs and/or benefits and, therefore, his optimum search time. (Is that good, or bad? Could you argue either side?) How might the viewpoint--about the costs and benefits of search--of a worker whose skills aren't very specific (and doesn't earn much but can work just about anywhere) differ from that of a worker who is highly productive in one narrow specialty?

Sherlock Holmes and "rational ignorance"

Another way of expressing our finding about optimum search time or "optimum quantity of information" is that it makes sense to deliberately choose to remain ignorant about some things.

There is always more that can be learned about any subject. I often think that as one learns more about anything, his sense of the scope or area covered by the subject seems to expand exponentially. The effect, which can be exciting or distressing depending on one's mood, is that the more one learns, the greater his sense of how ignorant he is. Nobody is as aware of how little he knows, as an accomplished scientist, artist, or scholar.

But we all have other things to do in life, and the acquisition of knowledge has its costs. When these costs are considered, it is sensible--after a point--to decide not to acquire additional information. This proposition is sometimes known as "the principle of rational ignorance."

As a college professor I always feel a little guilty about explaining this principle. Somehow it seems as if a person in my calling is supposed to maintain that knowledge is such a virtue that the most insignificant addition to it is worth the greatest sacrifice imaginable.

Well, I do value knowledge and understanding and scholarship highly. My own conviction is that there has been a shift, in perhaps the last thirty years, in American public opinion away from the significance that had been associated with academic achievement and scholarship in earlier periods of our history. It's been a terrible mistake, one that has caused and will be causing great harm.

Although I hope that this brief spate of ranting and raving has helped to re-establish my credentials as an old-fogy professor, the most fundamental nature of my subject does not permit me to teach that choices about learning are unique in somehow bearing no relationship to costs and benefits.

Among those who understood the basics of search theory and its implication of "rational ignorance" was Arthur Conan Doyle's fictional detective, Sherlock Holmes. Holmes's friend Dr. Watson was shocked to discover, by chance, that Holmes knew nothing of the Copernican theory of solar systems, and began to inform him that planets revolve around the sun. It was an affront to the learned Watson that Holmes, with his encyclopedic knowledge of the precise London neighborhoods in which soils of certain chemical compositions could be found and a wealth of other details useful to a criminologist, should be ignorant of such a basic fact of physical reality. But Holmes immediately interrupted Watson's lesson, explaining that he could see no way that such knowledge could help him detect criminals. "'You see,' he explained, 'I consider that a man's brain originally is like a little empty attic, and you have to stock it with such furniture as you choose.'"[2] Like any attic, the brain had only a limited capacity, and if part of it was taken up by useless facts like the operation of the solar system, there wouldn't be room for some truly useful detail about the criminal mind.

Holmes carried the notion that additional information has an opportunity cost to an extreme, no doubt an invalid one. (I suspect that a better analogy is between the brain and a muscle, whose capacity increases with use.) But his point is an amusing application of the principle of the marginal benefit and cost of information.

Advertising and search

Perhaps it occurred to you, in my discussion of search for the best car price, that I was missing the most obvious option: just look at the ads in the daily newspaper.

Advertising can be interpreted either as reducing the cost of locating a particular piece of information, or as sharply reducing the expected benefit from further time spent searching. If we put "time spent searching" on our "Quantity" axis, we should interpret advertising as a reduction of the marginal benefit from further search. After all, it does such a great job, making so much information available with so little search, that a further investment of time may promise very little return.

---

[2] The episode is from "A Study in Scarlet," reprinted in Sir Arthur Conan Doyle, The Complete Sherlock Holmes (Garden City, NY: Doubleday & Co., ncd), p. 21.

The more pervasive and truthful advertising is, the more it reduces the benefit that you expect from further search. Of course you do pay for this source of information--it's one of the seller's costs of doing business that he must be able to cover if he's to remain a seller. But what you pay is often a much lower cost than you would have incurred by direct search.

Try to imagine "search" without the assistance of the folks you're searching for. Is there a Mitsubishi dealer in Belair? If he doesn't advertise (which includes listing his business in the telephone book), you're going to have to go out there and see. But don't expect any signs--that's advertising too. Even leaving his dozens of cars where they're visible from the road may be considered "advertising."

Those who criticize advertising--say, billboards--often have the advertised information already. To them, it seems to be of no value but positive cost. They ignore the fact that advertising stimulates competition and often substantially reduces prices, partly by making demands more elastic. The critics don't bother to think of others to whom the information may be exceedingly valuable. Furthermore, their attack on advertising as a "waste of society's resources" commits the fallacy of the tribal premise, misidentifying "society" as the resource owner. Obviously their real owner doesn't consider it waste, which is something that he has every incentive to avoid.

Speculation, Information, and Profit

Among the most important information determining our actions is "information" about the future. It consists of our own expectations.

If I were to believe that all of my life's problems would be solved if only I had one of those $2.69 notebooks, that belief or expectation is part of the information on which I'll base my choices. "This $35 stock will double in a year" may be "information" to a stock-market investor just as surely as is the fact that his bicycle has two wheels. "This $35 stock will be $31 in a year" may be another investor's information about the same stock. In a year, of course, at least one of these guys will be proven wrong and, with 20-20 hindsight, will identify his year-ago belief as misinformation. But each acts, now, on what he believes now.

Information, in the sense of "knowledge" about future effects, is significantly related to economic profit. The only way that one can obtain profit is to anticipate the future more accurately than most others do, and to act on that anticipation. We can now interpret that as having better information than do others.

This kind of information is only tangentially related to search, though. Each of the investors above may have studied the very same charts with wiggly lines showing years of history of this stock's price, and the same corporate financial statements, yet drawn distinctly different conclusions from all of that data.
The term "speculation" is often used to identify activities that are related to our analysis of choice, profit, and information.

> SPECULATION is an attempt to profit by accurately anticipating the future.

We all think of "stock-market speculators" who try to get rich by buying stocks at low prices and selling them a short time later at much higher prices. But think about how any of us chooses and acts. The very process of valuation--of determining benefits and costs--requires hypotheses about the future, and we all try to make those anticipations as accurate as possible to improve the quality of our choice and avoid disappointment later. Since the general interpretation of profit is "benefit minus cost," every human action consists of speculation: an attempt to profit by accurately anticipating the future. Try applying this to your problem of where to eat lunch today.

Each of us, every human being, is a speculator. Some of us buy millions of dollars' worth of frozen pork-belly futures on margin (I think it's the pork bellies, not the futures, that are frozen), and some of us just buy redwood lawn chairs, but each of us attempts to profit by current action based on an accurate estimate the future.

Speculation has an undeserved bad press, for a couple of possible reasons. First, its effects are widely misunderstood. (I'm going to try to take care of some of that, shortly.) Second, envy is a strong (though negative and undesirable) emotion. When you work hard for your money, but some obnoxious hotshot makes ten times your annual wage in one week simply by buying and selling something, it's easy to understand envy and even hatred.

Envy is a dangerous and damaging emotion, one that simply has no redeeming features. Its greatest harm is to the individual who harbors it. (Respect and the desire to emulate another's achievement are not at all the same thing.) In economics, envy is not limited to income earned through financial-market speculation. It is significantly responsible for attacks on the "unequal distribution of income" in a free society. Just as an understanding of the nature and source of income provides the best antidote (there's no conceivable reason to expect everyone's freely-earned income to be the same), an examination of some of the economic effects of speculation may help to offset its undeserved reputation.

Speculation: an example

Wodgets are produced mainly from a vegetable derivative that comes from a particular crop. Although the wodget market is currently in equilibrium, Dave has been watching long-term weather forecasts and believes that the next harvest will be poor. The producers' supply of wodgets will then shrink and their price rise (to P_4; the other P's are used for other things later). Figure 12.6 offers a picture. (He anticipates no change in demand.)

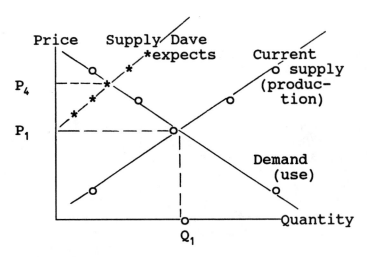

Figure 12.6: What speculator Dave expects

The terms "use" and "production" denote the demand by "normal" customers who wish to use wodgets in their everyday lives, and the normal supply by current producers. Both market demand and market supply will be affected by Dave's speculative activity, and we need this "normal" situation for a benchmark.

If wodgets are costlessly stored, Dave perceives a profit opportunity. It looks to him--though to nobody else--as if "Wodgets in six months" can be obtained far below their market price, simply by purchasing them now and holding them for six months. He will step into the current wodget market as a demander--not because he has any interest in using the wodgets himself, but because of his own expectation about their future price. Back in Chapter 2 we identified that as one of the causes of a change in <u>demand</u>. To help us to understand that the new demand consists of the old "use" demand by everyone except Dave, plus Dave's "speculative" demand, the demand curve in Figure 12.7 is labelled "u+s."

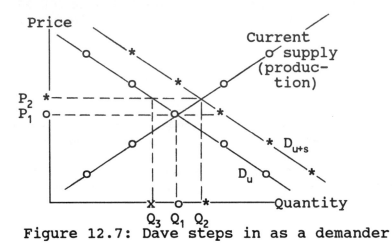

Figure 12.7: Dave steps in as a demander

Dave's action has a number of interesting effects. First, it drives up the current price from P_1 to P_2, and therefore slides the current users back up their "use" demand curve, reducing the "quantity demanded for use" from Q_1 to Q_3. Second, it stimulates current production as the wodget producers slide up their current supply curve to the new market equilibrium point at a quantity of Q_2. With more production and less consumption, something has to be happening to those extra wodgets. They're going into Dave's (costless) warehouse, $(Q_2 - Q_3)$ of them.

If you had just been hired to improve the public image of speculators, this story doesn't make your job look easy. So far, the effect of Dave the Speculator's activity has been to "artificially" raise the price of a useful commodity (somebody is sure to call the price increase "artificial," so I just thought I'd beat him to it) and lead ordinary, everyday citizens to use less of it. It's probably going to be called an "artificial scarcity."

Remember that few of the wodget users--perhaps nobody but Dave--sense that there's anything wrong. They have no idea about these weather patterns or the link between the harvest and the cost of producing wodgets. To them, Dave's action would simply seem purposeless if it didn't have harmful effects (the higher price and resulting smaller quantity demanded for use).

But this is only the first half of the story, and the second half makes the speculator look a little better.

Suppose that Dave turns out to be right about the weather and the future costs of producing wodgets. Figure 12.8 illustrates the market under these conditions. In this "future" time period, the "supply from production" curve lies exactly where Dave had expected it to, and the market equilibrium price would be high. But "lucky" Dave has a "windfall": a warehouse full of wodgets purchased at much lower prices. When he begins to offer them to the market, the market supply of wodgets consists no longer merely of current production but also of the units offered by the speculator. It's an increase in supply, which makes the price (P_5) <u>lower</u> than it otherwise would have been (P_4) and the quantity that wodget customers have available for use (Q_5) <u>higher</u> than it would have been (Q_4).

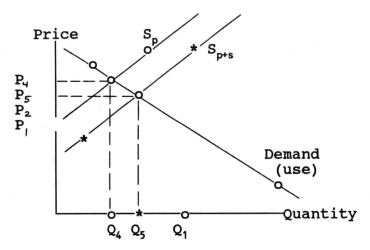

Figure 12.8: Speculator Dave was right

Because Dave's speculative activity has reduced the market price, the quantity that is actually produced falls a bit, as suppliers move down their "production" supply curve in response to the lower price. (To stem the proliferation of labels it's not shown; it's the "quantity supplied from production" at the new market equilibrium price (with speculation) of P_5.)

The populist critics of "speculators" (besides not realizing that they do it too) seem unaware of this second half of the story, and it presents the speculator in a considerably better light.

If Dave was clever, the price at which he bought the wodgets (P_2) was less than that at which he sold them (P_5), and he got rich. This is pure economic profit, earned by anticipating the future more correctly than did the majority and by having the courage to act on that anticipation.

Consider the broader implications of his action, though. His buying brought about an increase in production during a period in which production was relatively easy (low-cost), and provoked a reduction in consumption when the good was relatively plentiful. His selling caused a reduction of production during a period of high production costs, and made possible an increase in consumption in this period of relatively greater scarcity.

Economic profit comes from the creation of value, and Dave has done just that. His simple action has transformed goods for which others were willing to sacrifice only little ("wodgets before"), into goods for which others are willing to sacrifice much ("wodgets after the bad weather"). A quick way to think of Dave's successful speculation is that he has transferred goods in time, from a period of low value to a period of higher value.

> Successful speculation transfers goods IN
> TIME, from a period of relatively LOW value
> to a period of relatively HIGH value. This
> process CREATES VALUE.

The public may never see how high the new equilibrium price would have been. There is seldom a nice clear black-and-white picture demonstrating precisely what prices would have been, under conditions different from those that actually obtained. This is just another example of our repeated lesson that <u>understanding</u> comes from <u>theorizing</u>, and never from simple observation of "facts."

Concluding notes on speculation

Criticism of speculation sometimes emphasizes that it can be wrong. In our example, if Dave had been wrong about the weather, he would have suffered a loss, buying at P_2 and finding, to his dismay, that he must sell at a price below P_1. He has, essentially, used up resources ("wodgets before the 'bad' weather") with greater value, to produce goods ("wodgets after the 'bad' weather") of lower value. (The quotes around "bad" indicate that it really didn't turn out to be bad at all. And that was bad for Dave.)

But this problem is hardly unique to speculators. Every failed little restaurant, every business that can't pay its bills, every attempt to better satisfy consumer preferences that didn't work out, even everyone like you after you bought the motorcycle, is in exactly the same position. These entrepreneurs anticipated the future, acted on their anticipation, and turned out to be wrong.

We would all be better off if they'd been right, but how could they (or we) have known beforehand which new endeavors would later be discovered to have created, and which to have destroyed, value? How would one devise a law that permits only <u>correct</u> anticipations of future demands, technology, and resource availability?

Speculative activity is simply the quest for economic profit, and is responsible for innovation and dynamism in a free society. A system of voluntary exchange and money prices, that requires the innovators to risk their own resources, provides both the best available information about preferences and the strongest incentive for the entrepreneur to be right about the future.

ENTREPRENEURSHIP, ECONOMIC MODELS,
AND THE "NIRVANA FALLACY"

We spend a lot of time and effort in this book on the description of what a market looks like when it's in equilibrium.

There are plenty of ways of describing equilibrium. The most superficial, of course, is my "Law of Economic Graphs": the supply and demand curves intersect. If you're not quite satisfied with that level of sophistication, we can dig into meanings.

At equilibrium, individuals in the markets have adjusted the price to exactly that level at which quantity demanded (the number of units that some individuals prefer to buy) and quantity supplied (the number that others prefer to sell) are equal. That's a "horizontal" look, but we can also examine things from a "vertical" perspective. At equilibrium, every unit for which the demand price exceeds the supply price (that is, each unit that lies to the left of the equilibrium point) is produced, and none of the units for which the supply price is greater than the demand price (units that lie to the right of equilibrium) is produced. If we dig even deeper to what terms mean, "demand price" is the most money that someone is willing to sacrifice for a particular unit, and "supply price" is the most money that others are willing to sacrifice for the other goods that could have been produced instead. We could go even deeper, inquiring into the fundamental values that lead one to be willing to forego $10.52 but not $10.53, and that make it necessary for a producer to spend $11.74 on the resources he would need.

I hope that this all looks a little less unfamiliar now than it did a few chapters ago. Even if it still seems a little complicated, it's time to point out that the equilibrium analysis of markets bears about the same relationship to an understanding of a free economic system, as our derivation of the semicircular pattern of cars bears to a thorough understanding of the mall parking lot. It may be the place to start, but it sure isn't the place to stop.

Entrepreneurship and equilibrium models

In my discussion of market adjustment in Chapter 4, I asked you to picture a supply and a demand curve (with their standard up and down slopes), and to imagine that a price suddenly appeared that was either above or below equilibrium.

The simple fact that the temporarily existing price is "above equilibrium" is an important piece of information. We know it, because we drew the curves and picked the price. The manager of the shoe store, or the proprietor of the roadside widget stand, isn't in that position, and neither are his customers. The "information" about demands and supplies with which they must operate is much less satisfactory than our own. They don't know the quantity demanded and supplied per week at every single conceivable price, but we do. That's just because we've designed the problem, and in this little respect are playing the role of omniscient gods.

In another respect, the customers and business managers have information that's considerably superior to ours. After all, ours is just pretend information that we claimed to have so that we could illustrate some (and only some) of the features of the logic of market exchange. They really know how many shoes were bought yesterday, they remember little things like how eager the buyers (and window-shoppers) seemed, what kinds of shoes were of most interest, and the seeming reluctance of the supplier to commit to a firm price on the future delivery of three dozen pairs of a particular shoe.

> There is a BIG DIFFERENCE between the "information" that we economists ASSUME that we have when we construct our graphs, and the information that real, acting individuals are able to obtain.

Any time you think about all of the nice properties of market equilibria and are tempted to wonder why markets don't just go immediately to the intersection of their supply and demand curves, step out of the role of the pretend-omniscient economist and into the position of the manager of the shoe store. Where would he ever get the knowledge that we pretend we have? (Where would we ever actually get it?)

If the supply and demand curves really are where we economists think they are, and if they stay there for a while, the market adjustment processes that we discussed in earlier chapters will lead to equilibrium. The very suspicion that a price is a disequilibrium price, and therefore that a different price would make us sellers or us buyers better off, is entrepreneurship. Some seller (for example) must infer, from what he perceives in the market, that he could profit by the simple innovation of cutting his price a little, and then he must have the courage actually to do it. (By "profit" here I mean just that the seller decides that he's better off with "definitely selling, at a lower price" than "maybe selling, at the current price.") Suppliers or demanders who perceive--not from our curves but from the kind of information that's actually available to them--that a price is "too high" and then proceed to ask or offer less, are entrepreneurs in the very same sense as someone who creates a new product from scratch.

There is nothing "automatic" and insignificant about the adjustment of a market to its equilibrium. If we're going to understand how a free economic system works, we'd better not take that adjustment process for granted. It all looks pretty trivial to anyone whose level of sophistication doesn't go beyond my "Law of Economic Graphs." It hardly seems any more important to economists who, familiar with the need to "assume" perfect knowledge of demands and supplies to investigate their logic, forget that neither they nor the individuals whose actions they're trying to describe actually have any way of obtaining that knowledge.

Information and "market failure"

When do markets "work" and when do they "fail"? Before anyone can grapple with that question, we have to ask, "Well, what are they supposed to do, anyway?" Only after we've decided that can we judge whether they did it (and therefore "worked" or "succeeded") or didn't (and therefore "failed").

> Any judgment of "market failure" presupposes some belief about what constitutes the <u>successful</u> functioning of markets.

Are markets supposed to guarantee lifetime income to everyone (regardless of the value that others perceive in the services he has to offer)? Is a market system supposed to produce the same income for everyone (again, despite differences in the values others perceive in their services)? Is it supposed to provide each consumer with nearly-identical alternatives to every good (whether or not any producer chooses to produce them)?

By any of these criteria, markets "fail." But my parenthetical commentary was intended to indicate that these are not proper standards. Failure to meet a false standard cannot be considered "failure" at all. (We can't, of course, conclude from this that markets succeed. But we can conclude that what has really failed are these arguments that markets fail.)

Since "the market system" is a pattern of activities and relationships among individuals, any criticism of what "it" does is really a criticism of what <u>they</u> do. When an economist argues that a market fails, he asserts that other individuals should have acted differently.

Many of the outcomes that economists identify as "failures"--and the only ones we're going to address here--fail only because the economist thinks he knows everything about supply and demand (values, costs, and marginal revenues). Relying on this "knowledge," he is able to calculate equilibrium prices and quantities, to compare values and costs. He sometimes finds that real-world businesses do not seem to produce the outcome that he calculates as optimum.

Here's a reminder of an example that we discussed earlier. It's the price-searcher, and that marginal revenue curve is based on the assumption that he can't (or at least doesn't) discriminate.

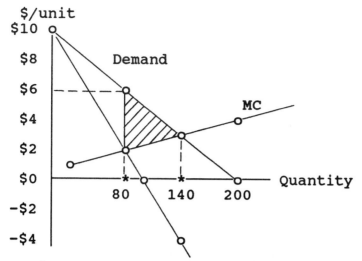

Figure 12.9: The "welfare-loss" fallacy
of market failure

This price-searcher will equate MR and MC, produce 80 per week, and sell each of them for $6. There are another 60 individuals, those demanding units 81 through 140, whose demand prices exceed the producer's marginal cost of production, yet he will not produce and sell these units. (We know why: although "price" exceeds marginal cost, "marginal revenue" doesn't--and is, in fact, negative for 40 out of those 60 units).

We've seen that "welfare-loss triangle" before, in Chapter 7. It's bounded by the vertical line at 80 on the left, the demand curve on the right, and the marginal cost curve on the bottom. It's made up of consumers' surpluses that consumers don't get. They're willing to pay (price) more than the units cost to produce (marginal cost), yet something about the operation of the market system "denies" them the goods.

Many economists identify the "welfare loss triangle" as evidence of "market failure," an indication of inefficiency and of a "monopoly problem." Is this fair? Is "the market" doing something <u>wrong</u> if such areas exist?

We discussed, in Chapters 6 and 7, some of the reasons that "welfare-loss triangles" exist, and I'm not going to rehash all of that now. A little refresher: The more elastic the demand curve, the smaller the triangle. Does that mean that consumers are doing something wrong if they don't consider other products to be close substitutes? Or that other businesses are misbehaving if they decide not to offer a product similar to that of our price-searcher?

The only other way that a price-searcher would produce the quantity at which price and marginal cost were equal, is if he could perfectly discriminate. If he could charge a different price to each customer, exactly that customer's demand price (shown, conveniently, by a neon sign hanging around each customer's neck), then the "marginal revenue" and "demand" curves would coincide (even though sloping downward). The price-searcher who equates MR to MC would, if he can discriminate perfectly, automatically also equate P to MC.

But there are no neon signs, and the only way most real-world sellers know to sell more is to lower the price to all. The cost of selling that additional unit is not only the cost of producing it, but also the "rebate" (in the form of a lower price) that has to be offered to all of the old customers. Instead of considering this "rebate" as a reduction of "benefit" (as we did with the concept of "marginal revenue"), some economists believe it is more insightfully interpreted as an increase in "costs." Specifically, it's a selling or marketing cost. We add it to the standard "marginal cost of production," obtaining a "marginal cost of selling." Although the best quantity and price are no different than under the more conventional "MR=MC" analysis, our revised interpretation of cost (including the old "production" MC and the new "marketing" MC) makes "marginal cost" and price equal, even for a non-discriminating price searcher.

The contention that gaps between price and marginal production cost constitute "market failure" is, essentially, an assertion that markets "succeed" only when sellers can perfectly discriminate at zero cost. They shouldn't have any of those "marketing costs," they shouldn't have to offer "rebates" in the form of lower prices to those willing to pay more. Well, the sellers certainly would discriminate if they could. But where do they get the required knowledge?

The common claim that downward-sloping demand curves inherently produce "market failure," and therefore that markets only "succeed" when each seller is a price taker or can perfectly discriminate, is an outstanding example of a false standard. When a standard labels every realistic market a "failure," it's time to begin to wonder if maybe it's the standard that's the failure.

The "Nirvana Fallacy"

In his fine article "Information and Efficiency: Another Viewpoint,"[3] Harold Demsetz refers to the "nirvana approach."

> In practice, those who adopt the nirvana viewpoint seek to discover discrepancies between the ideal and the real and if discrepancies are found, they deduce that the real is inefficient. (p. 1)

He identifies it with three fallacies: "the grass is always greener fallacy," "the fallacy of the free lunch," and "the people could be different" fallacy (p. 2).

I just use the phrase "Nirvana Fallacy" to identify the tendency--which seems especially prevalent among economists--to judge the real world against a standard which, by its very nature, is unattainable, and to conclude that it's the real world that has "failed."

---

[3] Journal of Law and Economics 12 (April 1969), pp. 1-22.

> The NIRVANA FALLACY is economists' habit of judging real markets against an unattainable standard, and concluding that it's the real-world markets that have "failed."

We economists have to assume--at the beginning of our analysis--that we know all about individuals' valuations, technological possibilities, and resource availabilities. That's what allows us to investigate the logic of individuals' voluntary exchanges in a free society. It's a little like the parking-lot assumption that "only walking-distance matters."

But we'd darn well better not allow ourselves to get stuck at that primitive stage in the quest for understanding. When an economist mistakes a necessary pedagogical technique (the assumption that we have perfect knowledge) for genuine knowledge of individuals' values (demands, costs, efficiency, comparative advantages), he's naively and dangerously claiming knowledge that neither he nor anyone else can have. When he calls other people "failures" because they don't act the way they would if they had the knowledge that he thinks he has, he's mainly fooling himself. Unfortunately, the joke's on us, because government policymakers take this "market failure" stuff seriously.

A truly careful study of the process of choice in a free society should protect us against the "Nirvana Fallacy." Nobody has better information about benefits and costs, and nobody has more incentive to use that information correctly, than the individuals whose actions determine market outcomes.

YOU SHOULD REMEMBER...

1. INFORMATION is a scarce good, with value and costs of production.

2. It is often preferable to BUY information from someone who already has it, rather than to incur the costs of producing it yourself.

3. People who already KNOW information, or can get it cheaply, are likely to have a COMPARATIVE ADVANTAGE in supplying it.

4. Middlemen don't change the physical nature of a good, but they sell services associated with it.

5. The most important of these services may be INFORMATION.

6. To "eliminate the middleman," you must either go without his services or produce them (at some cost) for yourself.

7. SEARCH THEORY states that an individual will invest in the search for information until he judges its marginal cost to exceed its marginal benefit.

8. Search theory is especially useful to explain UNEMPLOYMENT (the search for a job).

9. "Rational Ignorance" explains that the costs of information make it sensible to choose to remain ignorant of some things.

10. SPECULATION is the attempt to profit by accurately anticipating the future.

11. ALL HUMAN ACTION involves SPECULATION.

12. A successful commodities speculator creates value by transferring goods from a period of LOW value to a period of HIGH value.

13. When economists judge markets to have "succeeded" or "failed," their STANDARD is usually their own ASSUMED PERFECT knowledge.

14. What economists ASSUME they know about demands and supplies, and what real-world decisionmakers actually CAN KNOW, are often vastly different.

15. The NIRVANA FALLACY is the judging of the real world against an unrealistic, unattainable standard (like perfect knowledge), and concluding that "the real world" has failed.

Problems

1. Middlemen incur costs to provide their customers with certain services. How would you decide whether, in a particular circumstance, it would be preferable for you to "eliminate the middleman"?

2. The nature of information as a costly, scarce resource has considerable bearing on the issue of "product liability" and of risk and safety in general. Consider the following.

   (a) If airline safety were costless, is it likely that people would prefer that commercial air travel be 100% safe?

   (b) If airline safety is subject to sharply rising marginal costs, are people likely to patronize an airline that is absolutely as safe as is technologically feasible?

   (c) If a "consumer group" convinces the government to force all airlines to meet this standard of safety, what will happen to ticket prices?

   (d) If these prices lead a family of four to decide to drive its old sedan to Arizona instead of fly, has the legislation had the effect of making the family's travel safer?

3. You are invited to London for a week. How are you likely to <u>speculate</u> in the simple act of packing your suitcase?

4. (a) What information is conveyed by a Coors television ad that mainly focuses on attractive young people cavorting in their bathing suits?

   (b) Does the devoting of resources to the creation and broadcasting of this kind of ad seem like "waste" to you? Do you suppose it does, to Coors? Discuss, with reference to whose resources they are, and perhaps to "the tribal premise" (Chapter 9).

   (c) Is this kind of ad aimed at persuading instead of informing? If you think so, please try to clearly specify a difference between persuasion and information. Does a small black-and-white tombstone notice of the opening of a new furniture store constitute persuasion or information?

5. Doesn't advertising have costs? The price for thirty seconds on a prime-time network hit television show can be a quarter of a million dollars. Nonetheless, advertising often dramatically reduces the prices that customers pay. How is this possible?

6. How many instances in your normal, daily life can you think of in which you pay primarily for someone else's information, rather than for some physical good?

7. Is it fair for a middleman to charge you for information that it no longer costs him anything to produce (because he already has it)? Discuss. (If your answer is "No," please address this: Would it be fair for you to pay nothing for it, when it has considerable value to you and would cost you a lot to produce for yourself?)

8. Suppose that Speculator Dave manages to drive the current price up a bit, but the natural disaster that he foresaw never occurs. The "current production" supply curve stays right where it was at first. What happens? How does Dave make out in his endeavor?

9. A member of a nationally famous political family has become involved in a "co-op" to sell home heating oil much cheaper than "profit-making" businesses are able to.

   a) Assume that the private suppliers really are NOT making any economic profit. How could the co-op underprice them?

   b) Could the private suppliers really be making economic profit, year after year?

   c) If the private companies are earning permanent returns from the ownership of some kind of unique resource (whatever it might be that's required to distribute heating oil!), how can the co-op get along without it?

10. Suppose that, in the interests of fairness (of course), our legislators pass a law that prevents the holder of any kind of inventory (whether it's of crude oil, cans of beans, works of art, or salt pills) from making a profit from an "unanticipated" rise in its market value.

   a) First of all, "unanticipated" by whom? The legislators? What is the significance of this question?

   b) Now, what will be the effect, on individuals' future actions, of such legislation?

CHAPTER 13

ECONOMICS AND CAPITALISM

THE NATURE OF CAPITALISM

"The wicked witch is dead!," celebrated the East Europeans depicted in an editorial cartoon in the <u>Baltimore Sun</u> shortly after the collapse of the Soviet Union. The focus of the cartoon was their dragging away of a horrible witch identified as "socialism." But watching them surreptitiously from around the corner, with evident glee, was a witch of identical appearance, labelled "capitalism."

It is hard to imagine more ignorant commentary. This political cartoonist sees no significant difference between socialism and capitalism. He's not alone, though. I've seen cartoons with a similar theme in other newspapers.

Frankly, the fundamental differences between socialism and capitalism have been apparent to me for so many years that I have a little trouble understanding where these clever artists have gotten this idea.

People who live in capitalist societies have problems, and so do people who live under socialism, so there's no real difference? Is that the rationale? Or is it more like "there's no difference between being ordered around by a boss (or the rich), and being ordered around by the government"?

Then there's the problem to which I referred in Chapters 4 and 9: identifying the United States and western-European "mixed economies" with capitalism. One cartoonist, incredibly, included--among the problems he that attributed to capitalism--the Savings and Loan crisis. Crisis, yes, but few problems are more clearly and directly attributable to government (in particular, its program of deposit insurance). Anyone who insists on labelling every economy either socialist or capitalist would use one term to identify a 49-51 mix and the other for a 51-49. One loses a lot by insisting on that.

A more careful thinker might try to figure out which of the problems of the United States seem to originate primarily from its basic capitalist nature, and which arise from the aspects of its system that are socialist. The problems of Eastern European economies, in the process of painful transition from mostly-socialist to more-capitalist, can be analyzed the same way.

But this requires some understanding of the fundamental natures, the essentials, of the two systems. It requires <u>theorizing</u>, abstracting from details that, while present in either system, aren't fundamental.

This is where the editorial cartoonists fall down. Like the guy in Chapter 2 who doesn't understand the law of demand and concludes from two observed prices and quantities that "demand slopes up," they lack the <u>theory</u> that protects them from the error of fallacious generalization from simple, observable, fact.

People who live in the United States have problems, but not all of them are attributable to capitalism. Citizens of the former Soviet Union have a lot of troubles that aren't properly attributed to socialism. To figure out what's what here, we have to expand our introduction ("The fairness of markets") from Chapter 4.

The essence of capitalism

The basic idea underlying capitalism is that a system of laws that governs a society should treat each and every individual human life as an end in itself.

> CAPITALISM treats each and every individual life as an end in itself.

Whether one prefers to attribute this principle to a religious belief (our Declaration of Independence uses the phrase "endowed by their Creator") or to a non-theological "natural rights" philosophy, its consequence is a respect for each and every unique individual life. No individual--regardless of who his parents happen to have been--stands above any other with regard to this philosophical foundation.

This reverence for each individual's life implies that each person must be accorded, by law, the maximum possible freedom to determine how his own life will be lived. A sole castaway on a desert island has no particular problem; he can do anything that he wants, short of violating the laws of nature. But when there are two or more individuals forming a society, there are <u>logical</u> constraints arising from their interaction.

Remember that no individual stands above any other in this respect. If I feel like moving my fist rapidly through the air, but you're standing in front of me and you neither want to move nor be hit, there's a problem. Apparently the crude notion of "freedom" as "doing whatever you want" isn't good enough when more than one individual is involved. (And why would we need laws if there were only one person, anyway?)

The great challenge is to devise a set of principles governing individuals' behavior among other individuals that affords <u>each of them</u> the maximum possible degree of freedom over his own life and choices. Whatever rules we devise for one individual must be logically capable of applying, simultaneously, to all individuals.

The answer of the Founding Fathers of the United States, and of philosophers who preceded (like John Locke) and followed them, was the concept of <u>natural rights</u>. Whether or not one prefers to believe that each individual is granted such rights by God, they constitute a solution to this challenge. They establish conditions that provide the "maximum identical freedom for each individual," and serve as the philosophical foundation of capitalism.

> "Natural rights" represent the philosophical
> solution to the logical puzzle of "maximum
> identical freedom for each individual."

The primary such right is the ability to own and control the use of physical property--"private-property rights." The ability to preserve and maintain one's life, and the ability to use certain property (food? shelter?) are hard to separate. In Locke's approach, when an individual "mixed his labor" with previously unowned property, it became his.[1] Nowadays, "previously unowned property" is a little hard to come by, and these acts of "original acquisition" fade into pre-history. But the subsequent patterns of property ownership are legitimate if other individuals and later generations acquire it either through gift or voluntary exchange. These are the only legitimate ways to obtain property from another.

An individual's property is, in a sense, an extension or perhaps even a part of his life. That's why capitalism seems to make such a fetish of "private property."

> From the individual's right of ownership of
> his own life follows his right to own and
> control physical resources: "private-property
> rights."

It is seen--and properly so--as a part of its owner's life, something that is to be respected and protected by law. When a criminal steals the life savings of a couple nearing retirement, he steals their planned (and earned) leisure and sentences them to a future of continued labor. When anyone steals the rightfully owned property of another, he claims for himself part of the victim's life.[2]

---

[1] See John Locke, "An Essay Concerning the True Original, Extent and End of Civil Government" in his Two Treatises of Government (1690), Chapter V ("Of Property"). It is reprinted in many collections, including Edwin A. Burtt, ed., The English Philosophers from Bacon to Mill (New York: Modern Library, 1939), pp. 403-503 (see especially pp. 413-423).

[2] Critics who are either ignorant or deliberately deceptive sometimes depict "private-property rights" as rights that are possessed by inanimate property. When they claim that your property right to your own car is somehow the car's property right, they're trying to make the whole idea of "private-property rights" sound silly. You'll hear this ignorant confusion in debates about "human rights versus property rights." A property right is a right OF humans TO property.

The exchange principle

We learned, earlier, that any voluntary exchange must be mutually beneficial: each (that is, both; not just one) of the individuals must perceive the exchange to make him better off. A corollary that we applied to supply and cost is that: if you want someone else to take a specific action, you must make it worth his while. You must arrange for him to perceive that action as the best of his own current alternatives.

In our current context, the most important characteristic of voluntary exchange is that it maintains a mutual respect for the individuals' lives. No individual gives up his own property unless he voluntarily chooses to, and that happens only if he perceives the value of what he is offered to exceed the value of what he is asked to give up.

That means, in turn, that if we want property--a widget, a paycheck, or instruction in how to repair a bicycle--that is owned by another, it is <u>our obligation</u> to offer him something that he values more than he values the good or service that we're after. <u>It is our obligation.</u> If we don't, won't, or can't, then he keeps it.

When another person turns down our offer because it doesn't benefit him, we have to go without the good. But he violates none of our rights; he takes nothing from us to which we are entitled. Take my "This cup contains the terrible coffee they make at my office" coffee mug again. (Please.) If you were to decide that $3 is a fair offer, even though I would not consider myself better off with less than $15, your act of stuffing $3 in my pocket and dashing off with my mug is an act of theft. It is a forceful seizing, for your own benefit, of part of <u>my</u> life, and it has a good deal in common with slavery. Any victim of aggression, including theft, will know the feeling that someone has taken a part of his life.

Each of us views others as means to our own ends--that's what it means to perceive benefit through exchange, specialization and the pursuit of one's own comparative advantage. It is the structure of rights that supports the capitalist system that makes it possible for each of us to use the abilities of others to our own benefit, in a process that simultaneously benefits them.

> The real beauty of the capitalist system of
> voluntary exchange is that it permits each
> of us to use, for our own ends, the abilities
> of others... in a way that fully respects the
> life of each and every individual.

The process of voluntary exchange maintains respect for the lives of all individuals concerned. <u>That</u>, and not any details about market equilibria and quantity demanded, is the real virtue of the free economic system that we know as capitalism.

Love and friendship as voluntary exchange

The principle of voluntary exchange is much broader than we economists sometimes imply. Consider its application to friendship and even to love. In either type of relationship each party gives something and receives something in return. It's not always easy to pinpoint exactly what these "somethings" are, but it's hard to imagine a healthy friendship or love in which one party truly gives nothing of value to the other.

What happens to a long-standing friendship when, because either you or your friend has changed, you now have "nothing in common" and find that he's no longer pleasant to be with? He may hang on, deriving value of some kind from association with you, and you'll tolerate that for a while. But as you gradually realize that he no longer has anything to offer that you value, the friendship--or love--fades away.

Lasting love and friendship have to be built on this foundation of mutual respect and its corollary, voluntary exchange. Each party must value what he receives from such a relationship more than he values that which he puts into it. One obtains the affection of another by earning it, by offering in exchange something that he or she values, emotionally, more than its (emotional) cost. An attempt to claim another individual's affection in any other way reflects a lack of respect for that individual's life. It's the emotional equivalent of theft.

Don't interpret this as a coldly calculated business deal. The value that we offer to another to earn his or her affection is often very deep and complex. It may involve such things as simply being a nice person, honest, with a fairly good sense of humor, various shared interests, and a dimpled chin. Often it's reinforcement for whatever he or she believes is good about him/herself.

Especially, don't forget that value is subjective. Sometimes an individual-- perhaps a student of introductory economics, impressed with this "trading" discussion- -tries to calculate the values traded in a relationship, and concludes from the fact that he values what he gets more than what he gives, that the relationship is exploitive of his partner. Don't fall into this old "objective value" trap. (Remember the in-line skates and the bicycle?) All that means is that you benefit; as long as your partner has the reverse relative valuations, s/he benefits, too. You may not know, and you may never know, exactly what it is that your partner values. S/he might not be able to explain it, even if s/he wanted to. That doesn't keep the relationship from being strong and stable, of great mutual benefit.

It may seem as if I'm a little far afield here, as an economist. But it's important to perceive the significance of the principle of respect for the lives of other individuals. The only kind of relationship between individuals that preserves that respect is the process of voluntary exchange. And the only socioeconomic system that, in its pure form, permits only voluntary exchange, is capitalism.

A brief comment on socialism

The theory underlying socialism is that the system of laws that governs a society should focus on the well-being of the society. The life of each individual is considered significant only for its contribution to that goal. No individual's life is important for its own sake, and no individual can be permitted to make choices about his own life that are identified as opposed to the interests of society.

The principal theoretical clash with capitalism is socialism's claim that no individual's life is significant for its own sake.

While capitalism treats no individual as "more significant" than any other, it attempts to respect each and every life by maximizing each individual's freedom to select his own actions. Genuine "society," its advocates argue, requires that interpersonal relationships consist only of mutually respectful acts of voluntary exchange.[3]

The elevation of "society" to a position superior to that of each individual is questionable enough. In practice, the interests of <u>some</u> individuals are identified with those of "society," and the lives of <u>other</u> individuals (often the vast majority) are sacrificed for their benefit.

Wise economists (starting with the Austrian Ludwig von Mises in 1920) have long known that a genuine "socialist economy" is impossible. For a system to produce goods consistent with individuals' values, in which they are permitted no freedom to demonstrate, communicate, and even discover those values, is simply impossible.

The primary reason for a repudiation of socialism, however, is its disrespectful treatment of human life. It is simply a defense of slavery, of the use of government by individuals who have attained power to seize, for their own benefit, the lives of other individuals.

Blaming the waiter for obesity...

My little story about the theoretical foundation of pure capitalism may give one the feeling--for a moment, anyway--that all of life's problems would disappear if only individuals' property rights were enforced so that all exchanges would have to be strictly voluntary.

Not so, of course.

Anyone who claims that the adoption of a particular socioeconomic system-- be it pure capitalism, pure socialism, or any mixed scheme--will resolve all

---

[3] Another alert: There are critics of capitalism who argue that because <u>voluntary</u> association with others has beneficial effects, <u>forced</u> association would, too. I can hardly count the times I have heard this argument. Suppose a neighborhood group of volunteers, with generosity and friendship all around, cleans up a vacant lot for a playground. Would the same wonderful sense of community and good will toward others have really arisen if some kind of compulsory National Service had forced them, under threat of prison, to clean the property? The inability of some economists to understand the difference between voluntary choice and force never ceases to amaze me.

conceivable economic problems and turn Earth into a Garden of Eden, is not only badly misinformed. He's also establishing a standard by which that system--if it's ever implemented--is certain to be judged a failure. There is no system of laws and economic organization that can eliminate scarcity and its related problem of cost.

> No system of laws and economic organization can eliminate the problems that necessarily arise from the existence of scarcity.

If you're worried that people just can't have as much of everything as they want, don't blame either socialism or capitalism. Blame scarcity. Then accept the fact that you (and everyone else) has to live with it, and look into the best ways of dealing with it.

A perennial "problem" alleged to plague a society that accords individuals freedom to make their own choices, is that "they" don't make the right choices. Here's the problem, once again, of judging others' choices. All that it really means is that the actor's knowledge, alternatives, and/or values are not those of the critic. But the critic invariably is convinced that they know less than he knows--or that if their alternatives and/or values are not the same as his, they should be.

Perhaps the best known exemplar of this attitude is Ralph Nader, who has spawned a collection of "consumer advocacy" groups whose purpose seems to be to make sure that we ignorant consumers are not permitted to make choices that aren't "really" in our best interests.

The fashion of blaming freedom and capitalism when others make choices of which you disapprove has been called "blaming the waiter for obesity." The proper, life-respecting, solution is education: teach people that it's to their own benefit to turn down that second piece of pecan pie, and to buy cars with air bags. (Insurance premium differentials, offered by many insurance companies, may provide some voluntary incentive.)

To assert that individuals must be deprived of some of their freedom--that is, of a part of their lives--because we know, better than do they themselves, how their lives should be conducted, is to claim that we have some kind of exalted status over them, that our lives are superior to theirs. While "conservatives" are well known for this attitude, it is interesting that it is just as common among those who consider themselves to be "liberals." While they profess humanitarian concern for their fellow human beings, their "help" often consists of using the force of law to limit the alternatives from which others may choose. This snobbish elitism reflects a disdain, not respect, for the lives of others.

If you don't want to work in a cigarette factory, you're under no compulsion to do so. If you think that smoking is deadly and want no part of helping others to do it, capitalism respects your values by offering you the freedom to choose another alternative. But think twice before you attempt to deny some other worker, and the smokers who support his job, the opportunity for voluntary exchange.

There are, of course, many socioeconomic problems in American society today, and we hardly have the time, space, energy, or knowledge to examine them all. One of the purposes of this discussion has been to impress upon you how far the contemporary United States is from a truly capitalist country.

Some of our problems arise from the simple fact of scarcity. (If I insisted on living in certain pricey neighborhoods around Baltimore, I would be homeless. The houses there are too expensive for me to afford.) Some arise from poverty; since some individuals have little of value to offer in exchange, they receive little back.

But many problems are largely attributable to governments' refusal to permit voluntary exchanges. The envy-motivated "luxury tax" has thrown hundreds or thousands of boatbuilders and luxury-car salesmen and mechanics out of work. Zoning restrictions (benefiting existing residents) and building codes (benefiting construction-labor unions) and rent controls have limited the supply of low-cost housing. Mandated-benefits laws, which sometimes seem almost to require than an employer adopt any new full-time employee, have contributed significantly to the replacement of full-time with part-time workers. Price floors benefiting the domestic sugar industry have added hundreds of dollars to the family food bill and have helped to keep sugar-exporting countries impoverished. Pork-barrelling congressmen saddle you with another nickel a gallon gas tax, so that they can build a six-lane highway in their home district and get re-elected. The Federal Reserve System's mishandling of the economy's money supply robs purchasing power from those who hold dollars, and creates massive distortions in economic activity.

None of this has anything to do with capitalism. These problems and forced "solutions" are profoundly anti-capitalistic. They are absolutely contrary to the principle of voluntary exchange, of respecting the lives of others and not treating them as slaves to be sacrificed to the ends of those with political power.

Our analyses of economic profit and the functions of price teach that individuals identify profit opportunities and respond to them most quickly if they are free to bid and ask whatever prices they wish, and are free to receive the resulting income (or are obligated to suffer the resulting loss). But the principal virtue of a free society, and its correspondingly free economic organization (capitalism), is simply that its system of voluntary exchange respects the life of each individual.

THE PLACE OF ECONOMICS IN A LIBERAL EDUCATION

The close of a semester is not always the best time for reflective thought. You have final exams to prepare for, and before them term papers to finish (or start--don't forget, I was a student too!). Believe it or not, your professors often feel similar pressures. They may know of important topics that, somehow, they didn't fit into the course earlier, and that they feel obliged to try to pack into the last couple of days. One of my most dreadful memories is of an engineering professor who, with about two weeks to go, realized that he'd only covered half of what he was supposed to.

Nonetheless, this introduction to the study of economics would not be complete without an examination of its place in a proper liberal education.

We have come a long way. We began with the "Principles of Choice," building on them the concept of demand and its mirror-image, supply. We used supply and demand to study markets, and then returned for a more thorough examination of cost that focused on its future-oriented nature. The "Principles" helped us to determine the nature of efficiency and efficient exchange. We examined problems that all sellers face, caused by the downward slope of their demand curves (price searchers), and argued that the only public-enemy monopolists are those who are protected from competition by rights-violating government legislation. (Businesses know that, and actively seek it.)

Relying on the principle that "if you want someone to take a particular action, you must outbid his best alternative," we then used marginal productivity theory to discuss the determination of labor incomes. The time-preference axiom was the keystone of our examination of interest rates and present values, while entrepreneurship accounted for economic profit, that ghostly concept that evaporates as soon as people learn that it's there. An explicit study of information as a scarce good, and a caution about economic models that don't seem to allow for this, formed the last of our substantive chapters.

Summarized (or, at least, identified) in two paragraphs like this, it may seem a bit overwhelming.

The single most important lesson that you can learn from this book is that free individuals, acting within a legal system that protects property rights, produce an economic system--capitalism--whose efficiency simply cannot be improved by deliberate government design and control.

If that's too wordy for you: Freedom works.

> The simple lesson of a good first course in economics is that FREEDOM WORKS.

Remember that by "efficiency" we mean most successfully satisfying individuals' values. The only source of knowledge that we have of others' values is to see how they actually choose when they have the greatest freedom to make their own decisions. It's easy to imagine using government coercion to better satisfy one of your goals--if you like only Grape Nuts, get a law passed ("in the public interest, to make the industry more efficient") permitting no cereals except Grape Nuts (well, maybe Wheaties too). But this not only thwarts others' attainment of their values, but--by doing so--implies that your life has some kind of exalted status over theirs. Maybe... but good luck trying to prove it.

This leads me to another point which, though I firmly believe it, seemed a little too radical to include in my "most important lesson you can learn from this book." It is: Because the system of voluntary exchange (capitalism) respects the sanctity of each individual's life, it is not only the most efficient but also the most moral socioeconomic system of which man is capable.

Economics and other social studies

Economics provides a framework or structure, a <u>way of thinking</u>, about human behavior that is absolutely essential to any understanding of the human being and his social institutions. (You should be warned that there are, nonetheless, plenty of individuals pontificating on social analysis who obviously lack even the basic understanding provided in a book like this one. Listen carefully to them--if you can stand to--and you'll usually have no trouble finding their errors.)

But like any structure or framework or skeleton, the insights of economics have to be fleshed out with knowledge of human behavior that's provided by other social studies.

We treat rather cavalierly the issue of the source of individuals' values, for example. Although we commented briefly on possible determinants of attitudes toward time preference (the gusto-grabber vs. the Puritan), economists by and large recognize that <u>that</u> is someone else's business.

It's especially important that you not invalidly generalize your own values to everyone else.

> Part of the process of respecting the lives of
> others is to avoid invalidly generalizing
> your own values to them.

We all have a natural tendency to socialize with others who are much like ourselves, to live and work among people of similar socioeconomic class and general tastes. And we certainly are first-hand familiar only with people who are living at this particular period of history. It's very easy to develop this provincial attitude, convincing ourselves that all individuals' values must be basically like ours.

This error of unwarranted generalization is quite common among those who concentrate their study on the economic problems of businesses operating under modern capitalism. To protect yourselves from it, you must study human behavior in other cultures, other countries, and other times.[4]

A provocative and pertinent phrase, which I recently heard attributed to G. K. Chesterton, observes that: "The style of a period is always invisible." Certain practices, habits, customs, are so much taken for granted that we do not even notice them. It takes an outside perspective--perhaps an astute observer from another culture, or a retrospective look from a hundred years in the future--to identify these practices not merely as curious or unusual, but to identify them <u>at all</u>.

History and anthropology are the best sources of knowledge about the way that individuals live and act in societies outside our own. The timid might want to stay

---

[4] I presume--and hope--that all that I have written elsewhere in this book will keep this advice from identifying me with the "multiculturalism" trend that is sweeping United States universities.

with American history; even sticking relatively close to home, it can be illuminating to experience the thrill and joy brought to the isolated prairie town by the very steam locomotive that we might identify today merely as noisy, dangerous, and--above all-- an environmentalist's catastrophe. The more adventurous might examine the value structures of non-Western cultures: how do the "Principles of Choice," with their concepts of benefit and cost, apply in tribal societies...or do they? (I know _my_ answer, but you ought to come up with your own.)

You should be forewarned, though, that not all historians and anthropologists have even a basic understanding of economics. Fewer still have a clear grip on the nature and meaning of "capitalism." Issues in American history that seem particularly susceptible to distortion are the alleged "Robber Baron" period of the late 1800s and almost any tale of conflict involving labor unions (invariably depicted--with only occasional accuracy--as innocent victims defending "workers' rights").

Forewarned is forearmed, and don't let these cautions dissuade you. Both history and anthropology are essential complements to your study of economics.

Economics, mathematics, and
the physical sciences

The social sciences and humanities sometimes find themselves entertaining students who prefer feeling to thinking and believe they'll find more of a home in subjects that deal with people than in those dealing with things.

By now it's probably clear that economics is the wrong social science to pick if one is trying to avoid the unfeeling, unbending, strictures of logic. But the reason for trying to ward off this attitude goes far beyond its tendency to hinder your understanding of economics.

The attempt to substitute feeling for thinking, of trying to replace reason with "emotion," is an exceedingly dangerous and anti-intellectual attitude. If one wishes to take actions that are truly beneficial, either to one's self or to others, one must have more than warm, fuzzy feelings: he must understand the probable effects of his action. Among the more tragic stories are those of parents who, with the most loving of intentions but insufficient knowledge, have taken actions that imposed lifelong damage on their children. "We've got to help the low-skilled, low-wage workers" may be a laudable emotion, but "so it's imperative that we boost the minimum wage" reflects an ignorance of (among other things) the harm to those very workers that such a policy is actually likely to produce.

Probably the best way to train one's mind in the application of logic is to study mathematics and the physical sciences.

Mathematics, in particular, is hardly more than the pure application of logic. But the principal intellectual virtue of either math or physics or chemistry is that these subjects have nothing whatsoever to do with one's feelings. There is right and wrong, and you either get it or you don't.

That's quite stark and painful for many students, and it's not uncommon to find them avoiding these subjects like the plague. As I've suggested earlier, if you find yourself the victim of "math phobia," you owe it to yourself to tackle and attempt to overcome it.

Mathematics is used more and more in advanced economics, and particularly in the statistical testing of economic hypotheses. Many economists will advise you to study math for this reason alone--that you will find graduate work in economics difficult without it. I prefer to emphasize the general contribution of mathematics and the physical sciences to your intellectual development, your ability to reason.

My reason for this different emphasis is that I'm not quite as enthusiastic about the application of mathematics to economics as are many economists. In my judgment, the principal challenges of economics lie elsewhere.

Economics and philosophy

The single most important subject that anyone who is interested in human behavior can study is philosophy. (Economics runs second.)

Philosophy can help you, as a student of economics, to avoid some of the blind alleys into which economists sometimes get themselves. By highlighting the shortcomings of utilitarianism, it reinforces the principle that "interpersonal utility comparison is impossible," steering the careful economist away from utilitarian judgments about "social welfare" and "welfare-loss triangles." An analyses of the errors of the various forms of positivism emphasizes the importance of abstract theory, and warns the economist to beware of the claim that knowledge can be obtained only from the observation of quantitative data.

Philosophy offers us ethics, the theory of how individuals ought to treat each other. Its link with politics is the theory of rights, which applies the theory of ethics to determine the kinds of action that are appropriate among individuals and should be protected by proper legislation. We finally wind up with a set of implications about the proper relationship between economy (the process of individuals' voluntary exchanges) and government. What does it imply about "affirmative action," antitrust legislation, the "Americans with Disabilities Act," and "anti-dumping" tariffs?

Our discussion of the nature of capitalism, a few pages ago, demonstrated that rights are not just what anybody claims they are. It seems, these days, as if everyone uses rights simply as a debating tool: by asserting stridently enough that you have this or that "right," you've got the argument half won. But there are logical criteria that real rights have to obey. For example, they have to be "universalizable," capable of being held by each and every individual simultaneously. A lot of things that people claim to be rights just don't meet that test. (An example of such a non-right is the "right to a decent wage," regardless of whether anyone else values the labor service that you're offering for sale.)

Sorting out what you think about these matters of proper interpersonal conduct, of how others ought to be treated and of what it's fair for you to expect of them, is probably the most important goal that you could achieve during your formal education. (That's sorting out what you <u>think</u>, not simply what you <u>feel</u>. You don't need college for that.) Do not expect to reach a once-and-for-all solution; your views will change as you grow older and acquire different perspectives and more knowledge.

On the nature of economics

Economists in general treat the philosophical underpinnings of their subject rather lightly, apparently believing that if they ignore problems like the impossibility of adding different individuals' utilities, they'll go away. But values are subjective, and economists can no more read minds than can anyone else. They lack a standard for comparing different individuals' utilities.

These are facts of nature, and imply that economists lack the necessary knowledge to calculate <u>standards</u> for judging voluntary exchange and its results. We have no independent way to calculate specifically what kinds of actions are efficient, who has a comparative advantage in what, what the "distribution of income" or the rate of unemployment should be. Economics can offer no standard against which to judge whether or not a free society is "working."

What we <u>do</u> know is that, if accorded the freedom of choice that follows from the protection of individual rights, individuals will pursue their own values. They will take their own efficient actions, pursue their own comparative advantages, determine costs of production (by valuing alternatives), establish whether a particular seller's demand curve is fairly flat or fairly steep, and support a particular number of firms-- no more and no less--in an industry. We can show how market restrictions (whether or not well-intentioned) interfere with these processes. We can explain how the information and incentives conveyed, in a free system, by money prices encourage and assist individuals to create value wherever they perceive the possibility.

We economists lack the knowledge to compute all of these details beforehand, but we can explain the logic of the process by which voluntary exchange produces these outcomes. We can explain how "freedom works." That's more than enough to establish an essential role for our subject in a good liberal education.

Index